THE
LEGAL
GUIDE
FOR THE
FAMILY

Donald L. Very

Editorial Consultant
EUGENE F. KEEFE
Attorney-at-Law

DOUBLEDAY & COMPANY, INC.
Garden City, N.Y.

Donald Leroy Very

Donald Leroy Very was born in Pittsburgh on August 19, 1933. He received his Bachelor of Arts Degree from Duquesne University in 1955 and his J.D. from the University of Notre Dame in 1958.

He was admitted to the Pennsylvania Bar in 1959; Partner in the law firm of Campbell, Thomas and Burke of Pittsburgh from 1959 to 1970; Partner in the law firm of Tucker, Arensberg, Very and Ferguson since 1971.

Assistant Director of In-Dev-Or, the Insurance Development Organization Business School; member Admiralty Rules Committee U.S. District Court of the Western District of Pennsylvania; examiner of Pennsylvania Board of Law Examiners; Adjunct Professor of Admiralty Law University of Pittsburgh; President—1978—Allegheny County Bar Association; member American Judicature Society; member American Trial Lawyers Association; member Maritime Law Association.

Mr. Very was the Editor-In-Chief of the Pittsburgh Legal Journal, and Editor of the Pennsylvania Bar Quarterly Publication.

Foreword

I was impressed by the courage of the publisher when I was approached to read this book and write a foreword. There is as much art as science in the practice of law; in addition, attorneys, as with any other group, run a broad spectrum in their personal philosophies and approach to the practice of their profession. Moreover, the "law" in any particular area varies from state to state. Even where there is a "uniform" law such as the Uniform Commercial Code, there is not only an "Official" commentary but also an "Illinois" commentary to the official commentary to point out where the Illinois statute differs from the "model" statute. Finally, the law is constantly changing; witness the fact, that as this manuscript was going to press, Congress enacted the Economic Recovery Tax Act of 1981, thereby requiring last minute editorial work to ensure that various parts of the text reflected this latest development. Thus it is a bold stroke for a lawyer and a publisher to seek to present a book on the "law" to the public.

However, the strength of *The Legal Guide for the Family* is that it does not purport to be a definitive statement of the law in any particular area. Nor does it purport to be one of the "how to avoid a lawyer" type book; this latter category runs the risk of causing much mischief if people are encouraged to rely on superficial knowledge where expertise is required.

The purpose of Mr. Very's work is to offer the average reader a perspective on the legal system in general and upon particular aspects of that system with respect to which most individuals will be affected at some point in their lives. The book also provides a perspective for the reader upon the role of the attorney and the relationship between attorney and client. I would expect that a person who reads this book with awareness of the foregoing goals will not only have a better understanding of our legal system and the way it touches us in our daily lives but also will be in a better position to seek legal advice when appropriate and to work effectively, efficiently and harmoniously with an attorney when the attorney-client relationship is formed.

Dean Charles W. Murdock
Loyola University of Chicago
School of Law

To Norma because . . .

EDITOR'S NOTE

The Legal Guide for the Family is an extraordinarily informative guide to the laws that affect all of us at one time or another during our normal business and social activities. It provides useful guidelines for the reader's assistance when he or she is entering into any venture covered by statutes, whether it is forming a partnership, signing a lease, building a patio, or planning a will. In this book the reader will find a wealth of helpful information simply and concisely outlined in language the layperson can understand. The book is not, however, meant to be a substitute for a lawyer, and, in fact, the book offers guidelines on when to seek a lawyer's help, what assistance a lawyer will provide, and why it is usually essential to have a lawyer's services.

It must be noted that laws and customs vary from state to state and what is a rule in one state will not necessarily be the rule in another. Lawyers who are licensed by states understand the application of the law within your state.

CONTENTS

Part I
INTRODUCTION

In the words of Oliver Wendell Holmes, Jr., "The law is the witness and external deposit of our moral life. Its history is the history of the moral development of the race."

Its value in the life of every citizen, one might add, lies in its capacity to serve every citizen. To serve, in this case, means to provide the protections that all bodies of law must give if they are to continue in existence.

To serve also means that the individual citizen has the right and privilege to call on the law, courts, and lawyers in case of need.

This book deals with ways in which the law can be used more effectively. This is a goal that can be achieved whether one uses a lawyer or not. More effective use of the law can be promoted in at least five ways:

(1) by gaining a better understanding of the nature of law;
(2) by using lawyers more effectively;
(3) by proceeding without a lawyer when that is appropriate;
(4) by planning one's personal affairs so as to prevent legal problems before they arise; and
(5) by changing the law where that becomes possible.

Chapters 1 and 2 are concerned mainly with the first two ways of using the law. Later sections deal with the other three ways to make the law work for you.

In understanding the law, one can better appreciate the issues that involve the law and its methods. For example, a news item may involve freedom of speech or freedom of the press. The citizen can decide how the issue involves him and what action should be taken, if any. Even if he chooses to take no action, he will have made an informed choice.

In trying to ascertain when a lawyer is needed and what he can do for a particular problem, the individual faces challenges. He or she needs to know several things: how to find a lawyer, how to agree on a proper fee, how to use one's time with the lawyer effectively, what to expect from him, and what to do if dissatisfied with fees or services.

In discussing these and related subjects, Chapters 1 and 2 provide stepping stones to use of the rest of this book.

1 WHAT IS "THE LAW"?

What is the law? It represents many things to many people. To a consumer seeking compensation for a faulty product, it stands for one thing. To a corporation executive seeking patent protection for a new product, it promises something else. To the person arrested on criminal charges, it may have yet another meaning. For the lawyer representing each of these individuals, the law has still different meanings.

The law, in short, is complex, and has many facets. The phrase, "the law," simply offers a convenient way to deal with that complexity.

The law even represents something different from laws. As a concept and a reality, the law refers to the great heritage on which the rights, benefits, and privileges of Americans are based. The laws are the specific statutes and provisions that guarantee these rights and privileges.

The different facets of the law have their own characteristics. Each facet has its own origins in history, deals with certain kinds of cases or situations, and has meaning in certain kinds of courts. And, in fact, not all cases even go to a courtroom. This suggests that the law is a flexible tool.

The law's flexibility points to another quality: continuous change and growth. New laws appear all the time; old laws disappear. The new laws help citizens to deal with new needs and problems as they arise. Supreme Court decisions provide one example of how the law grows. But the decisions of other courts, bills or pieces of legislation, and many other legal developments forward the process of growth.

A set of rules for the common good

No matter how much the law grows and changes, it has a definite, unchanging meaning: the law stands as a set of rules or principles of conduct designed for the common good. The law specifies what behavior is desired and not desired in specific situations. It frequently spells out what remedies to apply when undesirable behavior is encountered.

Law has been described as a set of do's and don'ts. But such rules and regulations do not exist for their own sake. They are not intended to place obstacles in the way of freedom or the pursuit of happiness. Rather, they are designed to remove or at least smooth out obstacles: to make freedom a reality. The obstacles arise inevitably when people live together in a society. Some of the more obvious of these obstacles are crimes and disputes between people.

The law tries to walk the fine line between the rights of one person to act and of another person to enjoy protection. In the words of the adage, "My right to swing my fist ends where your nose begins."

Laws are thus designed to serve and protect in two ways. First, they are designed to protect the individual's interests so long as no one else is harmed. Second, the laws are designed to protect society as a whole. Society, in turn, is protected in three ways:

1. Order is maintained and progress is ensured.
2. Society is protected from harmful acts by individuals.
3. The general welfare and justice are advanced.

Laws function in accordance with at least two principles. The first centers on fairness: if a wrong has been committed, the remedy prescribed should make amends for that wrong as much as is humanly possible. The second has universal application: all individuals, without exception, are to be treated alike under the law.

Far from being just a set of do's and don'ts, the law represents a practical instrument for individual use. A citizen of the United States of America has obligations and duties; but he also has rights under the Constitution. U.S. law is vitally concerned with preserving Constitutional rights.

THE ORIGINS OF MODERN LAW

Law survives if it is accepted

Every society has some kind of law. In any social group the law survives because people accept and believe in it. Even the most ancient and primitive of societies have been lawful societies.

The American system of law has carried forward and refined this legal approach to solving problems. Modern man's heritage of law can be traced back to ancient civilizations.

Ancient Developments

Among ancient legal developments, several have significance today. For example, the Code of Hammurabi appeared in 1900 B.C. Basically a set of criminal laws, the Code prescribed a punishment for each crime. The Ten Commandments of Moses, dating from about 1200 B.C., provide the basis for many modern laws. Here a moral element appears: rather than stress punishment and the fear of punishment, the Commandments proceed from a conviction that certain acts are wrong.

The moral precepts of the Ten Commandments have been accepted down to the present day. Laws, it is assumed, have a moral basis. Citizens may resist or rebel against a law if they feel that it is wrong, morally or otherwise.

The Greeks developed the philosophy that a country should be ruled by laws rather than by men. The American government functions according to that belief. Typically, Greek laws dealt with property and commerce, particularly contracts. They also held trials before citizens—what are now known as jury trials.

Roman law incorporated Greek law

Roman Law incorporated Greek Law in a complete set of moral precepts published in 450 B.C. The Roman Emperor Justinian I, a thousand years later, published the *Corpus Juris Civilis* ("Body of Civil Law"). Roman law became the basis for canon law in the Roman Catholic Church. Napoleon carried this tradition forward in the Napoleonic Code. Louisiana, once a French possession, still uses that code as the basis of its civil law.

The civil-law tradition exemplified by the Napoleonic Code had its counterpart in areas that were historically under Spanish control. The Spanish *fuero juzgo,* or legal court, stood as a code of laws for those areas. The *fuero juzgo* was replaced by U.S. law as the Spanish possessions came under American control.

English Common Law and the Constitution

The American legal system owes much of its character to the English Common Law. Most of the earlier developments involved establishing codes of conduct. The Common Law offered a method of establishing new laws in the courtroom. The judge, or the jury, reaches decisions on the basis of previous decisions—precedents—in similar cases.

The origin of the term common law

The name Common Law comes from the fact that this form of law was commonly practiced throughout England.

Common law developed when a group of king's judges began to "ride the circuit" to hear cases. When the judges could not find any known principle to apply in a given case, they created a new one. Staying at inns, these judges would share experiences and opinions with one another. Summaries of many proceedings were written into legal *Year Books*.

Sir Edward Coke (1552-1634) analyzed many of these cases and developed a set of rules or standards. Sir William Blackstone (1723-1780) carried these analyses further. His *Commentaries* formed the basis for legal training in England through the nineteenth century. Americans have carried on this tradition of commentaries. Thus, both court decisions and commentaries on them form central parts of the common law.

Growing out of the English traditions, the U.S. Bill of Rights—the first ten amendments to the Constitution—embodies ideas expressed long before Thomas Jefferson put them down in organized form. The principles to which Jefferson referred reached all the way back to ancient Greece.

Many other thinkers contributed ideas that helped form Jefferson's thinking—and thus our Bill of Rights. One was England's John Locke. Discussing human nature and natural law, Locke wrote:

The State of Nature has a law of nature to govern it, which obliges everyone; and reason, which is that law, teaches all mankind, who will but consult it, that all begin equal and independent, no one aught harm another in his life, health, liberty or possession.

Two kinds of
American law

In discussing American law today, we are actually talking about two kinds of law: case law and statutory law. Case law utilizes the precedents reached by courts in similar situations. Statutory law functions on the basis of written laws, or acts of federal, state, or local legislative bodies.

THE PURPOSES OF LAWS

The law today comprises a thorough, comprehensive body of precepts and regulations. Laws deal with every aspect of a person's life. Some ways in which the individual is affected by the law include:
Marriage and rights of the marriage partners
Relations between parent and child
Buying a house
Household loans
Wills and the disposal of property
The rights of employers and employees
Injuries to one's body, property, or reputation
Civil rights
Protection against crime
Rights if arrested
The law operates in these and other areas to achieve four different goals:
1. It serves to prevent and settle disputes.
2. It enforces standards of social conduct.
3. It establishes relations between the government and the society.
4. It distributes various kinds of resources within the society.

Preventing and Settling Disputes

Preventing and settling disputes, or conflict resolution, provides a rationale for civil lawsuits between individuals. Examples of such disputes include divorce proceedings and conflicting claims over property. In many disputes, the "case" may never come to court. Both attorneys may agree that one of the parties is entitled to all or part of his claim. For example, one party may be rewarded with ownership of a property ("have title") while the other can use it under the "easement" principle.

If the lawyers disagree, the case may go to court. "Going to court" represents an effort to obtain an impartial decision, or judgment. One or both parties may later appeal the verdict of the judge or jury. The party receiving a negative verdict may *appeal* to a higher court. The legal pathway for handling a dispute is clearly marked.

Social Conduct

Law in modern society

The law serves also as a way to enforce standards of acceptable social conduct. Society has both informal and formal means of enforcing standards of behavior. In primitive societies, informal means such as social pressure and opinion were used for the most part. Law, the formal means, became more important as society became more complex. Today's society, especially, could not live without the law.

This use of the law applies in many areas. For example, the control of crime requires enforcement of standards of acceptable behavior. The handling of disputes involves similar enforcement of rules.

Government and Society

The U.S. Constitution is concerned with establishing overarching relations between the government and society. "Society" here means individuals as well as the group. The fifth and fourteenth amendments to the Constitution established the right of the individual to "due process." This means that the government can only take legal actions toward individuals.

The application of due process

Two kinds of due process have been identified. The first is procedural, meaning that the methods the government uses to deal with its citizens must be acceptable. The second is concerned with the content of the laws passed by government. In the 1930s, for example, the Supreme Court rejected many New Deal laws passed by the Roosevelt administration.

Distribution of Resources

Finally, the law helps to determine how society's resources are distributed among its members. One way in which this is done is by regulating the actions of citizens. Such regulation, in turn, may be effected through control of the criminally greedy. Regulation also takes place through supervision of contractual relations. In both cases, standards of acceptable conduct are being enforced.

Another way of effecting the distribution of resources is through taxation. Here, the government (1) takes a portion of a citizen's money or (2) finds ways to spend it. People may be taxed either directly or indirectly. In the latter case, as with sales taxes, the tax is first paid to a merchant. Sometimes members of society see the ways in which resources are distributed as unfair or unjust. Individuals or groups may try to influence the government to use some of its tax money to remedy that injustice.

These four uses of the law overlap. For example, enforcing standards of conduct affects both the settlement of disputes and the relations between government and society. Poor allocation of resources can lead to social disorder and enforcement of standards. Such enforcement can prevent disputes, which maintains social order. Resolving conflicts can smooth out relations between individuals and the government.

THE TYPES OF LAW

"The law," as noted, is not a unitary thing. Laws exist at federal, state, and local levels. These, in turn, can be classified according to whether they deal with civil or criminal matters. Finally, the law may be considered with respect to its origins: whether a law was passed by a legislative body or shaped in the courtroom because of a judge's decision. Of special importance is whether a law is civil or criminal, and how it originated.

Civil and Criminal Law

*Differences
between civil and
criminal law*

Civil and criminal law differ according to the identity of the "injured" party. In civil law the injured party is another individual. In criminal law the injured party is considered to be society. Civil law may involve either common law or statutory law while criminal law usually involves only statutory law. Criminal statutes define the offenses that are considered grave enough to be regarded as crimes against society.

Civil law typically involves a plaintiff and his lawyer, and a defendant and his lawyer. Civil suits may involve any of the following:

Auto accidents
Injuries at home
Injuries on the job
Injuries to one's reputation

In a criminal trial the defendant and his lawyer face a prosecuting attorney and his "client"—the state or federal government. Federal and state statutes describe the specific crimes and the permissible punishments for each. Violations of city ordinances are not classified as crimes, but can bring fines.

Some states have more than 200 crimes on their books. The most typical crimes are:

Murder, both first and second degree
Voluntary manslaughter
Criminal negligence
Larceny
Embezzlement
Rape
Robbery
Receiving stolen goods
Forgery
Burglary
Arson
Perjury
Kidnapping

Accessory after fact
Assault

Statutory and Common Law

In each state, legislatures pass laws, acts, or statutes from time to time. Cities, counties, townships, and other local municipal units have legislative bodies that pass ordinances. Nationally, the Congress passes laws which, as in the states, are called statutes.

Governments at all three levels have administrative agencies that make rules, regulations, and resolutions. These may have the force of law, and therefore are sometimes referred to as "administrative law." In each case, however, the agency's rulings have the backing or authorization of a specific statute or ordinance. Without that specific law, the ruling would be invalid. Thus, administrative law is often viewed as a branch of statutory law.

Administrative agencies control a wide variety of areas of public life. These include public utilities, insurance, banking, motor vehicles, taxation, and the regulation and licensing of professions and occupations.

The American system of courts

The common law is centered in the systems of courts. Every state has its own system of courts. At the top is a State Supreme Court or a Court of Appeals. Lesser courts include Criminal Courts, Civil Courts, Alderman's Courts, Justice of the Peace Courts, Mayor's Courts, and City Courts. Each court has the duty of interpreting the law and enforcing it. They do this by imposing fines and penalties in criminal cases, or by awarding damages in civil cases.

Because courts rely on decisions made in previous cases involving similar conditions, an attorney can use his research into previous cases to advise his client of the present status of the law in a particular case.

Court Systems

The federal court system is headed by the Supreme Court of the United States. Lesser courts include the Circuit Courts of Appeal,

U.S. District Courts, Tax Court, and the Court of Claims. Federal law, including statutory, administrative, and common, together with comparable kinds of law at state and local levels, comprises the sum total of what is called "the law."

Clearly, "the law" cannot be a simple thing. The average citizen may hesitate even to try to understand the total U.S. legal picture. But examination a little at a time can be helpful. For those concerned with civil matters, criminal law does not apply. If one is concerned with a federal matter, state and local matters have no immediate importance. If a case involves only statutory law, precedents may be of little concern.

Federal and State Courts

Two separate systems of courts, the state and federal systems, function side by side. State courts are established by state constitutions and state legislatures. Federal courts are established by the United States Constitution and the Congress. Both the state and federal systems have different levels of courts. These levels are classified according to their geographic jurisdiction and by the kinds of cases they try.

Federal Court System

The federal court system has three principal levels: (1) District Courts, (2) the Circuit Courts of Appeal, and (3) the United States Supreme Court.

The District Courts are known as the trial courts of the federal system. Every state in the nation is served by at least one District Court. Both Maine and Ohio have two District Courts each.

The role of
district courts

District Courts hear cases involving federal laws, the U.S. Constitution, and problems between citizens of different states. All kinds of criminal cases are tried, including felonies and misdemeanors occurring under federal statutes. Civil suits include:

• Matters governed by federal law, such as bankruptcies, patent and copyright cases, and admiralty cases, which involve laws of the seas and navigable waterways

- Suits involving the Constitution or federal statutes such as civil rights
- Suits to which the federal government is a party
- Suits by one state against another
- Trials involving citizens of different states and sums greater than $10,000

In the last instance, the kind of law used may vary with the case. For example, if a car accident occurred in Ohio between a resident of Ohio and a resident of Kentucky, Ohio law would be used. The reason for this is that the federal system has no common law of its own. It has only statutory laws and these do not cover accidents.

Each Circuit Court of Appeals covers one of the eleven "circuits" into which the country is divided. Such a court hears cases which have moved upward through the court system from a District Court within its circuit.

The Supreme Court is the highest U.S. court. The Supreme Court hears appeals of important cases from Circuit Courts. In addition, it may consent to hear appeals to decisions made in state Supreme Courts.

State Court Systems

State court systems vary from state to state. In Ohio, as one typical example, the court system functions on three levels: the Ohio Supreme Court, Ohio Court of Appeals, and Ohio trial courts. The last group includes Common Pleas Courts, Municipal and County Courts, Mayor's Courts, and the Court of Claims.

*The differences
among state court
systems*

Another state, Maine, has five distinct levels of courts. The Maine District Courts try traffic cases, civil cases involving less than $20,000, some adult criminal cases, and cases involving juvenile crimes. Small Claims Courts involve private disputes involving debt or damage of less than $800. Superior Courts try all state criminal and civil cases, and hear appeals of cases from District Courts and administrative agencies.

Maine has two other special courts. The Supreme Judicial Court of Maine, called the Law Court, hears appeals from Superior Courts. The Probate Court oversees the administration of estates of deceased persons.

THE ADVERSARY PROCEDURE

A court trial, in whatever court, is based on the "adversary procedure." The case may be either civil or criminal; the two "sides" contend. Each side tries to persuade a judge or jury that it is right.

In this contest the judge acts as a referee, or authority, on questions of law. The jury decides on questions of fact. A trial proceeds according to well-defined steps:

1. Selection of a jury, where there is one
2. Opening statements by the attorneys
3. Presentation of witnesses and evidence, with the plaintiff or prosecutor appearing first
4. Closing arguments by the attorneys
5. Instructions by the judge to the jury
6. Deliberation and jury decision

The jury system

Parties to civil suits and defendants in criminal cases are entitled to a jury trial. A trial jury is called a petit (or petty) jury; a grand jury in Criminal Cases decides in advance whether a trial should be held on the basis of available evidence.

A party to a trial is not always entitled to a jury. Even where one is so entitled, it may not be provided unless it is demanded. Jury trials are not allowed in cases involving minor offenses calling for penalties up to $100. Felonies and major misdemeanors usually call for trials by jury. In felony cases, twelve jurors are normally used; in misdemeanor cases, eight.

RIGHTS

The Bill of Rights

Under the United States Constitution, each American has certain guaranteed rights. Briefly, these rights include:

freedom of speech and freedom of the press,
freedom of assembly,
freedom of religion,
the right to vote,
the right to hold public office,
the right to keep and bear arms,
protection of individual privacy,
full enjoyment of one's property,
equal protection under the laws,
privilege against self-incrimination,
due process of law,
the right of habeas corpus,
protection against "double jeopardy" (two trials for one offense), and
the right to a jury trial.

The first ten amendments to the Constitution make up the Bill of Rights. Other amendments have a bearing on rights, however. The Fourteenth Amendment, dealing with due process, incorporates many of the features of the first ten amendments.

The Constitution grows and changes constantly. The written document itself undergoes additions; but interpretations are made repeatedly by the Supreme Court. The Fourteenth Amendment, as indicated, has been selectively absorbing the Bill of Rights over a matter of years. Essentially, it guarantees that many of the rights provided at the federal level have also to be protected at the state level.

The law has been developed to be used. Why not make it work for you?

2 LAWYERS AND THE LAW

As society becomes more complex, so does the law. As laws become more numerous, the need for lawyers grows. One can often conduct one's personal affairs without a lawyer. But it is important to know when a lawyer is needed and when one is not. Then more effective use can be made of lawyers. This chapter tells how and when to find and use a lawyer—and when not to. The nature of the legal profession is explained. Alternatives to the use of lawyers are noted, and the question of lawyers' fees receives attention. Finally, the reader learns what to do if he or she is dissatisfied with a lawyer's work.

WHAT IS A LAWYER?

In a single sentence, a lawyer is an officer of the court who is authorized to explain the law to clients and to represent them in and out of court. As an officer of the court, the lawyer swears that he will

uphold the law and conduct himself according to appropriate court procedures. The court may discipline a lawyer who fails in either role.

A lawyer has expert knowledge within the field of law. Sometimes he has specialized knowledge within the many subfields of law. A nonlawyer may know some aspects of the law, and may even be able to help himself in some instances, as this book will show. But the lawyer's expert knowledge may prove to be indispensable. Because of the very complexity of the law, his intelligent guidance of his client may make the difference between great or little expense and inconvenience.

Regardless of where a lawyer represents his client—in court or out —or what kind of advice is given, the purpose is to help the client (1) safeguard his legal rights and (2) fulfill his legal obligations. A lawyer has primary loyalty, thus, to his client. However, as he is sworn to uphold the court and the law, he will never counsel a client to break the law.

Different kinds of lawyers

There are many different kinds of lawyers. *Family lawyers* are the "general practitioners" who help with leases, wills, estate planning, contracts, real estate transactions, and divorce. Family lawyers try to practice *preventive law,* keeping clients out of court if possible. *Trial lawyers* possess special skills in courtroom procedures and the presentation of evidence. *Corporate lawyers* are salaried employees of corporations who often specialize in legal subfields important to their employers. These subfields include labor law, patents, consumer protection, and many others. The corporate lawyer may or may not become involved in court cases.

Among the many specialties in law, the most common in addition to those named are:

Negligence
Tax law
Banking and business law
Wills, estate planning, and probate
Real estate
Criminal law
Domestic relations

What Lawyers Do

Lawyers perform in many different roles to help their clients. The lawyer's principal tasks are preparing documents and agreements, negotiating out-of-court settlements of disputes, and representing clients in court and before government agencies. Lawyers have to develop various skills, including:

- *Reading.*   Lawyers must read constantly to keep informed. This is essential not only for a general knowledge of the law, but to prepare a client's case.
- *Writing.*   A lawyer's writing must be clear, comprehensive, and persuasive.
- *Creative thinking.*   Lawyers must be able to adapt their knowledge of the law to the particular client's needs. This may mean applying old precedents or trying to shape new ones.
- *Speaking.*   This vital skill comes into use when lawyers represent clients in court or before agencies, boards, councils, commissions, and other governmental bodies.
- *Counseling.*   Clients receive legal advice that can prevent legal problems and disputes.
- *Dealing with disputes.*   Lawyers must anticipate legal arguments once disputes have developed.
- *Negotiation.*   Lawyers try to settle legal disputes with an eye to preventing court appearances (litigation).
- *Serving the public.*   Many lawyers try to improve the profession and engage in civic activities.

Their Training and Qualifications

*Meeting
requirements for
practice*

Lawyers must meet certain requirements before they are permitted to practice law. Most or all of the following are required, with some variations among states:

- Four years of college.
- Three years in an accredited law school.

- Specialization in a particular area of law (optional). In a state such as California, before lawyers can advertise themselves as specialists in specific areas, they must be certified by the state.
- Clerkship or internship in a law office. While sometimes optional, this phase of training is usually required.
- Passing a state bar examination, a rigorous test of all areas of legal knowledge, administered and graded by personnel appointed by the state Supreme Court.
- Membership in some bar association, usually the state bar association. Memberships may also include the American Bar Association, the county bar association for smaller communities, or the local bar association for larger cities. Membership is not essential to the practice of law.
- Evidence of good character, whether vouchers of character from associates or affidavits of character from practicing lawyers or both.
- Waiver of the above requirements in some states, including Kansas, if a lawyer has been practicing in another state for over five years.
- A license to practice, upon completing all other requirements, issued by the state Supreme Court.

Discipline and Ethics

Codes and standards

Standards of conduct for lawyers are determined both ethically and legally. Standards seek to ensure prompt, adequate, and lawful assistance to clients. Key guidelines for the lawyer-client relationship appear below.

Various codes set standards for lawyers. The Supreme Court has adopted a Code of Professional Responsibility. The American Bar Association has its Canons of Professional Ethics that govern the behavior of members. In addition, individual state Supreme Courts and legislatures may have their own codes of conduct.

Bar associations work primarily in the public interest, not in the interest of individual lawyers. Offering voluntary memberships, such organizations also try to ensure high standards of ethics among lawyers and to improve the administration of justice. Most bar associations have a committee on *legal ethics* and *professional conduct*. Such a committee can recommend to a state Supreme Court the suspension, disbarment, or reprimand of a lawyer who has violated any standards or who has committed an act of moral turpitude.

Services provided by bar associations may include any of the following:

- Lawyer referral service or lawyer directory
- Continuing legal education
- Fee dispute arbitration
- Legal Aid
- Tel-Law, "Call for Action," and other free information and counseling services for the public

Lawyers' responsibilities

The American Bar Association began in 1980 to develop Model Rules of Professional Conduct. The Rules may be a definitive statement of lawyers' responsibilities. The preamble to the Rules spells out the lawyers' responsibilities, including statements that the lawyer:

- is an officer of the legal system, a representative of clients, and a public citizen with special responsibility for the quality of justice;
- should conform to the law both as a lawyer and as a private citizen;
- should serve the client's interests, but dissuade the client from wrongful acts against others;
- should be honest with any tribunal and respectful of the interests of other parties while asserting his client's position;
- should safeguard the client's interest when negotiating while showing fairness to others;
- may serve as intermediary between clients;
- is responsible to third parties where they exist;
- should act competently, promptly, and diligently;
- should seek improvement of the law and the administration of justice;

- is ethically bound to perform at his highest level of competence, to try to improve the law and his profession, and to try to meet the profession's ideals of public service; and
- should exercise his professional and moral judgment in resolving conflicts in his responsibilities where the Rules of Professional Conduct do not provide guidelines for such resolution.

The lawyer's obligations to the client are discussed more fully in a section below.

USING A LAWYER

How and when do lawyers become necessary? This section discusses why and when a lawyer is needed and how the citizen can utilize his or her services. The decision to use a lawyer is an individual matter, but some general considerations can help in making that decision.

Why a Lawyer May Be Needed

The individual may decide to hire a lawyer for at least three reasons. The law's complexity may require it, or the services of lawyers as officers of the court may be needed. Very importantly, lawyers can prevent bigger legal problems.

Law can be complex

The law's complexity may present too great a problem for the average citizen. Various laws may be relevant to a particular case. Moreover, as was noted in Chapter 1, the law has different sources—the Constitution, statutory law, common law, administrative law, and so on—and each kind has its own scope and effect. Certain kinds of cases may be relatively easy for a layman to handle without a lawyer —for example, small claims cases. In many situations, however, the "amateur lawyer" would be in over his head. An old adage holds that "the person who is his own lawyer has a fool for a client."

As officers of the court, lawyers understand the procedures and protocols of the courtroom. Not all cases need to go to court. When one does, however, the layman without a lawyer may needlessly delay proceedings. An "amateur lawyer" is also prohibited from representing persons in court; only an officer of the court may do that. Similarly, only a licensed lawyer can give "legal advice." So long as a person receives advice and representation from a lawyer, he has the court's protection because the lawyer remains accountable to the court. The court may protect the individual against his or her own lawyer!

Finally, lawyers serve both to prevent and to cure problems. What kinds of problems require the aid of a lawyer? Anyone faced with the following kinds of situations should absolutely hire a lawyer:

Being arrested for a crime
Facing a lawsuit
Wanting to sue someone else
Seeking a divorce
Filing for bankruptcy

Preventive law

Practicing preventive law can save time, trouble, and money. The ways in which early consultation with a lawyer can help include these:

- Preventing some legal problems entirely, for instance by signing an important paper
- Consuming less time on a case by consulting a lawyer beforehand
- Making information and evidence (including witnesses) more readily available when prompt action needs to be taken
- Avoiding complications by advising a client what or what not to do, say, or sign
- Having a legal matter taken care of before a "statute of limitations" blocks action
- Settling a dispute in negotiation phase, rather than letting it mushroom into a typically more expensive court case

When a Lawyer Is Needed

At many other times in a person's life he or she should at least consider seeing a lawyer. These include:

Buying a house
Selling a house
Getting an opinion on a real estate title

Making or terminating a lease
Dealing with troubles with a landlord
Choosing the right insurance
A change in legal status, such as marriage or coming of age
Adoption
Retirement planning
Preparing and revising wills and estates
Deaths
Administering estates
Calculating taxes and dealing with tax disputes
Organizing, buying, selling, or dissolving a business
Employer-employee relations
Consumer problems
Business transactions, such as collecting debts
Money problems
A significant change in financial status
Accidents, when there is damage to property or person
Taking out copyrights and patents
Signing a contract or making a verbal agreement
When arrested for a crime
Dealing with a governmental agency on an important matter
When one's rights are threatened
When one is not certain of the need for a lawyer

Minimizing problems

Lawyers cannot, of course, solve every problem. Some problems are so minor that additional legal expenses would not be warranted—for example, in a dispute with a merchant involving less than $50. The best time to see a lawyer is in a preventive situation. Often, the individual can minimize problems by engaging a lawyer in advance. Still other legal problems can be handled by alternative means. Some disputes can be removed from the jurisdiction of the legal system, for example, and "kept out of court."

What a Lawyer Can and Cannot Do

Examination of the extent of a lawyer's powers and capabilities may influence a final decision on hiring a lawyer. Such examination may also encourage more realistic expectations about the lawyer's future performance. But sometimes, clearly, only an initial consultation can provide an individual with information on whether to proceed further with a lawyer. Among the things that a lawyer can do are:

Confer with the client to pinpoint the problem
Gather and analyze all available facts and information
Interview those involved in the case
Study applicable laws and previous court decisions
Prepare legal arguments for presentation in court
Negotiate a settlement if both sides are agreeable
Present a client's arguments before the court
Appeal the decision of a court

A lawyer cannot . . .

Within that general framework, it is important to keep in mind the things a lawyer cannot do:

- Contact a client about a new case or new legal matter before the client has requested advice. Exceptions to this rule include cases in which a lawyer is specifically hired to handle all of a person's legal affairs at all times, and where a lawyer is a close relative or friend. If a lawyer who is a stranger approaches a person, that lawyer should be reported to the local bar association.

- Take action, for a client, that conflicts with a lawyer's duty to the court. A lawyer cannot introduce misleading or false evidence or assist a client in spiteful, malicious, stubborn, or obstructive actions. Nor can a lawyer represent a client where a conflict of interest exists between lawyer and client.

- Guarantee the outcome or result of a lawsuit.

- Speed up the time required by law for processing a lawsuit. A lawyer should, upon request, inform his client as to the time allotted by the court for each phase of the proceedings.

Thus, a lawyer can often achieve for a person what the person unaided could not achieve. At the same time, the lawyer is not all-powerful, since he must abide by his obligations to the court. He also has obligations to his client.

The Lawyer's Obligations to the Client

The lawyer's obligations

In order to do his job effectively and to ensure client satisfaction, a lawyer has certain obligations to the client. A client has a right to expect that all of the following obligations will be fulfilled:

- To keep the client's personal legal matters confidential. The lawyer can reveal only those facts that must become public knowledge when he pleads his client's case and offers evidence and testimony.
- To account promptly and completely to the client for money and other things of value that the client has entrusted to him. A lawyer cannot mix a client's funds into his own personal account. If a client asks for a return of valuables or funds, they must be returned promptly, without delay or excuses.
- To remain absolutely loyal to the client and his cause. An exception would be where such loyalty conflicts with the lawyer's ethical duties and responsibilities. The lawyer should then advise his client of the conflict and what to do about it.
- To file the client's action, or response to an action filed against the client, within the prescribed time.
- To record in timely fashion other legal documents that are intended to notify the public as protection to the client.
- To counsel the client to obey the orders of the court. If a court order is erroneous, it should be challenged on appeal and not disobeyed or ignored.
- To keep up to date on developments in law and the latest methods and models of practice.
- To investigate thoroughly the facts and laws that are relevant to the client's legal problem.
- To analyze carefully the client's problems and give a candid opinion of the probability of success or failure of the case.
- To make a thorough effort to settle a case and avoid the risks and expense of a lawsuit.
- To make adequate and timely preparation of the client's case

for trial and to prepare relevant documents and papers well in advance of a settlement or a closing of a transaction.

The Client's Obligations to the Lawyer

The client's obligations

The relationship between a lawyer and a client is not one-sided. If a lawyer is to work effectively on the client's behalf, the client must fulfill certain obligations as well. These include:

- To give full and complete disclosure of all facts, particularly regarding the client's conduct in a case. All information given is protected by the lawyer's obligation of confidentiality. A client can even confess a crime to his lawyer; such a confession is considered privileged communication.
- To consult promptly when a problem first develops.
- To adhere strictly to a lawyer's advice. Disregarding instructions could result in loss of a case.
- To have faith in the lawyer's opinion and judgment. In short, "let the lawyer run the case."
- To give adequate time to render satisfactory service. After a client puts a matter into a lawyer's hands, he should wait for the lawyer to make return contact unless there is an important new development.
- To feel free to ask about any relevant matter in the case.
- To give prompt notice to the lawyer of any dissatisfaction with his conduct of the client's affairs.
- To pay a fair and reasonable fee.
- To compliment the lawyer and give a good recommendation when the client feels that he has received outstanding service.

How to Conduct a Relationship with a Lawyer

To work with your lawyer . . .

Guidelines such as those just listed are directed at helping the client in specific dealings with his lawyer. The following guidelines will help the client establish a good overall atmosphere that may ensure a successful working relationship with his lawyer.

- The client should view his lawyer as another human being, not a god. The lawyer is not all-powerful; like all persons, he can make mistakes. However, he remains accountable for living up to his obligations. The client need not feel intimidated. If a lawyer appears intimidating, the client should feel free to complain or find another lawyer.
- At the outset, the client should tell the lawyer what he expects of him. If any of those expectations are unreasonable, the lawyer should say so. Similarly, the client should ask what the lawyer expects of him.
- The client should ask what steps are involved in handling the case and what kind of time schedule may be expected. This can reduce or eliminate impatience.
- The fee arrangement should be discussed at the outset. It should be made clear when the fee is to be paid. The client should know if and how he will be charged for making phone calls to ask questions. Guidelines for keeping fees down are presented later in this chapter.
- The client should help in any way he can—for example, by providing papers and evidence and finding witnesses. If the lawyer has not suggested it, the client should offer such help. In this way time is saved; the lawyer's fees may be reduced.
- The client should always choose the lawyer, not the other way around. An exception may be the class-action suit for a group or category of clients.
- The client should call with any and all questions. He should make sure that making frequent calls will not result in a higher legal bill. If it will, the client should make his phone calls count, grouping questions together on a given call.

What to Expect and Do During the First Visit

That first visit

On first meeting with a lawyer, and not before, an individual will usually decide whether or not he wants to hire that lawyer. If he decides to hire the lawyer, the meeting should be used to establish the relationship. The first meeting should therefore be approached with those objectives in mind. The following pointers should help the individual in the first meeting:

- Before going to the meeting, the potential client makes notes about the problem. He can then go over the important points when talking to the lawyer.

- He should bring the names, addresses, and telephone numbers of everyone connected with the case. Some lawyers may ask to see certain papers even before a meeting takes place.

- He should ask the lawyer to tell him about cases like his that he may have handled. Note: a lawyer's ability to handle a particular case may have nothing to do with his age.

- When dealing with a law firm, the potential client should ask the lawyer conducting the interview whether he will conduct the case personally. If another lawyer in the firm will handle the case, it would be advisable to talk to the other lawyer as well.

- Beware the lawyer who guarantees results. Most lawsuits are not "sure things." A lawyer should assess the chances of success or failure, however.

- If the lawyer says something that is not clear, the individual should ask for an explanation in simpler language.

- The individual should not hurry into a decision on hiring. He can decide at the first meeting or he can "think about it."

- Considerations in the hiring decision should include: feeling comfortable with that lawyer, the lawyer's experience and skill at handling a particular type of case (insofar as these can be determined), understanding of the lawyer's explanation of what the case involves, and whether the fee seems reasonable. A "no" verdict on even one of these criteria may rule out a particular lawyer.

- If an individual has decided to hire the lawyer, he should then follow the guidelines for conducting the relationship.

Compromise or negotiate?

Most cases, it should be noted, do not end up in court. Notable exceptions are when one is being sued or when one is arrested for a crime. In a civil case, a lawyer may see a court fight as futile or expensive or both. Litigation can then be a luxury. The lawyer may therefore recommend compromise or negotiation.

HOW TO FIND A LAWYER

If an individual does not have a lawyer, he can take several routes to find one. These include:

Recommendations
Referral services
Advertisements
Lawyer directories
Public interest groups
Prepaid plans
Various free or low-cost services such as Legal Aid, public defenders, Public Interest Bar, and various special projects for the elderly and other groups

The individual should initially develop a list of candidates from which to choose a lawyer. It may turn out that the first lawyer a person finds proves to be satisfactory on the basis of the criteria listed above. On the other hand, it helps to have a list from which to select —if only to avoid feeling pressed to take the first lawyer one finds. The various sources of lawyers are described below.

Recommendations

A lawyer may be recommended by a friend or relative who has had similar legal work done. This person can provide information on the lawyer's competence, personality, and fees. Recommendations may come also from professionals such as clergy, doctors, business executives, or social workers. Such individuals may have had to deal with a similar problem in their lives or in their professional work.

Sources of recommendations

Other possibilities exist. At one's place of work, co-workers and employers can also be important sources of recommendations. One lawyer may recommend another who specializes in the particular kind of legal problem. Where a person has moved, a lawyer known or used earlier may be able to provide one or more names of lawyers in the new community. A lawyer who happens to be a neighbor might be another source.

Referral Services

Lawyer referral services are operated by state, county, and local bar associations. They may also be called attorney referral services or lawyer reference services. Such services put individuals who have legal problems in touch with attorneys; the latter may charge a modest fee for a first consultation.

Consulting a referral service is usually not a complicated process. The individual who thinks he has a legal problem contacts the lawyer referral service office, most often using a toll-free number; any information given is held in strict confidence. Office personnel will then place the individual in contact with an attorney in his area. If the problem is not a legal one, either the referral office or the lawyer will say so. If the caller has a legal problem, the individual can decide for himself whether to make another appointment or authorize the lawyer to take appropriate action.

These services are found in the Yellow Pages of the telephone directory under "Attorneys," "Lawyers," "Attorney Referral Services," or some similar entry. Some referral services deal with special problems of groups such as artists, Spanish-speaking people, or the elderly.

Low fees for consultations

The lawyers obtained through referral services typically charge low fees for consultations. A typical fee would be $15. If a person thinks he cannot afford that much, he has other alternatives, such as Legal Aid and other legal services.

Advertisements

The Yellow Pages and newspaper advertisements offer other sources of lawyers' names. Most lawyers, however, choose not to advertise except to be listed in the Yellow Pages. Lawyers can advertise in the Yellow Pages, in newspapers and magazines, on radio and television, on billboards, or elsewhere as desired. The single restriction that applies is that the information in an ad cannot be false or misleading.

In addition to fees, ads may specify the legal fields in which lawyers specialize. "Legal clinics," law firms that deal with typical problems, often on a high-volume basis, may advertise their services for adoptions, divorces, bankruptcies, and wills. If an ad uses phrases like "simple will" or "uncontested divorce," it is important to ask what the service includes and what additional charges are entailed for more complicated cases or for expenses.

If the ad appeared in print, it should be clipped and kept. It tells much in few words about the lawyer's practice. If the ad appeared as a radio or television commercial, it may be helpful to take notes.

Lawyer Directories

Lawyer
directories

Some bar associations publish lawyer directories. These provide names and information, usually as furnished by the lawyers themselves. Included are educational background, fees (including those for initial consultations), areas of practice or specialization, office hours, and foreign languages spoken. Such directories are usually found in public libraries and bar association offices. A nationwide directory found in most public libraries is the seven-volume Martindale and Hubbell Law Directory, now in its 112th edition (Summit, N.J.: Martindale-Hubbell, Inc., 1980).

Public Interest Groups

Nonprofit public-interest organizations may either provide legal services in specific areas or refer persons to experienced lawyers specializing in those areas. The American Civil Liberties Union, for instance, can help if one's civil rights, such as freedom of speech or religion, are threatened or violated. The Women's Legal Defense Fund provides counseling and referral services for women with problems in domestic relations or sex discrimination. The National Association for the Advancement of Colored People Legal Defense Fund handles individual and class-action cases of discrimination against minorities.

In general, such groups may be divided into those that help individuals and those that only help groups in class-action cases. These organizations may be found in a variety of ways, for example by calling a city agency or contacting the "consumer action line" of a local paper, radio station, or television station. Checking the Yellow Pages under "Associations," "Consumer Protection Organizations," "Social Service and Welfare Organizations," or other similar entries may also produce lawyers' names.

Prepaid Plans

Legal insurance plans

Legal services are sometimes provided under "legal insurance" plans sponsored by an employer, by a labor union or credit union, or through individual purchase. Such a plan involves a prepaid fee or premium. An employer may establish the program on behalf of all covered employees or as an employee benefit provided either voluntarily or under collective bargaining. In some companies, an individual may join the plan by authorizing a payroll deduction.

Other characteristics may be noted. The premiums may be paid to (1) a trust fund that then provides legal services, (2) an insurance company, or (3) a private entrepreneurial group. Staff lawyers may work exclusively for plan members, or one or more law firms may handle plan services. A large group of lawyers may contribute services under the plan. Some programs offer the services of any licensed lawyer anywhere. Most such plans pay for specific service to the individual beneficiary or group member; services not covered by the plan require additional fees from the individual.

Plans offer advantages

The advantages of such plans are many. Members have access to lawyers, especially for preventive services, without paying high initial consultation fees. Methods of payment are easier, and sometimes painless, depending on the plan's benefits. Fee schedules are published. In general, members are assured of quality services and good treatment. The possibility that a lawyer may lose group business has been said to motivate many plan lawyers to deliver uniformly high-quality services.

THE SHREVEPORT PLAN[1]

The Shreveport Plan was established in 1971. One of the first of the prepaid legal plans, it was created in recognition of the fact that middle-income Americans have typically been deprived of adequate legal protection: the poor could get government-financed legal aid while the rich could afford to pay lawyers.

In 1969, the American Bar Association decided to use Shreveport, Louisiana, as an experimental site for creating a prepaid legal plan. The local bar association was responsive to the idea. A local group of workers, Laborers' Local 229, joined in the experiment.

Local 229 negotiated an arrangement under which two cents an hour from the salary of each worker would be paid into the plan. The American Bar Association and the Ford Foundation also provided funds. Shreveport Legal Services Corporation, a nonprofit corporation, was formed.

The members of Local 229, mostly rural blacks, did not trust strangers, especially those representing the law. The law collected bills, repossessed furniture, or put people in jail. Officials of the Local had been giving advice on legal matters for years, but could not call it "legal advice." Seeing a demand for real legal services and hearing about the American Bar Association's interest in starting a plan, a union official had contacted the local attorney handling the project. As a result, Shreveport became the site for the experiment.

Many members of Local 229 have been aided by the plan. In one case, a man was confronted by local, state, and federal officials with another person's check, apparently endorsed with his signature. Calling an attorney, the victim received help; a handwriting expert was able to state that it was not the man's writing. A woman neighbor was identified as the culprit.

In 1974, Ford Foundation funding was terminated. The union membership voted overwhelmingly to retain the plan. Were it not for the plan, many workers would have suffered serious financial losses or invasions of personal liberties.

[1] Adapted from Philip J. Murphy, Ralph N. Jackson, and David Chandler, *Lawyers for Laborers* (American Bar Association, 1975).

Free or Low-Cost Services

Inexpensive legal services are available for those who need help but cannot afford ordinary attorneys' fees. Such services include Legal Aid, law school clinical programs, public defenders, the Public Interest Bar, and Pro Bono, elderly, and other special projects.

Legal Aid, also called Legal Services, offers services for the indigent under funding by the federal and state governments and by bar associations. Lawyers in Legal Aid offices can represent clients in most legal situations. However, since the demand for services usually exceeds the supply of lawyers, Legal Aid will not handle criminal cases or cases in which a person seeks a money award (*see* Contingency Fees, below). A person must also meet an eligibility requirement by proving that his income is below a certain level. The level varies from one community to another.

Law school clinical programs

Law school clinical programs provide law students with practical experience with indigent clients. At any given law school, either the supervising lawyer or the program's referral individual may be contacted. Some programs make referrals to former students who are practicing in the area. Alternatively, the law school dean may provide the name of a faculty member specializing in the area of concern. That person may refer the potential client to other attorneys.

State governments make *public defenders* available to individuals accused of crimes who cannot afford attorneys' fees. The public defender can be found in the White Pages of the phone book under Public Defender. If an area or community has no public defender, a judge may appoint a private attorney to take a case without charge.

Public interest groups, as noted, sometimes provide legal services for individuals. Other special programs for particular groups may be provided by bar associations. The Lawyer Referral Service may also be a source of inexpensive, if not free, help.

AIDS AND ALTERNATIVES

The individual has some alternatives to lawyers or law offices in resolving certain legal problems. For example, the Small Claims Court makes it possible to file claims below certain levels. Some of the specific alternatives are described in later chapters.

Tel-law tapes

One aid is Tel-Law, a library of tape recordings that can be heard over the telephone. Such recordings are designed to convey an understanding of the justice system and of state laws, to aid in determining whether one has a legal problem, and to help in finding assistance. These tapes are not intended as legal advice or as a substitute for a lawyer; nor do they apply to all legal problems and situations. But diverse areas of law are covered, including adoption, bankruptcy, juvenile law, criminal law, civil law, public benefits, domestic relations, legal matters related to the handicapped, credit and consumer law, and estates and probate. The number of tapes may range from 50 to over 100 depending on the particular bar association.

WHEN A LAWYER MAY NOT BE NEEDED[1]

- When money is needed in an emergency; a better way is to consult a banker.

- Income tax problems; consult an accountant first.

- Routine purchase of a house from a reputable builder; use a real estate agent or title insurance company or an attorney for a lending institution (see Chapter 3).

- Problems receiving social security or unemployment compensation; see appropriate government agency officials (see Chapter 12).

- Claims for a relatively small amount of money under the limits set by the state; go to Small Claims Court (see Chapter 13).

- Traffic accident; in states with no-fault liability laws, conflict is minimized and matters are handled by the person's insurance company (see Chapter 17).

- Divorce; some states have no-fault divorce laws, making unnecessary the adversary procedure; elsewhere, do-it-yourself divorce kits may handle the problem without a hitch (see Chapter 8).

• Incorporation; in this area, do-it-yourself kits may have their pros and cons; indeed, incorporation may not even be the best way for some to organize a business (see Chapter 13).

• Consumer complaint; new consumer protection laws are being enforced by government agencies, and private consumer groups can exert pressure (see Chapter 14).

[1] Adapted from *You and the Law,* Copyright © 1977 The Reader's Digest Association, Inc. Copyright © 1977 The Reader's Digest Association (Canada) Ltd. Copyright © 1977 The Reader's Digest Association Far East Ltd. Philippine Copyright © 1977 The Reader's Digest Association Far East Ltd.

Another alternative to lawyers is do-it-yourself kits. These provide aid in such areas as wills, divorces, incorporation, and avoiding probate. In the case of probate, a group of lawyers sued the author of such a kit for illegally dispensing legal advice. The author successfully appealed the action, and has sold many copies of his plan along with the appropriate forms. The plan does successfully avoid the costs of probate. Even where a lawyer is used, the kit has features that are useful to both client and lawyer.

Not all alternatives may prove as useful or foolproof as the probate-avoidance plan. A kit may provide only minimum protection for the average person. But there is no average person as far as the law is concerned: each case is unique. A kit may not anticipate some kinds of legal problems. Consequently, one could end up with more cost and trouble than expected. The objective is to make an informed, thoughtful decision on whether and how to use a lawyer.

LAWYERS' FEES

Fees depend on services provided

Fees vary depending on the type of service provided. They vary also from lawyer to lawyer and community to community. Lawyers determine fees according to the following criteria:

• The fee customarily charged in the area for a particular type of service.
• The amount of time and labor invested.

- The skill of the lawyer, his experience, ability, specialties, and reputation.
- Business or office expenses, which vary from 35 to 50 per cent of the fee.
- Whether a fixed or contingent fee is established. Where a fee is contingent, the lawyer receives nothing if the case is lost.
- Results, in the case of the contingent fee.
- The amount involved in the settlement, in the case of a contingent fee.
- The complexity of the case.
- The nature and length of the relationship with the client. For example, a client doing casual business with a lawyer would be charged a higher rate than an old client doing steady business.
- Time limitations imposed by the client or by the circumstances of the case. If a lawyer is prevented from taking other employment that might have been available, he may charge more.

Types of Fees

Lawyers may charge different kinds of fees. In some instances, the client can negotiate the kind of fee; in others, it is already determined. Types include:

- *Fixed fees.* This constitutes a "standard" fee, used for routine legal matters such as drafting an uncomplicated will. Law clinics typically use this kind of fee.
- *Hourly fees.* Here, time determines the final cost. But the hourly rate varies from one lawyer and area to another. The client's objective is to obtain the best combination of hourly rate and efficiency in getting the work done more quickly.
- *Retainers.* A lawyer may ask for a retainer, or advance payment, to cover the fee or expenses. Clients requiring regular service pay monthly or annual retainers to ensure continuing service.
- *Contingency fees.* In cases where the client is suing for money, the lawyer receives a percentage of the award if he wins and nothing if he loses. The lawyer may assess his percentage according to the total amount or on the award after other costs are deducted. If the latter, the client keeps more of the award. The

client should determine beforehand the lawyer's method of charging.

- *Statutory fees.*   The cost of probate and other kinds of legal work is set by law, hence is "statutory." A probate court has a schedule of allowable fees. These are usually based on percentages of the value of different kinds of property.
- *Fees set by a judge.*   Probate may fall under this heading. Considering the size of the estate and the amount of time the lawyer puts in, the judge determines the fee to be awarded.

Keeping Legal Fees Down

Keeping fees down

Whatever the type of fee, the client can use a number of tactics to keep fees to a minimum. He can, for example:

- Write down the names, addresses, and phone numbers of all persons involved and all the relevant facts that he can recall
- Take any pertinent papers to the first interview
- Be as brief as possible in all interviews
- Keep emotion from coloring the facts
- Make a full and honest disclosure of all facts to the lawyer
- Avoid unnecessary phone calls to the lawyer

- Obtain legal advice before signing documents or taking legal action and then follow that advice
- Consider the financial pros and cons of a proposed legal action by discussing it with a lawyer

If the Fee Is Too High

If the client feels the fee is too high, he should tell his lawyer. Asking for an explanation may prove entirely satisfactory. Some states, including California, have arbitration services that are provided by the state bar association. The services charge set fees to determine whether the lawyer did the work he was supposed to do for the amount paid. Fees set by a court or by law are not subject to arbitration, however. Such a proceeding usually takes no more than 80 days and costs a maximum of $50. Lacking arbitration, a client may sue a lawyer.

Dissatisfaction with a Lawyer's Performance

*Before registering
a complaint*

Aside from fee disputes, a client may be dissatisfied with what the lawyer has delivered. Generally, a client does not have grounds for complaint unless the lawyer has violated standards of professional responsibility.

A formal complaint can be damaging to a lawyer even if he is not at fault. For that reason, and because dissatisfaction often springs from misunderstanding or poor communication between client and lawyer, the client should thoroughly air his grievance with the lawyer. The state bar can only discipline the lawyer; it cannot remedy any loss to the client. For that, the client must sue.

Each state has its own procedures for handling client grievances. The state Supreme Court has the power to discipline lawyers. Such discipline may include disbarment as a type of sanction. It is worth remembering that losing a case does not automatically imply incompetence or malpractice.

Part II
"ON THE STREET WHERE YOU LIVE"

The right to own real estate, or real property, provides the basis for many other rights in the American legal system. The Founding Fathers who framed the Constitution recognized that right. They believed that the "right of property" had to be secured or liberty could not exist.

Property rights remain a cornerstone of the entire complex of rights that Americans enjoy. But property rights have acquired public meanings. Where at one time a person's home and land were his castle, to be used as the owner saw fit, the situation has changed to a degree. The owner of land and buildings—real property—cannot use that property without considering his neighbors. He cannot, for example, befoul the environment unreasonably, pollute neighboring water or air, or violate zoning regulations and other restrictions.

What are the basic questions?

Within those limitations, most of which are outgrowths of a developing awareness that every person has duties as well as rights where real property is concerned, the owner of property enjoys important kinds of protection. One of them received new emphasis as recently as 1967. In that year, the Supreme Court of the United States ruled that the owner of a home has immunity under the Fourth Constitutional Amendment against a property search without a warrant. The case, *Camara* v. *Municipal Court,* bore out the principle that an official inspection of a home constitutes a search under the Fourth Amendment. Therefore, the Court said, a search could not be conducted without a warrant.

The Fourth Amendment, of course, guarantees the right of all citizens "to be secure in their persons, houses, papers, and effects, against unreasonable searches and seizures . . ."

So important is the body of law surrounding real property rights and duties that laws have been devised to cover many basic phases of the entire ownership process. In Part II, many of the ways in which those laws apply or can be put to work are described. Many common-sense rules and principles are also noted. Particular attention is given to the procedures by which real estate is bought or sold; to zoning and similar devices for controlling population density; to condemnation and other procedures involved in the assumption of property ownership by a public agency or body; and to renting and leasing.

3 "HOME, SWEET HOME"

Purchasing a home may be the largest investment that a person makes during his or her lifetime. Numerous legal questions relate to the purchase of an existing home, construction of a new home, various types of financing, the sale of a home, and similar transactions.

BUYING AN EXISTING HOME

Some persons find their "dream homes" the first time they go house hunting. Others, undoubtedly more typical, search for weeks or months before the perfect home turns up.

House hunting takes time, usually, because many factors, legal and

other, enter into the purchase process. Every home buyer should make certain that he knows exactly what he is buying. That means questions and more questions—to both the seller and his real estate agent.

Finding the Right Property

Finding the home that suits your needs is vitally important. Finding the right home in a strange area or neighborhood may add up to a major challenge. When moving into a new area without prior knowledge of the neighborhood, however, the home seeker has several possible ways to find out about the new neighborhood and the types of homes there.

Some obvious options are open. A friend who lives in the new area can show a prospective buyer the various locations and perhaps take the time to make a circuit of the city or town. A telephone call or letter to the local Chamber of Commerce or Board of Realtors can produce information on the properties in the areas of interest. Nothing, however, takes the place of a personal inspection trip.

What are the basic questions?

Some of the considerations that should be investigated are fairly self-evident. The size of the home; its price and how it fits with your budget; the area, especially with respect to schools, shopping, distance from work, and other such practical considerations—all have to be checked out. Often, consulting a real estate broker in the area found to be most attractive is the best method of finding property. In order to avoid wasting their own time and the time of the broker, house hunters should explain what they are looking for. Looking at photographs of various listings before making a personal inspection of the property can clarify key points.

Many persons make a very serious mistake in house hunting: they look only at the house itself. Naturally, if the house fits in with the buyer's needs, is structurally sound and of suitable size, and falls in the right price bracket, an offer to buy may be called for as promptly as possible. However, an inspection of the house alone is never enough. The owner or the broker should take the potential buyer on a "guided tour" of the property itself. An inspection trip should follow along the borders of the property. The property line should be defined at all points. The buyer should look up in the air to determine whether or not utility lines or other apparent uses or obstructions cross the air space over the property.

Most situations follow one or another pattern. Unless all utilities are underground, telephone and electric lines connect to the house from a pole or other utility installation bordering the street. But electric power lines or telephone lines may cross the property without connection to the house. That usually means that the utility company has an easement or right of way to cross the property. Such a use might be found later to constitute interference with the complete use and enjoyment of the property.

Don't forget to look down

Walking over the property, the buyer should also look down to determine whether or not visible pathways or walkways indicate that people use the property as a shortcut. A path suggests a need for full investigation—possibly by an attorney. The law in most states holds that the public can gain an easement or right of way by continuous, uninterrupted use of someone else's property for shortcut purposes.

Manhole covers could indicate the existence of a sewage system across the property. The owner or broker should be asked to explain such facilities.

It is thus very important not to overlook a physical inspection, not only of the house itself but also of the surrounding property on which it sits, including the boundary lines, utility lines, both aboveground and underground, and any other easement or rights of way that may exist.

Hand Money Deposit

Assume that a piece of property fits within the buyer's means and satisfies all other needs and desires. It may be wise to prevent the seller from selling the property to someone else before a contract of sale can be signed. In this situation a *hand money deposit* is usually made. The seller then gives the would-be buyer a deposit receipt.

Because most states require that contracts for the sale of real estate be in writing, the deposit receipt that represents the amount of hand money or *earnest money* deposited by the buyer should contain some essential elements. With these, the receipt becomes a legally enforcible contract in the event that a later long-form agreement of sale is not signed.

Earnest money equals part payment

The amount of the earnest money deposit is not set by law and is subject to negotiation between the parties. The deposit applies as part payment of the purchase price if the buyer later buys the land and completes the sale. Usually, the contract provides that the earnest money deposit may be retained by the seller if the buyer defaults and does not buy the land. Ordinarily a seller will require a sufficiently high earnest money deposit to cover the broker's commission and other expenses of the sale to the seller—including his loss of time and loss of opportunity to sell elsewhere if the buyer should default. The hand money deposit may be a percentage of the total purchase price, such as 5 per cent, 10 per cent, and so on.

THE PURCHASE AND SALE AGREEMENT: QUESTIONS THE BUYER SHOULD ASK BEFORE SIGNING[1]

The paper first given to a prospective buyer by a real estate broker is the purchase and sale agreement. Few people realize that this paper is the most important step in making the purchase of a home, for the details of this agreement determine what you buy and how you buy it. Before signing, read the agreement carefully and discuss with your family lawyer such items as the following:

1. Exactly what land, buildings, and furnishings are included in your offer? Are stove, refrigerator, and the like included?
2. What details regarding payments should be stated?
3. When can you take possession?
4. Is the seller to furnish you with a good, marketable title?
5. What kind of deed should the seller give?
6. Who pays for the examination of the title to the property in the event the offer is accepted? Who pays for the abstract of title or title insurance?
7. Have utilities been installed and paid for?
8. Should a surveyor be employed to determine whether the improvements are actually located on the property?
Who should pay for the cost of the survey?
9. If a mortgage is to be given, who will pay the intangible tax on the mortgage?
10. If termite, water, or other damage is found, shall the seller pay the cost of repairs?
11. What are the zoning regulations, or restrictions, on the use of the property?
12. What is the time within which the purchase should be accepted or refused? Is the date of such acceptance to be vital to the offer?
13. If your offer is accepted, what steps should be taken with respect to insuring the improvements to protect you, the prospective purchaser, pending the final closing?
14. What persons (husbands and wives) should be required to sign and accept the offer?
15. Are boundary lines properly specified?
16. Are timber, mineral, and water rights, if any, properly covered?
17. Who is responsible for payment of taxes?
18. How should the agreement be executed to make it binding?
19. What are the remedies if the buyer or seller defaults?

[1] Adapted from *So You're Going to Buy a Home* (Tallahassee: The Florida Bar, February 1980).

The deposit receipt given by the seller to the buyer should at least identify by name the seller and the buyer. It should also describe the property so that it can be identified easily. As an exchange of promises between the seller and the buyer to purchase and sell the property, the receipt should state the full price. All parties to the deposit receipt should sign it to make certain that it stands as a legally enforcible contract.

The deposit
receipt

A deposit receipt cannot substitute for an agreement of sale. The receipt only acknowledges deposit of the earnest money under all the basic terms. The deposit receipt should refer to the fact that an agreement of sale will be entered into by the parties as soon as possible after the earnest money has been paid.

THE AGREEMENT OF SALE

All the essential elements in the sale and purchase of a home converge in the agreement of sale. All these elements, including full cost, description of the property, the type of title that the owner has and will convey to the buyer, and so on, must appear in the agreement. A checklist of those items that should be in the final agreement of sale would include at least the following:

- Date of the agreement. The agreement should contain the date on which it is made.
- The name and address of the seller. These should be stated clearly, and the marital status of the seller should be stated, such as "James Smith and Mary Smith, his wife, of 121 Jane Street, Center City, State X."
- The name of the buyer. "Name" should include marital status, mailing address, and so on.

Specify the kind
of title

If the buyers are not husband and wife, and want to take title jointly, the nature of the title that they wish to take should be stated in the agreement of sale. Many states recognize a form of title owner-ship known as "joint tenancy." If the two persons, not husband and wife, want to take title as "joint tenants," such should be stated in the agreement. If they want to take title as "tenants in common," also a recognized form of ownership, this should be stated.

Agreement to Sell. The agreement of sale should contain a specific agreement by the seller to sell the property and the buyer to purchase it on a specified date. In other words, the agreement should state that the seller will "on or before 90 days from the date of this agreement, sell, and the buyer will buy" the property as described in the agreement.

JOINT TENANCY: PROS AND CONS[1]

Many misleading ideas about joint tenancy are passed from person to person, usually quite innocently. You have probably heard them— "Joint tenancy eliminates the necessity of a will" . . . "Joint tenancy saves probate costs" . . . "Joint tenancy reduces 'death taxes' " . . . "Jointly held property passes 'automatically' at death to the survivor" . . . "Your creditors can't reach jointly held property" . . . and so forth. To clear up misunderstandings on these and other misconceptions, read on.

What is joint tenancy? It is a way of holding title to personal property or real estate by two or more persons. There are three types of joint tenancy: "with rights of survivorship," "as tenants in common," and "as tenants by the entireties" (limited to husband and wife).

Why do many property owners favor joint tenancy? They think

the "survivorship" feature will save the surviving owner probate costs and inheritance taxes. The only costs saved are the small probate court costs and not attorney fees or transfer expenses. There is no inheritance tax due on property passing to a spouse, whether in joint tenancy or otherwise, and no inheritance taxes are saved if the property is held jointly with anyone else.

Is it a substitute for a will? No. Joint tenancy with rights of survivorship will pass that particular property to the other named owner or owners, and do nothing else. A tenant in common's undivided interest, absent a will, will pass to his or her heirs-at-law. A properly drawn will covers a number of items in addition to passing property. For example, it designates who is to handle the estate, names a guardian for minor children, etc. Joint tenancy may be the right thing for you today but the wrong thing tomorrow, but you cannot change it easily——as you can a will——to fit tomorrow's situation.

Does jointly held property pass "automatically" at death to the other joint tenant?   No. If the joint tenancy was "with rights of survivorship" or "as tenants by the entirety," the property does pass by operation of law (statute or contract), to the survivor, but not automatically. A Survivorship Affidavit with respect to real estate and Consents to Transfer (except for spouses), stock powers, affidavits of domicile and perhaps other documents are required to be prepared, signed and recorded or sent to banks and transfer agents to get the title placed in the name of the surviving owner.

Why is joint tenancy difficult to change?   Because one co-owner may refuse.

Can a man compel his wife to give back a joint title he has conferred on her?   No.

Can creditors reach jointly held property?   Yes, except possibly for real estate held by a husband and wife as tenants by the entirety if only one spouse takes bankruptcy. On death, the creditors of the deceased joint tenant can reach that person's contributions into jointly held checking and savings accounts, certificates of deposit, and other accounts if necessary.

What is common danger in joint tenancy?   Joint owners——even husband and wife——may disagree. After that it becomes difficult to make such necessary decisions as those concerning management, repairs, division of income from the property, public liability problems, insurance to be carried, and so forth. If tenants in common cannot agree on the sale of real estate, one party has to bring a partition suit which generally results in the court ordering the property to be sold at a time when the market may or may not be good.

What happens to a husband-wife joint tenancy in case of a divorce? If the parties cannot agree upon a split of the property between themselves, the tenancy is converted into a "tenants in common" type of joint tenancy.

Does joint tenancy reduce taxes? When one of two joint tenants dies, for federal estate taxes and many state inheritance taxes, the law presumes that the decedent was the owner of such property and taxes it in his or her estate, except to the extent that the survivor can prove his or her contribution to the cost thereof. Trouble may arise in perfecting the record title of the joint tenancy property. The real tax liability comes upon the death of the surviving spouse and often results in "double taxation" of some of the property.

Does joint tenancy save probate expense? Very seldom. If a deceased person owned other property besides that held in joint tenancy, the other property must be probated just the same. There is also expense in perfecting the record title to the property after the death of each joint owner.

If joint owners die simultaneously (as in an accident), what happens to their joint tenancy property? Without a will containing a "survivorship clause," the jointly held property is divided one-half into each joint tenant's estate, and probate proceedings are then required to pass the property on to the devisees or heirs-at-law of each joint tenant.

Does the creation of joint tenancy ever constitute a gift? Yes, if an appropriate election is made. If no election is made, the entire property will be taxed as a part of the estate of the first joint tenant to die, and then will be taxed again when the other joint tenant dies.

Is joint tenancy ever advisable? In some circumstances, and with respect to some types of property, but only after careful consideration of all the circumstances.

1 Adapted from *Joint Tenancy: Does It Fit YOU?* (Indianapolis: The Indiana State Bar Association).

Type of Deed to be Delivered. The agreement should specify the type of deed that the seller will give to the buyer. A deed of *general warranty* is the highest form of deed that can be conveyed and ordinarily is utilized in the sale of a residence. Other forms of deed, such as deeds of special warranty, are used mainly in situations involving a sale from the estate of a deceased person and in other special situations.

Type of Title to be Conveyed. The agreement should provide that the seller will convey "fee simple title," the highest form of title. The statement indicates that the seller has all the elements of title to the property that he is agreeing to sell. By specific terms, the sale should be made clear of all liens and encumbrances except as noted in the agreement, thus assuring the buyer that the seller is agreeing to convey free of any liens or encumbrances except those noted in the contract itself.

The good and marketable title

Good and Marketable Title.   The buyer wants to be certain that the title he is acquiring is good. He may later want to sell the property to someone else. The agreement should thus provide that the seller is conveying a good and marketable title, one that will be insurable by a title insurance company at its regular rates and that can be freely transferred in the marketplace.

Description.   The agreement of sale should contain a full-length description by "metes and bounds" and by courses and distances. This means that the description is the kind that a registered engineer would prepare from a survey of the property.

It is important that the buyer insist on a perimeter survey—one that examines the boundaries of the property only. The buyer should also insist on a survey showing the existence and location of all improvements on the lot, including the house, garage, swimming pool, toolshed, or any other building. These improvements should be located precisely on the lot. The surveys are important for determining:

(1) whether or not there are any encroachments onto the lot by an adjoining land owner;

(2) whether or not the buildings that exist on the property encroach on someone else's property; and

(3) whether or not the buildings and other improvements are consistent with local laws dealing with provisions for setback from the roadway, side-yard restrictions, open-space restrictions, and so on.

Who pays for surveys?

The parties to the sale should agree between themselves, after negotiation, on who pays for the surveys. Usually, the seller will have a completed survey that can be used by the buyer. The seller simply attaches a certificate stating that no changes, additions to property, or other structures have been erected since the date of the survey.

Under any circumstances, the buyer should have a survey that conforms to local ordinances and that shows any private covenants and restrictions that may exist if the property is within a plan of lots as well as any recorded easements or rights of way.

The legal description contained in the agreement of sale should be prepared, if possible, in accordance with the survey made by the registered engineer.

Title Reference. The agreement of sale should contain the deed book volume and page record under which the seller acquired title to the property. In all counties, a register or recorder of deeds office makes a formal record after a transfer of property has taken place. To assist the buyer in a title examination, or to give him the opportunity to inspect the title to the property, the agreement of sale should contain a title reference showing where the current deed to the property can be found in the public records.

"Under and Subject."   If the agreement of sale, after negotiation, indicates that the property is to be taken subject to certain restrictions, easements, or rights of way, these should be stated specifically in the agreement of sale. For example, if a right of way crosses the rear of the property, this should be stated specifically. The buyer should have an opportunity to decide whether or not he wants to buy the property with that right of way.

Buyer beware

Many agreements are signed with a provision like this: "Under and subject to all liens and encumbrances, easements, and rights of way that may appear of record." In this case the buyer should beware. In agreeing to such a provision, the buyer is agreeing to any liens, encumbrances, rights of way, or easements that might appear on the record before he has an opportunity to do a title search. Under no circumstances should a buyer—if he can avoid it—sign an agreement with such a provision in it except on advice of counsel. The covenant that the seller will deliver a good and marketable title gives the buyer a measure of protection in such a situation. All easements and rights of way should nonetheless be specifically itemized to the extent possible.

Any other special provisions should likewise be included in the agreement of sale. For example, if the buyer is taking the property subject to an existing mortgage—if he is assuming the mortgage of the seller—the agreement should so state. The assumption clause should be specific, should identify the mortgage and the name of the financial institution involved, the place where the mortgage is recorded, and the balance at the time of signature.

Appurtenance Clause. Why does an agreement of sale mention specifically such items as plumbing, heating fixtures and systems, laundry tubs and permanent fixtures, awnings, venetian blinds, and television antennas? Unfortunately, some sellers have removed from the property such things as blinds, fixtures, storm doors, and even light bulbs after the agreement of sale has been signed. The buyer moving into the property later finds a significantly different property from what he agreed to buy.

The agreement of sale should be specific. It should state that the sale includes all the buildings, improvements, and all plumbing and heating fixtures forming a part of the property. To be mentioned also: all built-in ranges, refrigerators, laundry tubs and other permanent fixtures, storm doors, windows and awnings if any, screens, shades, blinds, drapery rods and fixtures, television antennas, and all trees, shrubbery, and plants currently on the property.

Listing personal property

Personal Property. Personal property includes items that are not normally considered part of the real estate. If any personal property items are to be transferred with the house, they should be separately listed, not included in the purchase price. Personal property may cover such items as wall-to-wall carpeting, rugs, drapes, mirrors, chandeliers, refrigerator, deep freeze, dishwasher, window air conditioners, fireplace items, lawnmower, garden tools, workbenches, water softeners, automatic door openers, and similar items. If any of these is being sold with the property, it should be specifically listed if it is to pass as part of the purchase price.

A better alternative should be noted. Where personal property is being sold with real estate, a separate value should be given to the personal items. They can then be listed in a separate bill of sale. For example, if the wall-to-wall carpeting, drapes, chandelier, and refrigerator are included in the sale, and the parties agree that they are worth $3,000, then the agreement of sale for the house could reflect a purchase price of $27,000. A separate bill of sale ($3,000) would list the items of personal property passing to the buyer. Total price for the entire package: $30,000.

Here a distinction has been made between the real estate and the items of personal property. This becomes important later on since, in many cases, the real estate tax assessment on the land and the house is based on the price stated in the deed. If the price in the deed reflects items of personal property that are not really part of the real estate, the real estate tax assessment may be set at too high a rate—namely, on $30,000 instead of on $27,000.

The terms of payment

Covenant to Buy. In the agreement the buyer consents to purchase the property. The price is stated. All terms of payment should also be stated, such as the amount of earnest money paid and the balance and how it is to be paid—whether in cash or certified funds or otherwise. For example, if the price of the property is $30,000 and $5,000 has already been deposited as earnest money, the agreement should provide that the buyer agrees to pay the sum of $30,000 payable as follows: $5,000 as earnest money on the signing of the agreement, receipt of which is acknowledged by the seller, and the balance of $25,000 to be payable in cash at the time of final closing.

The contract must contain other provisions on payment of the purchase price if the buyer must sell his present home first in order

to secure funds to buy the home. This is also true if the buyer must
secure a mortgage himself to proceed with the purchase of the property. Too often a buyer signs without specifying that he has to sell his
present house first to obtain money to buy the new house. If he cannot sell the old house in time—before the closing date—he may be in
breach of his agreement with the seller.

A buyer might also have difficulty in getting a mortgage to finance
the purchase of the new house. When the time comes to close, he
cannot produce the money. In this case he can lose his earnest
money deposit.

The buyer who has to sell his present home or obtain a mortgage
to finance the new home, or both, should insist that the agreement of
sale protect him. He needs *conditioned liability* under the contract:
he has to be allowed to sell his existing home prior to the closing on
the new home.

An element of uncertainty

The seller may, of course, resist such a provision. It brings an element of uncertainty into the contract because the buyer may not be
able to sell his home within the time limit set in the sale agreement.
The seller should then insist on a time limitation. The buyer will
have to sell his old home by a specified date or the agreement will be
void, and the seller can proceed to sell to someone else.

If the buyer has to obtain a mortgage to buy the new home, he
should make sure that the agreement contains a provision stating that
purchase is subject to securing the mortgage. If agreeable to the
seller, the interest rate should be indicated and the number of years
to pay off the mortgage specified.

Such a provision is, of course, to the advantage of the buyer. It
gives him an opportunity to "shop" for a mortgage that suits his situation. Again, the seller may raise the legitimate objection that this in-
jects an element of uncertainty into the contract.

The seller who agrees to such a provision usually insists on a time
limit by which the buyer has to secure a mortgage commitment in
writing—to be shown to the seller. The seller is then assured that the
sale will go through on schedule. If the buyer cannot procure the
mortgage commitment within the time specified, the seller can offer
the property to others.

Contract provisions conditioning the sale in any way should be negotiated matters in which both the seller and buyer have legitimate interests. Where possible, however, the buyer should insist, to the extent possible, on having these protections written into the contract. If they are not there, he is breaching the agreement if he cannot buy for those reasons at the time of closing.

THE CONTRACT[1]

The contract should be simple and complete, covering such items as:

* Legal description of the property (not just the street address)

* List of all items included in the sale, including removable items such as drapes and appliances

* Purchase price, including down payment and any special terms and provisions as to the types of financing the buyer will accept

* Date abstract is to be furnished to the buyer for examination by his attorney, or terms relating to title insurance

* Dates of payments

* Date possession is to be given

* Date deed is to be delivered

* Apportionment of taxes and special assessments

* Whether property is to be conveyed free and clear of all encumbrances (mortgages, taxes, and assessments)

* Who is to bear the loss if the property is damaged or destroyed before the sale is completed

* Damages to be paid if the contract is forfeited

* How the costs, legal and other, are to be apportioned between the parties

This list is not intended to be complete. It merely illustrates the basic items that should be included. Failure to include all necessary items could result in problems for both the buyer and seller.

[1] Adapted from *Tips on Buying a Home* (Montgomery: Alabama State Bar Assn., January 1978).

Settlement. The agreement should provide a specific closing date. The agreement can be closed or settled any time prior to that date. But a definite terminal date should be fixed in the contract so that all parties know what the time limitations are.

What are the time limitations?

Any sale agreement should state that either party may, on written notice to the other, declare *time to be of the essence* of the contract and fix a date, time, and place for final settlement. In this way the parties are assured that a closing will eventually take place. Neither party can drag his feet or postpone the sale if the contract does not provide for such a contingency.

If, after written notice is given, either party fails to proceed with the sale or purchase, that party is in default under the contract. The contract should also provide for a method of giving notice to the other party, such as certified or registered mail at the addresses set forth in the contract.

To ensure a closing . . .

Possession. The contract should specify the date on which the buyer can take possession of the property or move into the property. The possession date is normally the same as the date of final closing. But this is not always the case.

In a typical case, a seller may need additional time to move out of the property, and may request that the buyer take possession 30 days after the date of final closing. If the buyer agrees to the provision, the contract should provide for payment of rent or other form of payment for the 30-day waiting period. Alternatively, the buyer may

want to move into the property before the closing in order to make repairs, paint, or do other work. In this case the seller should insist on some form of 30-day lease or other written agreement that would give him the right to eject the buyer if the latter cannot proceed with the closing after moving into the property.

Where possession is granted before delivery of the deed, or where the seller remains in possession after delivery of the deed to the buyer, and the party in possession does not sell or buy as specified, the contract should provide for the right of ejectment by the innocent party.

Tenants.   If any part of the property included in the sale is occupied by a tenant, the sale agreement should specify this fact. The lease or leases under which the tenants are holding possession should be identified. There is need also to provide for the assignment and the proration of rent.

Proration of rent

The agreement of sale should thus provide that the leases will be assigned at the closing to the buyer and that rent for the month during which the sale takes place will be prorated between the seller and the buyer.

Prorated Items.   Normally, such things as real estate taxes, water and sewer charges, rents, and interest are prorated—divided proportionately—between seller and buyer as of the date of closing. For example, if the real estate taxes for the current year have already been paid by the seller, then he is entitled to a refund of those taxes for the balance of the year following the date of settlement. If the taxes have not been paid by the seller, the buyer is entitled to a credit for the seller's portion of the taxes for the part of the year during which the seller was the owner of the property.

Realty Transfer Taxes.   Many states and local municipalities impose taxes on the transfer of real estate by sale. This tax has various names; it is in fact a realty transfer tax.

The transfer tax is usually based on a percentage of the purchase price. The agreement of sale should provide how the tax is to be paid and by whom. The amounts of these taxes can be a significant factor in the purchase of real estate, and often can be prorated between the parties. If the buyer agrees to pay all the realty transfer taxes, the seller is receiving much more than the agreed purchase price for the real estate. Thus after negotiation it is usually agreed that the parties split or divide the realty tax between them.

Accidental destruction

Risk of Loss. It happens sometimes, after an agreement of sale has been signed, that the property then is destroyed by fire or some other accidental event. In many states the buyer may nevertheless be required to perform the contract and pay the purchase price even though the house is no longer in existence.

Against that possibility, a *risk of loss* clause in the contract provides that if neither title nor possession of the property has been transferred to the buyer, and if all material part of the property is destroyed without the buyer's fault or is taken by condemnation proceedings, the seller cannot then enforce the contract. The buyer at his option can ask for return of the earnest money deposit.

Such an arrangement is fair to the seller. The real estate is ordinarily insured against fire or other casualty and the seller can recover the loss. If the property is condemned, the seller receives the condemnation proceeds awarded him. The buyer, however, needs the risk of loss clause so that he can get back his earnest money and declare the agreement void in the event of major loss.

Two types of arrangements

Insurance. The agreement of sale must definitely provide for insurance coverage. The arrangement between the parties is usually one of two types. In one, the buyer agrees to take out adequate fire and casualty insurance on the property to protect his own interest starting with the effective date of the agreement. In the second, the seller agrees to add an endorsement to his own insurance policy to refer to the agreement, with a loss-payable clause making the proceeds payable to the seller and to the buyer "as their interests may appear."

Why is this insurance clause necessary? A buyer, when he signs a sale contract, becomes an owner of the property—what is known as the "equitable owner." This means that the buyer can go to court to force the seller to sell the property to him and deliver a deed—if the seller otherwise refuses to do so. As an owner, the buyer has an interest in the property; he can insure it and his interest must be protected.

The buyer may therefore want to place fire and casualty insurance on the property as of the date of the agreement, usually through a "binder" with his own insurance broker. As an alternative, the parties can agree that the seller will add an endorsement to his own policy making the proceeds payable to either the seller or the buyer or both as appropriate.

Of the two types, the first arrangement is to be preferred. The insurance proceeds would go directly to the buyer. They could not become involved in a possible legal quarrel between the seller and the buyer over entitlement to the proceeds of the policy.

"Fair ordinary wear and tear"

Maintenance and Repair. Ordinarily, the agreement of sale should contain a provision that the seller will continue to maintain and repair the property until final closing. "Fair ordinary wear and tear," casualty damages from causes insurable under a standard fire policy, or any other loss that occurs without the fault of the seller would not, however, be covered. This clause has importance because many sellers, after they have found a buyer, do not maintain the property, but let it deteriorate until final closing.

Seller's Expense. Ordinarily the seller pays to have the deed prepared, to have all matters of title clearance taken care of, including liens, and to have other restrictions taken off the property.

Statement of Zoning Classification and Uncorrected Violations of Ordinances. Many states require that an agreement of sale, especially in large cities, contain a statement on zoning classification. The buyer then knows, on reading the applicable zoning ordinance, what uses can be made of the property.

A property may also be sold while subject to uncorrected housing, fire, building, or safety violations. The agreement should provide for disclosure of such uncorrected violations. If the seller improperly indicates that there are no such violations when in reality these exist, the buyer has a cause of action or lawsuit against the seller for breach of the agreement.

It is very useful if the agreement of sale can specify the use to which the buyer wants to put the property. The seller should guarantee that the property is properly zoned for that use. For example, in a residential area a buyer may want to use one room on the first floor of the residence as an office for meeting customers or clients. The buyer should state that intention in the agreement of sale and request the seller to state that such a use is permitted under the applicable zoning laws. The buyer cannot complain if he does not indicate what use he wants to make of the property—if in fact he cannot use the property for that purpose after the purchase is completed.

Additional
property
assessments

Improvements by Municipality. In many cases, the municipality in which the property is situated has served notice on a seller that certain work or improvements have to be carried out on the property. An ordinance or resolution may have been passed authorizing work that will improve the property. For that work additional property assessments will be made. It comes as quite a surprise to a buyer, after he has purchased property, to receive a bill from the municipality for a sewer that was installed six months prior to his purchase.

To avoid such surprises, the buyer should insist that the seller state in the contract that he has no notice of any municipal demand that work be done on the property, or that no ordinance or other municipal resolution has been passed authorizing improvements to the property for which an assessment might be made later. The buyer can then agree that any such notices or requirements received after the signing of the agreement of sale would be the buyer's responsibility.

Inspection of Premises. The buyer should have inspected the premises both inside and out, as noted. But the agreement should provide that the buyer has in fact made such an inspection. To protect the seller, the contract should also state that the purchase is being made with reliance on the inspection and that no representations were made except as stated in the contract. The buyer should be given the right, on reasonable notice, to enter the property to view it prior to closing.

Additional Provisions. If no construction or recent remodeling has taken place, the plans and specifications for the house should be given—if available—to the buyer. The buyer should also receive any useful survey that the seller may have in his possession along with any warranties on any equipment or structural parts of the property. A termite inspection may be necessary, particularly if the buyer's financing arrangement is being insured by a government agency. If a termite inspection is to be made, provision should be made for it and for payment for it by one or both of the parties.

The seller's options

Default of the Buyer.   The agreement should specifically protect the seller in the event that the buyer does not go through with the deal. Ordinarily the seller has certain options in the event of the buyer's breach of the agreement. He may, for example:

(1) keep the earnest money and all monies paid toward the purchase price as liquidated damages, thus rendering the agreement null and void, and go on to sell the property to someone else;

(2) apply the earnest money toward the purchase price and sue the buyer for the balance; or

(3) apply the earnest money toward the seller's loss if he resells the property, then sue the buyer for any other damages sustained.

Default by Seller.   If the seller breaches the contract by refusing to deliver the deed or close the sale, the buyer has the option to:

(1) take back the earnest money from the seller and waive any claim for "loss of bargain" damages;

(2) sue for delivery of a deed to the property; or

(3) sue for damages sustained by the buyer as a result of the breach by the seller.

Avoiding future problems

No Other Warranties or Agreements.   In cases on record, one or both of the parties has later said that provisions were made or agreements entered into that were not included in the contract. For that reason an agreement usually specifies that the document constitutes the entire agreement between the parties and that no other oral or written understandings regarding the sale were entered into. This avoids any problems in the future concerning so-called oral agreements made with the contract.

Other provisions may, in some areas, be required in a contract of sale. These could include provisions covering mineral rights in Pennsylvania, West Virginia, and other coal-producing states; drilling rights in oil-producing states; and water rights in some of the states

in the West. Such provisions are customarily inserted into agreements
in those states or areas.

The above, however, constitutes a reasonably complete checklist
of items that should be contained in an agreement of sale for real estate. The sheer number of these items should make it clear that the
purchase of a piece of real estate is not a simple matter—that it
requires considerable time and study. Negotiation and signing of an
agreement of sale are only the first steps in the sale process. Some
important additional steps essential to completion of the process
should be noted.

Title Examination or Title Abstract. Depending on the state in
which the property is located, either the seller or the buyer has to
provide a title abstract, or title search, leading to the issuance of a
title insurance policy. In some states, this obligation falls on the
seller. The title abstract indicates the exact condition of the title, the
existence of encumbrances, liens, easements and rights of way,
whether or not the mineral rights on the property have been sold to
others, and all other matters dealing with the quality of the title of
the real estate.

Conducting a title search

In some states the buyer can decide to conduct a title search. In
that case an attorney may issue a certificate of title or a title insurance company will draw a title insurance policy that preliminarily
describes the quality of the title. If the title report or title abstract indicates deficiencies in the title, and if these can be corrected before
the closing, the buyer has to notify the seller of the deficiencies at
once. The seller then has the opportunity to correct those defects
prior to closing. For example, a judgment may have been entered
against the seller without his knowledge. Unless he learns of the
judgment, he will not have an opportunity to do anything about it
prior to closing.

Ordinarily, the copy of the preliminary title report or preliminary
abstract should be delivered to the seller by the buyer sometime prior
to the closing. The seller can then clear up the defects in the title.

Final Closing or Settlement of the Sale

At this point everything comes together. The deed and final evidence of good title are delivered to the buyer. The buyer pays the balance of the purchase price. The mortgages needed by the buyer to pay the purchase price are executed and the charges against the property are prorated between the parties.

No mystery in "closing"

Some mystery seems to surround the "closing" in the minds of people who have never bought or sold real estate. Such persons may view the whole question of a "closing" with some fear. However, if the agreement of sale has been properly prepared and executed, and if a title examination has been properly conducted, the closing merely represents the culmination of all the various steps.

The closing usually takes place in the offices of the financial institution that granted the buyer a mortgage. In some cases the closing is held in the office of the title insurance company—if title insurance is to be placed on the property—or in the offices of one of the attorneys for the seller or buyer. At the closing, a closing sheet is prepared which lists all the various items, including:

The purchase price
Earnest money paid

Various judgments paid
Taxes and other prorated items
Net balances due the seller
Proceeds received from the buyer
The method of final disbursement of all funds

At the closing the buyer should receive a signed deed for record-ing. Alternatively, the deed, after being shown to the buyer, is re-corded on the buyer's behalf. The buyer also receives the following:

- A title report or title insurance policy or other evidence of good title
- A bill of sale on any personal property sold with the real estate
- A receipt for the purchase price of the personal property
- A survey of the property
- The insurance policies covering the property
- A statement from the mortgagee of the amount due on any existing seller's mortgage that has to be paid from the proceeds at the closing, or a release and satisfaction of the mortgage or other liens to be paid off and released from the property

What the buyer receives

- Leases and assignments of leases
- Letters from the seller advising any tenants to pay future rents to the buyer
- Receipts for taxes for the last three years
- Receipts showing payment of all utilities to date, including water, gas, and electricity, and especially those utilities that under the law of the state are entitled to be liened against the property for nonpayment
- Keys to the home

At the closing, the seller should also receive the balance of the purchase price as adjusted in the closing statement. If the seller is taking a "purchase money mortgage" from the buyer, to be discussed later, the seller will also want evidence at the closing that the buyer has insurance naming the seller as mortgagee. This policy protects the seller in the event that a fire or other "act of God" causes loss to the dwelling.

A COST CHECKLIST[1]

You may want to use the following real estate cost checklist while discussing costs with your attorney:

Purchaser's Closing Cost

(a) Reimbursement for Disbursements for:

County search .... $

Municipal searches ....

Judgment search ....

Recording costs ....

Survey ....

Mortgage policy of title insurance ....

Owner's policy of title insurance ....

Other ....

Total Reimbursement for Disbursements .... $_____

(b) Attorney's Fee.. $_____

(c) Funds Required by Lending Institution:

Application fee and credit report .... $

Taxes: month at $ per month interest from

to   ....

Review of documents, lender's counsel ....

Other ....

Total Funds Required by Lender........................... $_____

(d) Miscellaneous:

Premium, homeowner's insurance policy .... $

Other, such as adjustments to seller for taxes, water and sewer

charges, and fuel .... $_____

Total Miscellaneous .... $_____

Total Purchaser's Closing Costs (a, b, c, and d) .... $_____

Seller's Closing Costs

(a) Attorney's fee .... $_____

(b) Realtor's commission   % × price of $ ... $_____

(c) Realty transfer fee: $3.50 per $1,000.00 of price, or less if seller

qualifies for exemption .... $_____

Total Seller's Closing Costs (a, b, and c) .... $_____

[1] Adapted from *New Jersey Real Estate, the Law, and You* (Trenton: New Jersey State Bar Assn., February 1977).

IN A NUTSHELL: QUESTIONS TO ASK BEFORE SIGNING A CONTRACT[1]

As a precaution, you should know the answers to the following questions before you sign anything or pay any money for a piece of real estate:

• When should you sign a purchase contract?

• Is the price specified?

• Does the proposed contract provide for furnishing proper evidence of title?

• Does the seller agree to furnish possession?

• Does the contract provide for the property to be insured?

• Is there a good marketable title to the property?

- Does the contract specify who is to pay the real estate taxes?

- Have you had your own attorney check the title?

- Is there an "easement or restriction of record" clause in the contract?

- Have you checked for zoning restrictions affecting the use of the property?

- Have you decided whether to hold the property in one person's name or in more than one name?

- Are you relying on a warranty deed alone for title protection?

- Will you have to pay for the property even if you can't borrow the money?

- Can you get your down payment back?

- Who is to pay the escrow fees?

- When will the transaction be closed?

- Is someone else living on the property?

- Will you have to pay any hidden fees?

[1] Adapted from *Stop, Look and Check before Buying a Home* (Topeka: Kansas Bar Assn.).

What Is a Deed?

As noted, the owner or seller of the property has to give the buyer at the closing a properly executed deed on the property. The deed is the written instrument or document by which the owner of the property conveys the land, or some interest in the land, to the buyer.

Making a gift by deed

A person may make a gift of real property by deed as well as sell property by deed. A father, for example, could make a gift of a piece of real estate to his son or other person by signing it, having it notarized before a notary public, and delivering the deed to the person receiving the property.

At the time of sale the deed will identify the parties, state the price or consideration paid, and give a complete, accurate description of the property. The deed has to be signed by the seller—or sellers if there is more than one person involved—and must be acknowledged before a notary public. At the closing, the deed is delivered to the buyer for recording.

Recording the deed is very important to the buyer. That formality constitutes notice that the buyer now owns the property and that the seller no longer has an interest as of the date of recording. If the buyer does not record the deed, anyone with a claim against the seller who is unaware of the fact of the sale can put a lien on the property. The buyer may actually have paid the purchase price and may have a deed in his possession. For the buyer's protection, the deed should be recorded immediately following the settlement.

There are various types or classes of deeds. Two rank as important insofar as individual rights are concerned:

• The *warranty deed* transfers an interest in the property and guarantees to the buyer that such interest has in fact been transferred.

• The *quitclaim deed* merely transfers whatever interest, if any, the seller may have in the property.

The quitclaim deed

The latter has a special purpose. For example, as a result of the title examination a third party may be found to have an interest in the property that the buyer intends to buy. The third party may have the right to use the property as a shortcut. In order to clear the title of that possible defect, the buyer would insist that the party who claims the right of way sign and deliver to the buyer a quitclaim deed. This transfers to the buyer whatever right the third party may have with respect to the property. In this way, the buyer is assured that the third party cannot later claim an interest in the property.

At the closing the buyer should make certain that the deed conforms in all respects to the agreement of sale and all its provisions. The lawyer for the buyer should inspect the deed to make certain that all promises contained in the sale agreement are fulfilled.

After the closing, and after the deed has been recorded, the buyer should change to his own name all necessary utility services and the real estate tax records. In many instances, because the next billing cycle for the real estate taxes comes along before the ownership records are changed, a statement for real estate taxes may be sent to the former owner. The buyer should make sure he is informed when this occurs. He must obtain a statement for the tax bill or the taxes may be placed as a lien against the property. The buyer may never know that the taxes were liened.

If the seller does not pay the tax or deliver the tax bill to the buyer when he receives it, the buyer may have no way of knowing that the taxes for that year have been billed.

BUILDING A HOME

Building versus buying

Some of the problems and procedures involved in buying an existing home have been described. Methods of financing such a purchase and the types of mortgages that may be used will be discussed later.

Suppose now that a buyer wants to build a home on a particular lot. Building is a much more complicated matter, one that requires knowledge by the proposed buyer or builder of just what is involved.

First, of course, the person who wants to build a home has the problem of finding a suitable lot. He faces the same problems in connection with the title to the lot, and with making certain that the title is good, as the buyer of an existing home. Other concerns include the cost of construction, selection of a knowledgeable builder, protection against the claims of subcontractors whom he may never have met, supervision of the work as it progresses so that he "gets his money's worth," and his need for financing.

Assuming that he has found a lot on which he hopes to build a home, the buyer may proceed in several ways. If he is buying a lot from a developer, the latter may have sets of plans and specifications available for use by the buyer. The sale may proceed as a purchase of the lot only, with an agreement to build a house later. The sale may, as an alternative, be based on an agreement to purchase the lot and the house to be built upon it. The final closing would then be held when the house is completed.

Either of these two methods may be utilized depending on the circumstances of the case and the needs of the parties as regards financing.

If the buyer decides to utilize plans and specifications already prepared by the developer, certain dangers may arise. The buyer should find out the reputation of the builder or developer—and ask some questions. What other types of homes has he built? Are the homes structurally sound? Are the people who have purchased these homes satisfied with their homes and construction features?

Obtaining references

No one who is building should hesitate to ask the developer or builder for references. Not only the people referred by the builder or developer, but other persons who have purchased a home constructed by this particular builder should be contacted.

Most persons, it seems, will discuss such matters with people who inquire, especially if the homeowners are satisfied with their homes.

A lukewarm response regarding a house built by the builder should touch off suspicions and should lead to further inquiries before buying or contracting to build.

It is very important that the plans and specifications should contain as much detail as possible so as to eliminate future problems. Some things the plans should do:

* Specify the kinds of materials and the brand names of the fixtures to be put in the house
* Be specific as far as colors are concerned
* Be very clear where specifications refer to the use of a certain type of material "or its equal"

Models, trade names, types

The latter clause, of course, gives the builder the right to substitute materials that he says are equal in quality to those specified, but that may not be or that the buyer would not want in the home. The buyer should for this reason investigate models of the desired types of lighting fixtures, kitchen fixtures, furnace, air-conditioning units, and even the types of faucets or commodes. The plans can be specific as to trade names and types.

The buyer should spend as much time as necessary in the review and preparation of the specifications for the building. He will be living in that home for a long time; if it is not exactly to his liking, he will always entertain some regret or some bitterness in connection with it. Such problems can be avoided by having the specifications reviewed by an attorney and by a construction adviser if the buyer has no architect.

The architect, the agreement with the general contractor, and other subjects deserve additional close attention from the buyer.

The Architect

If you are dissatisfied with the plans and specifications furnished by the builder or developer, you can utilize the services of an architect in the planning and designing phases. An architect will submit sketches, on request, of plans that will meet all requirements.

Architect's responsibilities, buyer's obligations

Ordinarily, a contract with an architect is based on the normal uniform architectural agreements that the American Institute of Architects distributes. These require payments based on a percentage of the total cost of the project. The agreement with the architect should be thoroughly discussed with him and with an attorney before it is signed—for one thing because it normally contains provisions for payment of architectural fees even if the buyer is not pleased with the architect's designs. The contract should specify the architect's responsibilities and the buyer's payment obligations.

The architect's services normally include drawing up the construction plans and specifications, including those relating to the architecture, structural details, all mechanical work such as electrical, heating, and plumbing installation, and all outside work on parking areas, walks, fences, landscaping, and so on.

An architect normally draws up preliminary plans for approval by the owner or buyer. If the latter approves the preliminary drawings, the architect proceeds with the final drawings or "detailed drawings." These plans may then be submitted for bids to various contractors. The preliminary plans often save unnecessary work because they make possible advance agreement on construction designs and plans.

THE PURCHASE AND SALE AGREEMENT: QUESTIONS THE BUYER SHOULD ASK BEFORE SIGNING[1]

The paper first given to a prospective buyer by a real estate broker is the purchase and sale agreement. Few people realize that this paper is the most important step in making the purchase of a home, for the details of this agreement determine what you buy and how you buy it. Before signing, read the agreement carefully and discuss with your family lawyer such items as the following:

1. Exactly what land, buildings, and furnishings are included in your offer? Are stove, refrigerator, and the like included?

2. What details regarding payments should be stated?

3. When can you take possession?

4. Is the seller to furnish you with a good, marketable title?

5. What kind of deed should the seller give?

6. Who pays for the examination of the title to the property in the event the offer is accepted? Who pays for the abstract of title or title insurance?

7. Have utilities been installed and paid for?

8. Should a surveyor be employed to determine whether the improvements are actually located on the property? Who should pay for the cost of the survey?

9. If a mortgage is to be given, who will pay the intangible tax on the mortgage?

10. If termite, water, or other damage is found, shall the seller pay the cost of repairs?

11. What are the zoning regulations, or restrictions, on the use of the property?

12. What is the time within which the purchase should be accepted or refused? Is the date of such acceptance to be vital to the offer?

13. If your offer is accepted, what steps should be taken with respect to insuring the improvements to protect you, the prospective purchaser, pending the final closing?

14. What persons (husbands and wives) should be required to sign and accept the offer?

15. Are boundary lines properly specified?

16. Are timber, mineral, and water rights, if any, properly covered?

17. Who is responsible for payment of taxes?

18. How should the agreement be executed to make it binding?

19. What are the remedies if the buyer or seller defaults?

[1] Adapted from *So You're Going to Buy a Home* (Tallahassee: The Florida Bar, February 1980).

The agreement with the architect should contain a provision that the plans and specifications belong to the buyer or person intending to build the home. Without such a provision the plans remain the property of the architect.

Supervision may guarantee performance

Depending on the size of the home and the amount of money involved, the owner may want also to retain the architect to supervise construction. Such supervision of the general contractor and all subcontractors serves often as a guarantee that the contractor will follow the plans and specifications. Normally, additional fees are required if the architect is to supervise, but it may well be worth the expense.

If no architect is used, someone with construction experience should be hired by the buyer to inspect the property from time to time and to make certain that the contractor is following the plans and specifications. Normally, the financial institution that granted the buyer a mortgage loan will have an inspector check the property before allowing any periodic payment of construction funds to the contractor. But this type of inspection is made by the financial institution primarily for its own benefit. It cannot be considered the complete type of inspection that an owner would want to ensure that high-quality materials and workmanship are going into the project.

Agreement with General Contractor

Agreement should be in writing

An architect can either place a project with several general contractors for bids or suggest a builder who meets the buyer's standards. In either case, the buyer is now in a position to enter into an agreement with a builder for the construction of the home.

For obvious reasons the agreement should be in writing. It will contain the basic agreement on the construction project. The contract must provide that the home and land will be free of all liens from all contractors, subcontractors, laborers, and persons supplying material to the general contractor.

Why is the latter assurance necessary? In most cases the buyer deals only with one general contractor. The contractor in turn enters into contracts with other people to supply him with materials and to do portions of the work, such as plastering, electrical, and plumbing.

These are people the buyer may never meet or ever see. If, however, they perform services on the home site and are not paid, such sub-contractors, suppliers of material, and workmen can, in most states, file liens against the property, called *mechanic's liens*, even though the buyer had no agreement with them.

In specific terms the building contract provides that the general contractor, on behalf of himself and all subcontractors, laborers, and suppliers of materials, will not lien the property for nonpayment. In some states a contract between the person building the home and the general contractor may specifically waive the right to file a mechanic's lien. This contract can be recorded in the courthouse so that any contractor or other "mechanic" dealing with the general contractor can know that the general contractor has waived the right to file mechanic's liens against the property. In those states where such a contract is permitted, the contract waiving the right to file mechanic's liens must be signed and filed before any work is done or any materials are supplied.

In rare cases general contractors will try to retain the right to file mechanic's liens by having supplies delivered to the project quickly, or by doing a minimal amount of work so that they can claim later that they started the work or supplied materials before the agreement waiving the mechanic's liens was filed. This is called "spiking the work."

To prevent "spiking"

To avoid spiking, many financial institutions, in lending money on new construction, will insist that photographs be taken on the site on the day the construction agreement is signed. The photos prove that no work has been done on the project, and that no supplies have been delivered.

Every buyer should make certain that the building contract provides that no liens can be filed. In states where they are permitted, contracts waiving the right to file a lien should be signed and filed as soon as possible—certainly before any work is done or any supplies delivered.

The sole judge
of quality

The construction agreement will provide for payments to the general contractor in accordance with a fixed timetable. The latter is usually based on stages of completion of the dwelling. For example, one-fifth of the total price must be paid after the foundation is completed, and so on. Normally, such agreements should provide that no payment will be made until the architect or job supervisor is satisfied that the work has been completed to that stage and issues a certificate to that effect. In such agreements, too, the architect or job supervisor should be named as the sole judge of the quality of the work, of any damages that may have been incurred because of delays, of the timeliness with which the work is proceeding, and of the degree to which the plans and specifications have been followed.

The construction contract also provides for changes in the work, normally accomplished by a "written change order." To protect the buyer, the architect, and the general contractor, the construction contract should provide only for written change orders signed by all parties. The reason: change orders may increase or decrease in number depending on the circumstances and the type of payment due.

As an example, the builder may indicate that a certain type of furnace that was specified is no longer available. He may suggest a substitute. If the different model is available at a lower price, a written change order would be prepared indicating the substitution of the new furnace and a reduction in the cost of the dwelling.

Normally, of course, change orders call for an increase in the purchase price due to a change in market conditions. At that time the parties should decide whether or not the change order should be executed. The important thing to remember here is that provisions for change orders should be included in the original construction contract.

One of the most important parts of the building or construction contract is the clause that sets a completion date. Normally, the owner's permanent financing is based on completion of the dwelling before a certain date. The date agreed upon in the contract should make some provision for the unforeseen contingencies that may arise. For example, strikes may cause certain supplies to be delivered late to the site through no fault of the general contractor. Or bad weather might delay the contract completion date. If, however, a delay occurs through the fault of the contractor, the building and construction agreement should provide for damages to be paid by the contractor at a fixed rate per day.

The termination
for cause

Finally, the construction contract should contain provisions giving the owner the right to terminate the contract for cause. That means the contractor is not doing the work properly or is not following the specifications

These basic contract provisions and the advice of a family lawyer will protect the buyer and provide for remedies in the event the general contractor defaults. The provisions also protect the buyer if the general contractor, after receiving payment, fails to pay the subcontractors. The latter will not be able to file a lien against the property or force the buyer to pay twice for the same work.

Construction Bonds

A bond is a personal commitment by the principal, the general contractor, and the surety, usually an insurance company, that both are bound to the third party, the buyer or owner, in a certain amount. The bond is conditioned on proper performance of the contract and payment of all subcontractors and suppliers.

* In a *performance bond,* the general contractor and the insurance company guarantee that the contractor will perform properly his end of the contract. If he does not, and the owner has to find another contractor to complete the work, the insurance company will pick up the additional costs.
* The *labor and material payment bond* guarantees that the general contractor will pay all his subcontractors and material suppliers. If he does not, the insurance company will step in and pay the claims.

While these bonds are normally used on large projects, they are available and may be required by contract in the construction of a home. While the premiums for these bonds are normally added to the contract price by the general contractor, the bonds are well worth the money because they give valuable added protection.

Caveat on
construction bonds

A word of caution regarding construction bonds: when the construction contract or the building plans and specifications are altered or modified in any way, the written consent of the insurance company must be obtained on every change. If this is not done, and if the contractor does not perform properly, the insurance company can claim that the change increased the possibility that the company would have to pay without its consent. Since the risk was increased, the company is no longer liable on the bonds.

If the change in the plans does increase the risk to the insurance company, it will be relieved of liability under the bond. Consent to the change should be secured from the insurance company when change orders are made out. Consent may be obtained by an architect, job supervisor, or lawyer. But it must be obtained!

The construction contract should also require that the general contractor provide the owner with insurance certificates, issued by his insurance company, protecting all parties against accidents. The certificates state that the contractor has liability insurance and workers' compensation insurance in sufficient amounts to protect himself and the owner in case of a construction accident, injury, or death. The buyer should be named as an insured person in these policies. Also, obviously, materials will be delivered to the property and more and more value will be added to the structure as construction goes forward. These values could be lost if fire should destroy the incomplete home.

Fire insurance
coverage

The construction contract itself should provide for fire insurance coverage in the event of loss by fire or some other casualty. Again, the buyer should be named as an insured. A conference with an insurance counselor on the appropriate coverage is well worth the time. It will pay off in peace of mind and in dollars and cents should a loss occur. The agreement should require that the general contractor provide the buyer with the insurance certificates so the buyer will be assured of having complete protection.

Common Disputes During Construction

Disputes arising between an owner and a contractor during construction of a dwelling usually center on whether the plans and

specifications are adequate. Other questions may arise: whether the land was in the condition represented by the owner, whether the contractor suffered additional costs because of stone encountered in excavating, whether extras claimed by the contractor were properly ordered and charged to the job, and whether the contractor deviated from the plans and specifications. Many of these disputes can be avoided by careful preparation of documents, a complete investigation of the contractor's reputation and prior performance, and a common-sense effort to be fair and understand the other guy's problems.

Protection in Making Payments

After the architect or job superintendent certifies that the work has been completed, the owner should make the final payment. A "retainage," a certain percentage of each periodic payment, is usually held back from earlier payments to ensure that the work will be done properly. The retainage is also paid over to the contractor on satisfactory completion of the work.

Before the final payment

Before making final payment, the owner should obtain from the contractor statements signed by each subcontractor and supplier that he has been paid in full. No subcontractors or suppliers will then be able to file future claims. These statements, called "releases of liens," are standard documents.

The complicated process of building a home requires the owner's close attention. He will, after all, live there for many years. A little study and care can save much money, many headaches, and a great deal of heartache. To keep that dream house from becoming a nightmare, do not hesitate to insist that the construction contract include the provisions discussed here.

The best protection, however, is a solid, competent, reputable contractor who stands behind his work. Spend as much time as necessary to find the best contractor available.

FINANCING THE PURCHASE OR BUILDING OF YOUR HOME

No discussion of the purchase or construction of a home would be complete without some discussion of how one pays for it. Not everyone, unfortunately, is in a position to pay cash when purchasing a home. Most people have to give much thought to the ways in which they can pay for it.

The property becomes security

Mortgages have traditionally been used to finance the purchase of real estate. They are not the sole means; personal loans, with or without security, can also be utilized. But in most cases, mortgages are used. With a mortgage, the owner retains the benefits of ownership while offering the property as security for a loan from the lender. While mortgages are different in the various states, the lender's interest in all cases is solely to protect his loan.

Like a deed, a mortgage must be recorded. Then the mortgagee, the party holding the mortgage, has a protected security in the real estate against third parties who might not know of the mortgage loan. The mortgage represents a lien on the real estate; it creates no personal liability on the part of the owner of the land. The mortgage follows the land from one owner to another as long as it is not paid.

The owner may become personally liable for the total amount of the mortgage loan by means of a *note* or a *bond* that can accompany the mortgage. This means that the owner signs a personal promise to pay back the entire loan. He also, of course, signs the mortgage, which creates a *security lien* in the hands of the lender. These are different documents creating different rights and obligations.

Certain types of mortgages and ancillary documents are commonly used in buying or building a home.

Purchase Money Mortgage

Financing part of purchase price

Because of financial problems facing a buyer, he may be unable to secure financing to purchase a home from any conventional mortgage or finance company. At the same time the seller may be willing to finance part of the purchase price. In other words, the seller says to the buyer, "Look, if you can't come up with all the money you need, give me a down payment and I will take back monthly payments, at interest, over a term of X number of years. Give me a mortgage to that effect, and we'll go ahead with the deal."

What the seller is talking about is a *purchase money mortgage,* a mortgage running back to the seller that covers the balance of the purchase price after the down payment is made. The seller takes a position similar to that of a bank or financial institution. He gives the buyer an opportunity to pay the balance in monthly installments with interest over a term of years.

Like every other mortgage, a purchase money mortgage must be recorded. However, to protect the seller, many states, by statute, give priority to a purchase money mortgage if it is recorded within a certain number of days or weeks from the date of the settlement. This is true even though there may be other liens filed on the real estate between the final closing and the date on which the purchase money mortgage is actually recorded.

The purchase money mortgage method is a very important method of financing for those buyers who cannot secure conventional mortgages. In some cases, too, buyers may obtain mortgage money from a financial institution for part of the purchase price. These buyers then need additional funds to complete their purchases. Where the seller will take back a purchase money mortgage, that becomes a "second mortgage"—second in priority to the first mortgage provided by the financial institution.

Conventional Mortgages

To qualify for a loan

Savings banks, commercial banks, savings and loan associations, building and loan groups, credit unions, and other private mortgage companies may grant *conventional mortgages* if the buyer qualifies for a loan as regards occupation, income, credit history, and so on. If a buyer goes into the mortgage department of a commercial bank seeking money to buy a dwelling, he must qualify for the loan under the rules of the individual bank. These rules touch on such things as the amount of money the buyer will put down in cash, the number of years the mortgage is to run, the interest rate to be paid on the mortgage, whether or not the buyer can afford the monthly payment in view of his monthly income, and whether or not he is a good credit risk.

In brief, the financial institution looks to the property to make certain it is sufficiently valuable to support a mortgage in the amount sought. The institution looks at the individual buyer to ensure that he is qualified for a mortgage under the rules and regulations.

Mortgage "shopping"

Conventional mortgages change from time to time. They undergo changes, for example, in the interest rates charged, the total terms of mortgages insofar as numbers of years is concerned, and in many other respects. The economy in which we live has much to do with determining interest rates. Much has been written in recent years of the so-called "prime rate," the rate of interest that financial institu-

tions charge their most valued clients. If the prime rate of interest at Bank X is 15 per cent, then it is to be expected that the rate of interest charged to other than prime clients will be higher than that. The individual buying a home is usually "other than a prime client." The buyer seeking a conventional loan to buy a house should, thus, "shop" for his mortgage at various financial institutions to get the best deal he can as far as interest rate and number of years are concerned.

Mortgages may be deceptive. A mortgage at one bank or financial institution for a 25-year term may mean a monthly payment of principal and interest of $400 while a mortgage at a different bank for a 20-year term may cost $450 per month. While the monthly payment may be more in the latter case, the total amount paid over the life of the mortgage would be much greater on a 25-year basis than on a 20-year basis.

In "shopping" for a mortgage, the buyer should determine the exact cost of that mortgage over the entire term of the mortgage. Only then can he make an intelligent decision on the financing of the purchase.

Prepayment
without penalty

Other factors have also to be considered. Whether or not the mortgage has a *prepayment privilege* becomes very important. Many mortgages have a penalty clause: the buyer pays a penalty if the mortgage is paid in full prior to its expiration date. This penalty is usually stated as a percentage of the total mortgage loan. Where possible, the buyer should secure a mortgage that allows prepayment without penalty.

The lender may insist, however, that the buyer both sign a bond or note, as mentioned, and allow other property to be covered by the mortgage in order to further secure the loan.

In the case of an existing dwelling, the amount of a conventional mortgage is ordinarily based on an appraisal of the property. Either by law or by its own policy, the financial institution involved will loan only up to a certain percentage of the appraised value, whether it be 75 per cent, 66⅔ per cent, 90 per cent, or whatever figure may be involved. When money is "tight," the financial institution requires a much larger percentage of the total price as a deposit from the buyer and grants a lower percentage of the balance under the mortgage. In times of "easy money," a much larger mortgage can usually be found.

Alternative Mortgage Instruments

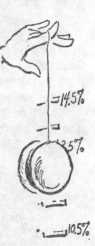

Home mortgage loans have evolved in new directions in the 1970s and early 1980s. The new forms sought partly to adapt the traditional fixed-rate, fixed-term, level-payment mortgage to new conditions. One type, for example, the *graduated payment mortgage* (GPM), was designed to accommodate payment levels to changing patterns of family income. Where the conventional mortgage cannot take account of the fact that a young family may see its income increasing over the years, the GPM can and does. Under this plan the payments on the mortgage start at lower than average levels and increase gradually over the years.

New mortgage formats also tried to take into account some basic economic facts in prolonged periods of inflation. The *variable-rate mortgage* seeks, for example, to protect lenders. It gives the lender the right to raise interest rates on existing mortgages as nationwide trends push interest rates up. Theoretically, rates can go down if local or regional rates drop.

Four new types of mortgages

At least four of the more common types of new or experimental mortgages should be described.

The "Rollover" or Renegotiable Mortgage. In effect, the "rollover" or renegotiable mortgage gives both the borrower and lender a means of re-setting the mortgage interest rate. The loan rate is set for a specific period—usually three or five years. At the end of that time it can be renegotiated to conform more closely with current mortgage loan rates.

Generally, the borrower has the option to find new financing if he and the lender cannot agree on the new loan rate.

The Variable-Rate Mortgage (VRM). The most widely used of the new mortgage formats, the VRM normally has provisions that make possible adjustments in the interest rate, the length of the loan,

or a combination of the two. Both can be changed as general interest
rates vary. In most cases the adjustments can be made once or twice
a year. A ceiling limits the extent to which the interest rate can be
changed. Customarily, this ceiling keeps aggregate changes at 2.5 per
cent—up or down—over the life of the loan.

VRM may extend
payoff period

The borrower using a VRM may have the option of extending the
payoff period while keeping monthly payments at a given level. But
the VRM favors the lender; it enables the institution to increase the
loan rates on existing mortgages within legally specified limits. A
loan taken out initially at 9 per cent can go to 11.5 per cent before
the principal has been paid off.

The Graduated Payment Mortgage (GPM). Young people starting families have provided the most receptive market for the GPM.
This type of mortgage sets monthly payments that start low, become
larger over a period of time, usually five years, and then level off.
The buyer of a home who takes a $40,000, 30-year mortgage at 9.5
per cent would, under a typical GPM, pay about $255 a month ini-
tially. The payments would increase by 7.5 per cent a year for five
years, then remain at that level.

But—a major but—the same borrower would have been making
payments at first that were $80 per month less than they would have
been under a conventional loan agreement of the same size.

Over the long haul of a 30-year GPM, the borrower would pay
substantially more ($127,601) than he would have with a conven-
tional mortgage ($121,083).

The Reverse Annuity Mortgage (RAM). Where the GPM serves
the young, climbing, ambitious homeowner, the RAM is adapted to
the needs of older men and women. The somewhat experimental
RAM makes it possible for the older person with a mortgage-free
home to recover some of the equity in his or her home without moving out.

The RAM works like this. The homeowner takes out a loan on the
home under an RAM. The lender pays out the loan in either a lump
sum or in pre-established monthly payments. The homeowner not
only continues to reside in the Old Homestead; he now has money
with which to take care of rising property taxes and home maintenance costs. He may have some money for that trip to Italy.

Legal, other questions

The RAM poses many legal and other questions. Among them: does the homeowner want to sacrifice part of his estate, to pay back the loan after his death, rather than leave it all to his heirs? If Aunt Jenny dies leaving the homeowner half a million, can the RAM be set aside—paid off in full?

The questions do not mean that the RAM has no real value. In specific cases it obviously can help older persons, retired or not. A plus is that it can be adapted almost entirely to the situation of the borrower.

Commitment Letter

Once the terms of the mortgage have been agreed on, the lender will ordinarily issue a commitment letter. The letter states the terms of the mortgage, such as interest rate, number of years, and other relevant facts. The commitment letter from the financial institution usually remains in effect for a specified period of time, such as 90 days or 120 days. If the sale is not completed within that period, the financial institution is no longer committed to give the mortgage, and no other terms remain in effect. The institution can refuse to proceed on the basis of its prior commitment letter. Where a conventional mortgage is secured, the sale should obviously be closed within the time limitation indicated in the commitment letter.

Financing the Construction of a Dwelling

Construction and permanent financing phases

Financing the construction of a dwelling differs from the financing of the purchase of an existing dwelling. In the typical case, financing a home to be built is divided into two stages: the construction phase and the permanent financing phase.

A short-term mortgage, for a year or 18 months, is normally written to finance the construction of a new dwelling or improvements on an existing dwelling. Some lenders cannot, by law, make short-term loans to finance construction; other lenders can do so. In other words, certain lenders can only issue commitment letters for "permanent" mortgages when the dwelling is completed.

Essentially, this distinction means that a construction mortgage involves a somewhat higher risk than a permanent mortgage obtained after the home has been completed. For example, the home may never be built; the contractor may default; the owner may run into difficulties; as a result, the financial institution may find itself with a home that is half built and a substantial investment already paid out.

Because of the higher risk, short-term construction loans are generally made at a higher interest rate than are permanent mortgages. Thus investors are attracted to this type of investment.

After preparing plans, specifications . . .

The buyer has his plans and specifications prepared. The next step is to approach the lender who, he feels, may give him a construction loan. The application for the loan usually requires financial information concerning the borrower, the architect, and others. Then come the appraisal of the property by the financial institution, inspection of the survey, and investigation of the credit ratings of the owner and the contractor.

The lender will also want to know where the balance of the construction money, if any, is coming from and who will be the "permanent" lender—who will provide the permanent mortgage after the home is built.

In many cases, the construction-loan lender and the permanent lender are one and the same institution. If so, the institution may simply advance funds from time to time on the basis of the mortgage. The mortgage may become permanent after completion of the entire project. The mortgage may also set forth the full amount needed at the beginning of the work, and funds may be advanced from time to time to complete the project; at final completion, a final settlement is made.

Construction-loan mortgages

Construction-loan mortgages may differ from permanent mortgages in many details. But the principles mentioned above ordinarily govern. The builder can sometimes aid in the securing of financing, but if the builder does extensive business with the financial institution, the owner should have his own inspector or architect follow the progress of the work from beginning to end. Otherwise, the financial institution's inspector could intentionally or unintentionally favor the contractor in a dispute arising over a progress payment. The attorney, architect, or job superintendent can assist sometimes in securing financing and in determining the type of inspection and supervision of the work on a day-to-day basis.

As noted, the financing institution will usually inspect only to determine whether or not, in its judgment, the progress of the work has proceeded sufficiently far to allow the next payment to be made to the contractor. The institution is not really as concerned as the owner with the day-to-day quality of the work. The owner should take all necessary steps to make sure the work is being done properly.

A commitment letter is issued by the financial institution on the construction-loan financing as well as on the permanent financing. Such a letter will spell out all the terms and conditions of the commitment on the construction loan.

Insured Mortgages

FHA and VA
insurance

Because the federal government issues mortgage insurance of several different types, an owner may qualify for a mortgage at a slightly lower interest rate than is normally possible. A smaller down payment may be required. Financial institutions will make loans under such circumstances because the federal government, through the Federal Housing Administration (FHA) or through the Veterans' Administration (VA), will insure mortgages. That means the lender will be paid the amount of the mortgage on default by the borrower.

An FHA-insured mortgage will usually allow a qualified borrower to receive 90 per cent financing. The borrower pays 10 per cent down and obtains 90 per cent financing at a slightly lower interest rate than that placed on the conventional mortgage. The same holds true for a veteran's mortgage.

The rules and regulations governing these types of mortgages are very precise and complicated; the advice of an attorney is essential in qualifying and proceeding with this type of mortgage. In "shopping" for his mortgage, the owner should not overlook the possibility that he may qualify for government-insured mortgages at lower interest rates and requiring smaller down payments.

Disclosure of Interest Rates

Recent federal and state laws, including the federal "truth-in-lending" and various state consumer-protection laws, require that mortgage and loan institutions disclose to the consumer all the terms of the sale insofar as financing is concerned. These terms include interest rates and annual percentage rate of interest charged. The borrower can then ascertain the exact amount and cost of securing a loan and making a purchase.

Making proper disclosure

The owner-borrower may be asked to sign a "disclosure statement" at a closing on his loan. The statement indicates that he has received all the necessary disclosures required by law with respect to interest, time payment charges, and all other required information. Failure on the part of the financial institution to make proper disclosure in cases where such disclosure is required may render the entire transaction null and void. Such failure may even make the institution liable in damages or penalty to the borrower or consumer.

Because of the nature of this legislation and its importance, the advice of a lawyer is essential to anyone dealing with these problems. A detailed discussion of truth-in-lending laws follows in a later chapter.

THE SELLER'S PROBLEMS

You may at this point be asking, "Whatever happened to the seller?" Everything appearing so far in this chapter has had to do with the buyer's problems: finding the property, obtaining an agreement of sale, checking the title, closing the deal, getting a proper deed, and finding the proper financing for both the purchase of an existing home and the building of a new home. What about the seller?

The seller in most cases has much less to worry about than does a buyer. The seller owns the property, and is primarily concerned with finding a buyer who is ready, willing, and able to purchase the property on terms that are agreeable to him.

If the seller has set a realistic price on the property—and this is important because being unrealistic leads only to delays in finding a buyer—the seller can proceed to sell in two different ways. First, he can try to find a buyer himself. Second, he may make use of a real estate broker to find a buyer.

1981 TAX BENEFITS

How can *the law work for you* in the purchase and sale of a home?

If you study the principles discussed in this chapter, you will be able to speak intelligently about real estate. You will also want to remember the changes that the Economic Recovery Tax Act of 1981 introduced. For example, starting in July, 1981, the seller of a principal residence could qualify for a capital gains deferral if he bought another home costing as much as or more than the "old" one within two years after the sale. Previously, the seller had 18 months to purchase a new home. Also starting in July, 1981, the seller over 55 years of age could claim a one-time capital-gains exclusion of $125,000 when selling a home and buying a new residence. Earlier, the exclusion was $100,000.

If he tries to sell the property himself, the seller may be successful in a very short period of time. He may also have to walk many prospective buyers through his house on a regular basis. Some of these persons may only be incidentally interested in the property, or just curious.

Selection of a Real Estate Broker

Finding a broker

If the seller decides to use the services of a broker, it is important to select a broker who is totally familiar with the area, who can answer the questions of prospective buyers, and who has a good record for moving properties.

How do you find such a broker? Again, consult other persons who have recently sold property and who have had good experience with a particular broker. Consult the real estate brokers' local board for help in this regard. Don't be afraid to ask questions to find out whether or not a particular broker is sufficiently interested in your property and is sufficiently knowledgeable in the area.

In interviewing a broker, one useful method is to quote to the particular broker a price that the seller himself knows is too high for the property. If the broker readily agrees that the property is worth what is clearly an exorbitant price, chances are he is only after the *listing* of the property. He will later come back to report that the price is too high and that it has to come down.

The broker will already have the written listing agreement. He will not have to worry about losing the seller as a client for the period of time covered by the agreement.

When the broker objects validly

If the broker truthfully and sincerely indicates that the asking price is too high, the chances are that he is more reliable. The seller can usually deal with him with a high degree of confidence. These are only assumptions, however. The seller's best protection is the reputation of the broker, his memberships in the professional real estate boards in the area, and his experience.

Exclusive Listing Agreements

Once the seller has found a broker, an "exclusive listing agreement" may come up for discussion. This means that the broker wants the property listed for sale with his firm exclusively for a fixed period of time, usually from 90 days to six months. The property cannot be sold through any other broker during that period.

THE JARGON OF REAL ESTATE[1]

Here, courtesy of Sylvia Porter, is a guide to the bafflegab of buying and selling real estate.

ABSTRACT. Short legal history of a property tracing ownership over the years and noting such encumbrances as unpaid taxes and liens.

AMORTIZATION. Reduction of a debt through monthly mortgage payments (or some other schedule of repayment in which the loan principal is reduced), along with payments of interest and other loan costs.

APPRAISAL. Estimate, made by the Federal Housing Administration, the Veterans Administration, a private lender, or other qualified appraiser, of the current market value of a property.

ASSESSMENT. Special charge imposed by local government on homeowners to cover costs of special projects such as street paving or new sewer systems from which the homeowners presumably benefit.

BINDER. Tentative agreement, between a buyer and seller of real estate, to the terms of the transaction—usually involving a deposit of a small amount of money.

BROKER. Professional who is licensed by the state in which he works to assist buyers and sellers of property.

CERTIFICATE OF TITLE. Legal statement to the effect that property ownership is established by public records.

CLOSING. The occasion on which the buyer and seller of a property—or their representatives—meet to exchange payment for the deed to a property.

CLOSING COSTS. Costs, other than the basic purchase price of a piece of property, which are imposed at the time a real estate deal is closed. Closing costs can include lawyers' fees, title insurance, taxes, and several other items.

COMMISSION. Fee which a seller of property pays to a real estate agent for his services—usually amounting to six to ten per cent of the sale price.

CONDOMINIUM. Individually owned real estate consisting of a dwelling unit and an undivided interest in joint facilities and areas which serve the multiunit complex.

CO-OPERATIVE. A form of real estate ownership in which each individual owns stock in a corporation, giving him the right to live in one of the units owned and administered by the corporation.

DEED. Legal, written document used to transfer ownership of property from seller to buyer.

DEFAULT. In this context, failure by a buyer to meet a mortgage payment or other requirement of the sale—which may result in forfeiture of the property itself.

DEPOSIT (or "EARNEST MONEY"). Sum of money, normally a small fraction of the sale price of the property, which a prospective buyer gives to a seller to secure a sales contract. See "Binder."

DEPRECIATION. Decrease in the value of property due to wear and tear, obsolescence, or the action of the elements. Differs from deterioration, which signifies abnormal loss of quality.

EARNEST MONEY. A deposit. See above.

EASEMENT. Right granted to one property owner by another to use the grantor's land for certain purposes—for example, a right of way for an access road or for power lines.

ENCUMBRANCE (or DEFECT OF RECORD). Claim against the title of a parcel of real estate by a third party, other than the buyer or seller (e.g., a lien due to unpaid taxes or a mortgage delinquency), which challenges the property's ownership and tends to reduce its value.

EQUITY. In real estate terms, value built up in a property over the years, including the down payment, repaid portion of the mortgage principal, and appreciation (or depreciation) in the property's market value. The amount of equity in a property is the total current value of the property minus debts against the property.

ESCROW. The placing of money or other items of value in the custody of a bank or other third party until the terms of a real estate transaction are fulfilled by the two parties involved. Also, amounts paid by a homeowner into an account, usually administered by the mortgage lender, to provide for recurring expenses such as real estate taxes and homeowner insurance premiums. This type of escrow usually is included in the total monthly payments to the lender.

FHA. Federal Housing Administration, which insures mortgage holders against losses from default on loans made according to the Administration's policies.

FORECLOSURE. Sale by a bank or other lender of a property on which payments are seriously in default in order to satisfy the debt at least partially.

LIEN. Claim against a property which sometimes is kept as security for the repayment of a debt.

LISTING. Registration of a property with one or more real estate brokers or agents, entitling the broker who actually sells the property to a commission. An exclusive listing gives one individual broker the exclusive right to handle the sale of a property; a multiple listing permits a special group of brokers to handle the transaction.

MORTGAGE. Legal claim on property, given as security by a borrower to the lender of the funds in case repayment of the loan is not made.

OPTION. Often sold by a seller of property to prospective buyer, giving the latter the right to buy the property at a specified price within a specified period of time.

PLAT. Pictorial plan or map of a land subdivision or housing development.

POINTS. Part of the settlement costs of exchanging real estate. One point is 1 per cent of the amount of the mortgage. Points are paid to the mortgage lender. In some cases, the term simply means a service charge imposed by the lender to cover part of the administrative costs of processing the loan. In other cases, particularly when an FHA loan is involved, the points amount to an adjustment in the interest rate to bring an artificially administered rate up to the market rate at the time. Points, in this second sense, technically are paid by the seller of the property. However, since the price of the house normally is adjusted to allow for this, points always effectively increase the interest rate on the loan to the buyer. They tend to eliminate the interest rate advantage of government-insured or guaranteed loans.

PURCHASE MONEY MORTGAGE. Mortgage granted directly by a seller to the buyer of the seller's property, in which the seller may take back the property if the buyer does not pay off the mortgage as agreed. In brief, the seller of the house lends the buyer the money with which to buy the house.

QUITCLAIM DEED. Deed which releases any interest a seller or other individual may have in a given piece of land. See "Deed."

REAL ESTATE (REAL PROPERTY). Land, and any structures situated on it.

REALTOR. Real estate agent who is a member of the National Association of Realtors. A copyrighted word, always capitalized.

SETBACK. A common restriction provided under zoning ordinances specifying the distance a new house must be set back from a road or from the lot boundaries.

SURVEY. The determination, by means of examination of land records and also field measurements based on these records, of the exact boundaries and location of a property.

TITLE. Legal document containing all necessary facts to prove ownership of property.

TITLE DEFECT. Fact or circumstance which challenges such ownership.

[1] Selections from *Sylvia Porter's New Money Book for the 80's* by Sylvia Porter, copyright © 1975, 1979 by Sylvia Porter. Reprinted by permission of Doubleday & Company, Inc.

Often, even though an exclusive agreement has been signed with Broker X, he will place the property on a so-called "multilist," a group of brokers who work together to sell a particular piece of property on a split commission basis. The multilist is also called a Multiple Listing Service (MLS). In this case the listing broker receives a percentage of the real estate commission regardless of which multilist broker actually sells the property.

Ordinarily, an exclusive real estate listing agreement contains a special clause. It provides that if the property is sold to someone who was introduced by the broker during the term of the exclusive listing agreement, then the broker earns his commission regardless of the fact that the property was sold directly to the buyer after the listing agreement had expired.

A hypothetical case

A hypothetical case shows what this can mean. You sign a six-month exclusive real estate listing agreement with Broker Brown. After three months have gone by, Broker Brown brings Mr. Smith to look at your house. You hear nothing from Mr. Smith for another eight months. If Mr. Smith comes back after the listing agreement has expired and says he wants to buy the property, you will owe the broker a commission since Mr. Smith was introduced to the property by the broker during the exclusive listing agreement period.

From the standpoint of the broker, the special clause prevents the parties from agreeing among themselves not to deal until the exclusive listing agreement period has expired. From the seller's point of view, however, the clause creates a difficult situation. A lawsuit could result if the seller and the broker disagree as to whether or not the individual to whom the property was sold was in fact introduced to the property by the broker.

For the seller's protection

Depending on the language used in the listing agreement, it becomes very important for the seller to protect himself in such a situation. Another provision in the exclusive listing agreement should require that the broker supply the seller with the names of all persons with whom the broker has discussed the property—or to whom he has shown the property during the term of the exclusive agreement. The list should be given to the seller at the end of the term of the agreement. This provision protects the seller in dealing with third parties after the expiration of the exclusive contract.

The requirement that the broker supply a list of names is fair to both the seller and the broker. It should not be objected to.

Multilist Plans

When a piece of property is placed on a multilist, the seller in effect engages the services of many more brokers whether he deals only through one or directly through the multilist. While some of these services have come under attack because of alleged antitrust problems, they do exist. They also bring in many brokers who will work to sell a property.

How long should an exclusive listing agreement run? Caution should be exercised. The period should not be too long. Six months, for example, is usually too long.

The circumstances of each particular case should, of course, be considered. A lawyer may be able to advise the seller. But in the normal situation, 90 to 120 days should be long enough. If more time is allowed on an exclusive agency agreement, the broker may have a tendency to push off the sale of the property while trying to "move" properties on which the listing agreements are about to expire. This is only human nature. But it may leave the seller with little activity on the sale of his property for a long time.

When Does a Broker Earn His Commission?

While the law differs from one state to another on this point, many states provide that a broker earns his commission once he finds a buyer who signs an agreement of sale. Even if the sale of the property does not go through because the buyer cannot qualify for the mortgage, or because he decides he does not want to buy for whatever reason, the broker nevertheless has earned his commission once a buyer signs an agreement.

Commission to be paid on closing

Once again the seller should protect himself. The listing agreement should specify clearly that the broker earns his commission only when and if a final closing takes place. The buyer must of course have been introduced to the property by that broker.

Where a seller decides to keep the earnest money as liquidated damages, as noted, disagreement over a broker's commission may be minimized. Many listing agreements provide that the earnest money be split between the broker and the seller where a sale falls through. Where, however, the broker's commission exceeds the amount of the earnest money paid, the seller may have to pay the commission to the broker from his own funds.

*The
"nonexclusive"
agreement*

Another form of listing agreement is the "nonexclusive" type. Here, the broker is given the right to sell the property on behalf of the seller, but other brokers have the same right. The nonexclusive agreement is similar to the multilist plans. But the seller can deal with several brokers individually, and each has the right to sell the property on his behalf. All that has been said before in connection with the exclusive agency agreement applies equally to the nonexclusive agreement.

Most real estate brokers work hard and diligently to secure buyers for residential property. While the commission earned in a particular case may seem high, usually 6 or 7 per cent, the broker may show the property to many persons before finding a buyer. Thus the selection of a qualified broker to assist in the sale of property can be of great help.

How can the law work for you in the purchase and sale of a home?

If you study the principles discussed in this chapter, you will be able to speak intelligently about real estate. You will also know what questions to ask, and can save money by understanding ahead of time what you are dealing with. You will be in a much stronger bargaining position, which, after all, is the name of the game.

Good luck in your new home!

4 "THEY WON'T LET ME ADD A PATIO TO MY HOME"

Every right that Americans possess under their system of laws has a corresponding duty. The right of free ownership of property carries with it the duty under the law not to interfere with the free use of someone else's property while exercising the right of ownership.

Under the policy power of the state to regulate the public health, safety, and morals for the general welfare, local governments enact and enforce "zoning regulations." As a result of zoning regulations, the free use of property is restricted. These restrictions, if reasonable, are deemed necessary for the public health, safety, and morals.

No matter where you live, you are affected by some form of zoning regulation. The regulations involve the determination by the governing body of the state, or the local government that receives its zoning authority from the state, that a zoning regulation is needed for a public purpose. That public purpose may be real or imagined in a particular case. While no clear-cut line separates arbitrary zoning from proper and legal zoning, the courts decide these issues as they arise.

COURT ACTIONS IN ZONING CASES: THE TEMPERING INFLUENCE

Court decisions have both upheld the zoning policies of local communities and attacked them. The net effect has been to moderate the social and other effects of zoning regulations.

Zoning that excludes certain groups of people, or people in certain socioeconomic categories, has come under attack. For example, the Supreme Court has stated its opposition to exclusionary zoning regulations that keep persons of low and moderate income out of specific portions of communities or entire areas. The Court has expressed the belief that developing communities have to make it possible for persons of widely diverse backgrounds and professions to reside within their boundaries.

Preserving a town's character

By contrast, the Supreme Court refused in 1974 to hear the case of *Construction Industrial Association of Sonoma County* v. *City of Petaluma*. In so refusing, the Court in effect upheld the right of the City of Petaluma, California, to preserve its small-town character by passing zoning ordinances. The city also gained the right to grow at an orderly and deliberate rate and to preserve its open spaces and low-density population.

The U.S. Court of Appeals had earlier ruled in the City of Petaluma case in favor of the city. The court said that "the concept of the public welfare is sufficiently broad to uphold Petaluma's desire" to preserve its basic character.

Other court cases can be expected both to underscore the rights of individuals to live where they want to and the municipality's right to establish plans for orderly community growth and development.

Zoning ordinances, to be valid and constitutional, must conform to a comprehensive plan of zoning in the area involved. The attacks on zoning ordinances that have been successful have been based on a community's failure to establish a comprehensive plan of development. Without such a plan, zoning restrictions can create undue hardship for the owner of particular real property, resulting in discrimination against that owner.

Constitutional protections

In addition, every zoning ordinance has to conform to the constitutional protections that keep a property owner from being deprived of his property without due process of law. If the ordinance bears no substantial relationship to the public health, safety, welfare, or morals, the ordinance can be attacked as unconstitutional.

Each particular case has to be decided upon its own facts. These include the circumstances surrounding the enactment of the ordinance, its purposes, the particular property involved, any undue hardship on the owner as a result of literal enforcement of the ordinance, and many other factors that go into determination of the validity of any ordinance.

DIVIDING PROPERTY INTO DISTRICTS

The purpose of a zoning ordinance is to divide a particular community into zoning districts. The ordinance specifies or limits the use to which property in that district can be put, and restricts or requires certain improvements and uses of land within the district. There are three main types of controls inherent in a typical zoning ordinance: control of population density, control of use of property, and control of height or other physical characteristics.

CONTROLLING POPULATION DENSITY

The ordinance will attempt to control population density by specifying the minimum lot area for a home or family, the number of square feet of open space required between structures, and the maximum number of homes per acre or per half acre or other given area.

Population density and zoning

The control of population density is a recent development in the law of zoning, and it has led to a method of developing property different from the normal, single-family residential dwelling-type development. The new developments, utilizing the townhouse or condominium-apartment ownership concept, have attempted to utilize a high-density population area with open space common to all the people living in the high-density housing development. For example, townhouses—individualized attached homes, sometimes on various levels but nevertheless having party or common walls—are built to include a common yard or parklike area immediately adjoining the residences. The net effect is to satisfy the total open-area requirement of the zoning ordinance and also permit high-density population within the area.

This concept will undoubtedly remain popular in future years if the cost of construction of single-family dwellings continues to rise and if the need for housing, at reasonable cost, continues to grow.

Control of population density becomes a matter of critical interest where an apartment building "goes condo," or is turned into a condominium. In this situation, a very common one in the cities in the 1970s, many apartment dwellers become homeowners. They usually have the opportunity to buy their apartments. Making such a purchase, most often by taking out a common type of mortgage, the new homeowner acquires a personal interest in limiting the population of his building or area.

Like the owner of a single-family home or townhouse, the condominium owner takes title to his unit by deed. He shares with other owners a common ownership of public areas. This means that each owner pays taxes on a prorated basis.

Upkeep of common areas

Each owner also contributes to the upkeep of common areas. Most condos are organized as corporations or associations. They have boards of directors, provide by-laws with which all owners have to comply, and decide on changes in the building or common areas.

Control of Use of Property

Zoning ordinance restrictions on use result in control of the particular type of activity or use that may be carried on in a building or on a piece of land. For example, a district may be limited to residential uses only, such as single- or multifamily dwellings. Another district may be limited to commercial uses. The ordinance may specify by

name the kinds of commercial uses that are permitted, such as bakery, professional offices, laundry, grocery store, and so on. Light manufacturing may be allowed in particular districts depending on the definitions contained in the ordinance itself.

Area and Height Restrictions

Area and height restrictions refer to the number of stories permitted in a building or dwelling by height in feet. The ordinance may also specify the minimum areas for side yard, front yard, and rear yard setback for any structures on the property. For example, if a particular district requires a 30-foot front yard, or 30-foot setback, the dwelling or building on any particular lot in that district must be at least 30 feet from the edge of the road or street right of way.

The side yard setback

Side yard setback means that the side of the building must be at least the number of feet specified from the lotline or dividing line to the side of the building. Rear yard setback means that the building must be at least a specified number of feet from the rear property line, unobstructed by any other structure.

The area regulations may go still farther. They may provide that a number of square feet or a percentage of the total lot be utilized or covered by a structure or a building. In some cases the ordinance will set a minimum size for lots that may be used as single units or individually owned units, or a maximum size or height for all buildings in relationship to the width of the streets adjoining the lot.

The typical zoning ordinance contains a definition of permitted or excluded uses in given, clearly defined blocks, areas, or districts. There may be residential, commercial, light industrial, heavy industrial, or special development districts. Still other types may be defined in the ordinance, each district classification spelling out the particular uses permitted.

Accompanying each zoning ordinance is a zoning map that shows the boundaries of the various districts. Each area is colored or shaded to indicate the district classifications. For example, an R-1 (Residential-1) district shown on a municipal map may be color-coded in red, the R-2 (Residential-2) district in blue, the C-1 (Commercial-1) district in yellow, and so on.

How to determine zoning by area

The color-coding or shading enables a prospective purchaser of real property to determine the zoning for the property. He simply goes to the local municipal building, speaks to the zoning officer, and looks at the zoning ordinance and the zoning map.

Anyone buying real estate should follow that procedure. Unless the law requires the seller to note the zoning classification in the agreement of sale, a purchaser is taking a chance if he fails to make absolutely certain that the property is zoned properly for his intended use, or that the dwelling or other structure can be utilized for his intended use. Otherwise he may buy the property and find out too late that he cannot use the property as he wants to.

SPECIAL EXCEPTIONS AND VARIANCES

The zoning ordinance attempts to be comprehensive regarding district classifications and other details. But provisions have to be built into the ordinance for property that does not precisely fit in with the general scheme of the ordinance. The typical ordinance thus contains exceptions to the general zoning scheme where the circumstances warrant. These special arrangements for problem property fall ordinarily into two categories: the special exception and the variance.

The Special Exception

A use of property that is specifically denied in the zoning ordinance, but that may be allowed if certain conditions are fulfilled, ranks as a special exception. For example, a zoning ordinance may forbid an auto repair shop in a light commercial district. However, the ordinance may indicate that the auto repair shop will be allowed by special exception if the proposed user or owner of the property appears before the zoning commission of the municipality, shows his plans and specifications, and gives assurance concerning the elimination of noise, odors, and so on.

Public hearings on uses

A public hearing may be held to determine whether or not the proposed use would meet with criticism from the inhabitants of the area. If all the requirements are met, a special exception use for the auto repair shop may be granted.

The special exception, in brief, permits a use ordinarily denied if the owner or user submits all the necessary information and if the zoning body rules favorably on the request.

The Variance

A variance is a procedure by which the literal language of a zoning ordinance is not followed. Usually, strict compliance with the ordinance requirements would cause unreasonable and unnecessary hardship to the owner of the property involved.

The *variance procedure* involves an application for a variance by the owner or intended user of the property. The application is filed with the local zoning officer or building permit officer. The user will receive a formal denial of his application, since his use for some reason will not conform to the strict literal language of the ordinance. The user then, after receiving the denial, will appeal to the local zoning board of adjustment or zoning appeals board.

In order to establish the hardship that he must show, the owner has to be able to establish several details in his application for the variance.

- Because of the nature of the property, for example because it is irregular in size, grade, or other feature, development of the property in accordance with the strict requirements of the zoning ordinance is unreasonable or impossible. Here it is stressed that the physical features of the site do not allow its use as specified in the ordinance.

Unreasonable cost
of development

- The nature of the site would involve an unreasonable cost of development. The reason may be the dimensions or shape of the property, its location, or the fact that strict adherence to the ordinance would make the property unprofitable.

- The owner has to show that he himself did not create the hardship problem. For example, a developer who lays out a plan of lots, leaving one plot irregular, would be denied a zoning variance on the basis of hardship because he himself created the hardship situation.

- The owner must show that the character of the neighborhood would not be changed if the proposed variance were granted. A factory might change the neighborhood in a residential district, for example; a three-flat might not. Construction of a parking area in a residential district might not in and of itself change the residential nature of the district, and could possibly qualify for variance treatment.

- Finally, the owner must show he is applying for the minimum change from the strict, literal terms of the ordinance that will give him the relief he seeks. Sometimes this requires proof of what the return on an investment will be, involving the use of appraisals and expert testimony before the reviewing body. While difficult to establish because of possible alternative uses of the property, the fact of minimal deviation must generally be proved.

The reviewing board of a municipality may refuse a variance even after the owner establishes all five points. He may then appeal to the courts for relief, claiming that the negative decision is arbitrary and capricious and not in accordance with the law.

Instructions on
variance
procedures

The zoning ordinance, to be effective, has to contain all necessary instructions on variance procedures and special exceptions. It must also provide for appeals procedures and the creation of zoning commissions and zoning boards of adjustment.

NONCONFORMING USE

When a zoning ordinance is first enacted, it often affects existing structures. For example, a commercial retail bakery that may have been operating at a particular location for a long time may find that its continued use is not permitted under a new zoning ordinance.

Existing buildings that do not conform to the newly established requirements of a zoning ordinance are called "nonconforming uses." If they have been proper uses under the regulations that previously existed, these will usually be allowed to continue under the new zoning ordinance as "legal nonconforming uses."

The buyer of real property should nonetheless ascertain whether or not the property he wants to buy constitutes a nonconforming use. If it does—if its use can continue because it was valid prior to enactment of a later ordinance—he takes a substantial risk in buying that property for several reasons.

A method of
nullifying

First of all, the nonconforming use may be nullified through abandonment or discontinuance of the particular use. It may be nullified by provisions of the zoning ordinance that require discontinuance of the nonconforming use after a certain number of years. In another situation, a new owner may change the use, however slight, and in that way give the municipal authorities the opportunity to claim that the nonconforming use had been discontinued.

Another danger is that the property might be destroyed or damaged by fire or some other "act of God." In most cases, if more than 50 per cent of the property is destroyed, the zoning ordinance will not permit the owner to reconstruct the same structure for the same use. Destruction would terminate the nonconforming use. An owner would rarely be able to obtain a variance or other exception to permit continuance of the use after destruction of the property.

For such reasons the purchaser of property will always investigate the zoning requirements completely. If a use is nonconforming, the owner risks loss of a substantial investment.

AMENDMENT OR CHANGE OF THE ZONING ORDINANCE

In addition to the procedures for seeking a variance or establishing a special exception, the owner of property has another option. He may decide to seek a change in the zoning classifications for the area covered by his property. This involves a request for a change to the zoning commission or planning commission of the municipality. The owner has to prove that the change sought will benefit not only himself but the community in general. He also has to establish that the requested change is in conformity with the comprehensive plan of development for the entire community.

"Spot zoning"

It may happen that the owner wants to make a change in a particular area of another district. That change will not affect the entire zoning district or even a substantial part of it. For example, he may want to erect a small shopping center in a residential district. The request may be attacked as "spot zoning," which means changing the classification only for a small area in a given zoning district.

Where spot zoning takes place to any great extent, it destroys the entire zoning scheme. It can sometimes upset the comprehensive zoning plan of the municipality. As a result, spot zoning is rarely permitted. It may be allowed, however, if the owner can establish a need for the type of use in the area and can thus establish his right to have the zoning changed. The proof required of the owner in a case of spot zoning is very heavy, however; an owner should proceed only with that awareness.

A change in zoning ordinarily requires a public hearing before the municipal plan commission. The meeting is announced publicly so that other residents or owners in the area can raise any objections that they might have.

From a practical standpoint, many courts are reluctant to consider zoning problems because they are considered the bailiwick of the local governing body representing the people in the area. A denial of a zoning change by the plan commission, or by the board of councilmen, commissioners, or supervisors, will very likely not be reversed by a court in the absence of clear proof of the need for the change. A permitted rezoning, if attacked by area residents, has a better chance of being upset by the courts.

PROCEDURES FOR APPEALS UNDER ZONING ORDINANCES

Assume that you are the person in this chapter title who wants to add a patio to your home. You will have prepared plans and specifications showing the area of your property where the patio is to be located, the patio's size, and the materials to be used. You will then take these plans and specifications to the zoning officer of your municipality for a *building permit*.

Two reasons for refusal

If the permit is refused, it will be for one of two reasons or both. The patio may come too close to, or impinge on, the rear yard, side yard, or front yard setback, or your specifications are not suitable under the building codes.

Refusal could be based on other factors. But once the refusal is made, you should insist that the zoning officer state his reasons in writing. Working with your family lawyer, you can decide whether you should apply for a special exception or for a variance under the terms of the ordinance. You may even decide to attack the ordinance on constitutional or other grounds; but since the law favors orderly

development of property, you should make every attempt to bring your request within the terms of the ordinance rather than attack it.

You will next file the necessary appeal forms with the zoning officer. Attached to your application you should have the following, if available:

- *Consent of neighbors.* It is important that the zoning officials understand that your neighbors have no objection to your application. If you cannot obtain their consent, at least try to get their assurances that they will not actively object to your request. Then you can truthfully tell the zoning board that your neighbors will not raise any objections.

- *A listing of other locations* where zoning officials have granted a request similar to yours. If you can point out that your neighbor down the street added a patio to his home recently, this will help your case. But previous allowance of a use similar to yours is not necessarily binding on the board. The board will normally be influenced by the prior allowance, however.

Presentation and master plan

- *Master plan.* Your presentation before the zoning board should show that your request is totally consistent with the master plan for the municipality. If you can establish this, your chances of success are greatly increased.

- *Evidence produced at the hearing.* It usually helps at municipal hearings if diagrams, photographs, and other documents are used to establish the need for a proposed change. The more complicated the request, the greater the need for "visuals" to show your request to the best advantage. You may also consider bringing in an expert to state his opinion that your request will add to the value and appearance of the property and enhance the neighborhood.

- *Financial evidence.* It may be helpful to your case to show that you may not get a fair return on your investment in the property unless you secure the change you seek. This is true even where you are not trying to establish financial hardship because of the physical characteristics of the property. If adding a patio will add to the value of the property, enhance the beauty of the neighborhood, and conform to the master plan, you have presented a good case for the new use.

After the hearing, the zoning board is required to make its decision known within a specified time. In rezoning cases, final action is taken by the elected governing body of the municipality. If the planning commission to which the rezoning petition is referred recommends the rezoning, it will be brought before the governing body. Another public hearing may be held before final action is taken. Only after all appeals within the zoning ordinance have been unsuccessful can you appeal to a court.

The example of the addition of a patio as a zoning "problem" has been used only for convenience. The methods discussed here apply equally to any other zoning problem that you might have.

ZONING CONSIDERATIONS FOR THE PURCHASER OF PROPERTY

Specific things to learn

As indicated, a purchaser of property should make sure he is totally familiar with the zoning situation. More specifically, the buyer must be aware of the following:

- *The existing zoning status or classification.* He should be familiar with the zoning district in which the property is located; the uses permitted in the district; the height of structures permitted; the rear, side, and front yard setback provisions; the area or percentage of the lot that can be covered by the structure; and the minimum sizes of dwellings.

- *Variance.* The buyer should know whether or not a structure or use can continue because of a variance issued at some time in the past. If so, the terms and conditions of the variance must be studied. Variances are usually granted under strict conditions that may change. If the variance was issued for a limited time, this would affect the buyer's use of the property.

- *Nonconforming use.* The purchaser should know whether or not the present use of the property is nonconforming. If it is, the zoning ordinance may contain terms that may affect the expiration of the legal nonconforming use. In addition, the buyer will be taking the chance that the nonconforming use may expire because of abandonment, change of use, or destruction of a building by fire or some other cause.

- *Certificate of occupancy.* Many municipalities require that a certificate of occupancy be issued before a building or structure can be occupied. The certificate ensures that the applicable building codes and zoning regulations have been complied with. The buyer who does not obtain a certificate of occupancy may be required later to make expensive improvements or tear out part of the structure before he can occupy it.

No vested right

- *Statement that use is permissible.* No property owner has a vested right in the continuance of a particular zoning classification for a piece of property. The zoning classification of the property may be changed if all the requirements of notices, hearings, and other protections are satisfied.

It sometimes happens that a change of zoning classification takes place between the time when an agreement of sale is signed and the time of the final closing or settlement. The courts have decided that a buyer cannot escape from his obligation to buy the property if the zoning is changed unless the agreement provides for that kind of alternative. Very properly, the buyer can insist that the agreement contain statements by the seller of the then-existing zoning classification and of the buyer's right to void the agreement if the property cannot be used as intended.

Such factors are important where the buyer is purchasing *improved* property that already has a dwelling or some other structure on it. If the purchaser is buying *unimproved* property, intending to build on it at some time in the future, his concerns are slightly different:

- *Zoning of intended use.* The buyer should check the zoning ordinance to make certain that the intended or future use is permitted in the district. The size of the plot, the height of the intended structure, and the area covered by the structure are all important.
- *Variance.* If the buyer's intended use of the property requires

a variance, the agreement with the seller should spell out clearly that "the deal is off" if the buyer cannot secure the variance before he completes the purchase. The application for the variance should be made in the seller's name because he is still holder of the legal title to the property. From a practical standpoint, his chances for success might be greater than the future owner's.

The seller must certify

- *Statement that intended use is permissible.*   The buyer should have the seller certify in the agreement that the intended use is permissible. Then zoning problems can be avoided.

PRIVATE DEED RESTRICTIONS

Another form of control over the use of land, other than zoning regulations, is based on *private restrictions* on use specified in the deeds to the property. These private restrictions may be called "protective covenants" or "restrictive covenants." But they involve contracts between a buyer and seller stipulating how land may be used.

In most cases, the purpose of a protective covenant or private deed restriction is to protect or preserve the character of the neighborhood. Examples of these restrictions include covenants against the sale of intoxicating liquors on the premises and restrictions against commercial uses.

A common deed restriction

Many years ago, many large tracts of land were sold with restrictions against the use of the land by churches and houses of religious worship, or with prohibitions on its sale to members of certain racial groups. These restrictions have since been declared unconstitutional and void by the Supreme Court.

The more common form of private deed restriction limits the kinds of structure that can be erected on a lot. A developer may want to maintain a certain "tone" on the lots he sells; to ensure that this tone or atmosphere is maintained, he will insert restrictions into the deeds to the lots. For example, a clause will state that all dwellings erected must be "brick to grade," with minimum livable floor space of not less than 3,000 square feet, with integral garages that face to the rear of the lot, and so on.

Each deed that the developer delivers contains the same restrictions. As an alternative, the developer may list all of the restrictions in one document, record that document in the local register or recorder of deeds office, and refer to that document in all deeds on all lots sold. In this way the developer can force restrictions on every property owner in the development.

These restrictions, if valid, may also be enforced by any owner of land that is subject to the restrictions. If the area has substantially changed from the conditions that existed when the restrictions were imposed, the court may, on application of one of the owners, set the restriction aside. This could occur where the deed restricts the use of the land to single-family dwellings in a situation where the area has become commercial in fact.

PROPERTY OWNERS' ASSOCIATIONS

Where cluster, condominium, or other high-density housing appears, a *maintenance association* may be established by the developer by means of the restrictive covenants contained in the deeds or in a separate document. These maintenance associations provide a vehicle for enforcement of the protective covenants in favor of all, for maintaining the open spaces and parks that are provided for all owners and residents, and for providing certain types of recreational activities. The latter could include swimming pools, community rooms, tennis courts, and club or meeting rooms.

An association of this kind can assess the owners of property in the development for benefits that the association provides. The association may be responsible for such tasks as paving sidewalks, painting common areas, paying taxes and assessments on property held for common use, and purchasing property from an owner desiring to sell. The latter applies if the restrictions require the owner to offer his property for sale to the association first. The association may also provide for garbage collection, snow removal, and even police and fire protection.

*Ordered developed
and individual
rights*

This discussion of zoning has focused on how zoning and master development plans of local municipalities have materially affected the rights of private landowners in the use of their property. But remember that while the orderly planning of a community is essential to the well-being and future value of the area, the right of private ownership must also be protected. The clash between the need for ordered development of land and the rights of the individual spotlights an area in which the law must find answers.

As the housing patterns of the country change, so will zoning regulations change to meet those changing patterns. The decrease in the United States birth rate that became particularly evident in the 1970s will undoubtedly lead to an increase in the high-density apartment-condominium type of construction and reduced construction of the single-family dwelling.

You, as a possible future buyer of real property, should be aware of the place of zoning in the scheme of land development. But you should also understand the principles and procedures used in the zoning process. As a possible investor in real estate, you should be aware of future housing trends to capitalize on those trends in seeking out available property. Then your decision to invest in land will be an informed decision.

In any event, good luck with your new patio!

5 "THEY WANT MY PROPERTY FOR THE NEW COURTHOUSE"

In the preceding chapter, it was shown that a comprehensive plan of development provided a community with a basic plan for growth. One of the considerations in community planning and development must include the right of governmental authority or other public body to "condemn" private property for public use. Condemnation, or "eminent domain," is the legal process by which a governmental body acquires private property from private citizens for public use on payment of reasonable and just compensation for the property. If no payment is made, the owner has been denied his right to his property without due process of law, an unconstitutional act.

Many typical condemnation situations could be cited. Additional property may be needed to widen a street. A new courthouse may have to be built on what was formerly private land. A limited-access highway may have to pass across private property. A municipal park or a municipal sewer system may have to be expanded through condemnation of some private property.

How do you, a private owner of real property who paid good money for that property, who lives in it or on it, and who wants to keep it, react to the intent of some governmental body to take your property? What are your rights? If you don't agree with the amount they offer you, what can you do about it? These are some of the questions that are dealt with in this chapter.

WHAT IS A "PUBLIC USE"?

In order to be valid, a condemnation has to have a public-use purpose. That means, today, that the proposed use must be more of a public necessity than the present use.

A "public use"
—originally

Originally, "public use" meant a use that was clearly public: one that all citizens could enjoy, or in which all could take part. A good example would have been a highway system, or a new courthouse, or a municipal park. But in relatively recent times, the concept of a "public use" has grown. It now includes such things as a public parking garage for the use of a limited number of people, the rental of airspace over a public garage to private users, or even a low-income housing project. The theory is that "public" includes both uses for the general public and uses for a limited number of citizens, such as low-income families.

The redevelopment of blighted areas has become a key means by which communities upgrade properties or districts. Redevelopment generally involves condemnation of private property by a redevelopment agency or authority, the payment of condemnation damages for taking the property, and then resale to other private companies or developers for the purpose of erecting new or improved structures on the condemned land.

Parenthetically, it should be noted that condemnation also refers to a governing body's right to declare a building unsafe or unfit for use. Where a structure is condemned because it is a menace to individuals or the public safety, use is usually ended until the defects have been remedied.

Redevelopment authorities were attacked at first because they took private property for public use and resold it to other private interests. Where was the alleged public use? However, because of the social desirability of redevelopment, the propriety of condemnation for that purpose has been universally allowed.

Charters for redevelopment

Redevelopment projects are usually undertaken by agencies under charter of state law. The agencies are called "authorities." By law, they have the right to issue bonds to finance their operations. By using these bonds and separately created authorities, a state can proceed with a program of redevelopment and rehabilitation without incurring any additional state debt.

WHAT IS INCLUDED IN THE "TAKING" OF PROPERTY?

When land is taken for a new highway, courthouse, or other public purpose, it is easy to see what land was actually taken and to acknowledge that the owner is entitled to compensation for it. But what about a situation in which a limited-access highway is built across a neighbor's land? The highway cuts off access to the property from one side. What if a flood control project results in the occasional flooding of a person's land even though none of his land is actually taken?

What if an airport is built near a residential area? On their approaches, the airplanes fly close to ground level, disturbing residents and interfering with the enjoyment and use of property for miles around.

Interference with
use or enjoyment

The courts have said that the affected property owners in all such cases are entitled to compensation: they should be paid. The owner who cannot gain access to his property because of construction of a limited-access highway has sustained a definite loss in value of his own property even though his property was not formally condemned. The owner whose land floods occasionally has had his land taken away—in the sense that he may not be able to use it or sell it under given circumstances. The owner who cannot enjoy his property because of low-flying airplanes is likewise entitled to damages for the "taking" of his property.

Even in the absence of a formal condemnation, if the use or enjoyment of property is interfered with by a condemnation or public construction on someone else's property, you may be able to make the law work for you. You may have the right to damages for the implicit taking of your property. A lawyer can find out if you have a valid claim.

PROCEDURES IN CONDEMNATION CASES

Depending on the nature of the improvement, the landowner will normally receive some form of notice. By mail or in a personal visit, he will learn that the improvement is on the drawing boards and that the property is in line for condemnation. Negotiations will follow regarding the amount of property to be taken and the compensation to be paid.

While these negotiations are going on, the condemnation body may file with the County Recorder, Register of Deeds, or other proper public official a condemnation plan showing the property to be condemned. Alternatively, a "Declaration of Taking," which amounts to the same thing, may be filed. The filing of this document, in whatever form is required by state law, constitutes the act of condemnation. It may be accompanied by a bond or some other type of security in the amount that the condemning body believes the property is worth.

The private owner will not necessarily agree with this figure; in fact, he usually does not. The bond or other security is posted to make sure that a fund will be available to pay the owner the amount of his award. The law of the state may require that the amount agreed to by the condemning authority be paid to the owner immediately rather than be posted in bond form.

After the condemnation plan or declaration of taking is filed, the legal title to the property vests in (passes to) the condemning body. But vesting is subject to any objections that the former owner may have regarding the right to take the property. There may be an error in the procedure used, or a question whether the use is a proper public use, or an objection that too much property was taken under the circumstances.

Five things to consider

The remaining considerations in a condemnation procedure normally number five:

1. Appointment of "viewers" or appraisers
2. Partial condemnation

3. Assessment of benefits
4. Recovery for additional items of damage
5. Condemnation of leased property

Appointment of "Viewers" or Appraisers

If the parties cannot agree on the value of the property taken, either the owner or the condemning authority may file a petition in court. The petition asks the court to determine the damages to which the owner is entitled. The court then appoints a group of citizens, usually called "viewers" or appraisers, whose duty is to go out, look at the property, and hold a hearing to determine the property's value.

While the viewers are looking at the property, the owner may be present to explain its features; representatives of the condemning body may also be present. At the follow-up hearing, evidence may be submitted by both parties regarding the value of the property immediately before the condemnation, unaffected by the condemnation. Expert real estate witnesses may also be called to give their opinions on values under oath. Documents such as deeds, plans, and photos may be used as evidence.

After the hearing, the viewers decide on the value of the property and hear any exceptions to their report. After disposing of the exceptions, they file their report in court. If one of the parties, or both, should be dissatisfied with the amount awarded, either or both may appeal—and may request a jury trial to determine the value of the land taken.

A test of value

The test for determining the value of any condemned property is the highest and best or most profitable use for which the property is used or could be used in the reasonably near future. In testifying, a real estate expert would use this test.

The property is valued as a unit. If there are different interests in the property, such as an owner, a tenant, and the holder of a mortgage, their individual interests, if any, will be decided after the value of the total property is fixed. In addition to the amount awarded, the owner may be entitled to interest from the date on which the property was taken.

Throughout all these proceedings, the owner and the condemning body may continue to negotiate on the value of the property. At any time they can settle the matter and end the proceedings.

Partial Condemnation

It sometimes happens that only a part of a piece of land is needed. That part may be condemned. Now a much more difficult problem arises. The damages for the owner's loss will involve the value of the part actually taken and may also include a substantial reduction in the value of the property remaining.

If part of a tract of land is condemned, the landowner will have to prove that the attractiveness of the part remaining has been reduced, that access has been interfered with, that the area remaining has been distorted in shape or area, that the cost of providing utilities such as gas, electricity, and water has been increased, or that the cost of constructing a building on the remaining property has been increased. The law will not allow mere speculation regarding damages of this kind, but demands clear proof.

TYPES OF REAL ESTATE VALUE[1]

Condemnation value represents only one kind of value placed on real estate. Experts in real estate law and practice recognize at least ten kinds of value, each of which is directly or indirectly related to the others. Also, each has its uses in specific contexts. The ten, including condemnation value:

Assessed value: a dollar amount assigned to taxable property by an assessor for the purpose of taxation; frequently a statutorily determined percentage of market value.

Condemnation value: value sought in condemnation proceedings is market value. In the instance of a partial taking, adjustments to the value of the part taken may be made for damages or special benefits to the remainder property.

Excess value: value over and above market value which is ascribable to a lease that guarantees contract rental income in excess of market rental at the time of appraisal.

Forced "value", liquidation "value": the price paid in forced sale or purchase when time is not sufficient to permit negotiations resulting in the payment of market value; should be called "forced price" or "liquidation price."

Going concern value: the value of the business enterprise and the real estate it occupies; includes good will.

Insurable value: the value of the destructible portions of a property.

Intangible value: value not imputable to any part of the physical property, such as the excess value attributable to a favorable lease, or the value attributable to good will.

Leasehold value: the value of leasehold interest; the right to use, enjoyment, and profit existing by virtue of the rights granted under a lease instrument.

Mortgage value: value for mortgage lending purposes.

Stabilized value: a long-term value estimate which excludes from consideration an abnormal relation of supply and demand; or a value estimate which excludes from consideration any transitory condition that may cause excessive cost of construction and an excessive sale price.

1 Adapted from *The Real Estate Handbook* edited by Maury Seldin, © Dow Jones-Irwin 1980. Reprinted by permission of Dow Jones-Irwin.

Assessment of Benefits

Public improvement and property values

An owner's property may actually benefit as a result of a public improvement. For example, the construction of a new municipal sewer system can involve the condemnation of easements across private property that entitles the owners to some compensation. The owners may at the same time benefit: they can now tap into a sewer system, thus increasing their property values.

Viewers or appraisers are used in such cases to determine the extent of such a benefit. The owner or owners will be assessed the value of the improvement. The procedures in the assessment of benefits are essentially the same as those involving the determination of damages.

Additional Items of Damage

While not all items of actual loss are recoverable in a condemnation case, landowners or tenants have in recent years been able to recover for additional items of loss. That trend will undoubtedly continue in the future. For example, assume that a person has owned and operated a small business for many years. He has built up extensive good will for the business. Then the building housing the business is condemned. The owner would be required to move to another location.

The owner might not be able to find a suitable building in an acceptable neighborhood at the same rental or value. He might have to start all over again to build up good will. In recognition of the problems the businessman faces in such a case, the eminent domain laws in many of the states now allow awards of *dislocation* and *relocation damages*.

Moving expenses
may be repaid

Moving expenses traditionally have not been compensable in condemnation cases. But under recent statutes, moving expenses are recognized, and the cost of moving business fixtures and heavy equipment from the condemned property may be recovered up to a specified amount. Legal fees and the costs of professional appraisers and appraisals can now be recovered by owners in some states.

Condemnation of Leased Property

A tenant in possession of property can recover for the loss of his lease if a condemnation results in his losing the property. In most instances, however, a lease would specify for the owner that the lease terminates in the event of condemnation. In that case the owner would receive the entire award for the property.

The tenant, in such a case, would receive his moving expenses and relocation expenses if state laws recognize those damages. If the lease does not provide for termination in the event of condemnation, however, the tenant may have lost the opportunity to sublease the property at a higher rent than he was paying under the lease, or he may have to rent another location at a higher rent. Both of these events could involve substantial losses for the tenant. Where state law allows a tenant to recover for the loss of his lease, he could, of course, recover those losses.

Differing
state laws

The laws of the states are very different. Some state laws permit this and some permit that. This is as true in the field of eminent domain as in other fields.

On receiving any notice whatsoever that property in which he has an interest is, or even might be, the subject of condemnation, the wise owner consults a lawyer. With the principles learned in this chapter, he knows what to expect, what the procedures will be, and what his rights are. But over and above that, if either the enjoyment or the use of property is interfered with because of a condemnation of another's property, the injured party may have the right to claim damages. The law can and should be used to protect property rights.

6 "LANDLORD, STAY AWAY FROM MY DOOR"

Suppose you have no desire to purchase or build a home. You would rather find a place to live on a somewhat temporary basis. In such a case, you will probably want to rent an apartment. This is particularly true of young married couples who may not have the means to purchase a home immediately.

What is involved in renting an apartment? What should the average tenant look for in the way of space, amount of rent, and other conditions of the lease? What is a lease and how does it operate?

FINDING THE RIGHT APARTMENT

Apartment-for-rent listings appear in the classified ad columns of local newspapers. A broker or real estate agent can often help in the

search for the right apartment. So can the various neighborhood or area services that exist for that purpose.

Is an entire home needed or only a part of a residence, such as the first or second floor of a duplex? Most persons know they need a certain number of rooms. Thus, in hunting for an apartment, they consider the amount of space available, the amount of rent to be paid, and whether or not the landlord is willing to renew the lease or will grant an option to renew the lease for a future term. Other lease provisions will be discussed later.

A CHECKLIST FOR APARTMENT HUNTERS[1]

	YES	NO
Is building sound, attractive, well built?		
Is it well managed and maintained?		
Are corridors and entranceways clean and well lighted? .		
Is protection from burglars provided?		
Is there a doorman?		
Is landscaping pleasant?		
Is there enough outdoor space?		
Are extras you want included (such as swimming pool, steam baths, a gym for men and women)?		
Is there parking space, indoor or outdoor?		
Is there a receiving room for packages?		
Is laundry equipment available?		
Are fire escapes adequate?		
Are there fire extinguishers?		
Is trash collected or disposed of?		
Are there storage rooms or facilities?		
Are there elevators?		
Are mailboxes locked?		
Is routine maintenance—window washing, decorating, painting—provided?		
Are servicemen available for emergency repairs?		
Is the floor plan convenient?		
Is the apartment big enough?		
Are rooms light enough?		
Are wall spaces adequate for your furniture?		
Is the apartment soundproof?		
Is decorating (if any) attractive?		

Are views attractive? . . . .

Are there enough windows, and are they well located? . .

Are there screens and storm windows? . . . .

Are major appliances you need installed? . . . .

Are appliances in good condition? . . . .

Is wiring sufficient? . . . .

Is ventilation adequate? . . . .

Will cleaning be easy? . . . .

Are there separate heat controls for each part of the
    apartment? . . . .

Are there enough electric outlets and are they well located?

Do windows and doors, including cabinet doors, open
    and close easily? . . . .

Is there air conditioning? . . . .

Is there a fireplace? Does it work? . . . .

Is there carpeting? . . . .

Is there a balcony? . . . .

Are there workable blinds or shades? . . . .

1 Selections from *Sylvia Porter's New Money Book for the 80's* by Sylvia Porter, copyright
© 1975, 1979 by Sylvia Porter. Reprinted by permission of Doubleday & Company, Inc.

Having found the right apartment, the prospective tenant should
understand the relationship that he or she will be entering into with
the landlord. The lease establishes that relationship.

What Is a Lease?

*The lease and the
right of possession*

A lease can be oral. Much more commonly, it is a written document that transfers the *right of possession* of real estate to a tenant
for a specified term. The term of the lease may be a month, several
months, a year, or more than one year. A lease may be *at sufferance,*
meaning that it can be terminated by the landlord at any time.

The lease should set forth all the terms and conditions of the tenant's occupancy of the property for the entire term of the lease.

Provisions Usually Found in a Lease

Leases for residential uses or occupancy, not business leases, are considered here. The terms that are discussed below are limited primarily to leases for residential purposes, not those for commercial purposes.

Rental Payments. The apartment is perfect, and vacant. The first question that comes up is, typically, the amount of rent. It is important to understand that rent is the price paid for the occupancy of the space described in the lease. If the lease is to run for one year, the amount of rent is determined, normally, on a total yearly rental basis. In other words, the lease will provide that "for the total rent of X dollars, payable in monthly installments of X dollars a month, being one-twelfth of the annual rent, you, as tenant, have the right to occupy the premises." You become legally obligated for the entire year's rent, even though you pay rent on a monthly installment basis.

This becomes important if for some reason, before the year is up, the tenant wants to vacate the property or to get out of the lease. He has committed himself, however, to pay rent for the entire year. Unless the lease provides an "out," he may be required by the landlord to pay the whole amount.

Negotiating
a lease

It is possible to negotiate with the landlord the proper term of the lease. The recently married person who wants to have a place to live for a year should probably ask for a one-year lease. The landlord will want to know that the property will be rented for a reasonable time. The tenant usually wants a reasonable period so that he will have time to find another place—if he is looking for a permanent home. He will want a sufficiently long term to make it unnecessary to go looking for another apartment in the near future.

How likely is it that the landlord will be prepared and willing to negotiate the terms of a lease—including the period for which it will run? In practical fact, most landlords know they want tenants who will "stay for a while." These landlords will offer the prospective tenant a one-year or two-year lease. The apartment seeker can then accept or reject.

The flat rental has just been described: a uniform monthly install-ment rate for the entire term of the lease. But other, less common forms of rental arrangements are available. Each of them, however, anticipates a total rent payable in some form of installment, perhaps in equal installments. The total amount of rent for the entire term is chargeable to the tenant and payable in various ways.

- A lease may provide for graduated rental payments at specified intervals. It is used normally to compensate the landlord for in-creasing expenses. Or it may be used where a tenant has inade-quate funds in the beginning but expects to be able to pay a higher rent later.

Rent increases at specified intervals

This type of lease provides for rent increases at specified intervals. For example, $250 a month may be charged for the first three months, $275 a month for the next three months, and so on to $325 or $350.

- A lease may provide that a specified portion of the real estate taxes, insurance, or costs of repairs be added periodically to the basic rent. This type of arrangement is normally part of a busi-ness lease; but residential leases also may provide for increases in the rent if the taxes on the property go up during the term of the lease. The rent may also go up with increases in utility charges caused by the tenant's use of the property.

The language of these leases usually provides that, "as additional rental," the tenant agrees to pay proportionate amounts of the real estate taxes or utilities. These charges are called "additional rental" to give the landlord the opportunity—if needed—to evict the tenant or sue for back rent.

- In a "cost-of-living lease," the tenant's rental obligation may fluctuate as the cost of living increases. More common in the commercial or business lease, this clause also finds its way into residential leases from time to time.

Discount for early payment

- Some leases call for a discount if the rent is paid before the tenth day of the month. This is designed to induce the tenant to make his payments promptly.

Whatever the total basic rent or the amount of the installments, the lease should specify the method of payment. If it is payable monthly, the lease should state where it is to be paid—at the home of the landlord or elsewhere. The date on which the initial rent payment is due should be set forth specifically. Then the tenant and the landlord know the date on which the rent is due every month.

Security Deposit. Most landlords try to protect themselves against a tenant's abandonment of the property, failure to maintain the property, nonpayment of rent, or other default. Usually, the tenant is required to deposit extra money with the landlord in advance: this security deposit is used to reimburse the landlord for any such default. In case of default, the lease usually authorizes the landlord to re-let the premises to someone else.

Most leases provide that the security deposit, if not applied by the landlord in the event of a default, will be treated as payment of rent for the last month or months of the lease. In other words, if two months' rent is required as a security deposit, this amount, if not utilized by the landlord because of any default or to pay for damages to the premises, will be refunded to the tenant upon termination of the lease.

Laws on security deposits

Many states have considered or passed legislation concerning the so-called security deposit. Some of the possible questions are whether or not the landlord should be required to pay interest on the security deposit; whether or not security deposits should be allowed at all; and whether or not the landlord should be required to refund the security deposit without suit at the end of a lease.

Any or all of these matters can be discussed with your lawyer where questions arise.

Options in Leases. An option in a lease is a right granted normally to the tenant. There are several type of options.

An *option to renew* is a right granted to the tenant to decide, within a specific period before the expiration of the original lease, whether or not he wants to renew it and, if so, to notify the landlord of that decision. For example, the original lease may provide that the tenant has the option to renew the lease for an additional term of one year. To exercise the option, the tenant has to notify the landlord of that decision at least three months before the expiration of the original one-year lease.

The renewal option

The renewal option is the most common type. The landlord will often require that the renewal term be at a higher rent level than the original term so as to make certain that the rental covers increased costs, taxes, and other expenses.

The lease may contain an *option to purchase*. In this case the tenant rents part of a home that he would like to purchase but cannot for financial reasons. The owner may be willing to rent the property for one year, granting an option to buy the property at a stated price at the expiration of that year or during the term of the lease. The owner may even allow all the rental that has been paid to be applied as a down payment on the purchase of the property once the tenant is ready to proceed with the purchase.

All of this can be arranged in an "option to purchase" clause. However, if the tenant wants such a clause, he should make certain that the option to buy contains all the necessary provisions of an agreement of sale because exercise of the option to purchase turns the lease into an agreement of sale of real estate; therefore, the lease must contain all the necessary provisions of an agreement of sale, including the purchase price and the closing or settlement date.

INTEREST ON SECURITY DEPOSITS?
YES, SOMETIMES

Some states, including Illinois, require landlords to pay interest on security deposits under certain conditions. The landlord of some residential real estate may, for example, have to pay 5 per cent interest on any security deposit held more than six months. This rule applies generally to landlords of larger buildings—containing, say, 25 or more units.

The "grace period"

The landlord who is obligated to pay security deposit interest will have a "grace period" in which to make payment. The period may be 30 days from the end of the rental term. The landlord can pay the interest in cash or credit the interest to rent due.

Few tenants will go to court to recover security deposit interest—in the event that the landlord does not pay—while they are still tenants. But they have that right, and can recover not only the interest but court costs and attorneys' fees. After the tenant moves, a different situation prevails.

In some states, the landlord may have to return the entire security deposit within 45 days after the tenant moves. The landlord can deduct the costs of repairing damage to the apartment. But he may have to give the tenant an itemized bill for such damages. Then the landlord has to return the balance of the security deposit.

Two types of law may be involved in these cases. One covers payment of interest on security deposits. The second applies to refunds of security deposits.

In either case the tenant—in given states—has the right to sue if the landlord defaults or if the landlord "chisels" on the amount of interest due or the extent of damage to the apartment. A solution may be to go to a Small Claims Court, where no lawyer is required. But some states, as noted, require a defaulting or chiseling landlord to pay attorneys' fees as well as court costs.

Two types of options

Options for additional space or for cancellation may be specified in the lease. A tenant on a long-term lease commonly faces the problem of unexpected events that may require him to vacate before the end of the term. Also, what happens if additional space is needed because of additions to the family? These situations can both be solved by provisions in the lease—if the landlord is willing to include them.

A *cancellation option* gives the tenant the right, at a designated time and with adequate notice, to either cancel his lease with the landlord or eliminate certain space that he no longer needs. The *additional space option,* on the other hand, allows the tenant to take over additional space at designated times, as necessary.

These options, like all other provisions of the lease, must be negotiated with the landlord. If they are granted, they can substantially help the tenant to deal with an unknown future.

Sublease. The right to sublease allows the tenant to give possession of the premises to a *subtenant.* A tenant decides to allow someone else to live in the premises. The subtenant then pays rental to the tenant, who is still obligated under his original lease with the landlord.

Most residence leases contain provisions restricting the right of a tenant to sublease. The reason is that the landlord does not want "unsuitable" subtenants in the premises—persons whom the landlord has not been able to investigate. Usually this restriction states that the tenant cannot sublease all or part of the premises without the prior written consent of the landlord. Where possible, however, the tenant should try to include a sublease agreement, or at least a provision that the landlord will not unreasonably withhold his consent to a sublease.

Prohibition of subleasing

Where the lease contains a clause against subleasing, the tenant should be prepared to remain on the premises under the lease for the full term—or pay the rent for the full term.

Identify the Premises Leased. It is important that the lease be very specific about what actually is being leased. If an apartment is being leased, the number of rooms and the location of the apartment should be spelled out. If permission to use the basement washer and dryer is granted, this should be indicated. If the right to use a garage on the property is given, this should also be spelled out. If the right to use a yard or recreation area is part of the lease, this should be clearly indicated. Any other similar permitted uses should be noted.

Right to Make Alterations. This is a very important clause in the lease. If the landlord agrees to make alterations for the tenant before the tenant moves in, this should be spelled out in detail. Specifications on the type of alterations should be listed very clearly. The tenant's obligation to pay rent should be conditioned on the landlord's performance of these alterations. Then the tenant need not move into the property until the work is done.

Where the alterations are to be made by the tenant, they are usually subject to the landlord's prior approval. It is, after all, his property. The landlord should understand that the alterations will benefit the property. If that is the case, his consent will usually be given freely.

*Questions
regarding
ownership of
fixtures*

Where alterations are made, questions may arise at the expiration of the lease regarding ownership of any fixtures attached or fixed to the property by the tenant. The normal lease provision states that such fixtures belong to the landlord unless he agrees otherwise. If possible, the tenant should seek to have the clause provide that he can take the specified fixtures away when he vacates the property.

The tenant may also want to leave specified alterations of fixtures because of the expense that removal involves. The lease should indicate that.

Alterations mean substantial changes in the premises or the addition of fixtures to the premises by a tenant.

Repairs. Perhaps no other provision of the lease causes more difficulty or more lawsuits than the one indicating who is required to repair and maintain the premises.

Normally, the lease provides that at the end of the term the tenant has to return the property to the landlord in the condition in which it was originally leased. Only normal wear and tear is allowed. So-called structural repairs—repairs to parts of the building itself, such as the roof and outside walls—are the responsibility of the landlord unless the lease states otherwise. Interior repairs, having to do with the use and occupancy of the premises, such as leaking faucets, interior plumbing, and a blown fuse, are normally the tenant's responsibility. However, the usual lease form provides that the tenant is responsible for damage resulting from such causes as short circuits, leakage of water, steam, gas, odors, frost, and bursting or leaking of pipes or plumbing.

A tenant signing such a lease is assuming a great deal of responsibility, especially where he may be occupying only a part of a dwelling rather than the entire building.

Minor interior repairs

Where the tenant is in a good negotiating position, he should demand a clause providing that he is only obligated to make interior repairs of a minor nature, or only such repairs as might result from his own misuse of the property. All other repairs, structural or otherwise, will then be the responsibility of the landlord.

Destruction or Condemnation of the Premises.   What happens if, during the term of the lease, the property is destroyed or is condemned for public use? Strange as it may seem, in most states the liability of the tenant to pay rent may continue. To protect himself, therefore, the tenant should insist on a clause in the lease stating that in the event of destruction, the obligation of the tenant to pay any further rent ends immediately. The landlord ordinarily will want a

provision specifying that, in the event of condemnation, the entire award for the loss of the property will go to the landlord. The tenant will then not share in the award at all.

While this clause is subject to negotiation in a residential lease, the landlord would normally have the right to claim the entire condemnation award. But it is important that the tenant should have the option to terminate the lease if the premises are destroyed.

Other Provisions of Residential Leases. Some other common clauses in leases deal with these questions:

Pets
Garbage or rubbish removal
Keeping the sidewalks free of snow and ice
Obstruction of sidewalks or doorways
Noises or disturbances in or around the building
The parties may negotiate other provisions from time to time.

DEFAULTS IN LEASES

*Two kinds
of defaults*

If a tenant cannot perform under a lease, what happens? What rights does the landlord have in such a case? Normally, a residential lease contains provisions dealing with defaults by the tenant. These defaults fall in two main classes: (1) failure to pay rent or any other sum provided for under the lease, and (2) removal by the tenant of any of the landlord's goods from the premises—or expression of an intention to do so.

In a third type of case, a lien may be filed against the tenant, or bankruptcy proceedings may be begun against him. The tenant may become insolvent, or a receiver may be appointed for him—someone appointed by a court to take over the tenant's business.

Should any of these defaults occur, the landlord under the typical residential lease has the right, first of all, to declare the entire balance of the rent for the remaining term of the lease immediately due and payable. The landlord also can evict the tenant in case any of these defaults should occur. In those states that still recognize it, the landlord has the right to enter a "confession of judgment" for the balance of the rent.

Confession of judgment and the landlord's rights

The confession of judgment clause gives the landlord the right to go to court to get a judgment against the tenant for the balance of the rent. The landlord files a paper; he does not have to bring a regular lawsuit. The latter would involve filing a complaint, whereupon the tenant would file an answer to the complaint. In the normal course of events a trial would take place.

The confession of judgment has for some years been under attack in the courts. In some cases it has been declared unconstitutional. The legality of such a lease provision should always be questioned.

The landlord himself may be violating the lease agreement. This occurs most often in a situation known as "constructive eviction." The landlord, failing to make repairs or provide necessary services, such as utilities, renders the premises uninhabitable. The tenant can then claim that he has been unlawfully evicted because of the landlord's breach of the lease. If the tenant can substantiate his claim, his obligation to pay rent ceases until the landlord corrects the default.

At present, state statutes are under consideration regarding the landlord's duty to make the premises habitable. Some states have even adopted, by court decision, a rule that the landlord, in leasing property, delivers a *warranty* to the tenant that the premises are habitable. In these states a tenant can sue the landlord for breach of that warranty where "constructive eviction" occurs.

The tenant may not have to pay rent where a breach of warranty takes place or during the period of a constructive eviction. But the tenant may also have a claim for additional damages if he has to leave the premises or find other housing because of the landlord's breach.

IN THE TYPICAL STATE:
THE LANDLORD'S OBLIGATIONS[1]

Various states have their own laws dealing with landlord-tenant rights and obligations. A typical set of state laws specifies the following obligations of the landlord:

A. The landlord is obliged at all times during the tenancy:
1) to comply with all applicable building, housing, or health codes, or

2) in the absence of codes, to maintain all structural components (e.g., roofs, windows, floors, exterior walls, etc.) in good repair; and to maintain the plumbing in a reasonable working condition. The landlord may alter or modify these obligations with respect to a single-family home or duplex by stating so in writing to his tenant(s).

B. Unless otherwise agreed in writing, in addition to the above requirements, the landlord of a dwelling unit, other than a single-family home or duplex, shall also make reasonable provisions for extermination of rats and bugs; supplying locks and keys; removal of garbage; heat; running water and hot water. He must also maintain the common areas in a clean and safe condition.

C. The landlord must disclose in writing to the tenant his name and address, or that of someone authorized by him to act as his agent. He shall disclose this in writing at or before commencement of the tenancy.

D. The landlord may enter the dwelling unit at any time necessary to protect or preserve the premises under the following circumstances:

1) with the tenant's consent;
2) in the case of an emergency;
3) when consent has been unreasonably withheld by the tenant; or
4) if the legal presumption for abandonment has occurred. The landlord shall not abuse his right of access nor use it to harass the tenant.

E. The landlord must observe and comply with the requirements of the rental agreement. He cannot make any agreements with the tenant which would take away any of the rights of the tenant.

[1] Adapted from *Landlord-Tenant: The Law* (Tallahassee: Florida Department of Agriculture and Consumer Services).

THE SALE CLAUSE

Clause covering possible sale

Every residential lease should contain a clause regarding the possible sale of the property while a tenant is in possession. Ordinarily, any buyer of residential real estate buys subject to all existing leases; the buyer should find out who is in possession of the property and the basis on which that person is in possession before he completes the purchase. If a tenant has possession, the buyer should find out on what basis that tenant has possession. The buyer can then buy the property subject to the tenant's rights to remain on the property.

IN THE TYPICAL STATE:
THE TENANT'S OBLIGATIONS[1]

Various states have their own laws setting out the rights and obligations of the landlord and tenant. A typical body of state law specifies the following obligations of the tenant. Every tenant shall be responsible for:

A. Ensuring that he does nothing to cause the landlord to be in violation of building, housing, and health codes.

B. Keeping that part of the premises which he occupies clean and sanitary, removal of garbage, and keeping the plumbing clean and in working order. This includes not flushing anything down the toilet or washing foreign matter down the sink drain which would have a tendency to cause these units to malfunction.

C. Operating in a reasonable manner all electrical, plumbing, sanitary, heating, ventilating, air-conditioning, and other facilities and appliances, including elevators.

D. Not destroying, damaging, or removing any property belonging to the landlord.

E. Conducting himself, and requiring those who visit him to conduct themselves, in a manner which will not disturb others.

F. Allowing the landlord entrance to the premises for purposes of inspection, repairs, or to show the dwelling unit to someone else. The tenant may not unreasonably withhold access to the unit.

G. Living up to all provisions made with the landlord when the rental agreement was made, particularly paying the rent on time. The law itself does not directly address the issue of late charges; however, it is customary and common for landlords to require a late fee for delinquent rental payments.

[1] Adapted from Landlord-Tenant: The Law (Tallahassee: Florida Department of Agriculture and Consumer Services).

If the landlord wants to change that situation, the lease should provide that in the event of the sale of the property, the tenant agrees to vacate after receiving a certain number of days' or months' notice of the sale. If the lease does not contain a sale clause, then the tenant is guaranteed possession of the property for the full term of the lease, regardless of whether or not the property is ever sold.

Waiver of protection

Most printed form leases contain a waiver of this protection by the tenant. These forms are usually drawn by the landlord, and a prospective tenant should understand what it means to waive the right to remain on the premises in the event of a sale. The tenant would ordinarily want the sale clause removed from the lease; the landlord may want to keep it. This again is a negotiated item.

HOLDOVER BY TENANT

A tenant retaining possession beyond the original term of the lease is a "holdover." Depending on the law of the state, the lease may or may not be renewed automatically for another full term, whatever the original terms of the lease. In some states, the holdover status only means that the lease is renewed for another month.

Because of this difference in the laws of various states, most leases contain a provision covering tenant holdovers. The lease usually specifies that if a tenant lawfully occupies the premises after the end of the term, the lease will be enforced for another year, or month, or whatever period is agreed to by the parties. The lease continues from month to month or year to year so long as the relationship of landlord and tenant continues. Such a clause clarifies the legal relationship where the tenant holds over beyond the original term of the lease. The clause also indicates the duration of the additional term— whether a year, a month, or another period of time.

To keep the landlord away from your door, it is important to sign a lease agreement that you understand and that benefits you. In looking for an apartment, take advantage of the comments in this chapter. Study them before entering into any agreement.

Part III
FAMILY MATTERS

The family plays so many roles in modern society that the law takes a basic interest in nearly all types of family matters. The family ensures the biological reproduction of the next generation and takes responsibility for the child's maintenance and education. Child training or socialization also falls in the family's area of responsibility, as does the provision of sexual controls. In effect, the family constitutes society's most basic unit.

The family performs all its social functions at once. In doing so, it gains in effectiveness and makes a fundamental contribution to a nation's or a society's survival. There can be little wonder that the law concerns itself with the ways in which a family is formed and what happens to it afterward.

Marriage is a
contract

The family begins with marriage, a step that commits both partners to legal responsibilities of a serious nature. The responsibilities rest in a contract. Marriage actually involves a contract in which three parties have an interest: the bride, the bridegroom, and the state in which the marriage is performed. The state is a party because under its laws the partners to the marriage assume certain duties toward each other and the state itself. For example, the husband is viewed widely as taking the primary duty of support for his wife and children. But that obligation may fall on the wife under certain circumstances.

The law girds the family around with both restrictions and protocols. Divorce or annulment requires specific procedures before the law recognizes any change—any formal dissolution of the marriage bonds. Insurance, the protection that can guarantee the family's survival in difficult times, is subject to close regulation under the law.

In one way or another, the law follows the family—and the individual who "goes it alone"—through life. The law safeguards personal security even after the individual's working years are done. Legislation has, for example, established the entire Social Security system. Other means of providing for the "golden years" come under the protective umbrella of the law, which seeks to ensure that pension, profit-sharing, and similar programs contribute to the comfort and dignity of older citizens.

All citizens share in the ambience created by the law. But in many cases the legal family is directly and deeply involved as a group, for example, where estate planning, wills, taxation, death, and burial are concerned. Part III examines all these areas of the law. By carefully reading this overview you can be better prepared to avoid many family-related problems and make the necessary adjustments in time.

7 "BE SURE, INSURE WITH SURE INSURANCE"

Think insurance for a moment. It has invaded every phase of the life of modern technological man.

The situations abound. A woman suddenly made a widow is asked, "How much insurance did he leave you?" Other similar questions may be asked:

- if someone slips and falls on the sidewalk in front of a friend's home;
- if the driver of a grocery truck runs into a pedestrian;

- if a bookkeeper absconds with money belonging to the firm or to others;
- if a fire destroys a home and/or its contents; or
- if a tenant fails to keep hallways clear and a visitor falls down the steps in the building.

In still another situation, a major illness strikes. Because of rapidly increasing medical care costs and ever higher charges for the delivery of medical services, a family's life savings can be wiped out by that one serious illness—unless insurance is available to meet the cost.

In this chapter, the normal types of insurance such as life, liability, and various types of business insurance come under examination. The typical provisions in these policies will be noted along with the risks covered. An attempt will be made to clarify the language of the policies. When deciding on more life insurance, or whether he has sufficient liability insurance, the individual should have an understanding of the basic terms used and the reason why a particular policy is needed to cover a particular risk. Everyone should be able to recognize a risk and know that insurance is available as protection against loss or disaster.

LIFE INSURANCE

Adequate life insurance is vital in any plan designed to provide for a family in the event of a parent's death. Insurance can give a family the means to live in an atmosphere of security. In addition to its normal use, life insurance can provide for the retirement of corporate stock or the purchase of a partnership interest from a deceased partner's estate. Insurance can be utilized to provide funds for pension and profit-sharing plans and many other family and business arrangements.

Payment in the event of death

In brief, life insurance is an agreement by an insurance company to pay an amount of money in the event of the death of the insured. The sum can be fixed, or based on some scale depending on either the age of the insured or some other element. Life insurance falls into three basic categories: term insurance, permanent or whole life insurance, and endowment insurance.

So-called "term" insurance is insurance written for a "term" or "period," rather than on a permanent basis. Term insurance normally remains in effect for one year, and is renewable on continued payment of premiums. It involves either a fixed *premium* with benefits reducing as the years go by—"reducing or decreasing term insurance"—or a fixed *benefit* with annual or other periodic increases in premiums over a period of time ("increased premium or level term insurance").

In other words, the benefits decrease (decreasing term) or the premiums increase (level term) as time passes. With decreasing term insurance, a policy can eventually expire.

Whole life insurance is generally taken out to cover a person for the remainder of his life. Payments may be made for a specified number of years. For example, a "20-Pay-Life" policy calls for payments for 20 years. Afterward, the insured is covered under his *limited-payment life* to the full extent of the policy for the rest of his life. Under *straight life,* or *ordinary* or *whole life* insurance, the insured is not only covered for the rest of his life; he can borrow against the *cash value* of the policy and can sometimes simply "cash it in" and take a cash settlement.

The question of cash value

The distinction between term and permanent life insurance also has to do with the question of *cash value*. Ordinarily, permanent insurance has a certain cash value after the policy has been in force for a certain period of time. That feature does not exist with term insurance. In purchasing term insurance, the insured is usually purchasing primary protection for his family. Whole life insurance has a cash feature that gives it some investment potential.

An *endowment life insurance* policy is designed primarily for the person who wants to receive a certain amount of money at a specific time in the future. Until that time, the person also has normal life insurance protection. The policy provides that a sum of money or income payments will go to the insured if he or she reaches a certain age. If the policy owner dies before reaching that age, the death benefit is paid to the beneficiary.

Young couples with small children sometimes find it difficult to afford permanent life insurance. These couples should probably buy as much *convertible term* insurance as possible—term insurance that, for a limited premium, delivers a high degree of protection in the dollar amount of death benefits payable. At the same time, such a policy can contain a convertible feature that permits the insured to convert the term insurance into permanent life insurance at any time. The premium rates will be those charged by the insurance company for similar insurance.

Other kinds of life insurance

This convertible feature ordinarily carries with it the right to convert without evidence of insurability: without taking a medical exam. Three other kinds of life insurance should be identified:

Credit life insurance will pay the balance of a debt, such as a loan, if the insured dies or is disabled.

Annuity life insurance is based on a contract under which an insurance company provides a regular income to the insured starting at a certain age, usually 65. An alternative to this *deferred annuity* policy is the *immediate basis* policy under which the insured pays the company a lump sum and starts receiving income payments at once.

Group life insurance is the kind provided typically by companies, labor unions, trade associations, and other organizations. Generally written as a form of term insurance, group life almost always gives the individual insured the option of continuing the insurance by applying 30 to 60 days after termination of employment or membership.

The standard provisions of the whole or term life insurance policy are important. So are those elements that give protection under the typical life insurance policy.

Grace Period

Premium due dates

Unless a policy is completely paid for, which may occur with some types of permanent insurance, premiums are due on a specified date. This is normally the anniversary of the date on which the policy was issued. Premiums are payable annually, semiannually, quarterly, or monthly. For accounting purposes and bookkeeping purposes the premium, if paid on an annual basis, is ordinarily slightly less than if the premium were paid on some other basis.

For situations in which the premium is not paid on the due date, the policy usually contains a "grace period" provision. That means the company will accept the premium if paid within, say, 31 days after the due date specified in the policy.

Automatic Premium Loan Provisions

If the premium is not paid within the grace period, under a permanent policy the insurance does not automatically expire. Rather, it ordinarily continues as term insurance for a period of time measured by the cash value earned by the policy over the years. In other words, if the permanent policy has cash value, that cash value will be utilized to pay the premium and keep the policy in force until the total cash value is exhausted.

The policy in that case will be treated as term insurance. No additional cash value will be earned as long as no premium is paid. Once the cash value is exhausted, the policy lapses for nonpayment of premium.

Many policies have an *automatic premium loan* provision. Such a clause provides that the insured can borrow, or request, against the cash value of the policy to pay premiums. This can be important if the insured is disabled and unable to pay the premiums as they come due.

Billing for loan interest

In this situation the insured is billed periodically for interest on the loans that are being made as premium payments. But the cash value of the policy continues to build. By contrast, where premiums are paid out of the cash value and permanent insurance becomes term insurance, no cash value is earned during the period of nonpayment.

In most cases, if a permanent policy's cash value is exhausted the policy can later be reinstated on payment of the unpaid premiums with interest. But the insured may have to show satisfactory evidence of good health. A physical examination may be required before the policy can be reinstated.

Death Benefit and Premium Adjustment

The amount of the death benefit is a matter of choice—and need. A young man with a wife and small children may want the highest death benefit at the least cost. For that reason convertible term insurance is usually a good buy in such a situation. Anyone "shopping" for permanent insurance should also consider the following:
* The premium base
* The amount of death benefit available for the particular premium
* The cost of various options or additions to the basic coverage
* The needs of the family after the insured's death

• Whether the amount of insurance selected fits the needs

More information on the last-cited point appears in the chapter on Wills and Estate Planning.

Death benefit
and premium
adjustment

In the event an insured dies, the beneficiary will receive not only the death benefit scheduled in the policy but also a *premium adjustment*. The latter is normally a refund of that portion of the paid premium that covers a period beyond the month of death. For example, if the policy runs from July to July and death occurs in September, the part of the premium representing the time from September to the following July will be refunded.

THE NEW LIFE INSURANCE:
"GRADED DEATH BENEFITS"
FOR HIGH-RISK CASES

In the recent past persons with serious health problems or risky jobs found it hard to buy life insurance. Today, by degrees, the picture is changing. The premiums paid on high-risk insurance may be 10 to 50 per cent higher than those on standard policies. But the individual may have no other source of protection.

Liberalized
approaches to life
insurance

The options open to diabetics, those undergoing psychotherapy, epileptics, and even persons with histories of cancer have increased substantially in number. People in high-risk jobs, including window washers and submarine testers, have encountered similar liberalization of life insurance underwriting.

A few companies today are offering "graded death benefit" coverage for individuals in high-risk categories. At those higher premium rates the companies offer "open enrollment" policies: they require no medical exams. The full face value of such a policy will not be paid if the insured dies from natural causes before a specified period of time elapses. By contrast, accidental death is covered in full at any time. The insurance policies generally take one of two forms:

- Those providing for an *elimination period*. If the insured dies after a certain number of years—usually three—from the date on which the policy became effective, the beneficiaries receive the policy's full face value. Before the lapse of three years, the insurance company would pay out only the money already paid in premiums plus interest. The interest rates run 5 or 6 per cent and up.

- Those providing for a *graded benefit*. Under this type of policy, payments to beneficiaries are tied to a rising percentage of the policy's face value. The total paid depends on how long the insured lives. If, for example, an insured were to die in the first year of coverage, the company might pay 5 per cent of the face value. The benefit might be 15 per cent if death occurs in the second year. The policy's full face value would be paid if the insured lives seven years.

Applications for graded benefit policies may ask some searching questions. The purpose is to avoid clear "deathbed" cases. As with other policies, the insurance company retains the right to cancel a graded benefit policy during the first two years of coverage.

Incontestability Clause

It used to be that an insurance company could refuse to pay benefits after the death of an insured, even though a substantial amount of time had passed since the policy was issued and substantial premiums had been paid. Because of this situation, the rule of *incontestability* was introduced into the laws dealing with insurance.

The beneficiary under the incontestability clause

The incontestability clause specifies that after a life insurance policy has been in force for a period of time—usually two years—the beneficiary of the policy must receive the insurance proceeds upon the death of the insured. The company cannot contest payment. This applies even where misstatements were included in the application for insurance.

Most often, insurance companies claimed that applications included misstatements regarding the health of the insured, his or her age, and similar factual questions. To avoid such defenses, the incontestability clause is required in all life insurance policies in all states. If the insured was actually older than was stated in the application, the benefits payable under the policy may be adjusted downward. On the other hand, if the insured was younger than was stated on the application, a slight adjustment upward will be made in the benefits.

Cash Value and Loan Value

As noted, permanent life insurance carries with it a cash value. The policy will contain a table showing the cash value of the policy for any given time in the life of the insured. In addition, the policy may set out various income options, giving the insured the opportunity to select one that will ordinarily provide for guaranteed installment payments for a fixed number of months or years. The payments start after a specified date.

Loans against life insurance policies

A real advantage of permanent life insurance centers on the loans that can be made against the policy. The policy itself states the interest that will be charged on a loan against the cash value of the policy. The interest rate stated in the policy is usually substantially lower than the prevailing interest rate on bank or other marketplace loans.

In times of high interest rates, as in the early 1980s, insurance companies usually report an extremely high number of loans against life insurance policies. Loans can be taken out at the lower interest rates stated in the policies and reinvested at rates that run more than double the policy rates. Thus the loan privilege becomes both a kind of resource for emergencies and a means of fighting inflation.

Surrender of Policy for Paid-Up Insurance

Most permanent life policies can be surrendered before the death of the insured. Rather than take the cash value, the insured elects to take a *paid-up policy* according to a table that is contained in the policy. For example, if he owns a policy insuring his life for $50,000, and at a given time he wants to surrender that policy for either its cash surrender value or an amount of paid-up insurance, he can select the paid-up policy as shown on the table rather than the cash surrender value. This means the insurance requires no further payment of any premium, but is paid up and has a cash value of its own.

In this case the insured no longer pays any premiums. But the insurance continues in force.

Ownership and Beneficiary Provisions

Naming the owner: a must

The owner of the policy is always named in it. The owner is usually the insured, but may be the beneficiary or some third party. In order to remove the proceeds of the insurance from the insured's estate, a common concern in the area of estate planning, the insured's wife or husband or a trust fund may be named as the owner of the policy.

The insured should always name a primary and a secondary or contingent beneficiary, usually specified as first and second beneficiaries. A third and even fourth beneficiary may be named.

Listing more than one beneficiary can avoid typical insurance problems. Many husbands, for example, name only their wives and forget about their children. If the wife dies before the husband, and the husband then dies, the insurance company has no named, living beneficiary to whom to make payment. The benefits then pass to the estate of the insured. The proceeds of the policy become subject to various death and inheritance taxes in many states. The taxes come out of the insurance.

You should review all your life insurance to make certain that you have named not only a primary beneficiary but a second and even a third. If you wish to protect your spouse and your children, your beneficiary designation should name your spouse as first beneficiary and your children, equally, as your secondary or contingent beneficiaries.

Dividend Options

The so-called "participating" life insurance policy entitles the policyholder or insured to dividends on earnings of the insurance company. These policies carry *dividend options*.

Options involve choices

In applying for insurance, the individual who wants such options may face choices regarding the dividend payments and their application. For example, one person may want to have the dividends paid to him in cash. He selects that option and later receives checks representing dividends as these are declared by the company. In another case the dividends can be used to reduce the premium payments, or to pay for additions to the policy. These are then paid up and require no further premium.

Dividends may also be utilized to pay interest on policy loans, to purchase additional term insurance, and to secure various other options available under the standard participating life insurance policy. The applicant chooses the desired option.

Conversion Privileges

Normally a life insurance policy will specify what other plans of insurance the existing policy can be converted into. The procedure to be followed to make such conversion will also be indicated.

Most term policies, as noted, contain a conversion clause that makes them very attractive. They can usually be converted into permanent insurance without a medical examination, unless the policyholder wants a lower premium program for the same or a higher death benefit. In the latter case the company may require a medical examination.

Assignment

Assignment and written notice

The typical policy spells out the procedures under which it can be assigned or transferred to someone else. The company is normally not bound by any assignment of the policy until it receives written notice of the assignment. The assignment has to cover all the outstanding loans to which the policy is subject; the responsibility for making a valid assignment falls on the insured or owner and not on the company itself.

In order to transfer ownership, the proper forms of assignment must be sent to the insurance company to make certain that the formalities have been satisfied.

Extra Coverages Available with a Basic Life Policy

Various endorsements can be added to the basic life insurance policy. Some or all of these may be very valuable. These endorsements, or "riders" to the policy, may entail extra charges, or they may be added without additional charge.

Ask your insurance advisor or agent

An insurance advisor or agent will know whether these coverages are available to an applicant for a policy. Depending on the purpose that the insurance is intended to serve—whether security, protection of one's family, retirement, or business—these special coverages may serve valid purposes and should be considered. The following are examples of some possible riders.

• *Accidental death benefit.* This endorsement provides that if the policyholder dies in an accident the company will pay the beneficiary an amount in excess of the face amount of the policy. This extra amount is usually some multiple of the policy's face value. For example, a double indemnity provision provides for payment of twice the amount of the face value if death occurs by accidental means.

Some *exclusions* of accidental death benefits should be noted. As in all types of insurance coverage, these exclusions apply to deaths due to war, certain types of airline accidents, and accidents resulting from illness or disability. Death must occur within a fixed period of time following the accident. In some cases, the double indemnity provisions expire when the insured reaches a certain age. Premiums for the accidental death benefit are ordinarily based on a flat rate per $1,000 of coverage.

- *Waiver of premium.*   If the policyholder becomes totally and permanently disabled, the insurance carrying a waiver of premium will remain in force without any further payment of premiums. A waiting period is required before this clause can take effect. Generally, the disability of the insured must occur prior to his reaching a specified age. A disability resulting from war or a self-inflicted wound is not covered and is specifically excluded.

A particular benefit of the waiver of premium provision is that the cash value of the policy continues to grow even though no further premiums are paid. As noted earlier, if the premiums on a permanent life policy are not paid the cash value may be used by the company to pay the premiums as if the policy were term insurance. Thus no further cash value accrues. With the waiver of premium provision, however, the cash value does grow even though no actual premiums are paid by the insured because of his disability. The disabled insured can also borrow against the cash value in such a case.

Extra benefit, low premium

Ordinarily, the premium for this extra benefit is low in comparison with the benefits provided. In fact, some companies do not charge an extra premium for it, but include it in the basic premium charge.

Obviously, the waiver of premium can bring substantial benefits. It protects the insured if he is disabled and safeguards his family by keeping his insurance in force.

- *Guaranteed insurability endorsement.*   Under this rider, the insured is guaranteed that he can take out additional insurance at standard rates without further evidence of insurability. That means he does not need to take an additional medical examination. Additional insurance would normally have to be purchased before the insured reaches certain age levels.

Guaranteed insurability can be a valuable addition to a policy. A young man may not be able to afford a great amount of life insurance at the beginning of his career. But he can obtain more insurance in the future at standard rates even if in the meantime he has contracted a serious illness that would prevent him from buying additional insurance on his own. The illness might cause him to be "rated"—meaning that the insurance would be much more expensive —if he did not have the guaranteed insurability endorsement.

Guarantees insurability to $10,000

In a typical case an insured may have guaranteed insurability to a maximum of $10,000 in additional coverage, if he applies before a certain age. He can apply for that additional coverage no matter how his health may have changed since he purchased the original policy. Premiums are inexpensive, and are payable, usually, until the insured turns 40 or up to the end of the basic policy payment period, whichever is earlier. Typically, the additional coverage has to be applied for within 60 days of the *option dates*.

- *Dismemberment benefits.* A typical group and association life insurance plan may contain, in addition to accidental death benefits, benefits for dismemberment—the loss of a limb, blindness, or other physical loss. Again, for an increase in premium payments the disability payoff provision may be included so that the face amount of the policy will be paid out in installments in the event of total disability.

Additional Add-On Riders for Term Insurance

The typical term life insurance policy may contain a great variety of riders and endorsements. These can provide additional low-cost insurance. Like those already mentioned, the *disability income rider* involves the payment of an additional premium, however small, for the additional coverage. The *automatic premium loan clause,* however, and those that follow it are free; no additional premium is charged. The add-on riders include the following.

Disability Income Rider. The disability income rider provides a monthly income to the insured if he becomes totally disabled. The amount of income is always stated in the policy. Some benefits are based on a percentage of the face amount of the policy—for example, 1 per cent, continuing to a stated age of the insured. A waiting period is usually required before disability payments begin.

HOW MUCH LIFE INSURANCE DO YOU NEED?

The somewhat bewildering world of life insurance changes constantly. New names for old policies make their ways into the marketplace. Some actually describe new life insurance gimmicks. Practically all of them confuse the issue and make choices difficult.

Questions and calculations

Remembering that there are two basic, popular kinds of life policy, ask yourself some questions and perform some calculations. The questions relate to what you want your life insurance to do—and for whom—and how many resources you have to play with. The calculations come out as rules of thumb:

• Estimate approximately how much income your family, close

friend, or other beneficiary will need after your death. "Need" means enough to maintain a current or better standard of living.

- Estimate how much the significant other or others will receive from dividends, interest, salaries, Social Security, and other sources.
- Calculate the difference. That difference represents the postmortem need that has to be met by life insurance or some other kind of protection.

Then ask yourself some additional questions to inject realism into the calculations and, if necessary, recalculate. Some of the questions:

- Have you figured in inflation, and, if so, at what rate?
- Will your beneficiary or beneficiaries be able to invest the insurance money made available after your death, and then live on the interest or dividends, or will they have to burrow into those benefits?
- What kind of interest will the insurance be able to earn?
- If a spouse survives, will he or she work? Be invalided? Handicapped? Will he or she need job training or education?
- Will the kids, if any, go to college? Can you estimate the costs of education in five years, or ten? Should there be special insurance for that purpose?
- And finally, is insurance the answer, or would investments be better, or something else you can more easily afford?

The lapse-proof policy

Automatic Premium Loan Clause. Under this clause the company is authorized to borrow against the policy to pay the premium if the policyholder fails to pay. The policy becomes lapse-proof while any cash value remains.

Settlement Agreement. Under the settlement agreement the method of payment of benefits is specified. The insured chooses one or more of the many payment options in an agreement that is attached to the policy.

Spendthrift Trust Clause. Some states have laws that automatically exclude life insurance proceeds from the claim of creditors. Other states require that a "spendthrift trust" clause be included in the policy to protect the proceeds against creditors' claims. The clause is designed to protect insurance proceeds that are to go, for example, to a trust fund for a spouse and children.

Where a policy contains a spendthrift trust clause, the creditors of the beneficiaries cannot reach the proceeds until they are actually paid over to the beneficiaries or their guardian, as the case may be.

Retirement Options.   An insured may want to use the cash value of his policies and any accumulated dividends to build a retirement fund or to provide an annuity to be paid monthly after retirement. The insured can in this case choose a lifetime income or installments for a fixed period of time. Together with his spouse, he can establish a joint and survivor annuity that pays monthly benefits until husband and wife are deceased.

These retirement options are open to the insured while he lives. In planning his estate, he should consider the use of life insurance to provide such retirement income.

The choice of a settlement option

Settlement Options.   Retirement options are available to a living insured who wants to use his cash policy value for retirement purposes. *Settlement options* refer to the options under which the beneficiaries of a deceased insured specify how they will take the proceeds of the policy.

The insured may select the kind of settlement option when he takes out the policy. Also he may select the option anytime during his life. After the death of the insured, the benefits can be paid in a lump sum. However, the insured may opt for other types of settlement to the spouse and children, trust fund, or another beneficiary.

These settlement options normally fall into several categories. *Interest only* settlements pay installments composed of only the interest earned by the available benefits. At the end of the specified installment period, the lump sum is payable. Under the *installment time option* installments are paid for a fixed period of time. At the end of that period, no further payment is made. The *installment amount option* pays a fixed amount until the total fund is exhausted. The *life income option* pays monthly checks for life. These life income options may be subdivided as follows:

- *Life income with definite guaranteed number of payments* provides income payable for the life of the beneficiary. But it provides for a definite number of payments. In the event of the death of the beneficiary before all the payments are made, payments are continued to the estate of the beneficiary.
- *Life annuity income plan.*   Under this plan, no fixed number of payments is guaranteed. Monthly payments are made to the date of death of the beneficiary, but there is no guaranty of the total number of payments. Thus if the beneficiary dies shortly after the date for payment arrives, the insurance company is "off the hook" for any balance.

  Alternatively, the beneficiary may live so long that the total number of installments equals the face amount of the policy. In this case the company pays more money than it would have under the lump-sum payment option.
- *Cash refund life annuity income plan.*   Under this plan, any amount not utilized under the life income annuity plan is refunded in cash to the estate of the beneficiary.

Annuity for the beneficiary and spouse jointly

- *Joint and survivorship annuity income plan.*   An annuity is established in joint names of the beneficiary and his or her spouse. After the death of the primary beneficiary, the annuity continues and the survivor collects payments until the benefits are used up.

Why would anyone select the life annuity income plan when the beneficiary might die shortly after the insured and no further payments would be made? The reason has to do with the amount of the monthly installments. The greater the risk that a beneficiary might not receive the full benefits because of a premature death, the higher the monthly payment. Many insured persons are only concerned with the primary beneficiary; they want him or her to get the highest possible monthly payment and to be secure during life.

WHEN AN INSURANCE POLICY GOES TO COURT:
A CASE CALLED "CORDER WINS"[1]

MATTHEW J. JASEN, Justice. This is a motion by plaintiff for summary judgment.[2]

An insurance policy was issued to deceased Anna M. Corder in the amount of $5,000.00 on April 26, 1960. The beneficiaries listed in said policy were Wesley D. Corder, husband of the insured, if living, otherwise Willa Eakman, mother of the insured. On April 15, 1963, the named insured died. Subsequently, the plaintiff brought action to collect said proceeds from the insurance company who in turn interpleaded Willa Eakman as Administratrix of the Estate of Anna M. Corder. The administratrix answered the complaint herein and interposed a counterclaim that the proceeds of the insurance policy in question be paid to her.

It is the contention of the plaintiff that he is the named beneficiary and therefore entitled to the proceeds.

The mother-administratrix in opposing this motion proceeds upon two theories. First, by reason of fraud of the plaintiff the proceeds of the policy belong to the estate of the insured, and secondly, that plaintiff was not the husband of the insured and that therefore the insurance contract is void by virtue of the deceased's breach of warranty in representing him as her husband.

It is conceded that the Wesley D. Corder who brings this action is the Wesley D. Corder named as beneficiary by the deceased in the insurance policy, and that he is the particular person intended by the insured to be the beneficiary of said proceeds.

(1) Where the deceased effects the insurance upon her own life, it is well-established law that she can designate any beneficiary she desires without regard to relationship or consanguinity.

(2) Since the undisputed proof shows that the application for the policy was made by the insured deceased, there is no issue of insurable interest on the part of the plaintiff.

The use of the term "husband" in the connection was merely descriptive of the relationship which the insured claimed existed between her and the beneficiary. Even though the named beneficiary was not actually the insured's husband, it does not alter the basic fact that the plaintiff is the person to whom the deceased had intended that the proceeds of the policy be paid.

For the reasons stated, motion for summary judgment granted.

[1] Corder v. Prudential Insurance Company, 248 N.Y.S. (2d) 265 (1964). Adapted from Law and the Life Insurance Contract by Janice E. Greider and William T. Beadles, ©

Richard D. Irwin, Inc. 1960, 1968, 1974, and 1979. Reprinted by permission of Richard D. Irwin, Inc.

2 An immediate judgment granted by the court without further proceedings, generally on the basis of the documents filed with the court and without the oral testimony of witnesses.

A choice of one of these settlement options will depend on many factors. The insurance shopper should pick that option that best fits with his estate plan and his family's needs in the event that he is not there to provide for them.

Federal Estate Tax Considerations and Life Insurance

As indicated, life insurance proceeds can be taxable to the estate of the insured. They thus become subject to the federal estate tax unless the insured puts the insurance benefits beyond the reach of the taxing authorities. This is usually done through transfer of ownership of the life insurance policy to the beneficiaries. This is how it works.

Transfer and
update

Most importantly, the policy is transferred and the designation of the beneficiary is kept up to date. If the beneficiary is dead, and if no living person is named in the policy as beneficiary, the proceeds will be payable to the estate of the insured at his death and will be fully taxable.

But note: with a properly named, living beneficiary, the proceeds will still be taxable to the estate as long as the insured holds "incidents of ownership" in the policy at the time of his death. That means the insured remains the owner of the policy; he has the right to cancel it, surrender it, or cash it in, and can change the beneficiary or borrow on the policy. But if, prior to his death, the insured makes a complete transfer of ownership of the policy and does not retain any of these incidents of ownership, the proceeds will most likely not be taxable to his estate.

In sum, where an overall estate plan makes it advisable, it is possible to avoid a larger federal tax against an estate. More money will go to those loved ones if the insured makes an irrevocable assignment of ownership of the policy to the beneficiary, retaining no ownership rights. Starting in 1981, it should be noted, federal taxes were levied on all estates totaling, with insurance benefits, $175,000 or more.

INSURANCE AGAINST LIABILITY AND LOSS OR DAMAGE TO PROPERTY

Have you ever read one of your insurance policies? Be honest, now. If you have, you are the great exception. Perhaps you are turned off by the technical language used, or the small print. Whatever the reason, most people do not read their policies. They depend on what their agent tells them regarding coverages.

The important coverages

This section discusses the most important coverages that are available in the fields of *liability and property insurance*. An effort will be made to explain simply the technical language used in the policies. The goal is to enable the reader to understand and be able to discuss insurance problems intelligently.

Both the homeowner and the apartment dweller are constantly exposed to possible losses that could wipe out all savings and assets. The types of risks are usually divided into two types: risks involving *liability,* that is, that may make one liable to someone else because of what he, an employee, or an agent does or has done; and *property losses or damage.* The latter includes loss of income and credit—personal loss resulting from property losses caused by oneself or someone else.

Liability Insurance

The ownership of property or the operation of a business may involve exposure to liability for one's own acts or for the acts of employees performing normal services. In general, a liability policy provides protection only if the insured is legally liable to pay a claim resulting from an accident or other event. There is no protection:

(1) if the insured is not legally obligated to pay the claim;

(2) if he has voluntarily assumed the risk; or

(3) if the occurrence is not really an "accident" (for example, where the other person becomes ill through repeated exposure to someone who carried the illness).

In brief, there must usually be some unintended event causing damage or injury for which the insured is legally obligated. Then the liability policy provides coverage.

Two basic parts

The basic policy is divided into two parts. One sets limits on the liability coverage for bodily injury claims—for example, claims by persons sustaining personal injuries while on one's property. The second sets limits on the coverage for damage to someone else's property.

The policy buyer chooses the desired limit of liability for each type of coverage: bodily injury or property damage. The many different kinds of policies available are designed to meet specific purposes and fulfill specific needs. The most important ones are noted below.

Owners', Landlords', and Tenants' (OLT) Liability Policy. This policy provides protection against claims that result from the ownership, leasing, and operation of property that is specifically listed in the policy. The property may include commercial buildings, both retail and wholesale, office buildings, and theaters. The policy lists the specific properties covered and the amounts of the bodily injury and property damage limits provided.

Comprehensive General Liability Policy. This is the broadest form of liability policy that can be purchased. It provides both bodily injury and property damage coverage, and may give additional protection against "personal injury" risks. These include such things as liability resulting from assault and battery, libel and slander, false imprisonment, and other types of "intentional" acts that may impose liability on the insured.

The "broad form" policy

The comprehensive policy is a "broad form" policy. It differs from the Owners', Landlords' and Tenants' policy in that it does not specify each risk covered. Rather, it is written on an all-risk basis and specific exceptions are listed.

Product Liability Policy. Product liability constitutes one of the most rapidly expanding areas of the law. If a soft drink bottle explodes, if a washing machine throws a bolt, causing injury to a member of the family, or if another manufactured product malfunctions and causes bodily injury or property damage, a claim can be brought against the manufacturer, wholesaler, or seller of the product.

In this area, liability insurance is essential today. The product liability policy provides coverage for what the manufacturer, wholesaler, or dealer may be legally liable to pay in damages for claims arising out of the handling or use of goods or products. The goods or products, of course, must be manufactured, handled, distributed, or sold by the insured. There must be a defect or unsafe condition in the product.

Product liability insurance can cover a service type of business as well as a manufacturing type. Those delivering services include barbers, painters, and contractors. A policy may insure against defects in installation as well as defects in equipment.

Like the product liability policy, the professional liability policy insures physicians, lawyers, accountants, architects, and other professionals against liability resulting from a defect in the performance of functions or the delivery of services. The malpractice insurance taken out by doctors is a typical professional liability policy format.

Contractual Liability. Certain obligations arising under contracts or agreements may result in legal liability. The contractual liability policy is intended to cover such liability; it usually involves manufacturers, distributors, and retailers of products as well as persons engaged in service businesses who, under their contracts, assume certain obligations.

For example . . . indemnification

An example may be noted. A homeowner may want to have work done on his home under a building agreement. The agreement would include a provision that the contractor agrees to *indemnify* the homeowner if anyone suffers bodily injury or property damage because of the contractor's performance of the work. In purchasing contract liability coverage, the contractor would protect himself against any claim against the homeowner. The latter simply refers the claim to the contractor under the contract.

Contractual liability coverage may be included in the comprehensive general liability policy mentioned above, usually for an additional premium. This assumption of liability, or an agreement to "hold harmless," appears in many different types of contracts, leases, and other arrangements. To be protected, the party making these promises of indemnity must have this coverage.

Owners' and Contractors' Protective Liability Policy. This policy is intended to give protection against claims arising out of work done by someone who is not under direct contract with the insured. An example is the subcontractor doing work for the insured, but under a contract with the general contractor.

In a typical case, homeowner Smith contracts to have contractor "X" put siding on his home. Contractor "X" may subcontract the work out to subcontractor "Y," who, in the process of doing the work, causes injury to another person. The protective liability policy will protect Smith against the claims of the injured person. Smith may have demanded that "X" provide this coverage as part of the contract, or Smith may secure this coverage himself.

Homeowners' policy—a recent development

Homeowners' Policy. The homeowners' policy is a relatively recent development in the field of insurance. Previously, a homeowner seeking protection against losses resulting from such events as fire, theft, or vandalism, or trying to protect himself against liability claims resulting from injury or property damage on his property, would have had to take out a series of separate policies to get total protection.

The homeowners policy is designed to give the homeowner in one package all the necessary protections. If the mailman trips and falls over cracks in the sidewalk, if a dog bites someone, or if a piece of your roof falls and injures someone, the homeowners' policy, under its liability provisions, would give protection. It would provide protection for what the homeowner would be legally obligated to pay if he or a member of his family were at fault. The property loss provisions of the homeowners' policy come under discussion in the section dealing with property insurance.

In any liability policy, the type and amount of coverage depends on the risks that concern the insured. In these days of six- and seven-figure jury awards, everyone should protect his home and business with an adequate, comprehensive general liability policy and a homeowners' policy. Thus the law governing contracts works for the private individual.

Additional Benefits Available under Liability Insurance. Not only does the liability policy give protection and pay money claims for damages; the typical policy also provides for additional valuable coverages. Often overlooked by an insured, these include:

What the company pays

- *Lawsuit defenses.*   Under a lawsuit clause the insurance company will defend the insured against all lawsuits brought against him, even where a suit is groundless and has no basis in fact or in law. It is essential, however, that the suit, if successful, would have been covered by the policy or would be considered a proper claim under the policy. In addition to paying any judgment or settlement falling within the policy limits, the company will pay attorneys' fees and other costs of defense, including those for investigation, securing witnesses, and other court costs. If required, the company would also pay interest on the judgment.

In defending an insured under an insurance policy, the company retains its own lawyer to handle the case. Where the amount of the possible recovery exceeds the amount of coverage, the lawyer for the company should so advise the insured. He should also suggest that the insured retain his own lawyer to protect him on the possible excess liability. This is another reason for making certain that coverage is adequate.

In a typical case, a policy would place a $50,000 limit on the insured liability. The amount that could be recovered might be $100,000 or more. The insured has the option of engaging his own lawyer to defend him against the amount of the claim in excess of $50,000.

- *Bond premiums.* The liability policy also provides for payment of bond premiums required in an appeal from an adverse decision, bonds to release legal attachments against property, and similar charges.

- *Reimbursement of expenses paid by insured.* If the insured incurs some expense at the request of the insurance company, such as travel or securing affidavits and notary fees, the policy may provide for full reimbursement.

- *Inspection and reimbursement for immediate medical aid rendered.* The policy may provide for inspection services to minimize the risk as well as to reimburse the insured for medical and surgical services. These may have been rendered by the insured to an injured party at the time of an accident.

Covering the injured party

- *Medical payments coverage.* This coverage provides protection against the cost of reasonable medical and surgical expenses incurred within a year after an accident. Each person who suffers bodily injury, illness, or disease as a result of an accident is covered regardless of whether the insured is legally liable or not. This protection covers the injured party, not the insured. It is usually limited to a specified amount per person and per accident. It is available under the liability policy for an additional premium.

Property Insurance

Property insurance protects the insured against direct damage to or losses of property such as real estate, furniture, fixtures, and equipment. The insurance can also cover loss of the use of damaged property. For an additional premium, consequential damages may also be covered—losses not to the physical property itself, but those resulting from losses to physical property of the insured or some other person. Consequential losses will be discussed in greater detail later.

There is no satisfactory way to list all the various types of property insurance. The modern trend is toward "package policies" providing multiple-peril insurance that incorporates many individual coverages into one package. However, as a help toward understanding the nature of property insurance, a basic listing follows.

Under the same policy . . .

Fire Insurance. Everyone knows about fire insurance that gives protection against direct losses caused by fire and lightning. The same insurance can cover certain types of damage caused by smoke where the damage results from a "hostile fire"—a fire not started by the insured in fireplace, stove, or other container. The latter is called a "friendly fire." Smoke damage caused by the fire in a fireplace is not covered because the fire is not "hostile." But smoke damage resulting from a hostile fire, whether on the insured's or someone else's property, would be covered.

Extended Coverage. Usually by endorsement, extended coverage can be added to the basic fire policy that covers risks of damage from windstorm, hail, explosion, riot, civil commotion, aircraft, smoke, and vehicle damage. Also, extended coverage may be provided for an additional premium against falling trees, glass breakage, malicious mischief and vandalism, and accidental discharge of water or steam from plumbing or heating fixtures.

Included also would be damage to vehicles owned or operated by the insured or his tenant as well as water damage and damage caused by ice, snow, and freezing.

The extended coverage endorsements do not increase the basic benefits of the fire policy. They only bring additional perils or risks under the coverage.

Endorsement Adding Earthquake Coverage. By special contract or by endorsement to the fire policy, protection can be obtained against earthquake, sprinkler leakage, hail that damages crops, and other risks.

Coverage and
rates vary

Motor Vehicle Damage. Collision, comprehensive fire and theft, and similar policies can protect an insured against physical damage to his autos, trucks, and other motor vehicles. The types of coverage and the rates will vary from place to place and from time to time. They will be affected by the make, model, and the way the vehicle is used. Automobile insurance policies are examined at greater length in a later chapter.

Burglary and Theft. Various types of burglary and theft policies afford protection against losses due to burglary of merchandise, fixtures, and equipment. The same applies to losses of money, securities, or other property through burglary of a safe or storekeeper's office. Special robbery policies give "package" protection to various kinds of business.

An example of the broad-form comprehensive coverage mentioned earlier is the money and securities form that provides all-risk protection against losses of money or securities.

Fidelity Bonds. A fidelity bond may be used to protect an employer against dishonest employees. The bond gives protection against losses of money, securities, raw materials, equipment and real property. Depending on the kind of bond used, the bond can cover either named individuals, all the incumbents in certain positions, such as the board of directors or officers of a corporation, or all employees of a firm.

Determining the
kind of
fidelity bond

The type of business, the number of employees, and their duties determine the kind of fidelity bond used and who is covered under it.

A business in which employees handle cash or securities should probably have these employees bonded for the employer's protection and that of his customers.

Package Policies and Floaters.   In recent years, as indicated, multiple-peril, or package, policies have proliferated. The package policy has a major advantage: it eliminates overlapping coverages in separate policies and reduces expenses and costs. It is important, however, to distinguish multiple-peril policies providing all-risk protection with specific exclusions from other policies covering only specifically stated risks and excluding all others. An insurance agent and family lawyer should probably be consulted on the type of package policy that will best fit a business and family arrangement.

A package policy in widespread use today is the homeowners' policy that provides basic fire coverage, extended coverage, and other insurance for the home and its contents. The property aspects of the homeowners' policy will be reviewed later in this section. The liability protection has already been discussed.

The floater for risk coverages

A *floater* usually provides all risk coverages on specified personal property such as jewelry and furs. Many floaters require the specific listing of all articles insured, with a description and valuation based on an appraisal or bill of sale. The types of floaters available are too numerous to list. They depend on the risk and the type of property to be protected.

Surety Bonds.   Many commercial transactions and contracts are guaranteed by the issuance of a surety bond. Here, the principal party guarantees that he will perform under a contract or the insurance company, as surety, will pay the party guaranteed. As indicated in the discussion of legal aspects of home construction, labor and material payment bonds and performance bonds are forms of surety bonds. There are others, however:

* *Contract bonds* guarantee the performance of a contract. These are written for the actual term of the contract and cannot be cancelled during the contract term.
* *Bid bonds* are bonds that accompany the bids of contractors for public and other types of contracts. The bond guarantees that the bidder, if awarded the contract, will sign it and furnish the

prescribed performance, labor, and material payment bonds
when required. If the bidding contractor defaults and fails to
provide the necessary bonds later, the insurance company becomes liable for the difference between the amount of the bid of
its contractor-principal and the next lowest bid.

* *Performance bonds,* such as construction bonds, guarantee the
faithful performance of work by a construction contractor. The
labor and material payment construction bond that guarantees
that the contractor will pay all bills for labor and material is involved in almost every large construction project.

* *Maintenance bonds* guarantee that the work performed by the
contractor will be free of defective workmanship or materials.
The bond may be separate or may be included in the performance bond.

Multi-peril coverage

Homeowners' Insurance.   As noted, this multiple-peril coverage
provides liability protection as well as protection against losses
directly caused to a home or its contents. The homeowners' insurance may include only the fire and extended coverage; but it may
also include specific additional risks or may be written on an all-risk
or all-property basis so long as no commercial property or use is involved. The premium, of course, depends on the type of homeowners' policy that the insured purchases.

The "all physical loss" form of the homeowners' policy is the
broadest form available. It gives protection against all physical loss
to the insured's property so long as it is a part of the insured's home
and is not commercial in character.

Consequential Loss Coverages.   Property insurance has been
mentioned as providing coverage for direct physical loss to property.
But with consequential loss coverage the insurance may also cover
losses sustained by the insured as a direct result of property losses.
For example, a business may be interrupted as a result of damage to
property. The owner has then suffered a real loss over and above the
loss incurred on the property.

This generally overlooked factor is very important. A restaurant
that has been severely damaged by fire reveals obvious physical dam-

age to fixtures and equipment. Will fire insurance alone take care of all the owner's losses? Of course not. Insurance may provide funds to replace and repair the damaged equipment; but what about the owner's loss of business and his obligation to continue to pay rent and other expenses while repairs are being made? As a rule, any property insurance is woefully inadequate if it has no consequential loss coverages. Such coverage comes in several different forms.

* *Business interruption insurance* covers losses resulting from the interruption of the insured's business because of fire or other accident.

When the insured is directly affected

* *Contingent business interruption insurance* covers losses resulting from the interruption of the business of a supplier or someone else whose activity or lack of activity directly affects the insured. A retailer may depend on a steady supply of goods from a wholesaler. If the wholesaler's business is interrupted by a fire, he may not be able to ship his goods to the retailer. The retailer then suffers losses that would be covered by the contingent business interruption policy.
* *Extra expense insurance* covers those expenses of a business that, because of its importance, cannot be interrupted and that produces additional expenses in remaining open during an emergency.
* *Leasehold insurance* covers a tenant's financial loss if he has a good lease from the standpoint of rent and loses it because of property damage. If the tenant has to rent other property at a higher rate, he has sustained a real loss that the insurance can cover.
  On the other side of the fence, the landlord may have suffered a loss because his building was destroyed and he lost a tenant. Rent insurance or rental value insurance protects the landlord by covering the loss of rents while a building is unusable because of some insured peril or accident.
* *Other consequential insurance coverages* also can be purchased to cover particular risks.

Co-Insurance Clause.   Suppose a homeowner has a policy on his

home. He is insured against all physical losses to a total of $40,000.
Suppose also that the policy contains a co-insurance clause. What is
it? How does it work? Can this clause actually cut back the amount
of your proceeds from the policy in the event of loss?

A misunderstood provision

Without doubt the co-insurance clause is the most totally unknown, or totally misunderstood, provision in insurance. The clause
makes the insured a co-insurer with the insurance company. If the insured should suffer a loss and is underinsured, he will be required to
bear part of the loss. The co-insurance clause requires that the insurance coverage total at least a stated percentage (usually 80 per cent)
of the total insurable value of the insured property. If the coverage is
less than 80 per cent of the insurable value, the insured shares in
"paying" for the loss.

A case illustration will show how this works. Assume that a home
has an insurable value of $50,000. The insurance policy provides
$40,000 worth of coverage with an 80 per cent co-insurance clause.
The homeowner has satisfied the requirements of the co-insurance
clause since exactly 80 per cent of the insurable value of the home is
covered.

The insurance company in this case will pay in full for any losses
covered by the policy up to the amount of the total coverage, or
$40,000.

Assume that the homeowner has insurance only in the amount of
$20,000, however. A dramatically different result can be expected. If
a loss is sustained, the company will pay only for one-half of the
total loss up to the limit of coverage. If the total loss was $20,000,
the company would only pay one-half of that amount, $10,000, and
the homeowner would be the co-insurer with the company on the
other $10,000: the homeowner bears that loss himself.

Note that the homeowner had coverage in the amount of $20,000,
and that was the amount of the loss. But he should have had coverage in the amount of at least $40,000. He thus failed to satisfy the
co-insurance requirements. If he had had the $40,000 coverage, the
company would have paid the entire $20,000 loss.

Keeping up with inflated real estate values

Many persons with inadequate insurance are surprised by the amounts they collect on losses when those losses equal or are less than the coverage. In almost every region of the country, real estate values have increased tremendously. Most people carry fire or homeowners' policies on a three-year basis; few even think about the insurance on their homes until they receive the next three-year premium statement from their insurance agent.

Where a mortgage company collects the insurance premium out of the monthly mortgage payment and pays the premiums directly to the insurer, the homeowner never has occasion to think about the insurance. Many agents are reluctant to "push" for an increase in coverage because they fear that the insured may take offense. It is becoming more and more obvious, however, that the insurance agent has to keep his clients abreast of the increases in property values. He has to impress on them the need for periodic increases in coverage to protect the property adequately.

Another method of handling this problem is to use the "replacement value" formula. The property is continually updated by appraisals and the coverage amount is maintained to meet the appraised values and cover replacement costs.

Adequate coverage on property, particularly a home, is essential. Without such coverage, no one can escape the effect of the co-insurance clause.

MORTGAGEE AND OTHER CREDITOR RIGHTS

Insurance pays the mortgage company first

In purchasing your home, if you needed a mortgage your insurance policy on the home contained a mortgagee clause naming the company as "First Mortgagee." In the event of a loss, the mortgage company would be paid first from the insurance proceeds. You, as the insured, would receive the balance after the mortgage was paid. By this means a creditor such as a mortgagee is protected by your insurance.

The ways in which creditors' rights can be protected by property insurance can be itemized as follows:

- The creditor takes out or receives from the debtor a separate policy protecting the creditor's interest; the property owner takes out a separate policy protecting his ownership interest.
- The owner assigns his policy to the creditor, but the insurance company may insist on its right to approve the assignment before it is effective.
- A "loss payable" clause is inserted into the owner's policy to protect the creditor. By endorsement or in the body of the policy, it is provided that the loss, if any, is payable to "creditor X" or "as its interest may appear." The creditor usually keeps possession of the policy. The owner then receives a *memorandum of insurance* indicating that the policy has been issued with a loss payee clause.

"As their interests may appear"

- Where several people or business interests have an interest in the same property, they may all be protected as named insureds "as their interests may appear." For example, two farmers who store their grain in the same grain elevator may insure it in both names "as their interest may appear." They cannot really separate the grain and identify what each originally stored.

Where a creditor wants to preserve his rights by using the property insurance of a debtor, the creditor should insist on an agreement that spells out:

- who should secure the insurance;
- how the premiums are to be paid;
- who receives the policy and who receives the memorandum of insurance; and
- how the creditor is to be designated as loss payee.

The agreement should also specify clearly how the proceeds are to be distributed. The policy itself should have the creditor as the party to whom the benefits are first to be paid.

Insurance protection is vital. In private life, it serves to protect the homeowner—to insure him against loss and liability claims. But insurance also plays a major role in business. For example, it can be used to finance buy-sell agreements, provide key-man protection, and accomplish many other purposes. These will be discussed in the chapter dealing with business organizations.

Check your personal insurance program

The present chapter serves as a checklist of a personal insurance program. Do those liability policies provide adequate protection? Should the limits of the homeowners' policy be increased? Do the life insurance policies contain all the necessary options and additional coverages, many available for a slight or no increase in premium?

Most people go through life reacting to events that they cannot control. Insurance is one means by which the individual can gain some measure of control over his life. By using insurance wisely, you can make the law work for you and thus inject more meaning, stability, and security into your personal affairs.

8 THE FAMILY THAT STAYS TOGETHER...

The field of law involving matrimonial matters—domestic relations law—is perhaps the most personal of all. It deals with the close personal relationships that exist between husband and wife and between parent and child. Key areas of the field include the questions that arise before marriage, the property rights of husband and wife, separation and dissolution of marriage, alimony, divisions of property, customary provisions for custody and visitation of children, and support payments.

Domestic relations law often deals with people under emotional stress. Who can be dispassionate when faced with a problem involving wife, husband, or children? Who can be objective when faced with a spouse who indicates he or she wants a divorce, or who has

aroused a fear of serious bodily harm as a result of his or her activities, or who is attempting to violate one's property rights?

Some solutions and answers are discussed in this chapter.

THE MARRIAGE CONTRACT: ISSUES AND ALTERNATIVES

Marriage as a civil contract has one aspect that sets it apart from other kinds of contracts: the parties cannot dissolve their marriage by themselves. They have to call on the sovereign power of the state if they want to obtain a divorce.

That fact suggests how important marriage is in the eyes of the law. The marriage contract brings legal consequences that can and often do affect the persons involved for the rest of their lives.

Valid and Invalid Marriages

Most states require that the parties to a marriage go through certain formalities before the ceremony. Typically, the following steps would be essential:

- A marriage license has to be issued. The license serves as legal permission to marry. Both the prospective partners have to sign an application at the offices of the appropriate local agency—Circuit Court, marriage license bureau, or other—to obtain the license.
- Before the license is issued, both applicants are required to undergo a standard laboratory blood test. The test certifies that each party is free of venereal disease.
- After the license is issued, most states require that the marriage be solemnized within a specified period. A judge, qualified clergyman, or other person appointed by a court can perform the marriage ceremony.

States specify marriageable ages

Both parties to a marriage have to have reached a legally specified age to be validly married. The age varies from state to state. Persons who have not reached the specified age—minors—can marry in most states with their parents' consent. In a typical case a girl of 16 or 17 can marry with her parents' consent; at the age of 18 she has reached her majority and can marry without consent.

A minor who lies about his or her age to get married has contracted an invalid marriage. A parent or guardian can go to court to have the marriage *annulled*—declared legally invalid. The court can annul the marriage without the parties' consent.

Common-Law Marriages. Common-law marriages are legal and valid in some states. In others, they are not recognized. But even in the latter states, the common-law marriage contracted legally in another state will usually be recognized.

In a common-law marriage the two partners simply agree to be married and to live together as man and wife. They do not take out a license or go through a formal ceremony. They consider themselves to be married.

Living Together. Social conventions have changed to the point where more and more couples live together in arrangements that replace marriage or that serve as "trial marriages." Such arrangements have become increasingly acceptable in a social sense. Yet many states still make living-together relationships illegal.

The laws against illegal cohabitation, where they exist, are rarely enforced. Thus the couples are generally free to form agreements, in writing or orally, on property rights, household duties, child-rearing

AGE AND OTHER MARRIAGE REQUIREMENTS BY STATE[1]

	Minimum Age With Parents' Consent		Minimum Age Without Parents' Consent		Blood Test Required	Waiting Period	Marriages Between First Cousins Prohibited	Common-Law Marriages Recognized
	Men	Women	Men	Women				
Alabama	17	14	18	18	yes	no	no	yes
Alaska	18	16		18	yes	no	no	no
Arizona	18	18	18	18	yes	no	yes	no
Arkansas	17	18	18	18	yes	3 days	yes	no
California					yes	no	no	no
Colorado	16	16	16	18	yes	no	no	yes
Connecticut	16	16	18	18	yes	4 days	no	no
Delaware	18	16	18	18	yes	24-96 hours		no
Florida	18	16	18	21	yes	3 days	no	no
Georgia	18	16	18	18	no	3 days	no	no
Hawaii	16	16	18	18	yes	3 days	yes	no
Idaho	15	15	18	18	yes	no	yes	yes
Illinois	16	16	18	18	yes	no	yes	no
Indiana	18	18	18	18	yes	3 days	yes	no
Iowa	18	18	18	18	yes	no	yes	yes
Kansas	14	12	18	18	yes	3 days	yes	yes
Kentucky	18	18	18	18	yes	3 days	yes	no
Louisiana	18	16	18	18	yes		yes	no
Maine	16	16	18	18	yes	5 days	yes	no
Maryland	16	16	18	18	no	48 hours	yes	no
Massachusetts	14	12	18	18	yes	5 days	no	no
Michigan	18	16		18	yes	no	yes	no
Minnesota	16	16	18	16	no	5 days	yes	no
Mississippi	no	no	17	15	yes	3 days	yes	no
Missouri	15	15	21	18	yes	3 days	yes	no
Montana			18	18	yes	5 days	yes	yes
Nebraska	18	18	18	18	yes	3 days	yes	yes
Nevada	18	18	18	18	no	no	yes	no
New Hampshire	18	18	18	18	yes	5 days	yes	no
New Jersey	18	18	18	18	yes	72 hours	no	no
New Mexico	18	18	18	18	yes	no	no	no
New York	16	14	18	18	yes	3 days	no	yes
North Carolina	16	16	18	18	yes	no	no	no
North Dakota	18	15	18	18	yes	no	yes	no
Ohio	18	16	18	18	yes	5 days	yes	yes
Oklahoma	16	16	21	18	yes	no	yes	yes
Oregon	17	17	17	17	yes	7 days	yes	no
Pennsylvania	18	18	18	18	yes	3 days	yes	yes
Rhode Island	14	12	18	16	yes	no	no	yes
South Carolina	14	16	18	18	no	24 hours	no	yes
South Dakota	18	16	18	18	yes	no	yes	no
Tennessee	16	16	18	18	yes	3 days	no	no
Texas	14	14	18	18	yes	no	no	yes
Utah	16	14	21	18	yes	no	yes	no
Vermont	18	16	18	18	yes	5 days	no	no
Virginia	16	16	18	18	yes	no	no	no
Washington	17	17	18	18	no	3 days	yes	no
West Virginia	18	16	18	18	yes	3 days	no	no
Wisconsin	18	18	18	18	yes	5 days	yes	no
Wyoming	16	16	16	16	yes	no	yes	no

[1] From *Your Introduction to Law*, Third Edition by George Gordon Coughlin (Barnes & Noble Books). Copyright© 1963, 1967 by Harper & Row, Publishers, Inc. Copyright© 1975, 1979 by George Gordon Coughlin. Reprinted by permission of Harper & Row, Publishers, Inc.

responsibilities, and other matters. Because no valid marriage has taken place, such agreements may be held to be unenforceable: many courts will refuse to sanction an agreement that has an illegal basis.

Legal Considerations

A number of other factors that can render a marriage void will be noted later. These factors rank among the legal considerations that the parties to a marriage should consider before the "knot is tied." Still other basic considerations that become important where a marriage is valid include the following:

- *Name change.*   On marrying, the wife usually assumes her husband's last name. But she is not legally required to do so. For professional or other reasons a wife may keep her maiden name. Many wives today retain their maiden names because, among other reasons, they have developed lines of credit with stores or institutions, often over long periods of time and at considerable expense.

"I now pronounce you Mr. Jones and Ms. Smith."

Hyphenated surnames

In other cases both husband and wife may assume hyphenated or combined surnames at the time of marriage. Mary Smith and John

Jones become Mary and John Smith-Jones. The husband should usually enter a court petition for a legal name change; the wife can make
such a change, often, without going through any formal legal procedures. Name changes should of course be given as soon as possible to
governmental agencies, including vehicle licensing authorities, and
institutions such as banks and insurance companies.

- *Insurance.* Marriage represents a change in status. Thus insurance companies that may be affected should be notified immediately. Where life insurance is involved, a change of beneficiaries
  —from a parent to a spouse, for example—may be called for.
  Auto insurance rates may change in the married person's favor.
  Combining the hospitalization coverages of husband and wife
  will usually result in substantial savings.

- *Wills and estate planning.* Everyone, and particularly every
  married person, should have a will. Even for a young couple
  with limited assets, the will constitutes the first step in estate
  planning. Of equal importance, the will helps the partners in a
  marriage to protect one another and their children in the event
  of the wife's or husband's death.

- *Tax status.* Once married, the couple become eligible to file a
  joint income tax return with both their state and federal governments. The joint return should be studied carefully, however. In
  some cases it can save money; in others, it will mean a larger tax
  "bite." The advantages and disadvantages are determined by
  each couple's financial situation.

Sales contract determines legal obligations

- *Buying a home.* Many couples look forward to owning a
  home of their own. When they buy, they should remember that
  the sales contract, not the deed, determines their legal obligations. The aid and advice of a lawyer should be solicited. The
  lawyer can do more than advise; he can also, if necessary, draw
  up or review the sales contract and examine the title to the
  property.

- *Record keeping.* Records become important as soon as two
  people marry. Documents such as insurance policies, the mar-

riage certificate, deeds, contracts, and birth certificates should be stored in a safe place. Almost inevitably, one partner or the other, or both, will have to refer to or use these documents. Even canceled checks should be retained for a period of time—if only as records for the Internal Revenue Service.

• *Children.*   Obviously, the children born to a married couple introduce entirely new sets of legal considerations. The same applies if the couple adopts a child. The key questions touch on support obligations, inheritance, and many others.

REMARRIAGE

A man has lost his wife of many years. He is lonely, despondent; he seeks companionship. He has a family, both sons and daughters, that is deeply concerned about him.

A woman has lost her husband. The deceased, concerned about her welfare, has left her with sufficient insurance and property to provide for her well-being. She can live very comfortably. She can remain close to her children.

Remarriage and property rights

Assume that this fictional man and woman meet. They find a companionship that satisfies a distinct human need. But they both have families. Because of the nature of the law dealing with property rights in marriage, they are concerned that if they marry, their own children will not receive the property they want them to inherit. Both fear that the property that each owns individually will find its way to the other and not pass on to their children.

This couple's situation is a common one today. Many organizations exist to bring people together: Parents Without Partners, for example, and other organizations that help widows and widowers to adjust to the fact that they are alone.

In other cases, an older widower wants to marry someone much younger than himself. Less frequently, an older widow wants to marry a man younger than herself. The same considerations apply insofar as the older person's children are concerned.

Can widows or widowers in these situations have the benefit of the companionship and love that they seek? Can they protect the rights of their own children to inherit their property? The law, always adaptable, offers a method by which this can be done.

Prenuptial Agreements

Defining interests
before marriage

An antenuptial agreement, or prenuptial agreement, is formulated before the marriage. It defines the interests that each will have in property of the other acquired before or during the marriage.

The prenuptial agreement might provide, first, that in contemplation of marriage and in consideration of a marriage to take place in the future, each party releases all the rights and interest he or she might have in the estate of the other. In other words, the widower would specifically release any rights or interest he might acquire by marriage in the property of the widow. The widow would do likewise.

The prenuptial agreement would also provide that if either partner dies, his or her property will pass under state law as if the person had died unmarried.

Where there's nondisclosure of assets . . .

The prenuptial agreement requires a full disclosure by each party of the assets owned in his or her own right. Thus each knows clearly and specifically what he or she is releasing. If a prospective spouse does not reveal the total extent of his or her property holdings, the other spouse can later claim that full disclosure was not made. The prenuptial agreement would be rendered null and void. The lawsuits arising over prenuptial agreements have almost always been based on nondisclosure of assets at the time the agreement was signed.

The Support Agreement

Where a widow or widower with property holdings marries someone who does not own property, the situation is somewhat different. As usual, the agreement will ordinarily consist of a release by the second party of all rights to the estate of the spouse. But the agreement may also require that one spouse make provision for the other in a will. A support agreement may provide for payments on a monthly or some other basis.

In this situation, as in that involving the widow and widower, full disclosure of assets is required to support the agreement.

The same type of agreement can be "postnuptial"—the parties can formulate it after the marriage. The full disclosure requirements still apply.

The agreement may provide for termination if the parties divorce or are separated. This is particularly important where the agreement provides for some form of monthly payments by one spouse to another—or where one spouse agrees to make out a will naming the other as a beneficiary.

For protection and peace of mind

Prenuptial and postnuptial agreements involve very serious federal estate and gift tax consequences. The family lawyer should be consulted regarding the method of preparation and the actual content of these agreements. They are important because they can protect the interest of children in the estates of their parents and give peace of mind to widows, widowers, and others. They can ensure that estates will be properly handled.

UNTIL DEATH US DO PART

The breakup of a marriage is a sad, sad thing. Psychologically, it affects the parties because they often feel they have failed in the most personal of human relationships. Practically, it means that they face a difficult period in their lives, economically and otherwise. Emotionally, it can mean a traumatic experience, especially if the marriage has lasted a long time and if children are involved.

Normally, divorce constitutes a last-resort measure, one to be taken only after all other means of saving the marriage have failed. The lawyer's first suggestion may be that the partners consult with their minister, priest, or rabbi. In many instances, this has already been attempted without success.

A next suggestion may indicate professional counseling by any of the excellent family or children's services supported by municipal governments, private foundations, and the United Fund and similar agencies. But, often, one or the other spouse refuses even to admit that a problem exists.

Some questions are commonly asked by a partner to a marriage that is breaking up. These include:

• *Who has to leave the house first?*   If the property is owned

jointly by the husband and wife, both have the right to remain
on the property. Neither can be required to leave before the
other. If one spouse fears that the other will inflict bodily injury
or harm, the aid of a court should be sought to force the other
party to leave the premises.

The obligation to support

- *Does the husband have to continue to support the wife?* The
  answer is yes. The husband's duty to support his wife continues
  until divorce. In those states that recognize alimony, the duty
  continues after the divorce decree is entered. Wives may also be
  required to support their husbands who may not have the same
  means. The same rules may apply equally to husband and wife.

- *What happens if one partner realistically and properly fears that
  the other may inflict serious bodily harm?* What about a wife
  beater? Practically, it may be impossible to deal with a wife
  beater. Counseling does not help; the only real protection for
  the spouse may be the protection that the law affords.
  Admittedly, this may not be adequate in all cases.

Where a wife seriously fears that her husband may injure her or
her children—where she has a "reasonable apprehension of bodily
harm"—she may have to face a very disagreeable, embarrassing con-
frontation. She may have to ignore what the neighbors may think.
She may have to bring charges against her husband, and take whatever steps are necessary to show that she will not stand for physical
abuse.

Extreme measures may become unavoidable. The wife in some
cases packs her husband's clothes, throws them out on the porch,
and locks the door, effectively driving him out. She should then be
prepared to call the police immediately if he attempts to gain entrance to the home. While he may have a legal right to possession
equal to hers, she has the right not to be assaulted, and may take
steps to protect herself and her children.

Wives in such situations sometimes take the children and leave the
house to seek refuge with a friendly neighbor or relative. The preservation of property rights becomes secondary to the safety of the wife
and children.

When legal advice
may be needed

A wife beater is generally recognized as a coward. When confronted by a defiant, angry wife, this husband usually loses heart. Many such husbands do not give their wives credit for having enough sense to consult a lawyer for legal advice in problem situations. The husbands are amazed to learn that their wives had enough "gumption" to seek legal advice. Often, the contact with a lawyer is enough to show the husband that the wife means business and will not stand being "pushed around" any more.

Some abusive husbands, of course, continue to act in the same boorish manner. In such cases the wife should make up her mind to resist; she should take any steps necessary to protect herself and her children.

The same considerations apply where a wife has been acting irrationally. It is always difficult for a husband to deal with a wife who shows no concern for the children, for him, or for herself; who stays out late at night; who drinks; or who otherwise appears incapable of taking care of herself or her family. The husband in such a case must assess how much unavoidable unpleasantness may result if he takes legal steps, particularly where the wife needs medical or psychiatric help.

Termination of a Marriage

In most states a marriage may be terminated in several ways. The marriage may be terminated by the death of one of the parties, of course. The marriage may also be terminated where a spouse is presumed to be dead after an unexplained absence for a fixed period of years. Here, the circumstances usually indicate that death is a reasonable explanation for the absence. The marital relationship may be suspended by separation, and it may be terminated by divorce or annulment.

Some states require proof of "fault"

Grounds for Absolute Divorce. The grounds for termination of the marriage relationship differ in those few states that still require proof of "fault" in one of the marriage partners. As a result, it is difficult to generalize in this area. However, certain common elements run through the state laws dealing with divorce as a way to terminate the marriage relationship.

GUIDELINES FOR NEWLY DIVORCED PARENTS[1]

1. Allow yourself and your children time for readjustment. Convalescence from an emotional operation such as dissolution is essential.

2. Remember the best parts of your marriage. Share them with your children and use them constructively.

3. Assure your children that they are not to blame for the breakup, and that they are not being rejected or abandoned. Children, especially the young ones, often mistakenly feel they have done something wrong and believe that the problems in the family are the result of their own misdeeds. Small children may feel that some action or secret wish of theirs has caused the trouble between their parents.

4. Continuing anger or bitterness toward your former partner can injure your children far more than the dissolution itself. The feelings you show are more important than the words you use.

5. Refrain from voicing criticism of the other parent. It is difficult but absolutely necessary. For a child's healthy development, it is important for him to respect both parents.

6. Do not force or encourage your child to take sides. To do so encourages frustration, guilt, and resentment.

7. Try not to upset a child's routine too abruptly. Children need a sense of continuity and it is disturbing to them if they must cope with too many changes all at once.

8. Dissolution of a marriage

often leads to financial pressures on both parents. When there is a financial crisis, the parents' first impulse may be to keep the children from realizing it. Often, they would rather make sacrifices themselves than ask the child to do so. The atmosphere is healthier when there is frankness and when children are expected to help.

9. Marriage breakdown is always hard on the children. They may not always show their distress or realize at first what this will mean to them. Parents should be direct and simple in telling children what is happening and why, and in a way a child can understand and digest.

10. The story of your marriage dissolution may have to be retold after the child gets older and considers life more maturely. Though it would be unfortunate to present dissolution as a tragedy and either party as a martyr, it would be a pity also to pretend there are no regrets and that dissolution is so common it hardly matters.

11. The guilt parents may feel about the marriage breakdown may interfere with their disciplining the children. A child needs consistent control and direction. Overpermissiveness, or indecisive parents who leave a child at the mercy of every passing whim and impulse, interfere with a child's healthy development.

[1] Adapted from *Parents Are Forever* (Richmond: The Virginia State Bar).

Adultery.   As a ground for divorce, adultery has essentially the same significance in all the "fault" states. Adultery occurs where one spouse has sexual relations with someone other than his or her wife or husband. It is generally not necessary to prove adultery by direct evidence. But it must at least be established that the spouse and the third party (corespondent) had the occasion and the inclination to perform the act.

Proof of a single act of adultery is enough to support a claim for divorce. But *condonation* may be raised as a defense. This becomes possible where the husband and wife have resumed marital relations after the other spouse has learned of the adultery.

Conviction of a Crime.   Statutory provisions establishing grounds for divorce often include terms such as the conviction of an infamous crime, a crime involving moral turpitude, or conviction for the commission of a felony. Conviction of a crime may have to be accompanied by an extended prison sentence that will constitute cause for divorce. Service of a one-year or an 18-month prison term would typically justify a divorce.

Cruelty. Cruelty may still constitute grounds for divorce or separation. But cruelty may be either physical or mental. Some states, for example, have viewed physical violence or cruel and barbarous treatment as one kind of cruelty. "Mental cruelty," or what have been termed indignities to the person of the innocent spouse, or incompatibility, represent another form entirely.

A single act, a course of conduct

A basic factor distinguishes cruelty involving physical violence from mental cruelty, indignities, or incompatibility. In the former, only one single act of violence usually justifies divorce if it endangers the life of the other spouse. Mental cruelty, indignities, or similar causes must usually involve a course of conduct. The offending spouse must continually have performed such acts, leading to mental anguish on the part of the other spouse, or to an intolerable condition for that marriage partner.

Some mental cruelty grounds have appeared repeatedly in court cases. These include:

* Habitual drunkenness—not merely a single act of drunkenness
* Habitual intemperance
* Repeated insults to the spouse in front of other people
* False accusations of immorality
* Habitual refusal to communicate or treat the spouse as a marriage partner
* Cruel treatment of a child in the presence of the spouse

Desertion and Abandonment. Desertion or abandonment for a continuous statutory period of time is another ground for divorce. The period varies from one state to another. To establish desertion or abandonment, the suing spouse must establish the necessary intent on the part of the other partner. A separation to which the marriage partners validly agree will not constitute desertion or abandonment.

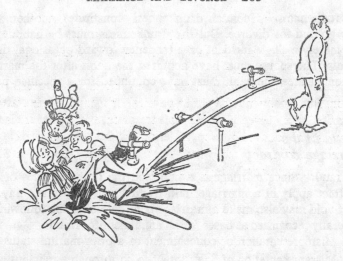

"Enoch Arden" laws

As noted, a marriage can be terminated where the unexplained absence of one spouse justifies a presumption of death. The circumstances must indicate that efforts to locate the spouse would be pointless. When the statutory period specified in state "Enoch Arden" laws expires, the remaining spouse may apply for a termination of the marriage. It is generally required, however, that the circumstances under which the missing spouse disappeared be shown. The remaining spouse must also have made efforts to locate him or her, unless the absent partner disappeared under circumstances indicating that efforts to locate him would be useless. For example, the absent spouse may have been last heard from in a war zone. No further word arrived throughout the statutory period. In this case the marriage relationship could be terminated under an Enoch Arden law without any further showing.

A spouse may remarry under an Enoch Arden law after the dissolution of the earlier marriage. If the first spouse later reappears, the validity of the second marriage would not be affected.

The Enoch Arden laws get their names from a poem, "Enoch Arden," by Alfred Lord Tennyson. The poem's hero, a sailor, is shipwrecked. Rescued after many years on a desert island, Enoch returns to find his wife happily remarried. He continues to live nearby, hiding his identity, and eventually dies of a broken heart.

Drunkenness. Habitual drunkenness constitutes another statutory ground for divorce. But the drunkenness must be habitual and not merely a single incident or a tendency toward occasional drunkenness. The spouse must have acquired the habit after the marriage. In some states, the habit must have continued for a specified period of time.

Fraud in the marriage contract

Fraud. Since marriage is a contract, the ordinary rules of valid contract apply in a marriage, and fraud that would make any contract void may also make a marriage contract void. The following are generally recognized as bases for an annulment for fraud:

- Misrepresentation or concealment of a prior marital status
- Misrepresentation of one's intent to go through a religious ceremony after a civil ceremony has taken place
- A secret intent not to have children or not to live with one's partner
- Concealment of a serious health impairment or a venereal disease
- Concealment at the time of the marriage of a pregnancy by someone other than the intended husband
- Misrepresentation as to prior morals

Insanity. A ground for divorce, insanity is also a ground for annulment in some states. If the sane spouse is seeking an annulment, he or she must prove that the condition of the insane spouse was unknown at the time of the marriage. If the wife is the insane partner, the court may require the husband to provide for her support.

Annulment

Annulment differs from divorce

An annulment differs from a divorce in a basic way. Where a divorce dissolves a valid marriage, an annulment states that a marriage is void—that it never legally existed. Some of the grounds for annulment may also be cited as grounds for divorce, as indicated. These include fraud and insanity or idiocy. In Indiana, a marriage will be held to be illegal or void if two Indiana residents are married in another state to avoid Indiana marriage license provisions. The same law applies in other states. A marriage to a minor, a person under the legal age of consent, can generally be annulled, as can an incestuous marriage. The latter is a marriage to a person within a specified degree of kinship.

Bigamy, a second marriage by a person who has a living spouse, will also render a marriage void. Because bigamy is not recognized in the United States, the second marriage can always be annulled, or held to be void.

In a few states, bigamy also constitutes grounds for an absolute divorce. Under any circumstances, a judicial decree of annulment will clear the record of the second marriage. Bigamy is also a crime, but ordinarily the bigamist can be prosecuted only in the state where the crime was committed. That means the state in which the second marriage was performed.

REQUIREMENTS OF RESIDENCE; SEPARATION AGREEMENTS

Residence requirements and state laws

Most states require that a person who wants to bring a divorce action must reside in the state for a specified period of time before starting the suit. All states recognize separation agreements under which the parties agree to live apart without divorcing.

"Public Policy"

Under each state's "public policy" regarding divorce, the residence requirement varies. For example, certain states seek divorce cases. These states have a residency requirement of several weeks to a month. Other states, however, take a different view, requiring at least a year's residence or more before the action can be started.

Residence requirements are strictly enforced because the state is said to have an interest in the marital contract. If for any reason the residency requirement is not met, any divorce can be set aside if attacked by one of the parties.

Separation Agreements

Under a separation agreement, the two parties to a marriage agree that they will live separately and not molest one another. In general, the agreement will provide for the disposition of the joint property of the parties and for support to be paid by one party to the other.

A separation agreement allows a husband and wife to live separate and apart from one another without getting a divorce. With an agreement, neither party has grounds for divorce on the basis of abandonment or desertion. The agreement spells out the parties' respective rights regarding shared property and, where children are involved, with respect to custody and visitation of the children.

A separation agreement requires all the legal steps that are involved in obtaining a divorce decree. Residence, grounds, pleadings, and court appearances become necessary. But a separation agreement leads to a *legal separation,* and the parties cannot remarry. Rights of inheritance and the duty to support may continue. A successful divorce proceeding leads to total dissolution of the marriage. The parties can remarry.

Separation after agreement

The partners in a marriage can separate immediately after signing an agreement. In most states, the agreement should not be conditioned on one of the parties getting a divorce. The reason is that many states have a policy against any agreements that interfere with the marital relationship.

The separation agreement usually involves matters common also

to divorce actions, including the obligation of support, custody of children and visitation rights, insurance and tax considerations, support payments or alimony, and methods of enforcing support provisions.

Obligation of Support.   The support obligation has changed as a result of equal rights legislation and amendments to various state constitutions. Today, both husband and wife may be obligated to support one another during their joint lives even where, in a separation agreement, one of the parties agrees to pay a stipulated amount instead of support. Each party may be liable for the other's support at least to the extent of keeping the other party from becoming another statistic on the welfare roles.

Some states restrict the right of either party to be released from the obligation to support the other. Other states permit a separation agreement providing a regular and substantial payment that will relieve the other party of his or her duty to pay support.

Many separation agreements provide for a *lump-sum* settlement to cover property rights, provide for the transfer of real estate from one spouse to the other, or release one spouse's interest in real estate to the other. An agreement may also provide for the distribution of personal property such as stocks, bonds, cash, furniture, fixtures, equipment, automobiles, and any other property.

Danger in lump-sum settlement

It should be noted that a lump-sum settlement involves some danger. The receiving spouse may lose the lump sum through an unfortunate accident or bad investment, and may then bring a further claim against the paying spouse despite the agreement. The danger can be avoided by payment of a substantial lump sum and acceptance of an obligation to pay on a monthly or other periodic basis such additional amounts as may be agreed on by the parties.

Custody and Visitation Rights.   By far the most important part of the separation agreement relates to child custody. Where an agreement has no provision for child custody, and where a court becomes involved in determining custody, the sole consideration will be the welfare of the child. Even if a divorce decree settles the question of custody, the court may alter the custodial provisions at any time because of changes in the circumstances of the parties. For example, a father who could not provide a home for a child when an agreement was signed may improve his status later. He may then go to court to try to obtain custody. He may ask for a writ of habeas corpus to

have the child brought to court for determination of custody.

Before the equal rights movement gained momentum, courts usually favored the mother where the child was of "tender years"—12 years of age or younger. The father had to go to court to establish that the mother was "unfit." That meant the mother had mental, moral, or physical limitations that could endanger the health or welfare of the child.

Today the courts generally hold that the father has as much right to custody of a child under the age of 12 as does the mother. No longer, in most states, is there a presumption favoring the mother. The welfare of the child is the only criterion applied.

A child's wishes not necessarily binding

Where a child is old enough and reasonably mature, the court as a general rule will ask what the child's wishes are; but that alone will not affect the decision if other factors indicate that custody should be awarded to the other spouse. In some cases, depending on the circumstances, custody may be awarded to another relative such as grandmother, aunt, or other third party.

A separation agreement may and should provide for custody. But such an agreement is not binding on the court. Normally it does carry considerable weight where custody is at issue.

Where a court awards custody to one parent, the other will be given visitation rights. Usually these rights of visitation will be limited to a particular time and place; or one spouse will have to give the one having custody notice as to when the visit will take place. The visitation arrangement thus acquires some degree of certainty. One party cannot claim later that the other is hiding the child or violating any visitation rights.

In many cases a court will allow a child to spend a summer vacation with the other spouse, perhaps for several weeks or a month. The child may be allowed to leave the jurisdiction of the court. In many cases, however, to avoid possible problems the court will direct that the child remain within its jurisdiction. One such problem is that the host parent may try to keep the child permanently.

If the spouse having custody of the child dies, the right of custody generally reverts to the surviving spouse. But that spouse must be able to provide a suitable home. Where the surviving spouse cannot provide a suitable home, custody awards may be made to other relatives or third parties.

The remarriage of either spouse does not automatically affect custody of children by a former marriage; but the remarried spouse may have acquired a proper home to replace the one broken by the divorce. Such arguments have been successful where the facts can be proved.

When children
become pawns

Heartbreak and an emotion-charged atmosphere may mar a custody hearing in which children become pawns in the struggle between divorcing parents. For that reason a separation agreement should provide for child custody. All details of custody and visitation should be spelled out. Notice requirements relating to visitation should be included so that the parties know precisely what their rights are and thus avoid court confrontations.

Insurance. To protect the children, again, the separation agreement should deal with the question of insurance. One spouse may want to keep the insurance on the other spouse in effect. The spouse having custody, or the children, may be named as irrevocable beneficiaries. This is done to prevent the other from agreeing to keep the policy in force and then changing the beneficiary.

Usually, the agreement will provide that ownership of the insurance policies is to be transferred to the wife or the husband, as the case may be; the other spouse will agree to continue to make the premium payments to keep the insurance in force. In this case the spouse paying the premiums cannot change the beneficiaries because the policy is owned by the other spouse.

Alimony. Most states recognize alimony, either temporary or permanent, as a basic part of a divorce action. Alimony should not be confused with support payments. The same principles apply, however, to support payments under a separation agreement and to a divorce decree that includes alimony, or provision of support by one spouse for the other.

Alimony while divorce action is pending

Temporary alimony may be awarded while an action for divorce is pending. In other words, the court will direct one spouse to pay temporary alimony to the other who may be in need before a final decree is entered. Again, it should be stressed that the court has to have jurisdiction over the paying party by valid service of process. That second party must have knowledge of the action, and have an opportunity to defend himself.

WHERE THERE ARE CHILDREN—AND PROPERTY[1]

Some basic factors are usually considered before a divorce decree becomes final. The fates of children born to the couple occupy a central place. So does the property owned by the marriage partners.

Factors to be considered where children are involved:

- The wishes of the children's parents as to their custody

- The wishes of the children as to their custodian

- The interaction and interrelationship of the children with their parents, brothers, and sisters and any other person who may

significantly affect the children's best interest

- The children's adjustment to home, school, and community

- The mental and physical health of all individuals concerned

Factors usually considered where property is involved:

- The contribution of each spouse to the acquisition of the marital property, including the contribution of a spouse as a homemaker

- The value of the property set apart for each spouse

- The economic circumstances of each spouse at the time the divi-

sion of property is to become
effective, including the desirability of awarding the family
home or the right to live therein
for reasonable periods to the

spouse having custody of the
children

• The conduct of the parties during
the marriage

1 Adapted from *Legal Facts about Dissolution of Marriage* (Jefferson City: The Missouri
Bar).

Temporary alimony is awarded where the court exercises its discretion in view of all the circumstances of the case. The award is
usually based on the reasonable probability that the suing party will
obtain the divorce. That party's needs and the ability of the other to
pay also enter into the decision. Lawyers' fees, which the suing partner may want to have paid, are not treated the same as alimony payments and are separate and distinct from alimony.

Divorce decree
and permanent
alimony

Permanent alimony is generally awarded as a part of the divorce
decree when all parties are present and in court. Where a separation
agreement has previously been signed, the court may consolidate the
separation agreement into the final divorce decree and make it a part
of the decree. The separation agreement may then be enforced just as
a direction to pay alimony would be.

The court considers various factors in determining the amount of
permanent alimony. The factors include the financial status of the
parties and their ability to pay, the anticipated future earnings of the
parties, their social standing, the conduct of the parties, and which
party was at fault. In most cases, permanent alimony will continue
until the death of either spouse or the remarriage of the spouse receiving alimony. Where a separation agreement exists, it may spell
out different conditions for termination.

Just as with provisions of a separation agreement dealing with custody of children, a decree of permanent alimony may be modified by
the court on application by either party. But the circumstances must
show substantially changed financial conditions, or one of the parties
must be shown to have concealed assets at the time the original

decree was entered. Any such modification must be made by the court that entered the original decree.

Support and temporary alimony

Not all states recognize permanent alimony, however. Some states hold that a final divorce decree terminates all duties of support between the parties. These states may recognize support payments while an action is pending, and may refer to such payments as "temporary alimony." But they do not recognize permanent alimony as such. The laws of the state should be checked before a marriage partner decides on a course of action.

Income Tax Aspects of Alimony. Important income tax considerations should be noted regarding alimony payments. Some of these include:

- Whether or not the person paying the alimony can deduct the alimony payments from his own personal income tax
- Whether these payments can be included in the gross income of the person receiving the alimony
- The tax result where alimony payments are contingent on the death or remarriage of the other spouse
- Whether or not the payments are in fact periodic
- The tax effect of insurance premiums paid by one spouse when the policies have been assigned to the other spouse

The separation agreement and the divorce decree raise similar tax and other problems. The family lawyer should be consulted to determine income tax consequences that may be considerable where a sizeable estate is involved. Division of the estate may be only one of those problems.

Some generalizations can be noted. The payments made as support by a husband under a written separation agreement will generally be taxed to the wife. But they will be deductible on the husband's tax returns where periodic payments are made and where the husband and wife file separate income tax forms. The parties may thus decide to take tax considerations into account in the separation agreement so that the wife will not have to report the support payments as income. At the same time the husband will not be able to claim tax deductions for those payments.

Legal effects of consolidation

Enforcement of Support or Alimony Payments. A particular benefit emerges where a separation agreement is consolidated into the divorce decree, or where the divorce decree sets the alimony payments. Consolidation allows a court to enforce the decree through contempt proceedings. A separation agreement providing for support payments is a contract; it can be used as the basis of a suit, like any other contract, if one of the parties breaches it.

A lawsuit may not always be the best remedy, however. The time involved in a lawsuit may, for example, be prohibitive if the other party defends. Where a separation agreement is part of a decree, a court can hold in contempt of court the party refusing to abide by its terms. The possibility of imprisonment for contempt constitutes a strong inducement to the other party to make the proper payments under the decree.

Imprisonment is actually unusual in such cases. The threat alone often convinces the offending party that he or she should meet the specified conditions.

Suit under a separation agreement

A spouse may sue under a separation agreement. If that spouse secures a judgment, the judgment may be collected by the normal means. These include attachment of the property of the other spouse, garnishment of rents or other funds owed the other spouse by third parties, and other methods established by state law. Decrees for the support of a spouse or children can also be enforced from one state to another under laws known as reciprocal support laws. These laws provide a means of following the spouse who owes support but skips town to avoid payments.

If marital problems as discussed in this chapter cannot be avoided, it is important that the parties to a failing marriage have full and complete knowledge concerning their rights and obligations. Thus they can make the law work for them. Not only can they settle on the best course of action, they will also be able to perform their obligations and enforce their rights with a minimum of heartache and discouragement.

ALTERNATIVE TYPES OF DIVORCE

A divorce action normally begins, as noted, with a complaint by one party against the other. The time required for completion of the action will depend on many factors. These include the degree to which husband and wife have agreed on financial and other problems and the backlog of cases in divorce court. Typically, from two months to a year or more can elapse before the divorce decree becomes final.

In some states an *interlocutory decree* may precede a *final decree*. The interlocutory decree will not become final for a period of time—30, 60, or 90 days or more. The parties are not divorced until the final decree is entered.

"Quickie" and no-fault divorces

Many couples and some states have sought ways in which to speed divorce actions. Two such methods are the so-called "quickie" divorce and no-fault divorce. The latter had been legalized in most states by the early 1980s; only five states—Illinois, Massachusetts, Mississippi, Pennsylvania, and South Dakota—did not have some kind of no-fault divorce.

"Quickie" Divorce Decrees

So-called "quickie" divorce decrees can be obtained in countries or states having little or no residence requirements. Are these "quickie" divorce decrees recognized everywhere?

Under the federal Constitution, the "Full Faith and Credit" clause requires that the courts of one state give full faith and credit to the judgments and decrees of the courts of another state. However, in an exception to this general rule, the court entering the original decrees must have had jurisdiction over the parties to that action. If the court did not have such jurisdiction, the second court does not have to give the decree full faith and credit.

The requirement of residence has been mentioned in connection with divorce decrees. The courts in several states have held that residence requires more than merely being present in the state for the period required to get a divorce. Rather, residence means physical presence plus an intent to remain within the state on a permanent basis. For example, divorce decrees have been attacked in some cases because the spouse did not indicate an intent to remain in the state. He or she may nonetheless have been in the state long enough to meet the residence requirement for a divorce.

In effect, some states take a stricter view of residence requirements than do others. An important question centers on notice—whether personal notice was given to the other party regarding the filing of the divorce action.

The foreign country divorce

Quickie or "overnight" divorces may be granted in a foreign country such as Mexico. Ads proclaim that "you can get a divorce overnight" by sending certain forms to the foreign country. The decree is allegedly granted the next day. Neither party has to be present.

The full faith and credit clause of the U.S. Constitution does not apply to judgments or decrees of a court in a foreign nation. Further, a foreign country's decrees must have a proper jurisdictional basis. Among nations, recognition of a foreign country's judgments and decrees is based in "comity," under which foreign courts will generally recognize the decrees of another country. But where the physical presence of the party is not required, American courts will almost universally refuse to recognize the foreign decree. That decree, after all, was not based on proper jurisdictional grounds.

A quickie divorce may not, in brief, be recognized in some states as a legal divorce. The situation varies from state to state.

Residence may change the situation

Again, some generalizations may be made. If a state's residence requirements have been met insofar as the original decree is concerned, if the spouse suing for divorce is physically present in the state issuing the decree for the required residence period, and if that spouse indicates an intent to remain there, normally such a decree will be valid and binding if attacked in another state. If a foreign country's decree is based on residence and the physical presence of the suing spouse in that country for a specified period, normally the U.S. courts will recognize the foreign country's divorce decree.

One-Party Divorces. In many cases one party receives a divorce from another when there is no indication that the other party was present or even had notice of the divorce action. These "one-party" divorce actions are possible because the laws of some states make it unnecessary to give the other party actual notice of the pending action. The court where the action is pending, in essence, has jurisdiction over the marriage and can change the marital relationship without notice to the absent party.

Like any other court action, a one-party divorce suit begins with the filing of a complaint or petition. An effort must be made to serve that complaint or summons on the other party. Many state rules of procedure permit service of the complaint on the other party by publication—through an advertisement in a newspaper noting the last known address of the other party. Other rules seek to ensure as much as possible that actual notice is given. But that step is not always necessary. The laws of any given state should be consulted.

Notice may be required

In other cases the second spouse must receive notice. This is true where a support order, an alimony decree, or any other decree or court order involving a judgment for money—or a direction to pay money to one's spouse—is concerned. The other party then has the opportunity to come in and defend.

No-Fault Divorce. The old "fault"-style divorce has been criticized because it encouraged deceit and lying for the purpose of obtaining a divorce. Beyond that, couples found it difficult to agree quietly to a divorce because one spouse had to prove guilt in the other. Unnecessary bitterness and resentment often resulted, forcing one person—where divorce was not a mutual decision—into a position of consenting to unreasonable terms.

How no-fault divorce differs

No-fault divorce, also known as no-fault dissolution, differs from the conventional divorce in the following respects:

No evidence of fault or misconduct on the part of either spouse is required in filing. Usually, the only ground needed is "irreconcilable differences," "irretrievable breakdown," or "incompatibility." Each state has its own standards for establishing the existence of this condition in a marriage. Some states require that a couple make an attempt, through counseling provided by the state or county, to repair the marital relationship. If that attempt fails, either party can file for dissolution. New York allows a spouse to file either under no-fault grounds or on the grounds of cruel and inhuman treatment, abandonment for one or more years, imprisonment for three or more years, or adultery.

Divorce settlements are not dictated by a finding on which spouse is "at fault" in a marriage. Alimony (or maintenance), property, child custody, and child support are based on need and other rational considerations rather than fault.

"THE GLEASON RULE"

In a variation of the "no-fault" rule, New York requires that the parties live apart for at least one year under the terms of a written, notarized agreement that is filed with the court. The so-called "Gleason Rule" states that it does not matter who filed for separation or whether fault was the ground for separation. Comedian-actor Jackie Gleason was granted a divorce on the ground that he lived apart even though his wife had obtained a separation based on a finding of fault against him.

A typical dissolution procedure

A typical no-fault dissolution procedure occurs through these steps:

- *An initial visit to a lawyer.* A spouse should provide his or her lawyer with the following: (1) a complete list of property owned by each spouse, jointly or with the children, including the value and how and when acquired; (2) an itemization of mortgages, debts, insurance policies, or other financial factors; (3) information about the children that would be affected by divorce; and (4) a copy of the latest income tax return. One should also discuss legal fees, as in all dealings with a lawyer.

- *Reconciliation.* One or both parties must consult with a party having expertise in marital problems. If a lawyer feels that not all efforts at reconciliation have been made, he will suggest further counseling.

- *Filing the petition.* Failing reconciliation attempts, a petition for dissolution is filed. At least 60 days will normally be required between filing and court hearing. This time should be used by both parties to reach a settlement. One spouse may be granted temporary child custody, support, or alimony.

- *Reaching a settlement.* This is based on the present and future needs of each party and on their respective abilities to meet those needs. For example, the spouse who gains child custody may require funds for child care and other needs. Child custody may be dictated by any of these factors: ages and sexes of the children; compatibility with each parent; the ability of each parent to take care of each child; and the personal characteristics of each parent. Some states, such as California, may grant either sole custody or joint custody.

- *Changing the settlement.* Division of property is one aspect of the settlement that cannot be changed. As circumstances change, however, support provisions can be altered except where the original decree did not include alimony; that cannot be added later. Negotiating a settlement that is agreeable to both parties can save time and expense later.

Reducing trauma, saving time

No-fault divorce reduces the trauma and bitterness of a proceeding as well as the time involved. Neither party is legally at fault. Formerly, the wife would usually be given custody of children. With no-fault divorce, however, more men are being awarded custody. In this respect, women not receiving custody may see themselves as somehow "at fault." This is one possible negative consequence of no-fault divorce. With the increase in no-fault divorces, the number of annulments has declined.

9 "COME TO RETIREMENT CITY FOR THE REST OF YOUR LIFE"

With the rapid rise in American technology, more and more employers have adopted retirement policies that allow employees to retire at specified ages. The feeling seems to be that once an employee reaches a certain age, his capacity to produce for the company diminishes, and "new blood" should be brought in to take over his job. Many companies require that employees retire at a certain age.

There is by no means total agreement on whether a person's productivity drops when he reaches the age of 65 or any other age. Many men and women who are forced into retirement go into a new

field and become very successful. Evidence to the contrary might also be cited.

From a practical standpoint, no employer should have a mandatory retirement age without some form of pension or profit-sharing plan that guarantees security to the retiring employee. So important has the whole question of pension and profit-sharing plans become that Congress has passed protective legislation, the Employee Retirement Income Security Act (ERISA) of 1974. The Act seeks to eliminate many of the problems resulting from the loss of benefits when employees change jobs or when they are fired or laid off just before they might qualify for pension benefits.

All too often an employee, feeling that he is secure in his pension rights, finds himself suddenly cast adrift when the company goes out of business, or is merged into another company. The employee may have no adequate provision for the future under existing pension plans.

The Employee Retirement Income Security Act guarantees greater security to the approximately 30 million workers who belong to private pension plans. But the Act also provides pension opportunities for another 35 million workers whose employers do not offer private pension plans. The self-employed person also benefits. The amount that he can set aside for his own pension plan, tax free, increased greatly after January 1, 1974. By 1980, he could contribute up to 15 per cent of his annual income to his personal retirement account, with a yearly maximum of $7,500. The tax benefits flowing from passage of the 1981 Economic Recovery Tax Act will be discussed later in this chapter.

Some ERISA provisions

The 1974 Act established age and length of service requirements. These entitle a worker who changes jobs or is fired before his retirement date to a part or all of the benefits he would have received after retirement—provided that he has put in at least five or ten years of service or that his age and years of service add up to 45. The employer has the option of which vesting procedure he wishes to choose for his plan and his employees.

Under the 1974 Act, if an employee quits, is fired, or changes employers after satisfying the minimum vesting requirements of the plan, he still retains his pension rights. His original employer will be required to pay him the pension benefits to which his service entitles him even though he has worked for someone else between his former employment and his retirement. If the company plan provides for it, the employee can take his vested or owned pension credits with him.

If his new employer agrees, the employee can invest the money from his former pension plan in the new company's plan. If not, the employee can invest that money in his own tax-free retirement account at a bank or other institution until he retires.

Additional important provisions of ERISA include funding standards. These ensure that there will be money in the plan to pay retirement benefits when they are due. Severe restrictions are placed on pension fund investment and management. All workers' pension plans are now insured against loss by the Federal Pension Benefit Guaranty Corporation, which is similar to the Federal Deposit Insurance Corporation that insures bank deposits against loss to the depositor.

A step toward pension reform

ERISA is not the final word on the matter. But it represents a first attempt to prevent forfeiture of pension rights when an employee is not at fault. The Act marks a good beginning in pension reform, one that was desperately needed. In a later reform, the Supreme Court ruled in 1978 that an employer was violating the Civil Rights Act of

1964 if he charged women more than men for participation in a retirement plan. By 1980, efforts to update ERISA were under way in Congress. Critics charged that the Act's complexity was forcing thousands of employers to terminate pension plans. The goal of proposed new reforms is the simplification of ERISA.

The standard private pension and profit-sharing plan and the federal Social Security laws require specific attention.

PRIVATE PENSION AND PROFIT-SHARING PLANS

A profit-sharing plan differs basically from a pension plan, particularly where employer contributions are concerned. The normal pension plan provides that the employer has a fixed commitment to make payments and contribute funds to the plan so that there will be sufficient funds to meet retirement claims. On the other hand, a profit-sharing plan contains no fixed commitment on the dollar amount to be contributed by an employer. Such a plan depends on the net profits of the company at the end of its fiscal year. A percentage is usually applied to the net profits to determine the amount to be contributed. If there are no net profits, no contribution is made.

*Method of
allocating funds
differs*

Another difference is the method of allocating funds to individual employees. Actuarial (age and life expectancy) calculations are required in a pension plan to make certain that the beneficiaries have the retirement funds needed at retirement. The 1974 Act provides for such adequate funding. Profit-sharing plans are normally based on the wages or salaries of employees, with some consideration given to length of service.

The actual forms that pension and profit-sharing plans take may also differ depending on investment objectives and the way the plan is administered. For example, an employer's plan may use mutual funds and direct stock investment (the so-called equity plans); it may also utilize annuities, life insurance, a combination of both, or debt obligations such as corporate, municipal, and treasury bonds and notes.

Administrators of pension and profit-sharing plans have to follow certain rules. Where investments are made in stocks or bonds, the plan will usually designate a trustee under a written trust agreement to hold and invest the plan's funds for the benefit of the employees. This agreement fixes the duties and obligations of the trustee. Where an annuity and life insurance program is used, a contract between the insurance company and the employer controls the method of administration.

Many people covered by pension or profit-sharing plans appear to have little understanding of their own plans. They may be aware that their employer has one and that he contributes to it, but other than that, they know nothing. Yet retirement security must be understood. How can you plan for your retirement if you don't know how your plan operates?

INCOME TAX BENEFITS

*Study your
own plan*

Aside from providing a means of achieving retirement security, pension and profit-sharing plans have a distinct advantage for both the employer and the employee. A "qualified" pension or profit-sharing plan—one that fulfills all the requirements of the federal Internal Revenue Code—offers definite tax advantages.

Within limits specified in the tax laws, a corporate employer can claim current deductions from gross business income for all amounts contributed to a qualified plan. This remains true even though no benefits are currently payable to employees in the year in which a contribution is made.

The employee, on the other hand, does not have to include in his own individual income tax return the amount contributed to the plan by his employer. The contribution is not considered income until the employee has actually received the benefits. Thus the employee will be taxed at ordinary income rates or at capital gains rates depending on the year when the contributions were made to the plan, as represented by the benefits paid.

In sum, the employee pays no income tax on the contributions until he actually receives retirement benefits from the plan.

Other tax benefits may be noted. If the employer's contributions are paid into an investment trust fund, any income from the investments is exempt from income tax during the entire period in which these investments are effective. If the contributions to the trust fund are allowed to accumulate, tax free, over the period of an employee's service to a company, the rate of accumulation is much greater since there is no withdrawal from the fund to pay income tax.

Qualified Plans

Four basic requirements

To take advantage of the tax benefits for both employer and employee, the plan must be "qualified" under the Internal Revenue Code. The plan must fulfill the following requirements:

* The plan must be permanent, not temporary.
* It must be for the exclusive benefit of the employees and their designated beneficiaries under the plan.
* It must be primarily a deferred compensation plan, a plan that recognizes the service of employees and compensates them on their retirement.
* It must not discriminate among different classes of employees.

Regarding the latter, the plan cannot favor high-salaried employees over other employees. Nor can the plan discriminate with respect to benefits distributable to employees. In other words, one employee cannot receive an amount that bears no relationship to the amounts received by other similar employees.

If a trust plan is used, the trust agreement must prohibit the trustee from taking money from the plan to benefit other persons who are not beneficiaries. The plan must also require the trustee to follow the investment restrictions of the law. It is important that the plan be in writing. It must be distributed and explained fully to all employees, and the papers filed with the Internal Revenue Service to qualify the plan must contain copies of all pertinent documents. These include the notices and reports given to the employees to advise them of the existence and terms of the plan.

Integration with Social Security

In most pension and profit-sharing plans, the benefits payable will take into account the amount of Social Security benefits that the retired or disabled employee, or his beneficiary, may receive. Thus the plans are said to be "integrated" with the Social Security benefits. A profit-sharing plan must also have a formula for allocating the contributions to the beneficiaries and should indicate a method for determining the net profit based upon which the amount of the contribution is figured.

Self-Employment

Self-employed persons and persons whose companies have no retirement plans cannot claim all the technical benefits that are available under corporate pension and profit-sharing plans. But Keogh plans and Individual Retirement Accounts (IRAs) do offer similar tax advantages. The number of these plans for self-employed individuals has grown steadily as increased benefits are made available. But note: plans for self-employed persons must also "qualify" for special tax advantages.

Keogh plans and IRAs actually give self-employed persons such as doctors, lawyers, and sole proprietors a form of tax shelter. Others who are employed full-time but who earn money by "moonlighting" may also set up such programs with the extra funds they earn.

Under the Economic Recovery Tax Act of 1981, the Keogh plan tax shelter works as follows: Retirement funds are invested in mutual funds, trust accounts with banks, U.S. Treasury certificates, or other programs. Starting in 1982, the individual could contribute as much as $15,000—instead of $7,500—to the plan out of his annual gross income. He cannot, however, contribute more than 15 percent of that income. All such contributions are deductible from income in the year in which they are made. No taxes are paid on the funds until after retirement. At that time, taxes are usually paid at a reduced rate.

The Individual Retirement Account brings tax advantages similar to those afforded by Keogh plans. But starting in 1982 the person with an existing IRA account can contribute up to $2,000 tax-free. The former limit was $1,500. At the same time the 15 percent-of-income rule was removed. A part-time teacher who in 1981 earned $5,000 and could only put $750 into her IRA account could in 1982 and afterward contribute $2,000. A husband and wife making joint contributions to an IRA account could in 1982 and after deposit $2,250 tax-free. The former limit was $1,750.

228 THE LEGAL GUIDE

The individual can start drawing on a Keogh plan or individual retirement fund at the age of 59½. But he can defer retirement—and drawing benefits—until 70½.

In Sum . . .

*What to
find out . . .*

If you are an employee of a company with a pension or profit-sharing plan, you should read all the literature about the plan carefully. Learn what rights you possess, the manner in which your rights are protected, and other details. Remember that the tax act of 1981 specified that if you are making contributions to a "mandatory" retirement plan, with the company putting money away only if you do too, your contributions won't be deductible.

If you are an employer without a company pension plan, you owe it to yourself and your employees to investigate the advantages of launching a plan. There is no better way to show your appreciation to your faithful, steady employees and give them the incentive to stay with you. The size of your company should make no difference; the tax savings and tax-deferred benefits that you may realize make it advantageous to examine the details immediately.

SOCIAL SECURITY BENEFITS

No discussion of pension and profit-sharing plans is complete without a discussion of the Social Security laws. As noted, private pension and profit-sharing plans take into account the Social Security benefits that the covered employee would receive on his retirement or disability. An understanding of the Social Security program fills in the picture regarding retirement benefits.

A series of programs offered by the federal government has the general heading of "Social Security." These include those programs operated directly by the federal government, such as the Old Age, Survivors' and Disability Insurance program and the health insurance program, including hospital and medical insurance for the aged.

State programs

In addition, programs involving unemployment insurance and public assistance and welfare services are operated by the several states. The programs include old age, aid to the blind, aid to needy families with children, aid to permanently and totally disabled individuals, medical assistance, maternal and child health services, services to crippled children, and child welfare services. The states run these programs with the cooperation and aid of the federal Department of Health and Human Services under the Social Security system.

A problem involving public assistance or welfare services can usually be solved by contacting a state or county public assistance agency.

This section deals with the benefits available under the program handled directly by the federal government under Social Security. Because benefits under other related programs change from time to time, no schedule of benefits will be cited. An up-to-date schedule can be obtained from any Social Security office.

Old Age, Survivors' and Disability Insurance Benefits

Key categories
of beneficiaries

The Old Age, Survivors' and Disability Insurance program involves monthly Social Security cash payments made directly to beneficiaries. The following list shows the key categories of persons who can participate as beneficiaries:

- A disabled insured worker
- A retired insured worker age 62 or older
- The wife (including the divorced wife in some cases) of a retired or disabled worker entitled to benefits, if the wife is age 62 or over or is caring for a worker's child who is under 18 or who is disabled and entitled to Social Security benefits
- The dependent husband of a retired or disabled woman entitled to benefits if he is age 62 or over
- The dependent, unmarried child of a retired or disabled worker entitled to benefits, or of a deceased insured worker, if the child is under 18 years or is age 18 or over but under a disability which began before he or she reached 18 years, or if the child is age 18 or over but under age 22 and attending school on a full-time basis
- The widow (including the surviving divorced wife, in some cases) of a deceased insured worker if the widow is age 60 or over
- The disabled widow (including the surviving divorced wife, in some cases) of a deceased insured worker if the disabled widow is at least 50 but under 60 and becomes disabled within the period specified in the law
- The widow (including the surviving divorced wife, in some cases) of a deceased insured worker, regardless of her age, if she cares for a child of the deceased under age 18, or a disabled child who is entitled to benefits
- The dependent widower of a deceased insured worker age 62 or over
- The disabled dependent widower of a deceased insured worker if the widower is at least 50 but under 62 and becomes disabled within the period specified in the law
- The dependent parents of an insured worker who died at age 62 or over

Monthly payment
plus lump-sum

In addition to the monthly cash payment made to a beneficiary, a lump-sum death payment may also be paid to the widow or widower who was living with the insured worker at the time of the worker's death. If there is no eligible widow or widower, the lump-sum death payment may be applied to pay the worker's funeral expenses. If the burial expenses are paid by someone other than the widow or widower, proof of payment must be made to the Social Security office before this payment can be made.

The rights to benefits depend on whether the worker was "insured" and became qualified during his lifetime. To be eligible for retirement, survivors' or disability benefits, the worker must have accumulated a certain number of "quarters of coverage." These are calendar quarters ending March 31, June 30, September 30, and December 31 of each calendar year in which a person has been paid $50 or more in wages for employment covered by the law. A self-employed person qualifies by earning $100 or more in self-employment income for a specified period. But, beginning after 1950, the self-employed person must earn at least $400 net in the taxable year before any quarters in the taxable year can be credited with self-employment income.

The method of computing the quarters of coverage needed under the program is very complicated. It is based on schedules and regulations in the law. Up-to-date information on the number of quarters of coverage required for qualification can be obtained from a local Social Security office.

Health Insurance Program under Social Security

"Medicare"
administration

The health insurance program, or "Medicare," is administered by the federal Social Security Administration with the assistance of "intermediaries" composed of insurance companies or the local Blue Cross agency. This program includes comprehensive hospital insurance and medical insurance features.

Medicare provides for payments for daily in-hospital benefits for persons 65 or over who are entitled to Social Security monthly cash benefits. The individual may not receive the payments for some reason. A person 65 or over who is a qualified railroad retirement beneficiary is also eligible. So are all persons 65 or over who do not meet the above two requirements but who have done some work covered by Social Security, are citizens of the United States or aliens who have been lawfully admitted to this country for permanent residence, and who have resided in the United States at least five years continuously before applying for benefits.

OLD AGE, SURVIVORS' AND DISABILITY INSURANCE: WHAT KINDS OF BENEFITS AND WHO RECEIVES THEM?[1]

There are three basic types of benefits available:

RETIREMENT BENEFITS: When a worker retires, he or she can choose to receive benefits at age 62 or age 65. The worker's spouse and dependent children, including stepchildren and adopted children, can be eligible for benefits as well.

DISABILITY BENEFITS: When a worker becomes severely disabled, monthly benefits can start even before age 65. Disability, for Social Security purposes, means having a severe mental or physical condition which prevents work and (1) has lasted for at least one year, (2) is expected to last for at least a year, or (3) is expected to result in death. Benefits can start for the sixth full month of disability and continue as long as the disability. The spouse and dependent children can be eligible for benefits too.

SURVIVORS' BENEFITS: When a worker dies, benefits can go to certain family members as monthly payments and a lump-sum payment, usually to the surviving spouse.

OTHER BENEFITS: In addition to the monthly cash payments under retirement, disability, and survivors' benefits, Medicare helps persons 65 and older and severely disabled people under age 65 to pay the high cost of health care. In some instances, a monthly premium must be paid for Medicare benefits. In other cases, you may receive it without paying the premium. If you are 65 or older or under 65 and severely disabled and do not have Medicare coverage, you should contact your Social Security office for information.

In addition to those situations noted above, which entitle a person to benefits under retirement, disability, and survivors' provisions, there are special situations which may apply to you:

COMMON-LAW MARRIAGES: Common-law spouses, widows, and widowers are eligible for benefits just as if there were a traditional ceremonial marriage.

ILLEGITIMATE CHILDREN: Illegitimate children are eligible for benefits just as legitimate children are, although there may be the additional problem of proving the relationship to the retired, disabled, or deceased parent.

GRANDCHILDREN: Unmarried grandchildren may be able to receive benefits if three requirements are met: (1) the child actually lives or lived with the grandparent, (2) the child receives or received at least half of his or her support from the grandparent, and (3) both parents are dead or totally disabled.

[1] Adapted from the brochure, *What Should I Know about Social Security?* Copyright June 1979, Pennsylvania Bar Association. Single copies of the brochure are available directly from the Association at the following address: Post Office Box 186, Harrisburg, PA 17108.

The law includes these transitional provisions for persons not otherwise entitled to hospital benefits. Benefits are not paid if the person has been convicted of treason or any other crime against the United States or is covered by a program providing health benefits to federal employees.

The Medicare coverage is provided on enrollment. In other words, application must be made specifically for the medical insurance coverage.

The amounts of Medicare benefits and the spans of coverage change from time to time. But the program does provide significant help to those individuals who have reached the required age and who do not have the means to maintain their own private hospitalization programs. In addition, certain insurance companies today provide hospitalization and medical coverages that supplement Medicare and provide longer spans of coverage.

Qualifying for "Medicare"

Persons who do not qualify for monthly Social Security cash benefits may nevertheless qualify for Medicare coverage. They have to be age 65 or over and fall within the provisions of the law.

The above represents an outline of private pension and profit-sharing plans and Social Security benefits available to retired or disabled persons and their survivors and beneficiaries. Additional questions should be referred to the administrators of a pension plan or to the local Social Security office. They are there to help; they are required to answer questions.

10 "I DECLARE THIS TO BE MY LAST WILL AND TESTAMENT"

An elderly couple requested that a lawyer stop at their home to discuss the task of writing their wills. The gentleman was 85 years of age; his wife 83. They had raised 12 children, all of whom had children of their own.

"How does this sound? Being of sound mind we are spending our money as fast as we can."

The lawyer explained the processes involved in making a will and what the couple should be thinking about regarding their property. But the old gentleman had a puzzled expression on his face. When asked whether it was his wish that all his property pass to his wife, the man said, "Yes, I leave everything to Mama, but if she marry again, she get *nothing!*"

Despite the fact that his wife had borne him 12 children and had been a good wife to him for many years, the old gentleman was worried about her marrying again. The case indicates the kinds of superstitions and fears that people entertain, even today, concerning the making of a will. The feeling occurs mostly among elderly people, but many younger persons do not appreciate the need for and importance of a will.

This chapter deals with the making of a will; what happens if you die without a will; what should be included in a will; and the process known as "estate planning" that is so much discussed today. This kind of planning seeks to ensure that your loved ones receive your property with a minimum of expense and taxes.

LAWS OF INTESTACY: DESCENT AND DISTRIBUTION

Every state has laws governing the ways in which property passes on the death of the owner who dies without a will. An "estate" is the sum total of all the property of a deceased individual. That property passes to the deceased's heirs at law, if he dies without a will, or to his beneficiaries under his will.

The laws of the various states differ regarding the transfer of property from a deceased person to his *heirs*, the persons who inherit from him under state law. If a man is survived by his wife and children, they become his primary heirs. However, in some states the wife does not inherit the entire estate of her husband if there are surviving children. Rather, she receives only a portion of the estate depending on the number of children. Or a wife may not inherit the entire estate if other relatives, such as brothers and sisters, parents, aunts and uncles, or cousins survive the deceased.

Wife may lose out

No one can assume, in short, that if he dies without a will, leaving a wife and children or other relatives, the wife will inherit the entire estate. The will in fact has this advantage: it ensures that one's wishes are carried out regardless of the state law dealing with inheritance. A will may also substantially reduce tax liabilities in the handling of an estate.

Under the laws of some states, if a person dies without a will the person appointed by the court to handle the estate must post a bond to ensure faithful performance of his duties. But the person named in a will need not post a bond in some cases. Depending on the size of the estate, a bond may involve a substantial expense. That money goes to a bonding company and is thus lost to the heirs.

A will is essential to your peace of mind. It also provides your loved ones with proof of your concern for them and shows your intentions regarding the property passing to them.

WHAT IS A WILL AND HOW IS IT MADE?

The will and disposition of property

A will is a written document in which the person making the will, called the "testator," specifies how and to whom his property will pass in the event of his death. It is commonly held that a will should be written, dated, and signed at the end. Some states require two or three witnesses to attest to the signing of the will by the testator. Other states do not require witnesses.

For safety, witnesses should be present when any will is signed. A will may be made out in a state not requiring witnesses; then the testator may later die in a state which does require them. Without witnesses, the will would not be valid in the second state.

WHAT ARE THE ADVANTAGES OF A WILL?[1]

- You can choose the executor you wish to handle your estate.

- The expense of bond premiums, required of the person managing your estate, as well as some probate costs, can be avoided.

- You decide who gets your property instead of having the law decide for you. You may wish to provide a larger share for a young or sick child, leave something to charity, or give all your property to your spouse. You may take into consideration gifts that you have made.

- A trust may be created to keep your property intact for the benefit of your family.

- Minors can be cared for without the expense of guardianship proceedings.

- You may avoid the forced sale of your business.

- You can save estate and inheritance taxes. Only your will can place the burden on the right parties.

- Your will is the final document that completes your lifetime of planning for your family.

[1] Adapted from *Legal Facts about Wills* (Jefferson City: The Missouri Bar).

Kinds of Wills

The most common type of will is the *witnessed will*. Whether handwritten or typed, this will should be signed by the testator and witnessed by at least two, and if possible three, persons. The witnesses attest that the testator signed his own will on a specified date. Other types of wills include:

- The *holographic will* that is written out by the testator in his or her own handwriting. The holographic will may or may not be witnessed. In the former case, the will would normally be held to be valid. If the will has not been witnessed, as when a trapper in fear of death scribbles his "last will and testament" while alone, proving the will may be difficult.

- The *nuncupative will* involves an oral declaration by a testator in extreme circumstances of what he wants to do with his estate. The testator may be in grave danger; he makes his declaration in the presence of witnesses; and the will may or may not be written down later. A court may decide that such a will is valid because the testator could not put down his final wishes in any other way. But all courts examine nuncupative wills closely.
- A *joint will* is the kind made out by the husband and wife to-

gether. The joint will is rarely used today because it has proved relatively inflexible.

* The *mutual* or *reciprocal will* offers much greater flexibility. The husband and wife make out separate but complementary documents. Mutual wills make it possible for the couple to provide specifically for most family needs, including unusual ones.

A will is effective at death

Any will is effective only at death. It can be changed at any time during the life of the testator. No one has any rights under the will of a living person since the will is effective only on the death of the testator.

Once death takes place, probate, the process of putting the will, in particular the witnessed will, on record, begins. The will then controls the settlement of the deceased person's estate. The will becomes a public record when it is probated.

Because the laws require that the will be signed, dated, and witnessed, it is always dangerous to put together a "home-made" will. A violation of any of the legal requirements concerning wills will render it null and void.

Can you scratch a name out of a will and just leave it in that form? No. Scratching out a name may effect what is seen as a *material alteration*. The validity of the entire document may come into question. That means no erasures, no scratching out, no adding is permitted.

A caveat: beware of the so-called "form wills," and of those who claim that anyone can write his own will without the advice of counsel. Many lawsuits have arisen because people have attempted to write their own wills.

Information Needed to Prepare a
Witnessed Will and Estate Plan

What information
is needed?

In order to draft a will properly, certain information should be made available to the family lawyer. A listing of all valuable papers, including birth certificates, deeds, mortgages, insurance policies, stocks and bonds, savings passbooks, and so on marks a beginning. This information or list is vital to the proper preparation of the will and should be kept with the will in a safe place. The information necessary is listed below in more specific form:

1.   Names, ages, and addresses of the testator and all relatives who might be beneficiaries under the will, including children, spouse, and others.

2.   Details concerning the testator and his immediate family, with ages, financial status, and any personal facts that may bear on the estate plan. For example, where a child has a physical deformity, a larger distribution may be necessary for that child than for the others.

3.   A complete list of all assets owned by the testator and spouse. The list should be complete and should include:

• Personal effects and household furnishings, with values; all real property and its value; all investments; names of corporations and denominations of stocks and bonds; bank accounts, both savings and checking; mortgages owned on other people's property; oil and gas properties owned; patents and copyrights owned; cash; and so on

• Property such as automobiles, works of art, libraries, coin or gun collections, and yachts

• All pension and profit-sharing plans to which the testator belongs, death benefits, any stock options that the testator may elect, and the Social Security benefits involved

• Life insurance payable at the time of the testator's death along with a listing of all policies by number and name of company, all annuities (monthly payment plans) and related policies

• A listing of all the testator's business interests, including any corporate, partnership, or sole proprietorship businesses, and all documents, stock certificates, profit and loss statements, and balance sheets connected with the business interests of the testator, for the purpose of determining the value of these interests

- Any interest in any estates or trusts created by others to which he is a beneficiary, and financial statements and back tax returns

This is a relatively exhaustive list. Putting it together serves a double purpose. First, the list shows all the assets that the will should cover. Second, drawing up the list necessitates a review of exactly what is owned and of the financial direction the testator is taking. The list should be complete and up to date.

Gathering documents for the family lawyer

All documents relating to property owned should be gathered for inspection by the family lawyer. The manner of ownership of property—by husband and wife, jointly with someone else, or otherwise—makes a big difference in planning an estate. The form of ownership of some properties may have to be changed.

To be complete, the list should include all debts and obligations of the testator, both personal and business. These would include mortgage obligations, long-term debts, short-term debts, charge accounts, and all currently payable items such as insurance premiums.

To assist the family lawyer, the listing should include the names and addresses of the testator's accountant, insurance agent or broker, bank trust officer, and stock broker. The lawyer can consult with these others as necessary in drawing up the total estate plan.

Goals of an estate plan

The testator should state his objectives clearly. What is the estate plan intended to do? If primary concerns are that the spouse and children remain secure, that children receive college educations, that funds be available to start them in business or buy them a home, and that their property be protected against the claims of creditors, the family lawyer should know that. He can then draft the will and estate plan with these objectives in mind.

Next some specific points should be considered:

1. *Specific instructions regarding funeral arrangements and burial.* These may be included in the will; but because the will is usually not read or probated until after the funeral arrangements have been completed, the instructions should usually be kept separate. A letter left with one's spouse and children specifying the testator's wishes regarding burial is usually a better method.

2. *Personal belongings.* Unless the testator makes specific reference to personal belongings, they will pass under the "residuary" clause of the will. This catchall section provides that anything left after specific bequests should go to the *residuary* beneficiary. An automobile, clothing, and any other specific personal property should be left to particular individuals. But if everything is left to the spouse, all personal belongings are covered. They should, however, be listed item by item.

3. *Cash gifts in the will.* A cash bequest can create problems. The executor—the person named in the will to handle the estate—may have to pay a specific amount of money despite the effect of that payment on the balance of the will. The executor may have to sell real property in order to obtain enough money to pay the specific cash bequests.

Bequests as percentages of the total estate

If an estate turns out to be smaller than anticipated, the cash bequests may exhaust the great bulk of the assets. Little or nothing may remain for distribution to other beneficiaries. Bequests can be made more appropriately in the form of parts or percentages of a total net estate rather than as specific dollar amounts. Thus the beneficiaries receive their percentages of whatever the total estate is when the testator dies.

4. *Real estate.* Various choices lie open to the testator in connection with real estate. He can leave it to his beneficiary outright, or direct that it be held in trust to provide income to a family member. He can have it sold, with the proceeds to go to the beneficiaries. The testator can give a *life estate,* the right of a beneficiary to live in the property or use it for life, with ownership automatically shifting to someone else after the death of the life tenant. Finally, disposition can be left to the discretion of the executor.

5. *The remainder of the estate.* Who receives the remainder of an estate after all individual bequests have been made? The testator makes that choice. But if more than one person is to receive the remaining portions, they should, again, be left shares (½ to X, ½ to Y).

6. *The guardian for minor children.* If assets are left to children under 18, on the testator's death a court has to appoint a guardian—usually a bank or trust company—for their persons and their property. As an alternative, the will can name a guardian for any minor children. The latter is often the preferred procedure.

Empowering the guardian

The terms of a will should give the guardian the power to use the property for the benefit of any minor children and to provide maintenance, support, and educational assistance.

Property left to minor children is their property. But because in the eyes of the law they are "under age," they cannot handle the property themselves. The guardian is needed to handle the property for them.

Another type of guardian should be named: the guardian of the person of each minor child. The guardian of the person takes physical charge of the children and raises them in the parent's absence. Serious consideration should be given to the appointment of someone who will raise the children, love them, and provide accommodations needed to keep them together in their younger years.

No guardians are required for adult beneficiaries. A testator who fears that an adult child will dissipate the assets received under a will can place that child's share in a special trust fund. The will in this case names a trustee to handle the property and provide for the beneficiary's maintenance, support, and education. The testator can specify the amounts to be distributed to him from time to time. The will can also include a special "spendthrift" provision that protects the trust assets from the claims of the child's creditors while the assets are being held for his benefit.

7. *The executor.* The executor, sometimes called an administrator or personal representative, is the person or firm named in the will to handle an estate to its conclusion. Depending on the state in which an estate is being settled, an executor can usually complete his work within a year of the date of death—or a year from the date on which the executor is appointed by the court. Some more complex estates, however, take years to settle.

The executor and
financial matters

An executor should have some understanding of financial matters. But he need not be an expert or a lawyer; nor does he have to be completely familiar with accounting or the handling of an estate. The more complicated the estate, however, the more important it is to select an executor who has experience in the handling of an estate. The best choice is, often, the trust department of a bank.

Witnesses to the Will

As noted, witnesses should invariably be provided. If other conditions are met, a witnessed will is valid in all 50 states. Also, the presence of the witnesses becomes important if the "testamentary capacity" of the testator is questioned later—if anyone asks whether the testator had sufficient mental competence or other legal ability to make a will at the time it was made.

The attorney who draws up the will can appropriately act as a witness. He stands in an excellent position to know the testamentary capacity of the testator and the intent of the testator at the time he signs the will.

Importantly, three disinterested persons—three people who are not named as beneficiaries under the will—should serve as witnesses. In certain states, if a witness acts as a beneficiary under a will, he may lose his bequest to the extent that it exceeds the amount he would have received without a will. If, therefore, a will is signed and witnessed in a state which allows beneficiaries to be witnesses, but is later probated in a state which does not, problems can arise. It is much better to have disinterested persons, in all cases, as witnesses to the will.

Formalities for Signing a Will

Protocols and formalities

The following is a list of protocols and formalities that should be observed in preparing and signing a will:

1. The will should first be written out.
2. The testator should sign it. If the testator cannot sign his name, he should place his "X" in the appropriate place. A witness should sign the testator's name and the words "his mark" over and below the "X". If the testator is physically incapable of even putting an "X" on the will, one of the witnesses should sign for him in his

presence and at his request. The fact that a witness has signed should be noted in the clause immediately preceding the signature, sometimes called the "attestation" clause. This clause would state that the testator is unable to sign his name and that the witness signed for him.

3.   The signature of the testator or the person signing for him must follow the text of the will immediately, with nothing in between.

4.   The testator should expressly declare in the presence of the witnesses that he is signing his will. He should ask the witnesses to witness his signature.

5.   At least three witnesses should sign their names and addresses in the presence of the testator and of each other, stating that they saw the testator sign the will and that they are signing as witnesses at his request.

6.   The will should be dated by day, month, and year so that no question can arise as to when the will was signed.

Signing and "conforming" the will

7.   Only the original copy of the will should be signed by the testator and witnesses. If more than one copy is signed, the testator might later change his will but not destroy both copies of the earlier will. Also, all copies of the will should be "conformed" copies: the names of the testator and witnesses and their addresses should be typed or printed onto the copies so that the testator cannot at some future time sign a second copy.

8.   The original copy of the will should be kept in a safe place, such as a home safe or strongbox. Many testators keep the executed or original copy of the will in the office of their family lawyer so that it can be referred to at any time. It may also be appropriate to give the original copy of the will to the named executor for safekeeping.

Because bank and other institutional safety deposit boxes are usually locked when a testator dies, a will should never be kept in such a box. The will could effectively be out of reach. A representative of a state tax commission might have to be called to stand by while the box is opened by bank officers. The representative would make sure that nothing is removed but the will.

Now that we have discussed the formalities of a will and some of the factors that make the preparation of a will important to you, the planning of your total estate, as it relates to your will, will be discussed.

ESTATE PLANNING AND ESTATE TAXES

A twofold goal of estate planning

The concept of total estate planning has developed in relatively recent times. It attempts to bring together all the factors relating to a man's or woman's financial status, his or her desires regarding family members, and their security. Estate planning combines these considerations by taking into account all federal and state death, inheritance, estate, and income tax laws. The purpose of estate planning, therefore, is twofold:

- To establish a plan to meet specific objectives insofar as family needs are concerned, including as parts of the plan the will and other necessary legal documents
- To take full advantage of all available tax avoidance or tax savings provisions of the various tax laws

Proper estate planning gives the family an important protective tool.

The family will need income in the future. Liabilities will have to be settled. Income will have to be shifted from one person to another or others. An estate-planning survey may indicate that additional life insurance is needed to meet tax liabilities that may arise when the head of the family dies. Provision may have to be made for additional income over and above that immediately available. That means Social Security and other pension benefits may have to be augmented for the family's protection after the breadwinner's death.

SOME QUESTIONS TO ASK—AND ANSWER—
ABOUT ESTATE PLANNING[1]

You want your assets and property to go to specific persons, or to fulfill specific purposes, after your death. You want to minimize the taxes that will be paid by your estate after you die. You want to leave enough assets that are readily convertible into cash to pay your death ex-

penses and protect your family until
your estate is settled. Why not consider these questions—and have
them answered—NOW, while you
can make plans for the disposition
of your estate.

1. Is there any better way of
holding my property to minimize my income taxes?

2. If I transfer some of my property to my spouse or children
during my lifetime, will I be
subject to gift taxes?

3. Are the beneficiaries properly
designated in my life insurance
policies?

4. Would my spouse be able to

carry on my business in the
event of my death?

5. In case of a partnership, do I
have any arrangements for the
survivor to buy my interests?

6. Does my estate have sufficient
liquid assets to cover the costs
of my death?

7. Have I adequately provided
for the support and education
of my children?

8. Would part of my estate pass
to minor children and be subject to guardianship pro-
ceedings?

9. Do I have my estate arranged
to minimize the death taxes?

[1] Adapted from *Estate Planning* (Des Moines: The Iowa State Bar Association, September 1978).

The complicated process of estate planning is usually approached in the following ways:

1. A complete inventory of all assets, current income, and any anticipated income is drawn up. Each asset should be listed with its cost, value, and projected future value. Insurance should be listed by its cash surrender value and face value. An "educated guess" should be made regarding the value of your business interests. The planner should have all the information necessary to make an independent business survey, including balance sheets and profit and loss statements for the last three years.

2. Cash, assets that can be readily converted to cash, and assets that are to be retained in their present form, such as real estate, should be specified. These should be analyzed to see whether noncash assets can readily be converted into cash or whether additional items should be listed.

3. All debts and liabilities, including anticipated funeral and final medical expenses and the costs of handling the estate, are reviewed and deducted from the assets of the estate.

4. After deducting all liabilities from total estate assets, the es-

tate planner estimates the federal estate tax liability that will be charged to the estate under the value and ownership conditions that presently exist. The estate planner also projects the dollar amount needed for the federal estate tax and the state inheritance or death taxes to calculate how much cash will be needed to pay these taxes after death. The estate planner will also indicate how these taxes may be reduced through the use of the "marital deduction," available in the federal laws.

Deduction of expenses from assets

5. The total expenses of the estate, including all taxes, costs of administration, and debts and liabilities, are deducted from the assets. If additional assets would be needed to meet various obligations, a forced sale of assets, usually at a loss, might be necessary to pay all the bills. Depending on the size of the estate, this comparison of assets and liabilities will usually reveal a need to make immediate cash available to meet postdeath expenses.

6. After making this comparison, the estate planner will discuss the distribution of the estate. He will want to know about beneficiaries and what is to be provided for them. Knowing what will be available, the planner may suggest a reevaluation of either the assets or the method of disposition.

While a great part of estate planning has to do with saving taxes, that should never be the main concern. The main goal is to provide for family members and other survivors.

7. A schedule is prepared to show the assets passing to each beneficiary and how much income is generated from those assets. The assets may be analyzed to ascertain whether they will be adequate to meet the living requirements of the beneficiaries.

8. The estate planner will explain how to reduce federal estate and other death tax liabilities through the use of lifetime gifts, provision of additional insurance or additional investments, and other means of increasing the net asset value of the estate. He may show how rearrangement of some assets may increase the value of assets passing to the beneficiaries and decrease taxes.

A key device in estate planning, lifetime giving offers a way to make gifts of assets to family members before death—to reduce the size of the estate, to provide for college educations, or for other purposes. Starting in 1982, the annual gift tax exclusion was increased from $3,000 to $10,000 per donee, with an unlimited exclusion for tuition and medical expenses. Gift taxes could also be paid on an annual rather than a quarterly basis. A husband could make the same gifts to his wife without incurring gift tax liability.

The spouse's gift exclusion

Under the 1981 tax-cut law, both spouses could make the same gifts to children or other family members, doubling the basic figures. The annual exclusion of gifts for any one person could then total $20,000.

The federal gift tax rates and the federal estate tax rates remain identical under the provisions of the 1981 law. But the top estate and gift tax rate was reduced from 70 percent to 65 percent as of 1982, to 60 percent in 1983, to 55 percent in 1984, and to 50 percent—the projected maximum—in 1985. Starting in 1985 the top rate would apply to gifts and estates of more than $2.5 million. Three cases illustrate the use of estate planning devices. In each case, the husband is assumed to be the person whose estate is being planned. He wants to provide for his wife and three children, all under the age of 18.

Estate Plan No. 1: $60,000 in Joint Assets

The federal estate tax exemption

In this plan, the husband and wife have joint assets of $60,000. Because of the limited size of the estate, there is no federal estate tax liability at all. Under the 1981 Economic Recovery Tax Act, the total amounts of estate and gift transfers that would be exempt from estate and gift taxes would be $225,000 in 1982 (from the 1981 level of $175,625); $275,000 in 1983; $325,000 in 1984; $400,000 in 1985; $500,000 in 1986, and $600,000 in 1987.

The plan for this individual includes a will providing that everything passes to his wife if she survives him for a specified period, usually 30 or 60 days. Should she fail to survive him for that period, everything passes in equal shares to his children. The reason for the 30- or 60-day survivorship requirement is to avoid a double tax if state law provides that the wife would take ownership under the husband's will if she survives him by even one moment. In this case, without a survivorship clause, state death taxes might have to be paid on both deaths. The survivorship clause eliminates that possibility by requiring the spouse to survive for the specified period of time; if he or she does not, the assets skip the estate of the spouse and go directly to the children. Only one death tax is imposed.

In Estate Plan No. 1, a witnessed will would be used to leave everything to the wife and, if she fails to survive, to the children equally. A guardian of the person must be named for the children. A guardian of the property should be named in case both parents die.

Estate Plan No. 2: Assets of $250,000

The "marital deduction" provisions

In this estate, the assets are considerably larger than those described in Plan No. 1. But basically the same strictures apply. Because of the changed "marital deduction" provisions of the federal estate tax laws, the estate would not be subject to any federal estate tax at all. The 1981 tax act simply repealed all limits on tax-free estate or gift transfers between spouses.

The plan for the individual here includes a will that leaves everything to the wife and, when she dies, to the children equally, with the same guardianship provisions mentioned in Plan No. 1. A trust may also be used for the benefit of the wife and children, or just for the children if both parents die.

In this testamentary trust, legal title to the estate assets passes to a trustee named in the will for the benefit of the spouse or children of the deceased. Unlike a guardianship, which ends when a child reaches the age of 18 or 21, depending on state law, a trust can continue beyond the age of 18 or 21 and even over the lifetime of the beneficiary if desired. The trustee generally has power to invest, sell, and handle the assets in the trust fund. He distributes the income to the beneficiaries at fixed intervals or at the trustee's discretion.

Distribution of principal

The trust provisions may also allow the trustee to distribute the principal of the fund to the beneficiaries at intervals or on termination of the trust. The trust has flexibility in other ways. For example, spendthrift protection can be built into the terms to keep the trust assets out of creditors' hands.

Under Plan No. 2, the testator may direct that the property pass to the wife. If she should fail to survive him, the assets go to a trustee for the benefit of the children. The property may be placed in trust for the wife's lifetime. On her death, the assets pass to the children.

The tax consequences of Plans 1 and 2 are basically the same. If the will in Plan 2 leaves everything outright to the wife and then in trust to the children, the property, beginning in 1983, would not be taxable at her death. If she has only a pure life estate in trust with no power to obtain any of the principal, but receives only what the trustee at his discretion may give her, and if, at her death, the trust assets are held for the benefit of the children, there would be no estate taxes to be paid at her death.

THOSE IMPORTANT PAPERS . . .
WHERE TO KEEP WHAT

Where do you keep important papers? The following checklist gives a basic breakdown of types of papers, including wills, and where they should normally be kept. Circumstances can, of course, dictate variations.

SAFE DEPOSIT BOX
1. Birth certificates
2. Citizenship papers
3. Marriage certificates
4. Adoption papers
5. Divorce decrees
6. Death certificates
7. Deeds
8. Automobile titles
9. Household inventory
10. Veteran's papers
11. Bonds and stock certificates
12. Important contracts

ACTIVE FILE
1. Tax receipts
2. Unpaid bills
3. Paid bill receipts

4. Current bank statements
5. Current canceled checks
6. Income tax working papers
7. Employment record
8. Health and life insurance information and policies
9. Credit card information
10. Copies of wills
11. Health records
12. Appliance manuals and warranties
13. Receipts of items under warranty
14. Education information
15. Inventory of safe deposit box (and key)
16. Loan statements
17. Loan payment books
18. Receipts of expensive items not yet paid for

LAWYER'S OR EXECUTOR'S SAFE

Wills

DEAD FILE

All active file papers over 3 years old

WHAT TO DISCARD

1. Salary statements (after checking on W-2 forms)
2. Canceled checks for cash or nondeductible expenses
3. Expired warranties
4. Coupons after expiration date
5. Other records no longer needed

A trust problem

The problem with using a trust for the wife's life is that, to avoid a tax at her death, she may, depending on the type of trust, lose the right to control what she receives from the trustee. This may be too harsh and restrictive. It may prevent the wife from receiving what she needs to maintain her standard of living. Again: tax considerations have never been, and should not be, the sole concern if the family does not have the freedom that the testator desires. The trust instrument should at least give the wife the latitude to obtain part or all of the principal during her lifetime.

Estate Plan No. 3: Assets of $1.5 Million

The federal estate tax resembles the federal income tax in one way: it is not a fixed percentage tax but a graduated tax. Many state death or inheritance taxes, by contrast, are based upon a percentage of the net taxable estate. For example, if a state imposes a death tax of 6 per cent of the net taxable estate, the tax is determined by multiplying .06 times the net estate. No matter how big the net estate is, the tax rate remains the same. Under federal estate tax laws, the larger the estate, the higher the tax—up to 50 percent in 1985.

Defining taxable property

The federal tax also differs from state taxes as regards the definition of taxable property or assets. Some states do not tax such things as the jointly held property of husband and wife that passes to one spouse on the death of the other, life insurance proceeds owned by the deceased, or the share of the surviving person in jointly held property not owned by husband and wife. The federal estate tax, however, includes all this property in determining the taxable estate for federal estate tax purposes. In short, any property over which the deceased had ownership, control, or any indication of ownership is included in the federal estate tax evaluation.

Because the federal estate tax is so all-inclusive, it may include much more property than is subject to probate under the will. Most states provide that jointly held property passes automatically on death to the surviving spouse. Life insurance proceeds are payable directly to the named beneficiary without going through the probate proceedings. It may, therefore, be misleading when newspapers report that Mr. Gotrocks died leaving an estate valued in the probate proceedings at $400,000. The estate was probably much greater than that, since life insurance, joint property, and other assets under Mr. Gotrocks' control would not be reported in the state proceedings.

The "adjusted gross estate"

While the estate tax includes all those assets that are not included in state probate proceedings, it does allow for exemptions and deductions that reduce the tax considerably. Beginning with the "gross value" of your estate, it permits deductions of certain debts and expenses to arrive at the "adjusted gross estate." These include the costs of settling the estate, debts and taxes owed by the decedent at death, and funeral expenses and casualty losses suffered by the estate during administration. Also, in theory, all of the estate can—effective in 1982—be transferred, untaxed, to one's spouse or to his or her control.

Plan No. 3. In Plan No. 3 the total estate of husband and wife totals $1.5 million. The wife has no property of her own purchased solely from her own funds. Assume that $50,000 of debts and expenses are allowable. The adjusted gross estate becomes $1,450,000.

If the husband in his will leaves his entire estate to his wife, he may, according to experts, be walking into a trap. The trap works this way: Assume that the year is 1987. The husband who, in taking care of his wife's future needs, leaves his entire $1,450,000 estate to his wife may in effect be leaving his children $249,000 less than if he did two things:

• Left his wife $950,000 under his will, and
• Took advantage of the full $600,000 exclusion that will be in effect in 1987 to put the rest of the estate into a marital trust.

In do doing, the husband would be avoiding all federal taxes.

If the husband fails to make a will, the estate passes under the laws of intestacy. The wife will not receive the full $1,450,000. Depending on the laws of her state of residence, she may receive only a share of the estate. The estate will have lost the advantage of the marital deduction.

When the Wife Dies. What happens when the wife dies? What effect does her death have on the estate tax? If the wife dies shortly after the husband, her estate will include all the assets she received because of the husband's death less the taxes that were paid.

The husband in planning his estate must take into account the effect on his children if the wife should die retaining substantially the same assets that he leaves her. The sensible estate plan takes into account the effects of both deaths and the possibility of reducing the total federal estate taxes to be paid. All beneficiaries can be provided for at the same time. Two basic approaches involve the *testamentary* and the *inter vivos* or *living trust*.

Testamentary and living trusts

Two Trusts. Trusts can take many specific forms depending on their terms. But all are either testamentary or living trusts. The former, as noted, is established in a will. The living trust is usually set up in a separate document made during the lifetime of the husband.

The testamentary trust goes into effect when the testator dies. The living trust can become effective at once.

Either basic kind of trust can utilize the marital deduction privilege. Whether the marital deduction is established by will or by a separate agreement, the method of distributing the property would have the following format:

* The husband directs in his will or in the inter vivos agreement that his estate or the insurance proceeds be divided into two parts, the part that qualifies for the marital deduction and the balance or residue.

* The husband then directs that the first part (Fund A) be placed in trust on his death for the benefit of his wife. The income from the property in the trust fund would be paid to the wife for life. She would have the absolute right to reach the principal of this part as well. She has the right to direct in her will how and to whom Fund A should be distributed at her death. But on the possibility that she may fail to exercise the right to direct to whom it should go at her death, the husband may direct that the property in Fund A will pass to the second trust, Fund B, on the death of his wife or later.

* The husband directs that the second part of his estate, Fund B, be established as a second trust or separate fund. The income from this second trust is likewise to be paid to the wife for life. But the Fund B property is to be distributed to the children on his wife's death or some other date. The wife has no absolute right to take any part of the principal of that part of the estate.

Fund B not taxable on wife's death

Fund B thus remains outside the wife's estate on her death. She has no absolute right to any part of it. The balance remaining in the first trust, Fund A, is taxable to the wife on her death since she has the right to withdraw all or any part of it during her lifetime and can also specify in her will to whom the balance of that trust fund should pass.

Net Effect. The net effect of this plan is to divide the estate into two different parts. One part, if substantial enough, is taxed at the wife's death, the other part at the husband's death. The portion that is taxable at the death of the wife, Fund A, is the marital deduction portion of the estate. This portion is entitled to the deduction, without tax, from the husband's estate and is taxed at the death of the wife. Fund B, in which the wife has no absolute right, is taxable at the husband's death and passes tax free to the children after the death of the wife.

The more varied the types of property owned, the more involved will be the estate plan chosen. Competent counsel can play an important role in the planning of an estate. So, in many cases, can an insurance advisor, accountant, broker, and bank trust officer.

Federal Income Tax

The estate planning process should include consideration of federal income taxes as they affect the administration of the estate. Because of the complexities of the income tax laws, tax advice is usually needed to handle the tax problems that the family will face after a testator dies. If the estate is sizeable, the executor will probably be required to file income tax returns on the estate, and will be faced with many of the same problems that the testator faces in the filing of his own income tax returns. A very brief summary of some of these considerations follows:

Ordinary income
and capital gains:
differences

Ordinary Income and Capital Gains. Most persons are affected most directly by the two different types or categories of income, ordinary income and capital gains. Ordinary income includes such items as salary, dividends, interest, bonuses, commissions, and so on. Ordinary income is taxed on a progressive scale. Capital gains, on the other hand, receive preferential treatment.

With certain exceptions, everything one owns is a capital asset. Stock in trade for sale to customers, accounts receivable, and many other categories are included. If a capital asset is held for six months or less, its sale or exchange may result in a capital gain or loss.

Generally, any short-term (six months or less) capital gain is treated as ordinary income. Any short-term loss must first be used to offset short-term gains and then to offset long-term (more than six months) gains.

Executors' and Administrators' Tax Duties. Executors and administrators may have a number of tax-related duties. One of them is to pay any income taxes that are unpaid when the estate owner dies. Estate tax returns must be filed with both federal and state tax authorities. Heirs may have to be informed of the basis for computing capital gains on inherited property.

Procedure for computing value

The Tax Reform Act of 1976 changed the regulations governing computation of the tax basis for all inherited assets. Before the Act, the value of any asset was its value on the date of the owner's death. Afterward, the tax basis for the heirs on all assets acquired by the deceased before December 31, 1976, became the value as computed on that date. Marketable stocks and bonds were excepted because their market value fluctuated and could be determined at any time. Computation of the value of all other assets followed an established procedure:

- It was assumed that the *rate of appreciation* remained constant from the date on which the deceased acquired the asset and the date of his death.
- The proportion of gain in value or growth would be a determinable fraction of the overall growth.
- This fraction would be: the number of years and days between the purchase and December 31, 1976, divided by the number of years and days between the purchase and deceased's death.

Other regulations further complicated the problem facing executors and administrators trying to establish asset values for tax purposes. By 1980 the U.S. Congress was considering means of simplifying these laws, which placed heavy burdens on many trustees as well as executors and administrators. An executor might have hundreds of valuable items—from boats to paintings to stamp collections —on which, in effect, individual histories might have to be compiled.

In a relatively simple instance, an executor might have to inform an heir of the value of an oil painting purchased in 1966. The cost to the deceased at that time was $60,000. The deceased owned the painting for 10 years on December 31, 1976. The fraction by which the painting has appreciated in value is estimated at $20,000. The value of the painting would then be calculated at $80,000, the original purchase price plus $20,000. The trustee, executor, or administrator would use that overall figure in computing capital gains of the estate.

The Economic Recovery Tax Act of 1981 introduced basic changes in the personal and business income tax rates. The trustee or executor would also have to take those new rates into consideration. The personal income tax reductions were to total 5 percent starting October 1, 1981, 10 percent additional on July 1, 1982, and a final 10 percent on July 1, 1983.

An estate is a taxpayer

Other Taxable Income. Executors, trustees, and administrators have to pay estate income taxes because an estate is considered a taxpayer. Thus taxes have to be paid on income from interest-yielding bonds, savings accounts, and other investments. Municipal bonds and similar securities that are tax free are usually excluded but may be taxable under state or local income tax laws.

The sale of a corporate bond may require payment of income taxes. The amount of appreciation will be taxed, for example, if the bond was held more than six months. The Internal Revenue Code contains a formula for determining the taxable gain or loss from the sale of a corporate bond where the issue price of the bond is different from its redemption value. Competent tax advice may be required where this situation obtains.

Income from securities issued by the U.S. government, such as Series E and Series II bonds, is taxable. But these securities have advantages because the owner can choose to take the interest income in a year in which he has a reduced income or losses that put him in a lower tax bracket. No one needs to pay taxes on the accrued interest on these bonds until they are redeemed or the interest actually received. One can also exchange Series E bonds for Series H bonds which pay cash interest on a regular basis.

What isn't taxable
income?

Certain types of income are not includable in the definition of "income" under the tax laws. Social Security and veterans' benefits are not taxable. A relief provision applies to stock dividends, excluding the first $100 of corporate dividend income. If a joint return of husband and wife is filed and the stock is owned in both names, a stock dividend exclusion of up to $200 can be claimed.

Many of these provisions apply whether assets are held by the estate of a deceased person or by a living person. Extensive regulations involve the federal income tax laws as applied to estates and the filing of the "fiduciary" income tax returns by the executor.

THE ADMINISTRATION OF AN ESTATE

What happens when someone dies? What are the duties of the executor? How long does it take to settle the estate of a deceased person? What steps are taken to settle the estate?

Many persons recall that when "Uncle Joe" died, it only took the attorney six months to close the estate. When "Aunt Emma" died, it took over two years.

Obviously, the time involved in settling an estate depends on many factors:

* The size of the estate
* The identification of the beneficiaries if they are hard to find and if tracers are needed
* The presence of trust provisions that would require the services of a trustee
* The sale of assets to preserve the value of the estate (the timing of the sale is very important)
* Claims against the estate
* The filing of tax returns and payment of taxes. No two estates are alike, and the time spent in settling one estate has nothing to do with the time spent in settling another.

Some duties of executor and lawyer

Some of the duties of the executor and family lawyer, who works closely with the executor, are as follows:

- To notify all the savings institutions where the decedent may have had accounts and obtain the necessary account numbers and balances as of the date of death

- To arrange for the custody of the decedent's personal property
- To maintain and see that all the decedent's property is covered by insurance, and change the "insured" in the policies to the "estate" of the deceased person
- To estimate the size of the estate to determine whether the estate has to go through formal probate and administration proceedings or whether the estate can be settled under the "small estate" (usually under $5,000) provisions that apply in many states to short-cut the more involved, full administration
- To obtain additional copies of the will for distribution to the beneficiaries and arrange a meeting with all of the beneficiaries as soon as practical and proper after the funeral of the testator
- To advise the beneficiaries of their interest and assure them of his intent to keep them advised
- To inventory the contents of any safe deposit boxes held by the

decedent, usually in the presence of state taxing authorities who may be required by law to be present

- To find out whether any beneficiary wants to take any asset "in kind," that is, in its present form, rather than have it sold and the proceeds distributed
- To have the beneficiary sign an "election to take the property in kind" as soon as possible, providing a choice in the event that the property—corporate stocks, for example—drops in value before it is sold

An executor needs information

The executor has also to find out whether any beneficiaries want to renounce any gifts or object to any provisions of the will. He must, with the help of the family lawyer, prepare the petition to probate the will and file it in court, and make copies available to all parties. Copies of the death certificate have to be obtained; beneficiaries may need help in the collection of life insurance proceeds, including provision of any necessary forms from the insurance companies. The executor will need information on salaries, wages, or commissions owed to the deceased, and will inquire about the pension or profit-sharing plans of the company employing the deceased and the amounts due the estate, if any. Other duties:

- To decide on continuing the operations of any businesses of the deceased and to arrange for collection of loans, rents, dividends, or other obligations owed to the decedent
- To follow local requirements concerning advertising the estate and asking all debtors to pay claims and all creditors to present their claims
- To collect and keep all information needed for tax returns, file for Social Security and veterans' benefits, and assemble all data on joint property, life insurance, trusts, and other assets for tax purposes
- To file any "fiduciary" bonds that may be required of him under local laws
- To obtain certified copies of his appointment for presentation to those requiring evidence of his authority to act for the estate

"DEAR ANN LANDERS" LETTER TELLS THE NO-WILL STORY[1]

A letter to columnist Ann Landers tells the poignant story of "Thorns among the widow's weeds," a wife whose husband died leaving no will. The letter, and Ann's answer:

Dear Ann Landers:

Why would a bright, loving man who showed every consideration for his wife and children during his lifetime die without leaving them protected by a will?

It's too late for your answer to help us, but please, Ann, print this letter because both my attorney and funeral director have told me that an unbelievable number of men, responsible and competent in fiscal matters, behave as if they are going to live forever. They make no preparation whatever for the eventuality of death.

I am now faced with a financial mess beyond belief. Attorney fees and inheritance taxes are hor-

rendous. I am also having heartbreaking problems with my husband's brother over some property —the ownership of which is unclear.

I know my husband loved me and the children with all his heart. Why didn't he take care of us properly?

Thorns among the widow's weeds

Dear Thorns:

Why? Because, like so many others, he hated to think about death—as if by ignoring it, it would ignore him.

I hope every man who reads this column will ask himself, "If I died tonight would my family be protected financially?" If the answer is yes, you deserve to sleep like a baby. If not, get busy and put your affairs in order. You owe it to those you love.

Ann Landers

[1] From *Your Will* (Lansing: State Bar of Michigan). Letters from Ann Landers' column in the *Detroit Free Press* reprinted by permission of Ann Landers and Field Newspaper Syndicate.

An important duty of the executor is to keep the beneficiaries advised of progress in settling the estate. More misunderstandings result from lack of communication in this area than from any other cause.

After his appointment, the executor must prepare an accurate inventory of all estate assets and then make certain that the property passes to the beneficiaries named in the will. He should secure receipts from each beneficiary showing that they have in fact received the property or the cash directed to them. Eventually, the executor has to account properly to a court, to the creditors, and to the beneficiaries of the estate for all payments, receipts, disbursements, and distributions made by him in settling the estate, including payment of taxes.

Working with your family lawyer

The executor should work closely with the family lawyer in handling an estate. The law of the particular state may require that the executor perform many functions; he should know what these obligations are. In practice, the lawyer prepares most of the papers for the executor and guides him in this process.

Where a testamentary trustee is named in a will, his duties begin where the executor's duties end. Most of the trustee's duties are specified in the will. State law gives the trustee certain powers and duties as well. But basically, a properly drawn will notes these powers and duties specifically.

Once the estate is closed and a final distribution of assets is made to the beneficiaries, the executor transfers the assets to be held in trust to the trustee and takes back a receipt. The trustee then takes over the administration of the trust property. In the ordinary case he is required to invest for income, pay taxes and expenses of the trust fund, exercise all obligations as set forth in the will or trust agreement, and exercise his discretion for the benefit of the trust assets and the beneficiaries.

The trustee also has to render accounts to the beneficiaries periodically. At the conclusion of the trust, he distributes the trust property to the beneficiaries. He must keep the trust property separate from his own, and pays any income from the trust assets to the beneficiaries as required by the will, trust agreement, or the law. A corporate trustee, such as the trust department of a bank, has the same rights and obligations as an individual trustee.

Compensation with court approval

Both the executor and trustee are entitled to compensation or commissions for handling estates and trust assets. The amount of compensation depends on the time spent and the work performed, and is subject to the approval of the court that has jurisdiction over the administration of estates and trusts.

Estate Tax Returns

As indicated, both the estate and the trust have to pay taxes. In some cases, the executor and trustee can be personally liable for taxes unpaid or improperly paid.

The returns that have to be filed may include:

Federal Estate Tax Return. The federal tax return must be filed within nine months from the date of death of a decedent who is a U.S. citizen and who leaves an estate in any given year whose gross worth exceeds the figures noted earlier. As indicated, the total amount of estate and gift transfers that would be exempt from estate and gift taxes in 1987 would be $600,000. Starting in 1985, the maximum estate and gift tax rate would be 50 percent, not the 70 percent of 1981.

Three types of gifts

Since federal estate taxes are levied on the *gross estate,* the executor or administrator has to account for all the assets and property owned by a decedent at the time of death—less, of course, debts and other obligations. The gross estate includes three main types of gifts:

* All gifts made outright after January 1, 1977
* Gifts over whose income the decedent has retained control for life, or those for which the decedent reserved the right to name the ultimate donee

- Gifts that remained revocable or amendable by the donor during his lifetime

Not included in the gross estate after 1981 are tax-free gifts of up to $10,000 a year per donee—or $20,000 if given jointly by husband and wife. Such gifts may have been made to anyone. They remain outside the gross estate under the 1981 Act.

Federal Income Tax Return. If the estate or trust during the period of administration has income in excess of $600, a federal income tax return must be filed. A taxable year for the estate or trust must be chosen and income reported accordingly. The year need not be a calendar year. The return must be filed by the fifteenth day of the fourth month following the end of the tax year. The choice of the proper fiscal year is very important and may have serious tax consequences. The federal law contains regulations concerning the proper taxable year.

Reporting to the beneficiaries

Since the income tax return may show amounts that are distributable to beneficiaries, the executor or trustee should report these amounts to the beneficiaries for inclusion in their own personal in-

come tax returns. The executor or administrator has also to report to the Internal Revenue Service all income distributed to the beneficiaries during the taxable year.

Final Federal Income Tax Return. The executor must also file the final federal income tax return of the decedent along with any returns that the decedent had not filed in prior years. It may be difficult to reconstruct the affairs of the decedent for the year of death or for prior years, but the duty nonetheless falls on the executor. If the decedent was married at the time of his death, a joint return may be filed as his final return unless the surviving spouse remarries before the close of the tax year or if some other exception applies.

The executor or trustee has the task of making sure that all taxes are paid before he makes any distribution of the assets of the estate or trust to the beneficiaries. If he fails to do so, he can be held personally liable for those taxes, plus penalty and interest. The only exceptions would be payments of allowances to the widow or widower, the funeral expenses, and some others that the law allows the executor to pay out before payment of federal taxes due.

An executor normally takes a "clearance" from the Internal Revenue Service before making final distribution to the beneficiaries. He also requests a prompt audit of the returns filed on behalf of the estate and previous years' returns filed by the decedent to ensure that no later audit will result in a claim for additional taxes after the estate is closed.

Tax Planning by Executor and Beneficiaries

*Tax avoidance,
not evasion*

Certain steps can be taken by the executor and beneficiaries to reduce the tax impact on the estate and the beneficiaries. For example, as indicated, the correct choice of a taxable year for the estate may have a significant impact on the total tax liability. In addition, decisions regarding the timing of distributions of income from the estate to the beneficiaries may be vital. Income payable to beneficiaries and distributable to them is taxable to them personally. The individual tax status of the beneficiaries must therefore be considered by them and by the executor in deciding when to make distributions.

A TEN-POINT CHECKLIST OF THE DUTIES NORMALLY PERFORMED BY AN EXECUTOR[1]

- Notify heirs and creditors of the probate proceedings.

- Take possession of, inventory, and preserve the probate assets of the decedent.

- Collect all income, such as rents, interest, and dividends, and make demand for and collect all debts, claims, and notes due the decedent.

- Determine the names, ages, residences, and degrees of relationship of all heirs at law and next of kin of the decedent.

- Complete any pending lawsuits in which the decedent has an interest and represent the estate of the decedent in any will contests.

- Determine, prepare returns for, and pay all state and federal inheritance, estate, and income taxes.

- Pay the valid claims of creditors of the decedent and, when necessary, sell property to raise funds to pay such claims as well as taxes and expenses of administration.

- Transfer decedent's title to real property to his or her beneficiaries through a decree of distribution (no deed or other formal document of transfer is required).

- Transfer decedent's title to certain personal property, such as stocks and bonds, to his or her beneficiaries.

- Distribute the remaining assets to the proper persons.

[1] Adapted from *Why Probate?* (Portland: Oregon State Bar).

The basic assets of the estate are not "income." No income tax is payable on those assets by the beneficiaries or by the estate. Only the income earned from these assets is taxable under the income tax laws.

The federal estate tax law contains provisions for an alternate valuation date. Under this provision the executor can select a date different from the date of death (six months later) for determination of the value of assets in the estate. The choice of a different valuation date is the most important means of saving on estate taxes, especially if the assets are mainly stocks, bonds, or other assets whose value is subject to shifts in value.

If the assets are worth less on the alternate valuation date than they were on the date of death, the executor will choose that date for determination of value. He thus reduces the tax liability. If the assets gain in value, he will use the date-of-death value.

Another method of tax planning to save on estate and income taxes has to do with the handling of deductions. The executor has a choice of deciding whether certain deductions should be taken against the gross estate value to reduce the federal estate tax or of taking the deductions against the estate's federal income tax liability. A correct choice may save considerable money for the estate or the beneficiaries.

Some allowable deductions

The deductions that may be allowed from the gross estate include the following:

- Burial expenses
- Claims against the estate, including legitimate debts
- Unpaid mortgage balances on properties owned by the decedent
- The expenses of administration of the estate, which may include commissions
- Losses resulting from casualty or theft
- Charitable bequests within the limits imposed by federal and state laws

Special rules also deal with any income earned by the decedent prior to his death, referred to as "income in respect to a decedent." Such income should be included in the estate tax return and deducted by the beneficiaries on their income tax returns.

Obviously, a testator has to use care in selecting an executor. The executor may have to work closely with the family lawyer to ensure that the beneficiaries receive the highest amount possible from an estate. Tax evasion is a crime; but tax avoidance is perfectly legal and proper.

Dozens of articles, books, and pamphlets tell the world how easy it is to write one's own will, how estate plans can be handled without help, and so on. However, the people who try to act as their own lawyers, accountants, and insurance advisors only create additional needs for professional help once they get in trouble. The legal profession has a cliché that expresses the truth neatly: "The lawyer who handles his own case has a fool for a client."

11 "THE ONLY THINGS CERTAIN ARE DEATH AND TAXES"

From the point of view of the law, death is related in at least one way to coming of age, marriage, divorce, and retirement: it represents a change in status for the individual. Where Chapter 10 discussed ways of using "preventive law" to prepare for death, this chapter discusses other ways.

Death often involves severe stress for family members. Making burial arrangements ahead of time can eliminate one source of stress. Also, decisions made calmly frequently emerge as wiser decisions that bring fewer legal complications.

Death has many legal aspects. Advances in medical science have resulted in the prolongation of life. The problem is that in many cases it has become difficult to determine when death has occurred. Once death has occurred, the legal questions become paramount.

WHAT IS DEATH?

Death has been defined variously. Most commonly, it has been held to be the moment and state when:
- there is loss of spontaneous respiration and of respiratory effort;
- that loss becomes irreversible; and
- the loss occurs during a coma judged to be irreversible.

There are important reasons for developing comprehensive and workable policies to help in determining the moment of death. Four such reasons are:
- Prolonging "life" through medical devices beyond the point of real or actual death can result in needlessly high medical bills for the patient's family.
- Terminating medical attention before the "point of no return" may result in needless and grievous loss of a loved one.

- In cases where the dying patient had made a commitment to donate an organ for transplantation, his survival is more important than the welfare of a potential organ recipient.
- On the other hand, where the donor is truly dead, the donee's welfare is vital.

A Legal Definition

Death: a definition

For centuries human societies have accepted the common-sense definition of death as the cessation of breathing, heartbeat, and brain functioning. For most purposes, this definition was all that was necessary. With advances in medical science, especially in the use of organ transplants, people began to take a closer look at the moment of death. Some people who were incurably ill insisted that they had the right to take their own lives.

These trends have exerted pressure on state legislatures in the United States to draft new death statutes. Kansas, for example, adopted a new definition of death in 1971, and Maryland followed suit in 1972. The Kansas statute states that a person is medically and legally dead when, in the opinion of a physician and based on ordinary standards of medical practice, either of the following conditions is met:

- There is an absence of spontaneous respiration and heartbeat because of disease or, because of the passage of time since they stopped, attempts to resuscitate are considered hopeless.
- There is an absence of spontaneous brain function, and despite attempts to maintain circulation and breathing, it appears that further attempts will not restore the brain.

Under the Kansas law, death is to be pronounced before artificial breathing and circulation functions are terminated. Such pronouncement must be made before any vital organ can be removed for transplanting.

The Maryland law differs little in basic respects from the Kansas law. Both laws have been criticized for making it too easy for a surgeon to take an organ for transplant from a person who is still alive.

Medical Definitions

Ambiguity in the
legal definition
of death

The legal definition of death suffers clearly from some ambiguity. This comes into sharper focus when medical viewpoints are considered. One has to speak here of "viewpoints" because no single medical definition of death applies universally.

One medical definition holds that *total human death* is characterized by the death of every cell in the body. In this irreversible state, there is in each cell a total absence of chemical, physical, or electrical activity. But, admittedly, not all cells need to be dead before a person may be said to be essentially dead: the nails and hair may continue to grow after death.

Another definition seeks to describe *essential death*. Here, both the heart and the breathing system have stopped functioning. But, again, qualifications may be noted. In a state of essential death, people can still be resuscitated, especially where the organism has suffered no brain damage. The brain may appear to show no life; but this can occur when the body temperature drops or when some nervous system poison enters the body.

In the absence of low body temperature or poisoning, it is possible to consider *irreversible death,* which occurs at some point between essential death and total death. Here, the progress toward death is irreversible; so are final coma and loss of breathing.

"Coming back
from the dead"

Even irreversible death raises some ambiguities: the basis of an illness, along with its diagnosis and prognosis, may come into doubt. People pronounced dead have spontaneously "come back from the dead." Where breathing has stopped, death is usually considered irreversible only under these conditions:

• A comatose patient cannot make an effort to breathe without mechanical assistance. In one test, a breathing apparatus may be removed for a specified period, perhaps two minutes.

GUIDELINES FOR PRONOUNCING DEATH[1]

In 1968, the major medical associations of the world convening at the twenty-second World Medical Assembly in Sydney, Australia, established the following guidelines for pronouncing a person dead:

- Total lack of response to external stimuli, even the most painful permissible

- Absence of all spontaneous muscular movements, notably breathing; a respirator can be turned off for three minutes to determine whether spontaneous breathing takes place

- Absence of reflexes; dilated pupils should not contract when a bright light is shown directly into them; the eyes must not move when ice water is poured into the ears; biceps, triceps, or quadriceps do not contract

- Flat electroencephalogram (EEG) or absence of brain waves

Other guidelines have been developed by committees at the Harvard Medical School and the Duquesne University Law School. These guidelines resemble those described above; but they also differ in some respects. This underlines the fact that no agreement exists on the exact moment when death takes place.

[1] Adapted from *The Right to Die* by Milton D. Heifetz, M.D. with Charles Mangel, copyright © 1975 by Milton D. Heifetz, M.D., and Charles Mangel. Reprinted by permission of the Putnam Publishing Group.

- There is no question of simple nerve damage or loss of control of the muscles used in breathing, as in polio.
- The possibility does not arise that the portion of the brain controlling breathing has irrevocably ceased to function.

Protecting the rights of the dying

The concept of irreversible death comes closest to serving both the medical and the legal requirements. It is important to know where each state stands, whether the irreversibility concept is used, and how that concept is spelled out. Thus the rights of the dying patient are protected; alternatives become clearer for him and for his family.

CERTIFICATION OF THE CAUSE OF DEATH

Every state requires that a certificate of death be issued. Depending on the state, either the physician or a coroner may sign and issue the certificate. This document must then be filed either with the county registrar or with another public official, as designated, in the place where the death occurred. The certificate indicates the time, place, and cause of death.

Where the cause of death is unknown, a temporary certificate may be issued. Burial would not be prevented or delayed if the temporary certificate was issued by a coroner or medical examiner. Issuance by a private physician or hospital would, however, forestall immediate burial.

Generally, several copies of the death certificate are required. Some of the purposes to which copies of the death certificate are put include:

Arranging probate of a will

Securing Social Security benefits

Claiming life insurance proceeds, pensions, or other payments

The death certificate constitutes proof of death. Without it, it is impossible to proceed with any of the above arrangements. The certificate should be checked closely for errors.

A death certificate will always specify the cause of death. Possible entries include death by natural causes, by accident, by homicide, by suicide, and "by cause unknown."

Uncertainty as to Cause of Death

When the cause of death is unknown, it is usually necessary to make an effort to determine the cause. Depending on the state or locale, the coroner or medical examiner has this responsibility. Either an informal or a formal inquest may be held.

Powers and Duties of Coroner or Medical Examiner

*The coroner is an
elected official
—usually*

Coroners and medical examiners differ from one another as regards their required credentials and how they attain office. A *coroner* is an elected official in most places in the United States; he is appointed in others. The office of coroner originated almost 900 years ago in England, and originally meant "King's officer." As such, he not only investigated unexplained deaths but also disposed of property following a suicide or homicide.

A CHECKLIST ON WHAT TO DO AFTER A DEATH OCCURS[1]

—Obtain a death certificate from the attending physician or from the coroner or medical examiner.

—Determine whether the deceased wanted to donate his body or any organs for medical purposes; ask the lawyer to see if the will contains reference to such wishes.

—Engage a mortician to handle the body, or notify the burial society if deceased was a member of one.

—Notify the insurance company or agent if there is burial insurance; make a list of the burial allowances available from various government agencies or private associations and make applications for them.

—Obtain a burial plot, unless deceased already had one.

—Arrange for the funeral and interment.

—Inform friends and relatives of the date, time, and place of the funeral and interment.

—Locate the deceased's will and turn it over to the executor to start probate proceedings; it should be in a home strongbox or the family lawyer's vault, and the executor may already have a copy of it.

—Review documents left by the deceased with the executor and his lawyer; give them the ones they will need to set in motion the settlement of the estate.

The common
law heritage

As part of the heritage of Anglo-Saxon common law, the coroner's office eventually found its way to America. The office has been part of the formal law, and even of constitutional law, in many areas. No specific qualifications for the office existed for many years. A coroner may or may not have the professional expertise to carry out his job—either legal or medical.

For such reasons the office of *medical examiner* is becoming more important. The medical examiner is appointed by the chief executive of a city, county, or state jurisdiction. He may also be appointed by a commission. In order to qualify for the job, he must meet these qualifications:

- Pass a competitive examination, along with other applicants
- Have a medical degree and five years' residence in the fields of general pathology and forensic pathology, the fifth year to have been spent at one of 15 medical-legal training centers in the country
- Obtain formal recognition as a diplomate from the American Board of Pathology by passing a national examination
- Show achievements in the chosen profession
- Optionally, earn certification by the American Board of Pathology in forensic pathology
- Also optionally, have training in law

The coroner or medical examiner assumes jurisdiction in cases such as the following:

- Where a doctor was not in attendance
- Where a doctor is unable to certify the cause of death with certainty
- In all homicides, accidents, and suicides
- In all deaths of a sudden or suspicious nature
- Where deaths occur in prisons and similar governmental institutions
- In industrial deaths
- In unexpected deaths at hospitals, particularly if medical negligence is possible or suspected

- In poisonings
- In drug overdoses

Some post-mortem
tests and analyses

Once the coroner or medical examiner assumes jurisdiction in a given case, he may decide to perform appropriate scientific studies. He may also see that such tests or studies are made. These include:

Autopsy
Toxicology tests
Microscopic slide examinations
Bacteriological tests
Chemical analyses
Blood and teeth tests
Physical measurement recordings
Fingerprinting
Any other tests deemed necessary

The coroner or medical examiner may also call in experts in these fields, as he sees fit. He then prepares his findings in an official way and makes them available to persons or institutions interested in them for one reason or another. These may include lawyers, hospitals, doctors, courts, law enforcement agencies, prosecuting and defense attorneys in criminal cases, families, and insurance companies.

All deaths from whatever causes are reported to the coroner or medical examiner by police, hospitals, doctors, and even private citizens. The coroner or medical examiner immediately conducts an investigation to determine whether an autopsy or other tests are necessary. It is usually necessary to conduct such tests. If the individual was under a doctor's care, the requirement may be waived.

Causes of Death

Coroner's inquest
plus jury

Inquests are formal legal examinations into the causes of death. They are usually not held in jurisdictions where medical examiners hold office. Where a coroner has local responsibility, he must conduct an inquest even when the possibility of a criminal charge exists.

When a coroner conducts an inquest, he often appoints a six-man jury to render a verdict. Some jurisdictions, especially those in which a medical examiner serves, do not have inquests. A medical examiner may conduct an inquest with or without a jury, depending on the jurisdiction.

The inquest constitutes a semijudicial proceeding. The coroner, the medical examiner, or the latter's lawyer may preside over it. Witnesses are called to testify. They may include law enforcement officers, the pathologist who performed the autopsy, any lay witnesses who can contribute information, and, in criminal cases, the defendant.

Where the coroner or jury determines that the death involved a criminal act, he or they will turn the suspect over to a grand jury for indictment. In some cases or jurisdictions, a preliminary hearing will achieve the same results as an inquest.

The question of
final disposition

Whether a coroner or medical examiner has jurisdiction in a given case, the question of final disposition of the body remains. Even when the cause of death is unknown, a temporary death certificate may be issued, permitting funeral services and burial or other arrangements to be made. Where the identity of the body remains unknown, the local government will make final arrangements. This could include giving the body to a medical school for anatomical studies in cases where the body is not disfigured or decomposed.

FUNERALS AND FUNERAL DIRECTORS

The funeral director handles all aspects of a funeral from embalming to funeral services to interment or burial. He is trained to deal with all these final steps as well as to deal with people in their times of grief.

To be licensed, the funeral director must meet these requirements:
• Have at least a high school diploma
• Have completed one year of college (in four states)
• Have at least one year of study in a professional curriculum in a college of funeral service education or mortuary science

• Have completed a period of internship or apprenticeship, ranging from one to three years—usually one year

All states except Alabama require that funeral directors be licensed before they can practice. Embalmers must be licensed in
every state. Most states provide a single license covering all aspects
of the profession, excluding embalming. Some states include embalming in the single license. About three-fourths of all funeral directors have a license that covers embalming.

Four types of charges and fees

The costs of a funeral can vary considerably. Some charges or fees
contribute to the total of funeral costs. There are four main categories:

1. Those relating specifically to the funeral director: his professional services and those of his staff, the use of his premises and
equipment, and the casket and vault selected by the family

2. Those involving disposition of the body: the cost of a grave if
interred in the earth or the cost of cremation and of an urn if desired

3. The cost of memorialization: a grave monument or marker,
or a niche in a columbarium for the cremation urn

4. Miscellaneous expenses paid by the family directly or through
the funeral director: honoraria, flowers, newspaper death notices, additional limousines, burial clothing, and out-of-town transportation
of the body

The costs of funerals may vary from community to community.
They will also vary according to the ethnic and religious customs of
the family involved. In discussions with the funeral director, it is usually possible to arrive at an agreeable price in advance. Prearranging
or prefinancing a funeral may offer certain advantages:

• Those living alone will be assured that they will have the kind
of funeral they want.

• Survivors will be relieved of some responsibility at the time of
death.

• The survivors will thus be able to make last-minute arrangements under less pressure, possibly saving some expenses.

PROFESSIONAL CODE OF FUNERAL DIRECTORS

The National Funeral Directors Association, the largest group of its kind in the United States, has adopted a code that underscores the following provisions:

• A card or brochure is placed in each casket in the selection room.

• Such card or brochure lists the services offered; services not included should be listed as separate items.

• After a family decides on the kind of service they want, they are given a memorandum or agreement to approve or sign. It should include:

    1.   The price of the service selected and what is included

    2.   The price of each of the supplemental items of service and/or merchandise requested

    3.   The amount involved in purchase of each of the items for which the funeral director will advance funds or credit as an accommodation to the family

    4.   The method of payment agreed upon by the family and the funeral director

*Before
prearranging your
funeral . . .*

In prearranging and prefinancing a funeral, certain factors should be taken into consideration:

• The possible effect on survivors.

• The logic and economics of planning for a situation that may not occur for many years. For example, many persons feel that they have other expenses at the moment that are more important.

• Selection of a funeral director and burial merchandise for some future time must be tentative at best.

• Money paid in advance is governed by law in most states. Where it is not, the funeral agreement should include provision for a trust fund. The person paying should maintain control.

The fund should include money already paid. The agreement should retain the right to terminate the contract without forfeiting any funds paid or interest accrued.

Importantly, the subject of financial resources for funeral and burial, whether prearranged or not, should be kept in mind. Money for these expenses can come from any of a number of sources:

- Some life insurance policies
- Allowances paid by governmental agencies, including Social Security, the Veterans Administration, worker's compensation, welfare, and others
- Union and fraternal organization benefits
- Savings and estate funds
- Specially designated insurance such as funeral insurance and burial insurance

BURIAL AND CREMATION

State laws
on burial

Each state specifies the number of days within which a body must be buried or cremated. If a person's will indicates a wish that his body be disposed of in a particular way, his family is not legally bound to abide by those wishes. The law does honor the person's right to donate his body or any organs thereof for medical purposes.

A body left unclaimed for a specified time must be buried by the state or given to a medical institution. The bodies of people killed *en masse* in natural disasters are buried or cremated by local authorities to minimize the risk of contamination.

If a person wants to donate organs or his entire body to medicine, he should be guided by a number of considerations. For example, a donation agreement, properly signed and witnessed, is legally binding on the person's heirs. In actual practice, relatives may object. When this happens, medical institutions are reluctant to go to court. In any case, delay would likely render the donated organ useless.

A person who is determined to donate an organ should discuss the matter with his family. They may then accept the decision. An organ should be removed before embalming. Organ removal does not in any way interfere with a proper funeral.

Cremation

In cremation, a body is reduced to ashes in a high-temperature oven. An old custom, cremation is far more prevalent in some other countries than in the United States. Following cremation, the ashes may be disposed of in a variety of ways. The urn and the ashes may be placed in a columbarium. The urn may be placed in an earth grave, either in a family grave or in a special plot connected with a crematorium. The ashes may be strewn or scattered by one means or another. Whatever method is used, a final service may be held.

Legal controls on cremation

Special legal circumstances attach to the process of cremation. Where a suspicion of criminal involvement exists, a cremated body cannot be exhumed for examination. Cremation is therefore not permitted until the cause of death has been specifically determined. The waiting period before a cremation can take place varies from state to state. Moreover, some states require the permission of a medical examiner or health authority before cremation becomes permissible.

No state requires that a body be embalmed and placed in a casket before cremation. Yet funeral parlors and crematoria may insist on these processes—to raise the disposal costs. For this reason, cremation in the United States costs about the same as burial. Some localities forbid the scattering of ashes. The remains then have to be placed in a columbarium. The cost of a niche in such a memorial may be as expensive as a grave.

Under common law, the body of the deceased is regarded as being under the control of the next of kin. This usually, but not always, ensures that the body will receive proper treatment.

Burial Grounds

The law requires that a burial or *interment* take place in a plot of land officially designated as a cemetery or graveyard. By special permission, that requirement may be waived. All cemeteries are subject to regulation and supervision by local and state governments as well as federal authorities.

Different kinds
of cemeteries

In terms of ownership, there are different kinds of cemeteries:
- Small churchyard cemeteries
- Mutual cemeteries, owned by the families who were using or going to use them and run by boards of trustees
- Municipal cemeteries, run by local governments for those residing within their jurisdictions
- Privately owned cemeteries established by philanthropic citizens desiring to meet a public need
- Cemeteries owned by religious and fraternal groups, ethnic groups, and craft organizations
- Memorial parks run as businesses, with perpetual care funds and memorials close to the ground, facilitating upkeep

Burial space or plots can be bought either in advance or at the time of death. Advance purchase has the same benefits as prearranging and prefinancing funerals. As with funerals, it is important to negotiate carefully to ensure fair treatment. In choosing a cemetery, the following considerations are important:
- The reputation of the cemetery
- The service it renders to the community
- How well it is maintained
- Whether it is guided by responsible citizens
- The availability of management with which to discuss problems
- How care funds are handled: whether money is set aside on a regular basis for care; whether the support fund is supervised by well-known and trustworthy citizens or banks; and whether accrued interest is used to provide care for grass and shrubbery

Once the purchase agreement is signed, the cemetery is obligated to live up to it. This applies in particular to care. Cemeteries often have rules about such matters as resale of burial space to the cemetery. A potential buyer should inquire if he will be permitted to do so, and at what price relative to the original purchase price.

Regulations on
vaults and liners

Other cemetery regulations apply to the use of vaults and liners. These keep the earth from sinking as a casket deteriorates. Most cemeteries require them, and that adds to the burial costs. Here, the buyer has no choice. He should also remember that a memorial park permits only low markers; if he prefers a monument, he should look elsewhere.

In today's mobile society, the purchaser of a cemetery plot may move away from the locale of the burial plot. There are two main solutions. In one, the individual makes arrangements with a funeral home in his new location, perhaps his place of retirement. The undertaker can make arrangements with an undertaker in the old location. The body can then be sent back and buried.

A second solution requires an organization that will permit one to transfer ownership from the old burial lot to one in the new locale. One such organization, the National Exchange Trust (NET) of Beckley, West Virginia, can arrange acquisition of property comparable to the original purchase. The original must be in a cemetery belonging to NET. The new plot can be in any cemetery over 50 miles from the original cemetery.

Under the Lot Exchange Dollar Credit Plan of the National Association of Cemeteries of Arlington, Virginia, it is possible to transfer dollar-for-dollar credit up to $1,500 between member cemeteries. But the two cemeteries must be at least 75 miles apart. The organizations can supply details.

Part IV
ECONOMIC MATTERS

You've lost your job as a secretary in a large industrial plant.

The itch to get into business on your own has convinced you that now is the time. You're searching for ways to go about it.

That new water heater has konked out completely and you're wondering whether the warranty really means anything.

In America's business society each of those kinds of problems has become common. Nearly every American faces these or similar situations in the course of a lifetime. Hundreds of other economic problems and questions occupy the average citizen; many, or most, involve elementary or complex principles of law.

Key economic areas

Understanding the principles that operate in four basic areas—the rights of the unemployed, starting a business of one's own, consumer affairs, and patents and copyrights—provides a basis for economic survival. Some knowledge of the background of modern legal dispensations takes one a step farther.

In the field of unemployment compensation, to name one example, history indicates that the worker at one time had to deal with laws that protected his employer against lawsuits more than they protected him. The worker could be injured on the job, or on the business premises. He would have great difficulty recovering any kind of compensation. That situation began to change when Germany, in 1883, then England, in 1897, passed compensation laws. In 1911, the U.S. Congress passed a similar law protecting federal employees.

Similar changes have taken place in other economic areas. A new copyright law was passed in 1976 and became effective in 1978. The consumer has become a protected species in hundreds of ways. The person going into business for himself can still find the United States a land of great opportunity. Part IV details some key aspects of the laws in effect today.

12 "THE UNEMPLOYMENT RATE FOR THIS YEAR IS UP"

Most people spend a great part of their lives at work. While work ranks as a source of pleasure to many, it is a necessity for millions.

Work may equate with economic security: receiving a steady income from a job. But it also brings—or should bring—a feeling that one will continue to have a job. In times of depression or recession, that feeling can be threatened.

The person who loses his or her job may still have ways of salvaging the situation, or at least of making the best of it. This chapter deals with some of the key remedies.

WHO ARE THE UNEMPLOYED?

The term "unemployed" applies to many different types of people and many different situations. It makes sense, moreover, to distinguish between the *unemployed* and the *underemployed*. These categories, in turn, differ from that of the *disadvantaged*. Examples of people in these three situations are as follows:

* Underemployed people include workers employed below their skill level; people outside the labor force seeking work; and people engaged in involuntary part-time work.

* Unemployed people include workers laid off temporarily or permanently because of recession or other economic reasons; workers laid off because of low productivity or misconduct on the job; people who are injured or sick because of their job, temporarily or permanently; unskilled and uneducated workers; seasonal workers; and people who have traditionally had difficulty finding adequate employment in America, such as teenagers, older workers, and women workers.

* Disadvantaged workers include many members of minority groups, such as black Americans, Spanish-speaking Americans, and American Indians; ex-convicts; hard-core unemployed; and people who are handicapped, due either to congenital or early illness.

Factors causing unemployment

A variety of factors operate to create these various categories. Prejudice, population changes that create excess labor markets, and apathy may result in unemployment. Poor training or education may combine with poor guidance to make some persons almost unemployable. Unhealthy working conditions and economic cycles may simply force some people out of jobs.

EMPLOYER AND EMPLOYEE

Whether on the job or without a job, the worker under the common law had minimal protection in the past. Over the past several decades, however, organized labor has obtained protection for the worker through collective bargaining. Today, the worker can find various kinds of assistance in the private and public sectors to cope with unemployment or the threat of unemployment. A number of federal and state statutes also provide additional protection.

The Civil Rights Act of 1964, amended in 1972, prohibits employers, labor organizations, and employment agencies from discriminating in employment or membership on the grounds of race, religion, national origin, or sex. Enforcement of this law takes place through the Equal Employment Opportunity Commission (EEOC) or through the appropriate state or local agency.

Age discrimination prohibited

The Age Discrimination in Employment Act of 1967 prohibits discrimination against older workers because of age. Excepted are jobs where age is an important criterion, as where heavy physical work is required.

FACTORS AFFECTING LAYOFFS DURING A RECESSION[1]

Based on statistics from the past few recessions, the chances of being laid off may be affected by any of the following factors:

- *How well a person does his or her job.* During a recession many companies weed out poor performers.
- *What field a person is in.* People working in manufacturing, mining, construction, agriculture, transportation, communications, and utilities will fare worse than those in wholesale and retail trades, personal and business services, finance, insurance, real estate, and government.
- *How much a person earns.* The chances of losing a job decline as one's salary rises. At the $28,000 to $30,000 levels and above, in 1979 the chances be-

came minimal. Thus professional, technical, and administrative people are less vulnerable than others. Exceptions are salesmen on commission and executives receiving performance bonuses.

• *Where a person lives.* Key industries can be affected by recession. So can the communities in which they are located. Locations in which layoffs may become epidemic: Detroit and Flint, Michigan, auto industry; Cumberland County, New Jersey, the glass industry; Miami, construction; New England and San Diego, tourism; Pennsylvania's steel areas. Least vulnerable: the Sunbelt, Rocky Mountain states, and the midwestern farm belt.

• *A person's age.* People under 25 are especially vulnerable even in prosperous times. Seniority protects older employees on the job. Even where an employer hires college graduates, they are not immune to an ensuing recession.

• *A person's sex and race.* In previous recessions, women and blacks suffered disproportionately. Because of affirmative action hiring, and the consequent buildup of seniority, these groups may not today be so adversely affected.

---

1 Adapted from "How Safe Is Your Job in a Slowdown?" by Patrick Flanagan, *Money* magazine, July 1979, by special permission, © 1979, Time Inc. All rights reserved.

The Rehabilitation Act of 1973, which became fully operative in 1978, encourages government agencies and institutions receiving federal funds to hire handicapped workers, provided they can perform. Many states have similar laws.

The Fair Labor Standards Act limits the kind of work children can do. People under 16 cannot, for example, work as public messengers, use power-driven machinery, work on construction jobs, or work in public utilities, transportation, mining, manufacturing, and other industries. Violators cannot sell their products in interstate or foreign commerce.

The Wage and Hour Law, a 1974 amendment of the Fair Labor Standards Act, puts a ceiling on the number of hours worked and a minimum on wages. The law applies to all workers engaged in interstate or foreign commerce. The minimum wage is scheduled to go from $2.90 in 1979 to $3.35 in 1981. Exceptions include executives and administrative employees, outside salesmen, certain types of transportation employees, employees in seasonal industries, and handicapped workers and students, with government permission.

Violations of the Wage and Hour Law are handled by the Wage

STATE LAWS PROTECTING WORKERS[1]

State	Fair Employment Practices Act	Civil or Human Rights Commission[2]	Right-to-Work Law	Workers' Compensation Act[3]
Alabama	No	No	Yes	Yes
Alaska	Yes	Yes	No	Yes
Arizona	Yes	Yes	Yes	Yes
Arkansas	Yes	Yes	Yes	Yes
California	Yes	Yes	No	Yes
Colorado	Yes	Yes	No	Yes
Connecticut	Yes	Yes	No	Yes
Delaware	Yes	Yes	No	Yes
D.C.	Yes	Yes	No	Yes
Florida	No	Yes	Yes	Yes
Georgia	Yes	No	Yes	Yes
Hawaii	Yes	No	No	Yes
Idaho	Yes	Yes	No	Yes
Illinois	Yes	Yes	No	Yes
Indiana	Yes	Yes	No	Yes
Iowa	Yes	Yes	Yes	Yes
Kansas	Yes	Yes	Yes	Yes
Kentucky	Yes	Yes	No	Yes
Louisiana	No	No	Yes	Yes[4]
Maine	Yes	Yes	No	Yes
Maryland	Yes	Yes	No	Yes
Massachusetts	Yes	Yes	No	Yes
Michigan	Yes	Yes	No	Yes
Minnesota	Yes	Yes	No	Yes
Mississippi	No	No	Yes	Yes
Missouri	Yes	Yes	No	Yes
Montana	Yes	Yes	No[5]	Yes
Nebraska	Yes	Yes	Yes	Yes
Nevada	Yes	Yes	Yes	Yes
New Hampshire	Yes	Yes	No	Yes
New Jersey	Yes	Yes	No	Yes
New York	Yes	Yes	No	Yes
North Carolina	Yes	Yes	Yes	Yes
North Dakota	Yes	No	Yes	Yes
Ohio	Yes	Yes	No	Yes
Oklahoma	Yes	Yes	No	Yes
Oregon	Yes	No[6]	Yes	Yes
Pennsylvania	Yes	Yes	No	Yes
Rhode Island	Yes	Yes	No	Yes
South Carolina	Yes[7]	Yes[8]	Yes	Yes
South Dakota	Yes	Yes	Yes	Yes
Tennessee	Yes	Yes	Yes	Yes
Texas	Yes[7]	Yes	Yes	Yes
Utah	Yes	No[9]	Yes	Yes
Vermont	Yes	Yes	No	Yes
Virginia	Yes	No[10]	Yes	Yes
Washington	Yes	Yes	No[11]	Yes
West Virginia	Yes	Yes	No	Yes
Wisconsin	Yes	Yes	No	Yes
Wyoming	Yes	Yes	Yes	Yes[12]

[1] Adapted from *You and the Law*, Copyright © 1977 The Reader's Digest Association, Inc. Copyright © 1977 The Reader's Digest Association (Canada) Ltd. Copyright © 1977 Reader's Digest Association Far East Ltd. Philippine Copyright 1977 Reader's Digest Association Far East Ltd.

[2] This includes Equal Opportunity Commission and Human Relations Council.

[3] Known in some states as industrial insurance.

[4] Not compulsory, but elected by employers and employees.

[5] A law prevents union interference with a sole proprietor or two-person partnership in the retail or amusement business.

[6] Complaints heard by the Commission of the Bureau of Labor.

[7] Only state employees are protected by a limited antidiscrimination law.

[8] The Human Affairs Commission deals only with discrimination against state employees.

[9] The antidiscrimination division of the Industrial Commission handles discrimination complaints.

[10] The Commission of Labor and Industry hears complaints.

[11] An agricultural laborer may not be denied work on the basis of whether he is or is not a union member.

[12] Applies only to workers in extra-hazardous industries.

and Hour Division of the U.S. Department of Labor, which has field offices in most states. A worker may sue for double the wages not paid him, plus court costs and attorney's fees, but must do so within two years from the time of the violation. Serious violations can bring heavy fines or imprisonment by the Department of Labor. An employer may not fire an employee who files a complaint or suit. States that also have wage and hour laws should be consulted for details.

Minimizing hazards on the job: OSHA

The Occupational Safety and Health Act (OSHA) of 1970 sets standards designed to minimize exposure to hazards on the job. All states have similar laws. Areas covered include buildings and furnishings, construction, equipment and machinery, fire hazards, and industrial safety.

The National Labor Relations Act of 1935 was passed to help workers who were organizing unions and to prevent domination of those unions by employers. It also helped to obtain employer recognition of unions as collective bargaining agents. The NLRA is administered by the National Labor Relations Board (NLRB).

Some provisions of Taft-Hartley

The Taft-Hartley Act of 1947 covers the same ground as the National Labor Relations Act, but goes farther, establishing prohibitions against the following:

- Forcing workers to join a union. This is the so-called "closed shop" situation. In a "union shop," however, a nonunion member can be hired, but must join the union within a specified time period or risk losing his job.
- Forcing employers to discriminate against an employee.
- The refusal of a union to enter into collective bargaining with an employer.
- Jurisdictional work stoppages, secondary boycotts, or forcing an employer to assign certain work to certain unions.

- Featherbedding, or forcing an employer to pay for unperformed work.
- Excessive initiation fees or dues in union shop plants.

There are also laws requiring various kinds of insurance, as specified by federal or state statutes. These include workers' compensation insurance for disabilities incurred on the job; nonoccupational disability insurance, required by a few states; Social Security; and unemployment insurance (UI), paid for by employers and administered by state and federal governments. Federal employees and members of the armed services are also covered on discharge. These and other plans are covered in greater detail later in the chapter.

Common law protections

The law of employer and employee, under common law, deals with the contractual obligations of the two parties. Features include:

- The employer's right to fire with good cause, and to refuse to pay wages for the period beyond the time of firing even if there was a contract for a longer period of work
- The employer's obligation to ensure the safety of employees, provide suitable tools, and warn of hazards
- Liability for damages due to a worker's negligence where such negligence occurred outside the line of work
- The employee's rights to an invention only if he used his own time and materials
- The employer's obligation to withhold and deposit income and Social Security taxes
- The employee's right to know what kind of insurance coverage he has, and when that coverage changes

To sum up, these laws give workers various forms of protection. For example, they prevent discrimination in hiring or promotion on the basis of race, sex, age, or physical handicap and establish minimum levels of pay and maximum numbers of work hours, with suitable extra compensation for extra hours. The laws also seek to prevent exposure to occupational hazards, and safeguard the right to join or form a labor union and be represented by it in collective bargaining.

Today an employee cannot legally be fired because he joined a union or brought suit against an employer for violation of a law or for negligence. Workers are also protected against union abuses. Various kinds of insurance are provided, including unemployment and disability.

UNIONS AND STRIKES

Labor unions are worker organizations established to obtain higher wages and improved working conditions and generally to protect worker rights and interests.

Three kinds of union organization

Craft unions are composed of workers in a particular craft, trade, or occupation. *Industrial unions* are generally mass organizations of people who work in particular industries, irrespective of their own special crafts or occupations. Unions within a single plant, or *plant unions,* are founded by and for one group of employees. Unlike the first two types, these unions are not usually affiliated with larger national or international unions.

The National Labor Relations and Taft-Hartley acts govern the relations between management and unions. Under the rules of the National Labor Relations Board (NLRB), each side has certain rights while collective bargaining is in progress. Management, for example, can express its opinions to workers on each side's proposals. But in that expression management can never make threats or engage in intimidation. In particular, workers who disagree with management cannot be threatened with firing or disciplinary action. The union must also avoid intimidation—of both management and the workers.

In most cases, a collective bargaining agreement emerges from union-management negotiations. In the event that no agreement is reached, a strike may be called. In industries engaging in interstate commerce, a union must give 60 days' notice before calling a strike.

Unions were formed to protect workers from unjust firings and other prejudicial actions. A collective bargaining agreement usually includes a section dealing with firing with "just cause" as well as protocols for handling grievances. If a worker complains to his or her union, the union then weighs the merits of the case. If it feels the worker has a legitimate grievance, the union takes the responsibility of defending the worker or taking action against the employer. The law requires that the union handle the case even if the worker is not a union member.

Union shops are legal in most states

Under the Taft-Hartley Act, *closed shops* are illegal. Firms engaged in interstate or foreign commerce cannot be required to hire union members. However, *union shops* are legal, and are permitted in most states. In these states, nonmembership cannot keep a person from being hired. But he must join the union within the time specified by the union-employer agreement, usually 60 to 120 days. If he does not join, the employer has to discharge him.

Both closed and union shops are prohibited in *open shop* states that have "right-to-work" laws. In these states every worker has the *right to work* whether he wants to join a union or not. A worker moving to another state that has no such law is no longer free of union shop rules.

Unions make their own admission rules. However, most unions admit as members all eligible workers who apply. It is to the union's advantage to have as many members as possible. Where a union shop agreement is in force, the union has to accept all who are eligible and apply. Under the Taft-Hartley Act, if the union in this situation does not take all applicants, it cannot enforce the union shop clause. If a union expels a member, an employer must keep him on as an employee.

Many states have fair employment practices laws that prevent discrimination in granting union memberships. The Equal Employment Opportunity Commission (EEOC) handles individuals' grievances, but in the states that have fair employment laws, state authorities also handle them.

Starting with the union's grievance machinery

A person with a grievance against a union should first use the union's grievance machinery. The union should also make available a copy of the collective bargaining agreement with the company. Failure to do so entitles the complainant to file a complaint with the federal Department of Labor. If the union gives no satisfaction, the worker can sue the union or its officials, and he is protected against union retaliation.

NLRB rules applying to workers

Under NLRB rules, if a union goes on strike, the following strictures apply to workers:

1.   Employees taking part in legal strikes remain employees. The NLRB can force an employer to take back an employee and to compensate him for any time he was not allowed to work after the settlement was reached. However, the employer does not have to rehire workers if new employees are legally engaged as replacements during the strike. The discharged workers retain voting rights in the union.

2.   Employees in illegal strikes are not protected by the NLRB. An employer is not obliged to rehire them.

3.   Employees of the federal government are not allowed to strike; most states also prohibit their employees from striking. Under the Taft-Hartley Act, a striking federal employee is subject to immediate discharge.

PROTECTION PLANS

Some of the laws described above indicate conditions under which a person may legally lose his job. These include incompetence, illegal strikes, and failure to join a union in a union shop. In still other situations, neither laws nor collective bargaining agreements can guarantee that a person will retain his job. Notable examples are conditions of recession or seasonal business.

Management and unions have developed a variety of protection plans in collective bargaining agreements. The federal and state governments have also devised plans and programs for the protection of workers in various categories. The remainder of this chapter deals with government programs and one private plan that dovetails with a government plan. The government plans include workers' compensation, nonoccupational disability, unemployment insurance (UI), veterans' rights under the GI Bill, and Social Security disability. The single private plan is known as supplemental unemployment benefits (SUB).

Workers' Compensation

How workers' compensation was born

Workers' compensation evolved as industrial injuries became an increasingly serious problem in the early twentieth century. Under common law, an employer had only to provide safe premises and equipment, competent fellow workers, and proper warnings of hazards. An employer could be held exempt from liability on the ground that the employee accepted the conditions of work when he accepted employment.

WHAT EMPLOYERS AND UNIONS CAN DO TO PROMOTE AN EMPLOYEE'S SECURITY[1]

Measures to promote group security

—Control over job functions, methods of production, technology
  * work rules, including output or pace
  * tight job definitions
  * prohibitions on using some types of machinery

—Restrictions on management in directing production
  * restrictions on subcontracting
  * manning requirements
  * required ratios of learners to journeymen
  * controls on scheduling overtime, or other work scheduling

—Regulation of individual worker hours

- shorten workweek by
  —increasing daily breaks, "make-ready" time, union business time
  —altering shiftwork patterns; short shifts
  —shortening workday directly; reducing number of days in standard workweek

- shorten workyear by
  —increasing vacations or holidays
  —adding to paid weeks of training, jury duty, etc.

Measures to allocate and specify the individual's security
—Seniority control over layoff and recall, job assignment, transfers, bumping, etc.

—Special rights provided by contract to

- training and retraining, in order to remain on the payroll

- interplant transfer

- wage retention after bumping or transfer

Income security, after unemployment has occurred
—Severance pay
—Supplemental unemployment benefits (SUB)
—Individual account benefit plans
—Savings plans

1 Adapted from Audrey Freedman, *Security Bargains Reconsidered: SUB, Severance Pay, Guaranteed Work* (New York: The Conference Board, 1978).

The federal government passed a workers' compensation act for federal employees in 1908. In 1911, New York became the first state to pass such a law. Most states had equivalent laws by 1921, and all states have them today.

Although state laws vary, all workers' compensation laws have characteristics in common, including:

- Employer negligence need not be shown.
- If an employee is injured in a work-related accident, injury or death is compensated according to a fixed schedule of benefits, no matter who may be at fault.
- Benefits are payable weekly for a set number of weeks, computed as a percentage of a person's weekly wages, with a maximum limit.
- Injuries subject to compensation include temporary and permanent disability (either partial or total), fractures, total or partial

loss of use of various body parts, disfigurement, other permanent injuries, and many occupational diseases.

* Death benefits are payable to designated dependents.
* The employee, in addition to cash compensation, is entitled to all necessary medical care.

Filing a claim, notifying the employer

When injury or illness has occurred, the employee seeking compensation should file a claim with the appropriate administrative agency. The employer should be notified immediately. Neglecting to notify the employer or delaying such notification can result in denial of the claim.

A person needing medical attention can obtain it on his own even when the employer does not provide it. The claimant simply includes the medical bills with his request for compensation.

After a person notifies the administrative agency, an arbitrator makes an initial determination of whether the injury can be compensated, and in what amount. This decision is reviewed by an administrative board, followed by approval, disapproval, or modification. The worker who is dissatisfied with the decision can obtain a judicial ruling in the next step.

State restrictions on claims

Some states set restrictions on the payments for injuries incurred in especially hazardous occupations. Some states also set restrictions on claims arising from occupational diseases. These states list only those diseases that are covered. A person may not be covered where the particular type of illness or injury is not covered in a particular state or where the regulatory agency does not rule in a person's favor. Coverage may also be lacking where an employer has fewer than three people on his payroll. If a person is not covered, he can bring a suit against his employer for negligence.

A brief waiting period is usual before a person collects workers' compensation. Benefits are classified as *medical* and *income*. Some states make partial medical payments; some provide for full compensation. All states make provision for rehabilitation training as well as surgery and prosthetic devices designed to restore limb and other functions to the greatest degree possible.

Disabilities are generally classified as *permanent total, temporary total,* and *permanent partial* disabilities. Two-thirds of a person's average earnings usually establishes the limit for income benefits. Death benefits, in the form of a pension for beneficiaries, also have the same limitation. But they may be less than the two-thirds level.

Nonoccupational Disability

Nonoccupational disability insurance is provided in only four states: California, New Jersey, New York, and Rhode Island. About 90 per cent of all illness is non-job related, but can still keep a person from working. A separate nonoccupational insurance plan covers railroad workers. The unemployment insurance (UI) program in each of the four states administers nonoccupational disability insurance.

The core features of the typical program, regardless of the state, include:

* Both employer and employee contribute to the plan.
* The amount of compensation depends on regular weekly earnings within fixed minimum and maximum levels.
* Payments continue up to one year, commencing after a one-week waiting period.
* The right to benefits depends on the type of disability, on how many weeks one has worked, and on whether one has earned the minimum amount stipulated by the state.

Unemployment Insurance (UI)

*UI—a main form
of unemployment
compensation*

UI constitutes the main form of compensation for unemployed workers. UI has historically ranked as the youngest member of the family of protective programs. Various countries have tended to establish programs for work injuries, old age, and sickness before they established forms of UI. When the United States established the Social Security system in 1935, the UI section came closest to being declared unconstitutional. UI still tends to enjoy least favored status among programs. The main objectives of UI are to:

provide cash during involuntary unemployment;

maintain a worker's standard of living;

give him time to locate or regain employment; and

help him find a specific job.

In addition, UI serves to:

counteract the effects of business cycles;

improve the utilization of workers;

encourage employers to stabilize employment; and

maintain a skilled work force.

State and D.C. administration

UI is administered individually by each state and the District of Columbia. It is supported by taxes paid by employers and by federal funding. Eligibility of workers for UI stipulates a need to meet such requirements as qualifying wages or employment, ability to work and availability for work, and actively looking for work. Eligible employees have also to prove freedom from disqualifications. The latter may include quitting one's job, discharge for misconduct, and refusal of suitable work.

Taking part in labor disputes—strikes—may also disqualify a worker for UI. Other causes could include student unavailability for work because of class schedules, pregnancy (in 23 states), quitting to marry (in 15 states), and fraudulent misrepresentation.

When a worker loses a job covered by UI, he should apply immediately to his nearest state UI office to file a claim for benefits. Promptness is vital; several weeks may elapse before the first compensation payment arrives. The person filing should have with him his Social Security card and discharge notice. Payments last up to 26 weeks; under extra hardship conditions, they may last a year.

UNEMPLOYMENT INSURANCE:
THE STATE-BY-STATE PICTURE[1]

In these states the base period is the first four of the last five completed calendar quarters. Your earnings in your highest-paying quarter in that period become the basis for your benefit.

	weekly benefit amount minimum	maximum	weeks of entitlement minimum	maximum	high quarter earnings to qualify for minimum	maximum
Alabama	$15	$90	11	26	$ 348	$2,136
Arizona	30	90	12	26	625	2,238
Arkansas	15	124	10	26	118	3,198
California	30	120	12	26	188	1,160
Colorado	25	142	7	26	188	3,666
Connecticut	15-20	134-201	26	26	150	3,458
Delaware	20	150	11	26	520	3,874
District of Columbia	13-14	181	17	34	300	4,140
Georgia	27	90	4	26	275	2,225
Hawaii	5	144	26	26	38	3,575
Idaho	17	121	10	26	416	3,120
Illinois	15	133-177	26	26	250	3,445
Indiana	35	74-124	3	26	400	1,698
Iowa	17-18	131-148	15	26	400	2,803
Kansas	30	123	10	26	—	2,871
Kentucky	22	120	15	26	500	2,749
Louisiana	10	149	12	28	75	3,700
Maine	12-17	96-144	3	26	367	2,101
Maryland	10-13	106	26	26	192	2,520
Massachusetts	12-18	131-197	9	30	225	3,380
Mississippi	10	90	12	26	160	2,314
Missouri	15	105	8	26	300	2,311
Montana	30	119	12	26	767	3,081
Nebraska	12	106	17	26	200	2,550
Nevada	16	115	11	26	375	2,850
New Mexico	22	106	18	26	546	2,730
North Carolina	15	130	13	26	150	3,367
North Dakota	36	131	12	26	910	3,380
Oklahoma	16	132	20	26	250	3,275
Pennsylvania	13-18	162-170	30	30	120	3,988
Puerto Rico	7	72	20	20	75	1,846
South Carolina	10	111	10	26	180	2,860
South Dakota	28	109	13	26	600	2,376
Tennessee	14	100	12	26	338	2,970
Texas	18	105	9	26	125	2,600
Utah	10	137	10	36	175	3,536
Virginia	38	122	12	26	342	3,025
Virgin Islands	15	90	26	26	99	2,225
Washington	17	137	8	30	325	3,413
Wyoming	24	131	12	26	600	3,250

[1] States listed here use as a base period either four of the last five quarters or another recent 52-week period, perhaps the 52 weeks before you lost your job. Your total earnings in the base period then become the benefit basis.

	weekly benefit amount		weeks of entitlement		high quarter earnings to qualify for	
	minimum	maximum	minimum	maximum	minimum	maximum
Alaska	$18-$28	$90-$120	14	28	$ 750	$8,500
New Hampshire	21	114	26	26	1,200	10,500
Oregon	35	127	6	26	700	10,120
West Virginia..............	18	166	28	28	1,150	15,650

These states use the 52-week system, too, but figure benefits roughly as a percentage of your average weekly wage during the base period. In Michigan, Minnesota and New York, for which a range of percentages is shown, the higher figures apply to those with lower earnings and vice versa.

	weekly benefit amount		weeks of entitlement		minimum earnings to qualify	% of average weekly wage
	minimum	maximum	minimum	maximum		
Florida	$10	$95	10	26	$ 400	50%
Michigan..................	16-18	97-136	11	26	350	63-55
Minnesota	30	150	11	26	750	60-50
New Jersey	20	123	15	26	600	66.6
New York.................	25	125	26	26	800	67-50
Ohio	10	128-202	20	26	400	50
Rhode Island..............	30-35	120-140	12	26	1,060	55
Vermont	18	115	26	26	700	50
Wisconsin................	29	155	1	34	840	50

From "Unemployment Insurance: Who Gets What for How Long," August 1980 *Changing Times* Magazine. Reprinted with permission from *Changing Times* Magazine, © 1980 Kiplinger Washington Editors, Inc.

"Unemployed and looking for work"

Under UI regulations, the worker has to report regularly to the state employment service office to prove that he or she is both unemployed and looking for work. The compensation check has to be picked up in person. If a claimant is doing any work, the wages are deductible from benefits.

The unemployed worker earning less than his usual weekly pay may be entitled to partial benefits. To qualify, he should obtain a payroll voucher or other document showing the gross pay received. Benefits will nonetheless be determined according to regular-job earnings.

Refusal to accept a suitable full-time job can result in loss of benefits. Ineligibility may also result from acceptance of workers' compensation, dismissal payments (severance pay), a pension, or other remuneration. Refusal of benefits can be appealed; the UI office will provide guidance on the procedures to be followed.

The state employment service can provide assistance in finding a job. A given state can refer applicants to employers, administer tests, provide counseling, prepare individuals for job interviews, or refer applicants to training programs.

Generally, the more of these services provided, the better are the chances of finding a job. One survey has shown that workers not temporarily laid off and not due to be called back to their old jobs received more assistance. Younger workers received much more attention than older. The more skilled the worker, the more attention given by the employment service. The most crucial service provided for job seekers was referral to a job interview.

Supplementary Unemployment Benefits (SUB)

Criticism of UI

UI has been criticized for a number of reasons. Its coverage has been said to be incomplete and its benefits inadequate. Only a small proportion of unemployed have received benefits. Disqualification standards have been termed harsh. Benefits are exhausted too quickly and the taxable wage base is inadequate.

Disqualification can occur, as noted, when one receives other government benefits. This cannot occur, however, when supplemental unemployment benefits (SUB) are provided. SUB is intimately related to UI, both in administration and in what it provides. SUB was developed privately as a reaction to the inadequacies of UI.

Many labor unions initiated SUB plans to supplement UI benefits. The United Auto Workers started the first plan in 1955. A number of major industries, afflicted by recurring unemployment, now have SUB plans—for example, the auto and steel industries, in which the threat of unemployment is especially great during recessions. SUB plans have proved acceptable to employers because they reduce worker resistance to change and displacement. They tend to reinforce the uses for which UI was intended.

SUB plans are of two types:

• *Pooled funds.* The more common type, pooled funds "pool" losses on behalf of all eligible employees. The employer contributes so many cents for each hour worked to a central fund. Pooled SUB plans, combined with UI, can cover from 60 to 95 per cent of a worker's former salary. Payments can last up to 52 weeks.

Two kinds of SUB plans

- *Individual account plans.* Under an individual account plan, a separate account is established for each employee. The result is a form of compulsory saving. Plans vary in details. If an employer does not contribute to the plan, a higher wage may replace the benefit. In other plans, the employer matches the amount deducted from the worker's salary. Still other plans have profit-sharing funds from which withdrawals can be made during periods of unemployment.

SUB offsets unemployment benefit differences among states. In states with low UI payments, SUB makes up the difference with higher payments. The chances that UI benefits will increase are small. SUB therefore serves a useful purpose for a large number of unionized workers: meeting the threat of unemployment.

Veterans' Rights

Under the GI Bill, veterans are entitled to a number of benefits. These include:

- Educational assistance at various educational institutions at the rate of one and one-half months for each month served up to a limit of 45 months. For those serving after Vietnam, the ratio is two months for every month served. The Veterans Administration (VA) gives a monthly allowance varying according to the number of dependents. The allowance is designed to cover tuition, books, and living expenses. The wives and widows of disabled veterans are also eligible. The veteran has to use his or her benefits within 10 years after discharge.

A veteran can reclaim his former job

- The right to reclaim a former job. A veteran is legally entitled to his former job after discharge. He even acquires seniority for the time spent in the service. A veteran must, however, apply for his old job within 90 days after discharge. Where an employer refuses to rehire, the Veterans Reemployment Rights Office of the U.S. Department of Labor should be contacted.

- Home loan guarantee. The VA cannot guarantee the entire price of a property—home, mobile home, condominium, or farm —since the law limits the amount of the mortgage that the government will insure. In some rural areas where there are few lenders, the VA will make loans directly.
- Medical care for service-connected disabilities. Even for a disability that is not service-connected, a VA hospital will admit a veteran if he cannot pay for care elsewhere. VA clinics are also available, and a veteran can be authorized by the VA to be treated by his own physician.
- Compensation and pensions for disabled veterans. Eligibility for such benefits arises from disability incurred or disease contracted or aggravated while in the service. Payments vary with the kind of disability. Even if the disability was not incurred in the service, the veteran may still be eligible if he served 90 days or more.

Social Security Disability

Social Security is not supposed to provide retirement benefits only. A person working in a job covered by Social Security can acquire eligibility for disability benefits at any age. To be eligible, one has to be unable to earn a living. Also, the condition must have lasted, or be expected to last, for at least a year. The disability may be mental or physical. There must be sufficient credit in one's Social Security account and the applicant must have worked for five of ten years or ten of 20 quarters preceding the onset of the disability.

Contacting the local Social Security office

To claim benefits, one should contact a local Social Security office. A five-month waiting period elapses before issuance of the first monthly payment. Physicians involved in treatment will fill out forms provided by Social Security; hospitals can provide records. Disability benefits are the same as old-age benefits at age 65; benefits may be reduced if one is under 62 and receiving workers' compensation. Denials of benefits can be appealed.

13 "BUSINESS OPPORTUNITY— YOUNG COUPLE— MINIMUM INVESTMENT"

Everyone has read, at one time or another, that opportunities in the United States are less numerous than they used to be. Stories abound—about the small business person, his or her problems, the bankruptcies that occur with greater frequency, and other data that seem to support the basic proposition.

The Business Opportunity section in the daily newspaper nonetheless lists numbers of enterprises that appeal to the small businessman, the person who is thinking of adopting a new way of life, and others. Franchise operations offer just one example of a field that expanded rapidly, creating thousands of opportunities.

More and more professional and business people are changing their lifestyles and their occupations. Despite whatever business or financial success they may have achieved, they launch new searches for occupations with more meaning for them and their families. Not

unusually, a husband or wife may decide to start a family business and to make whatever adjustments in lifestyle may be necessary.

This chapter deals with the problems of the individual seeking to operate a small business or to start out on a new line of work. What form of business enterprise will be best suited for one's family or for others who may come into the business later? How to raise capital and do all the things that have to be done in order to make a business operation succeed. Some basic answers will provide guidelines.

THREE TYPES OF BUSINESS ORGANIZATIONS

Three forms that a business may take will be considered here: the sole proprietorship, the partnership, and the corporation. Other forms will be touched on passingly.

The Sole Proprietorship

The sole proprietorship is perhaps the most simple organizational format. It may be the best way for an individual to start out on a small scale.

In a typical situation, a person wants to operate a franchise. It is likely that he will be the sole owner. Just as likely, he will not need additional capital, at least in the beginning, and the business will probably not grow to the point where the owner will need outside help.

One company,
one boss

The sole proprietorship is the answer. One person is the boss; he has only himself to answer to. He can give orders freely if he has employees, and has only his own tax situation to worry about. If the business remains small, he can keep a finger on the growth pattern and operating costs. Many of the complicated matters that arise under the corporate form of doing business, or even the partnership form, can be controlled.

Under the laws of many states, operating a business under an assumed or fictitious name requires, initially, that the necessary information be filed with county and state authorities. The information includes the name to be used and the names and addresses of all persons interested in the business. Filing is required so that individuals dealing with the business will be able to ascertain which parties actually have an interest in the business should the need ever arise. Typically, a state law might be called an Assumed Names Act.

For example, to do business under the trade name "Acme Food Market," it would be necessary in most states to register the company name and the names and addresses of all persons interested in the name. If ownership changes, an amendment to the filing will have to be made. New information would include the name of the new owner, whether a partnership is created, and the names of any new partners.

The Partnership

A partnership is composed of two or more persons working together in a business enterprise, usually on the basis of a partnership agreement. A relatively simple way to do business, the partnership is not as complicated as the corporation. Also, the partnership has advantages and disadvantages vis-à-vis both the sole proprietorship and the corporation.

When two or
more work
together

As in any new business venture, in the early stages capital will be needed. The partners may have to use their personal credit. Each partner is personally responsible for the debts and credit arrangements of any other partners and of the business itself. After a partnership has accumulated assets and can show an earnings history, credit will usually be extended to the enterprise without the personal guarantees of the principal parties.

Each partner may act for all the others. The partnership form of doing business is governed in most states by statute. These laws set out, in detail, the rights and obligations of partners where no formal partnership agreement exists.

However, most partnerships do—and should—operate under the

terms of a partnership agreement. The agreement spells out all the relative rights and obligations of the parties, describes the business in detail, enumerates its objectives, and indicates the investment or contributions of each partner.

General observations

Some general observations can be made regarding the typical partnership as it is ordinarily set out in a partnership agreement.

Duration.   The length of time a partnership will endure depends on the terms of the agreement. Ordinarily the agreement provides that the partnership will continue for an indefinite period until it is terminated by the death of a partner, by voluntary act of the partners, by the insolvency or bankruptcy of one of the partners, by improper activity on the part of a partner, or by other means.

THE THREE BASIC KINDS OF BUSINESS[1]

There are three basic kinds of business in our society. The first is the individual proprietorship or ownership, the second is the partnership, and the third is the corporation. Each of these types of business organization has unique characteristics that make it more or less suitable for a specific kind of operation.

The Individual Ownership

More than half the business concerns in this country are owned by a single person. This kind of business is known legally as an individual ownership or proprietorship. It may be small, like a newsstand or a candy store, or it may be a fairly large company. The individual owner has great flexibility; he is responsible only to himself and he alone reaps the rewards of a successful operation. By the same token, however, he is entirely responsible for any debts or losses his company incurs in the course of business. Many such businesses are started from scratch by the owner. Others are purchased from a previous owner. In either case, the individual owner may operate under his own name or under a company name.

The Partnership

A partnership is a more complicated form of business than an individual ownership. Any number of people may enter into a partnership (of course there must be at least two), investing their money or their services or both in the business of which they are co-owners. Usually there is a written partnership agreement between them that sets out their rights and duties under the partnership. Unless the agreement provides otherwise, the partners share equally in the profits or the losses of the company. In a general partnership all the partners are liable for any business debts, and they may be obliged to make up deficits out of their own personal property. A partnership may be for a limited or for an indefinite term.

The Corporation

While only a small percentage of American businesses are corporations, they are by far the largest and most important ones. The corporation is a group of people who have banded together to do business and who have been granted a charter by the government which gives them, as a unit, some of the legal rights and powers of an individual. In other words, the law regards a corporation as a person. A corporation may own, buy, sell and inherit property in its own name. It may even commit a crime and be tried and punished for it. Most corporations get the capital necessary for their operations by selling stock ——units or shares in the ownership of the company. If the business is successful, the profits are distributed to the stockholders in the form of dividends.

[1] From *You and the Law*, Copyright © 1977 The Reader's Digest Association, Inc. Copyright © 1977 The Reader's Digest Association (Canada) Ltd. Copyright © 1977 Reader's Digest Association Far East Ltd. Philippine Copyright 1977 Reader's Digest Association Far East Ltd.

The partnership agreement may specify that the partnership does not terminate or will not be dissolved on the death of a partner. Such a partnership continues so long as there are two or more partners. The remaining partners have the right to purchase the share of the deceased partner from his estate. Business insurance can help to facilitate the financing of the buy-out agreement in such a case.

Unlike a corporation, the partnership is not separate and distinct from the partners. The liability of the general partners in a partnership is individual to each of them and applies to all partnership obligations throughout the life of the agreement. *Limited partners* or other special partners may, however, have their liability limited to their investment only.

Changes and Limitations. If an existing partnership decides to take in a new partner, the "old" partnership should be terminated and a new one created. All of the former partners should give their consent. If one of the partners wants to retire, arrangements have to be made to protect him insofar as partnership debts are concerned. Thus no creditor can recover from the partner who has resigned or retired.

Ring out the old . . .

The partnership agreement must either provide for such contingencies or it must be amended. A new partnership agreement may have to be drawn up to incorporate changes.

The partnership can raise capital only in certain ways. Loans may involve the individual guarantees of all the partners. New partners may bring in additional capital. Additional contributions may be required of the present members of the partnership.

Management of the partnership ordinarily requires the unanimous agreement of all the partners. But one partner may be appointed *managing partner* under a partnership agreement, giving him responsibility for the day-to-day management decisions. Policy-making authority may thus reside in all the partners together or in the managing partner alone. Problems may, of course, arise, especially where the partners have equal management responsibility.

A partnership has flexibility

A partnership has a degree of flexibility in conducting business operations. But the basic agreement should specify the nature of the partnership and the work to be done. The partnership should not engage in any activity not specified in the agreement.

Taxation. Insofar as taxation is concerned, the partnership has only to file a federal *information return* for income tax purposes. The partnership itself pays no income tax, in brief. Rather, it distributes its income to the individual partners who are taxed on their own proportionate shares of the partnership income. That income may or may not be distributed to the partners during the taxable year.

Partners are taxed on distributed earnings, on accumulated earnings, and on their proportionate shares of all gains and losses of the partnership. Partners also use the same methods of determining capital gains and losses that they would use in individual sole proprietorships. The partnership return shows the amount distributable to the partners; they in turn report this income on their own individual income tax returns.

As regards charitable contributions, partners again figure in their proportionate shares of any partnership contributions when computing income. Pension and profit-sharing plans are available to partners, but only in the limited amount permitted to self-employed persons under the current federal income tax laws. An income tax deduction may be permitted for a limited pension and profit-sharing program (see Chapter 9).

Like self-employed persons, partners have to pay their own self-employment tax. If a partner wishes to sell his share, or assign income or interest in the partnership, he ordinarily has to have the consent of all the other partners. A new partnership may result.

Exemption from state income tax

With respect to state taxes, the same considerations usually apply. A partnership does not have to pay any state income tax. But again, income is distributable to the partners themselves, and they have to report it as income if the particular state has such a tax. Sales taxes and other business-type taxes may be chargeable to the partnership. These are paid, usually, as ordinary and necessary business expenses.

Caveats. A partnership implies a very close relationship. It should be entered into only with someone in whom you have the utmost confidence and faith, someone who gets along well with you and whose spouse gets along well with your spouse. Make no mistake: more partnerships have been dissolved for reasons of personal animosity that arises during the partnership period than through lack of business success.

Examples of partnerships that failed are numerous. Some famous show-business partnerships have been broken up because of conflicts between the spouses of the partners.

The human element is as important as the business element in the successful operation of any partnership. Before entering into such an arrangement, the potential partner should know the person he wants to enter into business with, know the spouse, and reach an affirmative conclusion after study of all the business and personal ramifications.

The Corporation

The corporate way of doing business is much more complicated than the sole proprietorship or partnership. But where the business is such that the corporate form makes sense, it can be very flexible.

The shareholders own the company

Basically, a corporation is made up of its *shareholders,* who are the owners of the company; the *board of directors,* which handles the management and policy of the company; and *officers* who handle day-to-day affairs. This division between ownership and management gives the corporation its flexibility. In addition, the corporation guarantees limited liability to the shareholders: their liability is limited to their investment only. Ordinarily, the individual shareholders need not concern themselves with the possibility that they can be held personally liable for debts of the corporation over and above their investments.

Does the corporate form of doing business apply only to a large enterprise, or to a large business operation? Not at all. The laws of many states provide for so-called "close" or "closed" corporations that have few shareholders, usually five or fewer. A corporation can have one or an unlimited number of shareholders. Thus a corporation format can be utilized by one person even if he is the only shareholder. He may thus have all the benefits of the corporate form, including these:

- A corporation may continue on a perpetual basis, until dissolved by law, unless a specific state statute limits the time. Ordinarily, however, a corporation can be organized to exist "forever."

- A corporation has an existence separate and apart from its owners, the stockholders. It has the legal capacity to sue and it can be sued, and it has the capacity to own property in its name.

- As far as liability is concerned, the corporation is liable for all of its own debts and obligations. But once its assets are exhausted by creditors, each shareholder's liability is limited to his capital contribution to the corporation.

Organizing. In organizing, a corporation as a creature of state law must adhere strictly to the laws of the state. Most states require that a corporate charter be issued after application to the appropriate state official. Usually, a corporate purpose must be stated in the charter. That purpose often sets limits on the activities of the corporation. In recent years, however, states have allowed corporations to include very broad statements of purpose in their charters.

Announcing the corporate charter

Some states require that the prospective issuance of the charter or the application for the corporate charter be publicly announced. Once the charter is issued, the corporation is legally organized. The application for the charter is accompanied by necessary filing fees, initial tax statements, and other required documentation.

Ordinarily, the first board of directors, or the first stockholders who will elect the board of directors, must also be identified in the application. Some states require that all limitations on the transfer of stock or issuance of shares of stock, or classes of stock, be set forth in the charter.

Small Corporations. If the corporation is a closed one, the creditors may attempt to look beyond the corporation and go after the personal assets of individual shareholders. The creditors may claim that the corporation is merely a sham designed to protect the shareholders who are in fact the owners and managers of the company.

In many cases, clearly, the corporate officers may be the same as the corporate directors. They may even be the same as the shareholders: the same individuals hold all positions. Unless all corporate records are maintained accurately and precisely, according to law, the creditor may be able to support such contentions. All corporate state and federal tax returns must be filed and minutes of corporate stockholders' meetings, corporate board of directors' meetings, and executive committee meetings must be maintained.

Keeping minutes

Accurate minutes must also be kept on all actions required by law of the board of directors or the stockholders. Only in this way can a small corporation protect itself against claims that it is not operating according to law and that the shareholders should therefore be responsible for company debts.

Raising Funds. The corporate form of doing business has a very practical advantage when funds are needed for capital expansion. Also, since the ownership of the corporation is represented by shares of stock, ownership can be transferred simply by selling the shares of stock. Unless the company's by-laws contain *stock transfer restrictions,* the stock is ordinarily freely saleable.

Some stock transfer restrictions are relatively common. For example, a stockholder may be required to offer stock shares for sale to the corporation before selling to a third party.

In larger corporations whose stock is traded on a national or local exchange such as the American or New York stock exchanges, transfers are made by brokers, based on the average price of the stock on the day of transfer. Where a small company is involved, however, it becomes more difficult to assess the value of stock shares. A closely held corporation whose shares are to be sold may have to rely on company records, such as earnings and other financial reports, since there is no ready market for these shares.

Where stock is sold in this way, no new agreements need be filed. A change in stock ownership does not change such factors as corporate assets, the operation of the company, or its title to real estate.

Money-raising options

In raising additional funds for a corporate business operation, the corporation has several options. It can sell an issue of *new stock*—stock that it issues for sale to the general public in addition to that already outstanding in the hands of stockholders. It can issue *bonds,* interest-bearing certificates of corporate debt, or other forms of securities such as preferred stock and debentures. The latter also represents corporate debt. With more options open to it than an individual proprietor or a partnership, the growth business established as a corporation can often provide periodically for expansion.

Management. The management of the corporation is in the hands of its board of directors, which ordinarily acts by majority agreement. The stockholders of the corporation elect the board of directors, usually on an annual basis at the annual stockholders' meeting. The board of directors normally appoints the top officers. Min-

utes of all meetings of the board of directors and stockholders are maintained. In some larger corporations, minutes are kept of all meetings of the executive committee and the officers.

As the legal owners, the stockholders may vote by proxy in electing the board of directors. The stockholders in effect give the right to vote to some other party who then votes for members of the board. However, the board of directors does not have the right to delegate its duties and must exercise its obligations directly. A director cannot, by proxy, give some other person or group his right to vote at the directors' meeting.

Taxes and Tax Reports. Many more state tax reports are ordinarily required of a corporation than of a partnership or a sole proprietorship. The various states have enacted different tax laws affecting corporations. Capital stock taxes, initial excise taxes, and a corporate net profits tax are usually levied. These may require the assistance of an experienced accountant.

Paying taxes directly on income

Unlike the partnership, the corporation pays taxes directly on its income. The stockholders pay taxes only on the dividend income they receive less the dividend tax credit. If the corporation does not distribute its dividends, and has a surplus available for payment of dividends over and above that allowed by law, a penalty or surtax may be charged for the accumulation of income beyond that permitted.

As a major advantage, the corporation under present tax laws can set up full-scale pension and profit-sharing plans. A current deduction is allowed for payments into the pension or profit-sharing fund. The members pay no taxes on the profit-sharing or pension benefits until they actually receive them—usually after retirement.

Pension/profit-sharing plan limitations

The tax laws limit the amounts that can be paid out under corporate pension and profit-sharing plans. But these benefits are much more liberal than those available to partners or other self-employed individuals. The sick-pay provisions of the tax laws typically allow regular employees a limited tax deduction on such payments. A corporation can also deduct its own charitable contributions up to a specified amount.

Officers and employees of a corporation are entitled to all the benefits enjoyed by employees. The corporation must withhold from the pay of officers and employees the necessary Social Security and other taxes, including income taxes. Even though they may also be shareholders, the officers are employees of the corporation and not self-employed individuals, and must report income as employees.

A final tax-related advantage is the ability of the corporation owner to make gifts of stock as part of an estate plan. A sole proprietor would find it very difficult to bring his children into his business in an ownership way. If he is incorporated, however, the individual can transfer shares of stock from himself to his children on a regular basis. In doing so, he reduces the size of his estate and increases each child's ownership interest in the business.

Things to Remember. Considering incorporation? Remember that the corporation is separate and apart. That remains true even if you are the sole stockholder and the president of the company. The corporation exists as an entity; it has a separate legal existence.

Mr. President's employment agreement

Remember also that even the owner-president of a small corporation has to have a working arrangement with the company. For example, he should have an *employment agreement* with the corporation that indicates his compensation and stock rights, his pension and profit-sharing rights, if any, and so on. It may seem unnecessary to have an employment agreement when there is only one stockholder. But the value of the agreement becomes clear if additional stockholders join the corporation later. The agreement protects the original owner's status as an officer of the company and his compensation level.

An employment agreement may have major impact on tax liability, particularly where a question arises involving the valuation of stock or the reasonableness of an officer's salary. In reviewing the income received by a corporate officer, and measuring it against the duties performed, the Internal Revenue Service sometimes finds that the officer is receiving a dividend, not compensation. The dividend could then be taxed twice—once while in the corporate account and again after it reaches the stockholder.

An employment agreement that specifies the total compensation to be paid to the officer and the duties required can often eliminate such problems.

Many other considerations relating to the corporate form of doing business should be kept in mind. These can depend on the nature of the business, the company's size, its growth potential, the degree of flexibility required, and so on. The need for competent legal and financial advice is ever-present. If set up properly, the corporation can serve as practical application of business principles to bring success to an enterprise.

OTHER FORMS OF BUSINESS ORGANIZATIONS

From limited
partnership to
joint venture

In addition to the sole proprietorship, the general partnership, and the corporation, there are other ways to go into business. These are combinations of some of the forms already noted. All should have a place in the process of determining the appropriate way to go into business.

The Limited Partnership

A limited partnership combines some of the elements of a general partnership with those of a corporation. A limited partner makes an investment in the partnership; but he ordinarily has nothing whatever to do with the management of the business and he enjoys a limitation on his liability for partnership debts. The limit is the amount of money that he has invested. The partnership form remains, but the limited partner has liability similar to that of a stockholder in a corporation.

The limited partnership is controlled by statute in the various states. The statutory requirements have to be followed very closely if each limited partner is to enjoy the advantage of limited liability. Major tax advantages can also be claimed by limited partners.

A limited partnership and a corporation may be joined in a single enterprise. Each of the entities performs a separate function. In such instances, it is important to keep all records of the two organizations separate and apart. All agreements, arrangements, and contracts between the two are treated as though the partnership and corporation were unrelated entities and totally separate business enterprises.

The limited partnership has been widely used as a vehicle for conducting long-range, risky, and costly operations of a highly technical nature. An example would be oil and gas exploration and drilling. The partners usually do not want to take a direct role in management. They have funds to invest; in making an investment, they see the risk of loss as secondary. More importantly, the investment usually gives them a *tax write-off*. The funds in many cases would have been paid to the government as income taxes.

One general partner required

Every limited partnership has to have at least one general partner who organizes and runs the partnership operations. One or more limited partners—up to dozens and even hundreds—join the partnership and invest in it. If the partnership makes a profit, it is distributed to the partners according to a formula set out in the limited partnership certificate that each partner receives.

The "Sub-Chapter S" Corporation

The federal tax laws permit the so-called "sub-chapter S" corporation to be treated as a partnership insofar as taxation is concerned. The requirements arc that the corporation have no more than 10 stockholders to qualify. The corporation then retains all the advantages that make the corporation form advisable, such as limited liability of stockholders. At the same time the "sub-S" corporation is not taxed as a corporation.

Taxing Sub-S shareholders as partners

The shareholders of a sub-S corporation are taxed as partners. They include all the distributed income in their own income tax returns, reporting it as income.

Under the income tax laws a partnership or a sole proprietorship, if qualified, can elect to be treated as a corporation. Ordinarily, the purpose would be to reduce taxes. Typically, the corporation has unreasonably high income and wants to take advantage of certain lower tax rates.

The Joint Venture

A joint venture is similar to a partnership. Two or more individuals or a combination of individuals and companies undertake to perform certain services or do a certain job. Unlike a partnership, however, the joint venture is not a continuing arrangement. A joint venture is entered into only for one specific project. On termination or completion of that project, the joint venture terminates.

The parties to a joint venture enter into an agreement that spells out all rights and obligations and the nature of the work or project to be undertaken by the joint venture. The test of a joint venture is whether it has been formed for one specific project only.

CONTROL OF THE BUSINESS ENTERPRISE

A particular field of business has been selected. A specific form of organization—sole proprietorship, partnership, or corporation—has been decided on. How about the problem of control? How can you be assured that, having set up the business, you will be able to protect it—or keep out people whom you may not want to be in it? How do you keep the management and control of the business in your hands or subject to your approval?

The question of control

The question of control involves a number of considerations. The type of business, the method by which interests can be transferred to others, restrictions on the transfer of ownership, employment contracts, and other factors become important. This is why the necessary agreements, contracts, charters, by-laws, and other documents should be prepared by a lawyer. All rights and obligations of the parties have to be spelled out clearly and precisely or questions of control may arise in the future.

The nonlawyer may not be able to assess the importance of some factors. Specific questions may turn on the provisions of state law regarding restrictions on transfers of shares, what can be included in the charter of a corporation, the attitudes of the local courts toward management, and restrictions on the transfer of control of the business. The wording of some documents may affect an owner's power to control his own business.

Some possible ways of maintaining control include the following:

Limiting transfers
of interest

1. *Restrictions on transfers of interest.* As noted, an absolute restriction on the transfer of an interest in a business enterprise may be considered unreasonable. The law generally does not favor restraints on the selling or assignment of business enterprise or property rights. This legal hurdle can be overcome, however, by a *stock transfer restriction agreement* among the shareholders. The agreement gives the other partners or stockholders an option or right of first refusal before stock shares can be sold to a third party outside the business.

An example may be noted. A partnership agreement could specify that a partnership interest could not be sold unless the partner wishing to sell first offered his partnership interest to the other partners. If the others refuse to buy under a formula established in the agreement, then the partner would be free to sell to someone else.

Other agreements might provide that before a shareholder can sell his stock to the general public, he must first offer it to the corporation itself—or to the other shareholders. The latter could buy the offered stock in proportion to the total number of shares each owns. If the stock is not purchased, the shareholder would have the right to sell to the general public.

Stock transfer
restrictions: valid
but not absolute

Such stock transfer restrictions are valid and enforceable. They are not considered absolute restrictions on transfer of shares. This type of restriction is often set out in a clause in the agreement among the shareholders in a by-law provision, and in a statement on every stock certificate. Anyone who buys the stock in violation of the restriction is regarded as having been put on notice by the provision on the certificate.

2. *Employment contracts.* Continued control of a business can be assured by drawing up an employment agreement between a partnership and its partners or between a corporation and its officers.

The agreement can specify the rights, duties, and obligations of the corporation or partnership and of the employee or officer.

3. *Voting rights.* Most business enterprises involve a number of people. Usually, the parties want some assurance that the business will go on as originally planned. Where the possibility exists that a majority could act contrary to the wishes of the founders and forget what the business was designed to do, voting provisions can be used to maintain control. Various approaches are utilized to protect the business operation in such cases:

- Arrangements may be made for voting and nonvoting stock, for voting rules that ensure that the minority group is represented on the board of directors, and for elections of different directors in different years.

- Shareholder agreements may be written so as to require the shareholders to vote their stock in a certain way. For example, the agreements could require all shareholders to elect each other as directors of the corporation and no one else. The stockholders would then be able to prevent others from taking control of the corporation. It should be noted, however, that such restrictions on voting or on transfers of shares will naturally inhibit someone else from buying that stock. If the intent of the corporation is to create a market for its stock and to attract additional shareholders, such restrictions will adversely affect that intent.

Use of the voting trust agreement

- Where a number of shareholders want to join together to give a lesser number the right to vote all the shares, a *voting trust agreement* may be utilized. The voting trustees are designated by the agreement. They themselves can agree on how the votes will be cast.

- Depending on the law of the state, the charter and by-law provisions of the corporation may provide for the requirements as to quorums and the number of persons required to vote. Different percentages of the total number of shares may have to be represented at meetings before votes can be taken on certain acts. For example, a two-thirds vote of all shareholders may be needed to change the by-laws of the corporation. In a small corporation, the by-laws or a separate agreement among the shareholders may specify that all shareholders must agree to any change in the company by-laws.

Arbitration to settle disagreements

- Arrangements may be made to provide for arbitration. Where disagreements arise, preventing the orderly operation of the business, the partnership agreement, the by-laws of the corporation, or a separate agreement among the shareholders should provide for some means of breaking any deadlock. Arbitration, dissolution of the company, or a provision allowing one party to buy out the other are all possible methods. All can be useful, especially where only a few shareholders or partners are involved.

Not uncommonly, a partnership agreement or stockholder agreement involving a few partners or stockholders will provide that one party offer his stock to another party at a certain price. The other person then decides whether to sell or buy depending on the price. One party sets the price, and the other party decides whether to sell his own stock at that price or to buy the other person's stock at the same price.

4. *Buy-sell agreements between shareholders in a corporation.* The founder of a corporation would usually want to ensure that on his death the corporation would have an opportunity to buy his interest for the benefit of his estate or beneficiaries. These *buy-sell agreements* ordinarily establish an obligation on the part of the corporation to buy. The estate of the deceased shareholder has to sell the stock.

Sometimes such agreements are called "options" to buy and sell. They may require that if the estate wants to sell the stock, the stock must first be offered to the corporation or to the other surviving shareholders before it can be offered to others.

Stock retirement and cross-purchase

In order to finance the purchase of the stock of a deceased shareholder, the corporation must have a *stock retirement program* providing funds for this purpose. A *cross-purchase plan,* by contrast, gives the other stockholders the right to purchase the shares of the deceased. The corporation cannot then buy the shares.

One problem faced by a corporation in retiring stock is that under the laws of most states it must have funds for such purchases in its surplus account. It may be difficult for the company to set aside such funds. A cross-purchase plan for stockholders solves the problem. Funded through an insurance program, with each shareholder owning an insurance policy on the lives of the other shareholders, the plan makes it possible to buy the stock of a deceased shareholder with the insurance proceeds. Such funds go to the estate of the deceased to purchase his stock.

If the corporation buys the stock, the ownership interest of the other stockholders remains the same. No change has taken place in the numbers of shares owned by the surviving shareholders. If those survivors buy the decedent's stock, a change in the stock interest of the surviving shareholders does result.

How do you set the price of stock for the purpose of carrying out a corporate buy-sell agreement? If the stock is traded on a regional or national stock exchange, the price can be easily determined from the quotation for the day on which the stock is offered. In a close corporation, however, where there is no ready market for the stock, the problem of evaluation becomes critical. A mandatory buy-sell agreement must outline an effective method of determining the price of the stock or the agreement is not worth the paper it is written on.

Incidentally, an effective formula may help in determination of the value of a decedent's stock for federal estate tax purposes. The price as determined according to the agreement could be used to calculate the estate tax valuation.

Ways to establish the per-share value of stock

A buy-sell agreement in a closely held corporation may utilize any of several different ways of determining the per-share value of stock. The shareholders can set a fixed price per share, adding provisions for revising the price on an annual or some other basis. Calculations of value would be based on the performance of the company and other criteria. The controlling price would be the last stated price set before the death of the stockholder.

Where stock values have not been updated under a buy-sell agreement, problems may arise. The stock may have inflated or deflated in value since the last stated price was set. Where a fixed price has not been calculated for more than a year, an *appraisal method* of pricing the stock may be used. Other methods are also available.

The appraisal method leaves the price of the stock open pending later appraisal by a disinterested appraiser. On the death of the stockholder, the appraiser comes in and evaluates the stock. That decision is binding on the several parties.

The *book value method* of determining stock values utilizes both the last corporate balance sheet prepared before the death of the stockholder and a "net worth" adjustment to the date of death. The book value method does not take into account the value of the business as a going concern. The net worth method, however, will serve adequately:

- if inventory, for example, is determined at its actual worth rather than at cost;
- where accounts receivable are adjusted to take care of those that are not collectible;
- where the book value of machinery and equipment adequately represents their fair value and present worth;
- where real estate and buildings reflect current market values; and
- where insurance proceeds are considered as part of the evaluation.

Various other methods combine different valuation techniques that attempt to average corporate proceeds over a period of time and either *capitalize* the proceeds or *average out* the proceeds to determine a fair price for each share of stock.

Where a valuation formula is limited to book value only, the fair market value of the depreciable assets will be ignored. Only the depreciated value will be determined. The beneficiaries may receive much less for the stock than it is actually worth.

When survivors can buy the deceased partner's shares

5. *Partnership buy-sell agreement.* A partnership has problems similar to those of corporations. The partnership agreement should therefore establish the circumstances under which the surviving partners can buy the interest of the deceased partner. The obligation of the decedent's estate to offer the partnership interest for sale on agreed terms should be specified.

All partners and the partners' spouses should sign the partnership agreement—or the separate buy-sell agreement if such exists.

The valuation of the partnership interest for purposes of the buy-sell agreement involves some of the same considerations as the valuation of corporate stock. A value for good will should be placed on the partnership interest in the agreement. Provisions for payment should be spelled out clearly. The income tax laws provide for different treatments of payments depending on how they are made and the nature of the agreement. Thus care should be used in preparing the agreement to take advantage of the best possible tax thinking of professional advisors.

Four elements of a life insurance buyout agreement

Where life insurance is used to fund the purchase of a partner's interest, the agreement should spell out at least the following:

- Exactly how much life insurance is to be purchased
- Whether the partnership or the other partners own the policies on the lives of individual partners

- How the premium is to be paid
- How the transfer of the policy held by the deceased to the survivors is to be handled

INSURANCE UTILIZED IN BUSINESS OPERATIONS

Chapter 12, on insurance problems, noted some situations in which the insurance advice of professionals is needed. Such advice is absolutely indispensable where business insurance is concerned.

The insurance industry has recognized its obligation to provide expert advice in a professional way in recent years. Programs have been set up to train agents and brokers. Continuing education programs of the insurance industry include programs, seminars, and courses leading to the certification of an individual as a *Chartered Life Underwriter* (CLU). Other programs lead to the professional designation of *Chartered Property and Casualty Underwriter* (CPCU). Thus the business community has available top-notch experts who have the ability, the training, and the experience to apply their knowledge to current problems.

Insurance advisors can analyze risks. They can also read a partnership agreement or an agreement among shareholders to determine whether insurance protection is needed. They can give advice on the kinds of protection required and on costs.

In many cases, insurance offers the most economical and feasible method of funding programs for the purchase of stock of a deceased shareholder or the partnership interest of a deceased partner. The insurance advisor can explain how such programs work. The method to be used depends on the nature of the plan involved and the needs of the parties. If the number of shareholders or partners is large enough to require one, a trustee may be named to own the insurance policies and see to the distribution of the proceeds. The trustee becomes the designated beneficiary under the insurance policies so that he can carry out the terms of the agreement.

The trustee
becomes the
beneficiary

In other respects the trustee plan works much the same as that involving ownership of the policy by other partners, stockholders, or the corporation. The trustee can, however, be helpful where a great number of persons is involved and where distribution may be difficult.

A key factor in determining the best method of using life insurance to retire or purchase the stock of a deceased shareholder relates to the older and the younger shareholder. In a cross-purchase plan, the younger shareholder may "take a beating." This shareholder may have to pay premiums on a policy on the life of an older shareholder. These premiums, of course, can be very high. Where this situation exists, a corporation may use a stock retirement plan rather than the cross-purchase arrangement.

Premiums paid by corporations or individuals on insurance carried on the lives of stockholders are generally not deductible from income under the federal income tax laws. But in each case the insurance proceeds will be received by the beneficiaries free of tax. In most cases the corporation will receive the proceeds from the insurance and then buy up the decedent's stock. Where the stockholders own insurance on one another, the individual stockholder receives the proceeds and then purchases the stock.

Partnership
insurance

Partnership insurance is treated in similar fashion. The insurance policies can be owned by the partnership, which can later purchase the partnership interest of the deceased. Or the insurance can be owned, and the premiums paid, by the partners, who insure the other partners. Again, premium payments are not deductible by the partnership or by individual partners. But the proceeds are not includable in income or subject to income tax.

The decision to go into business raises complex questions. These relate to the form of business organization, the element of control of the business operation by various lawful means, and the funding of various plans to protect the interest of the businessman and his estate in the event of his death. What emerges constitutes a complete business plan. The need for sound business planning goes hand in hand with the necessity for consultation and advice from those whose profession or business it is to provide such assistance.

Protect your "minimum investment" by reviewing this chapter and consulting your family lawyer before taking the first step.

Despite claims to the contrary, the United States offers many opportunities for small businessmen and women. Recognition of the pitfalls and problem areas ahead of time can make your venture into the business world successful and enjoyable.

14 CAVEAT VENDOR—THE AGE OF THE CONSUMER

Without doubt the age of the consumer has begun. The consumer is king. Until recently, the maxim "caveat emptor"—"let the buyer beware"—was the rule of the marketplace. The purchase of goods of any kind, or an application for any kind of credit, put a consumer on his or her guard. No special treatment, no warnings, no protective information could be expected.

The complaints of consumers in such areas as exorbitant interest rates, defective goods, repossession of purchased products in cases of minor defaults, and many others reached such a crescendo that something had to be done. Both Congress and the various state legis-

latures have now passed laws protecting the consumer. The purpose of this chapter is to examine some of these laws and the citizen's rights as a consumer.

The consumer protection movement is based on the concept that the consumer is not in a position to protect himself against unfair practices. Because of their economic clout, companies can exert pressure against the consumer—or take advantage of him. He is vulnerable when buying goods, borrowing funds, or investing for financial gain. He also "consumes" the environment in which he lives—in various ways. In all these instances, he is today entitled by law to certain protections. If these protections are not honored, the consumer may have the right to a remedy against the party at fault.

The early 1980s saw far-reaching changes taking place in the consumer movement. From a relatively spectacular series of isolated controversies—car warranties, flammable children's underwear, dangerous drugs, and so on—consumerism has been transformed. It has become a true movement, one that seeks continually to generate legislation, change the ways in which institutions work, make companies responsive to popular needs.

How is the consumer protected?

One need remains to be underscored more thoroughly: the consumer's need to know how he or she is protected and how the protections can be used.

CONSUMER PROTECTION

The citizen's protection as a consumer of goods reaches into many different areas. These include:

Methods of presentation of goods, among them advertising

Packaging and labeling of goods

Methods used in selling the goods

Sales on credit

Protection of consumer defenses

Many more such areas might be listed. Each can be discussed under a separate heading.

Deceptive Practices

The statutes, rules, and regulations of various governmental agencies forbid or restrict deceptive practices in the sale of consumer goods. Some of these practices are:

False or Misleading Endorsements. An endorsement of a product is a statement by someone, usually someone with high public exposure and identity, that he or she approves the product. The endorser may be an athlete, a movie performer, a TV personality, or anyone else known to the public. Where the person making the endorsement has no way of knowing whether the product endorsed lives up to the ad statement, deception may be involved.

Endorsement may involve liability

In a typical example, a move star endorses a lawn mower, claiming that it is safe in all respects. But the movie star has no way of knowing whether the product is in fact safe. The endorsement may then be deceptive. The public figure who has loaned his or her name, for a price, to a product or business in the hope of stimulating sales

may have incurred liability if the product does not perform as advertised. The same is true if the advertising is otherwise deceptive.

At one time a salesperson could "puff up" his product. He could not be held responsible for such statements because the law assumed that no one would take them seriously. Today the salesman no longer has latitude to talk up a product without fear of liability: he must exercise caution to avoid deceiving the customer.

Deception in Advertising. Until recently, only a fraudulent act on the part of the seller of goods could serve as the basis for a remedy on the part of the consumer. In today's context deception on the part of the seller does not necessarily involve an intentional, fraudulent act designed to induce the consumer to buy. The test, now, is whether the buyer was misled, regardless of the intent or lack of intent of the seller. Note that the seller now has the task of showing that the consumer transaction was reasonable and fair.

Retail advertising is policed by the Federal Trade Commission (FTC), which reviews advertising materials to see whether a buyer would likely be misled. The FTC's Bureau of Consumer Protection also "rides shotgun" on illegal sales tactics, violations of the federal Truth in Lending law, and many other fraudulent or deceptive practices. Claims that overstate the life of a product, the superiority of one product over another, and other characteristics are outlawed unless they can be proved. The advertiser has to maintain records to substantiate his advertised claims regarding the quality of the product, its safety, its comparative price, and its contents.

Challenging advertisers

The FTC continually challenges advertisers regarding misleading or deceptive advertising. In a 1970s case the FTC discovered that a national advertiser was making false claims to encourage sales. The FTC ordered the offending company to launch a $10 million advertising campaign to correct the false claims. In 1978 the Supreme Court upheld the FTC's right to issue such orders for the protection of consumers.

Governmental efforts to protect the consumer touch on many aspects of life. For example, the Public Health Cigarette Smoking Act requires that a health warning appear on each package of cigarettes sold. Cigarette advertising has been banned on radio and television, and other forms of cigarette advertising have to contain the health warning in conspicuous print. The cigarette companies are also required to state the exact nicotine and tar content of their products. They cannot simply give a general statement that the product is low in nicotine and tar.

"Better, lighter, smoother than what?"

Paying some attention to radio and TV commercials, and to the advertisements in newspapers and magazines, will pay dividends. An effort should be made to analyze exactly what the advertiser is saying. If it is not clear what the advertiser is saying, or if the ad states that the product is better, lighter, smoother, mellower, more fragrant, harder-working, the consumer has the right to ask: "[li] better, lighter, smoother than *what?*"

If the ad deceives you, you have the right to complain. In some cases, you may have a right of action against the advertiser.

"Bait and Switch" Tactics. The FTC has outlawed "bait and switch" advertising. In one case a food store advertised a "special" without having on hand a sufficient stock of the special item to meet anticipated demand. The advertiser knew that by "baiting" the customer into the store with the advertised special, he was probably selling something else. The customer would usually buy a substitute item while in the store.

A "bait and switch" variation involves a merchant who advertises a low-cost item to get the customer into the store. The merchant then disparages or "talks down" the low-cost item in favor of a higher-priced item.

Are you really going out of business?

Many states outlaw such tactics. For example, state laws may forbid the "going out of business sale" when the store is not actually going out of business. Also prohibited in some states: the "fire sale" when there has been no fire, the "water damage and fire damage sale," or the "lost our lease sale," when none of these has in fact occurred. The laws of states or municipalities may require special licenses to conduct such sales to ensure that they are legitimate.

Games, Drawings, and Similar Contests. An obvious and frequently used advertising method is the sweepstakes or game-type promotion. The merchant tries to induce the customer to enter a contest or drawing. Where a sales promotion plan is involved, as is usual, the FTC has taken the position that there must be disclosure of the numerical odds of winning a prize, the approximate values of the prizes, the fact that all announced prizes will be awarded, and that they have in fact been awarded.

Requirements of Packaging and Labeling

What appears on the product label or package may be as important from a consumer rights viewpoint as the advertising that promotes its sale. Many federal laws have dealt with this area in recent years. They include the Fair Packaging and Labeling Act; the Fair Products Labeling Act; the Food, Drug, and Cosmetics Act; the Cigarette Labeling and Advertising Act; and the Flammable Fabrics Act. In addition, various federal and state laws forbid the use of such deceptive terms as "full," "jumbo size," "giant size," or "family size" in describing package dimensions. Such terms, it is held, create the impression that more is contained in the package than is actually there.

Under pressure and as a result of legislation, merchants have increasingly dated their products. They have tended more and more to describe contents in terms of commonly understood weights and measures—to avoid deceiving the consumer.

Labels have to be specific

Legislation now requires specifics on labels. The Fair Products Labeling Act, for example, requires that a product bear a label stating the identity of the product, the name and place of business of the manufacturer, the packer or distributor, the net quantity of all of the contents, and the net quantity of one serving when the number of servings is stated on the label. In addition, the Act gives the FTC and the Department of Health and Human Services the authority to require more information or additional disclosures on a label.

Where food, drugs, and cosmetics are involved, the federal Food and Drug Administration (FDA) regulates labeling and packaging. "Quackery" in medicine and drugs and the so-called "miracle drug" claims also come under the policing power of the FDA.

Approval or Testing of Goods

*What does the
"seal of approval"
mean?*

Stop and think. How many products can you name that are sold with a guarantee, tag, or other indication that the product has been tested and approved by some testing agency or organization? If the product has a seal of approval, this ordinarily means that the product has been tested and approved for normal consumer uses. If it has not in fact been tested and approved, the seller has violated a warranty made to the consumer and may be liable for fraud.

Products involving fire and electrical safety features may be tested by manufacturers' associations and testing companies for insurance purposes. Successful testing indicates that the product has been manufactured in accordance with industry safety standards and will pass muster. The consumer can rely on tests made by someone who knows more about the product than the consumer does, and thus is assured that the product is safe.

Some private and industry testing agencies report factually what the tests reveal but draw no conclusions. This is true also of private consumer organizations that report test results in various consumer magazines. On the other hand, certain magazines accept product advertising and agree to refund product costs or replace an item if it should prove defective.

Such approval would usually carry only the liability to refund a price or replace a defective article. But if the consumer is injured by the defective article, there may be liability in the expanding area of *product liability*. The magazine or organization giving its approval or guarantee might be held liable. The buyer might have a right of action against the seller as well. Should deception or injury result from a defective, guaranteed product, it is usually wise to consult a lawyer.

Control of Methods of Selling Goods

The sale-closers

The methods used by merchants in selling their products have been sharply limited in recent years. The reason: those methods may involve violations of consumer rights.

Read the classified ads section of the daily newspaper. Various ads call for salesmen who are specialists in closing a sale, called "closers." These are people who are trained to get the customer to sign on the dotted line. Many of them can take a "lead," the name of a prospective customer secured from someone else, and close the sale with a minimum investment of time and effort. These closers, who are highly trained and experienced, usually work on a straight commission basis. They try to induce the lead to sign immediately, rather than allow him or her to think about the purchase before signing.

Because the law seeks both to protect the consumer and to punish the fraudulent or unlawful merchant, various selling practices have been either placed under legal controls or outlawed.

Fair Disclosure of Contract Terms. The person taking out a loan and paying interest, points, service charges, or any other extra charge must have full disclosure of such charges. The person buying furniture, an automobile, or home improvements on the installment plan, or charging meals, gasoline costs, or repair charges is entitled to full disclosure of all contract terms. So is the buyer of hundreds of other items who buys on time or credit and pays interest. The law does not apply if no interest or other charges are added to the basic cost of the item even if installment payments are allowed.

The Consumer Credit Protection Act, better known as the "Truth in Lending Act," is the source of such protection. It is designed to let the consumer know exactly what the credit offered by the merchant will cost. Comparisons of the credit arrangements of other credit sources can then be made. The consumer can shop for the best "deal."

Finance charges and annual percentage rates

The landmark Truth in Lending Act guarantees the availability of information on the two most important factors in the cost of credit—the *finance charge,* or the amount paid to obtain credit, and the *annual percentage rate* (APR), the percentage of interest paid over a year's time. Both the finance charge and the annual percentage rate must be prominently displayed on the forms used by the merchant, banker, or other lender. With that information, the consumer can exactly compute what he or she will be paying.

THINK BEFORE YOU BORROW OR BUY ON TIME![1]

The wise borrower or buyer on time will pause a moment before signing anything. He or she will ask questions: Is it necessary to buy now? Can the loan be taken out later— when more cash will be available to repay or reduce it? Can interest or carrying charges be reduced in other ways?

Whatever the answers, some steps should be followed for one's own protection.

—Read and understand the contract; don't rush.

—Never sign a contract with blank spaces.

—Be sure the contract spells out in plain language:

• exactly what you are buying (make, model, size, type)

• purchase price

• down payment and trade-in allowances, if any

• amount borrowed

• total amount due

• interest and service charge in dollars and annual percentage rate

—Know to whom and where you make payments, as well as when the payments are due. What happens if you can't pay on time? Or if you pay ahead?

—What are the seller's obligations for delivery, maintenance, service, or replacement?

—Do you get a copy of the contract to keep?

—Do you suspect a violation of the Truth in Lending Act? It should be reported to the Bureau of Consumer Protection, Federal Trade Commission, Washington, D.C. 20580, or to a local consumer protection group.

[1] Reprinted with permission of Macmillan Publishing Co., Inc. from *Consumer Complaint Guide 1979* by Joseph Rosenbloom, copyright © 1979, Joseph Rosenbloom.

How does this work in practice? Suppose you borrowed $100 for one year and paid $6 in interest. If you had the full use of all of that money for a full year and did not have to repay it until the end of that year, you would be paying an annual percentage rate of 6 per cent. The finance charge would be $6. But if you repay the total $106 in 12 equal monthly installments, you would not have the full use of the $100 over the entire year. You would have an average of about one-half of the full amount. The $6 interest charged for the credit extended to you thus becomes an annual percentage rate of 11 per cent.

Some creditors apply a service charge or carrying charge instead of interest or in addition to interest. Whatever they call them, they must total up all of these charges, including interest, and call the total amount the "finance charge." Then they have to list the annual percentage rate on the total cost of credit.

Remember that the Truth in Lending Act is not designed to establish interest rates or other charges. Most states have laws that set the legal rates of interest for various types of transactions. The Act does apply to all business and financial institutions dealing in consumer credit.

An important subfeature of the law deals with advertising. If a business mentions one feature of credit in its advertising, such as the amount of the down payment, it must also mention all the other important terms. These range from the amount of each installment payment to the total number of such payments.

A violation of the Truth in Lending law by a lender can result in criminal penalties as well as civil money damages. The consumer can sue if the lender fails to make the proper disclosures, claiming an amount that is twice the finance charge or a minimum of $100 to a maximum of $1,000 for each violation. The lender may also have to pay court costs and reasonable attorney's fees.

Sales by Mail. More and more goods and services are being offered to the consuming public through the mails. If the mails are used to defraud, however, federal laws protect the consumer.

State statutes may also forbid deceptive practices by companies that use the mail as the primary means of advertising or delivering their products. Because the amounts involved in mail-order sales may be small, the consumer may find himself unable to recover the amount lost on the sale. If there is no attempt to defraud on the part of the seller, federal law would not ordinarily give any relief to the party buying by mail-order.

The consumer has the right, in mail-order sales, to know or do certain things. He is entitled, for example:
- to know when he can expect shipment of the merchandise;
- to have the merchandise shipped within 30 days;
- to cancel an order where merchandise is not shipped as promised or within 30 days;
- to be notified of delays and have a free means to reply, such as a postage-free postcard;
- to agree to a new shipping date; and
- to have any payments returned if 30 days elapse and the merchandise is not shipped.

Free sample and charitable mailings

Only two kinds of merchandise can be sent through the mail without the recipient's consent or agreement. The two are free samples, clearly marked as such, and items mailed by charitable organizations seeking contributions. In either case the merchandise can, at the option of the recipient, be regarded as a gift.

Control of Methods of Payment

The methods by which payment may be made or demanded by a creditor on a consumer sale comprise another area in which protective laws are common. Under the laws of some states, if a creditor accepts payment in a form other than cash or check, the creditor takes a chance. For example, if he has to sell the sales contract to a bank or finance company, the consumer can raise various defenses against the bank or finance company to block collection. A check gives the consumer adequate protection since he can stop payment if an item appears defective.

Application of Payments. In addition to payment by cash or check, *application* of the payments to the debt becomes important.

In the past it appeared proper for a creditor to require payment on any item on a continuous charge basis. Payments were to be applied in any way he wished. The result: if a debtor who was three months delinquent on his open credit account sent in a monthly payment, the creditor could apply that payment to the newest monthly charge. He could then hold the debtor in default on the payment due three months ago.

Right of repossession limited

Today, the laws of a number of states provide that in the event of default, any right of repossession by the creditor is limited to the later unpaid items. He must apply the payment to the oldest monthly installment due.

Accelerated and Large Final Payments. Under consumer credit contracts, the final payment in a monthly installment series could at one time have been larger than any of the previous monthly payments. In this way, unscrupulous creditors tried to make the last payment in the series larger than the debtor could pay. The debtor would then be in default on the last payment.

The laws of various states now ban this type of practice. The laws provide that if the final payment is double the average of the earlier scheduled payments, the debtor has a right to refinance the final payment on terms similar to those of the original transaction. The creditor is thus required to accept the refinancing of the final payment and cannot claim a default.

Federal law has similar provisions. Under these, the creditor has to identify any large final payments and provide in the contract for the terms under which the financing of this last payment may be handled.

Acceleration of payments refers to provisions in contracts that give creditors the right to declare an unpaid balance entirely due and payable in the event of default of one installment. In other words, the creditor can say, "All right, Tom, now you owe me the entire balance because you missed the August payment."

*Default must
really have
occurred*

While the creditor still has the right to accelerate payments, most states require that the acceleration be based on a good faith decision by the creditor that a substantial default has actually occurred. This eliminates the "trivial" default that previously could militate against consumers. All earlier payments were lost in many cases because of some minor deviation from the contract. In sales of furniture, appliances, and many other categories of products, the buyer even today should study both the fine and the large print.

Control of Credit Card Sales

Commentators have noted that American society is rapidly becoming "cashless." This means that instead of cash, transactions are increasingly being handled by such things as credit cards, entries in bank records, and so on. Cash appears to be going out of style.

Credit cards may now be used for just about everything, including travel, entertainment, and purchases of furniture and appliances. Certain credit cards can be used for all of the above and for loans, deposits to other accounts, check cashing, and many other bank transactions. Yet controls on the issuance, use, and liabilities of credit cards exist—and necessarily. Users of cards should be aware of these controls for their own protection.

Limits on credit
card issuance
and use

A credit card can no longer be issued to someone who has not applied for it. When the push for cards first began, the bank, store, or other issuer would commonly flood their customer lists. Credit cards were sent to almost anyone. There was little or no control over who actually ended up with the cards, and signed applications for cards were rarely on record. Tremendous problems resulted. The prohibition against issuance without an application resulted.

You lose a credit card. Someone else uses it without your permission. You are not liable for the purchases made on the card beyond the sum of $50.00. Even then, to hold you liable for that amount, the company issuing the card must show that the card was accepted by you, either through your use of the card or your application for it. You must also have been given notice that you might be liable up to $50.00; you must have been given a self-addressed, prestamped form to notify the issuer of the loss or theft of the card; and the issuing company must have provided a method of identifying you as the authorized user of the card—by providing a space on the card for your signature, photograph, fingerprint, or some other form of identification.

To hold you liable for the first $50.00, of course, the improper use of the card by someone else must have occurred before you notified the issuing company of the loss or theft. If the use occurs after you notify the company, you are not liable even for the first $50.00.

To protect yourself against any such claim, notify the issuing company immediately on discovery that your credit card has been lost or stolen. Send the notification by certified mail, return receipt requested. Then you have proof that you sent the notice and that the company in fact received it.

*Credit card
insurance
unnecessary*

In one ripoff scheme of recent years, credit card holders could buy insurance against loss of a card—and subsequent misuse of it by unauthorized persons. Because of the $50 limitation of liability, the insurance is no longer necessary—if it ever was.

Defenses of the Consumer

Because the consumer and the merchant have had unequal bargaining positions, the merchant at one time could include provisions in a contract under which the consumer waived many protections that the law then provided. If the consumer could not understand what he was surrendering, the merchant could point to the "small print" on the reverse side, indicating that the consumer had given up many legal defenses he might have had.

A buyer cannot waive some defenses under recent consumer's statutes. For example, specific provisions permit the buyer to protect himself against the seller or against a financial institution that purchased the installment sales contract from the seller. Where a household appliance is defective, under the consumer protection statutes of many states the buyer has the right to withdraw from the contract. This is the case regardless of what the terms of the contract provide.

State law must be investigated to determine the rights or defenses that a consumer cannot waive. The methods used to defend against a third party who has purchased a sales contract from a seller should also be studied. The state laws are not uniform.

Control of the Sales Contract

*Some "confession
of judgment"
clauses outlawed*

The consumer protection laws are not designed to interfere with the rights of people to enter into contracts with others. But the laws do attempt to override certain terms or clauses in sales contracts that tend to deceive the consumer or place him in an unfortunate position as opposed to the merchant. For example, in some states the "confession of judgment" clauses in sales and other contracts have been outlawed. These clauses attempt to give the creditor the right to obtain an immediate judgment against the debtor in the event of an alleged default in payment. The creditor need not file a formal complaint in court and go through the normal trial procedures.

Under the confession of judgment procedure, the debtor has to come forward and try to have the judgment opened. Such clauses are still valid in some states—or can be valid depending on the circumstances. Where a sales contract contains a confession of judgment clause, the buyer should at least know what it means and make an intelligent decision on signing or not signing.

A court may declare other kinds of sales contracts invalid. For example, a contract involving grossly exorbitant prices would show clearly that the consumer was cheated. On application of the consumer, a court could rule against the seller.

Protecting the right to earn a living

Wages and salaries comprise yet another sensitive area. Both are considered so important to the individual and his family's well-being that state statutes in most states forbid or restrict the attachment of wages for payment of debts. The controlling public policy in such cases is the protection of the right to earn a living. For the same reason, most states hold that no one can assign his wages or direct that they be paid to someone other than his spouse or dependents. In those states that forbid assignment, no creditor can claim a person's wages before they are paid to the employee.

Finally, consumer protection laws sometimes require that sales contracts include certain clauses or fulfill certain conditions. The consumer may not be legally allowed to sign a blank contract. All the terms may have to be filled in completely before the contract is signed and delivered to the consumer. The contract may have to show exactly what the payments are composed of—the amount of the principal payment, the amount of interest, total finance costs, and the annual percentage rate of interest charged. The number of installments, the total amounts due, and the due dates may have to be specified.

Such laws may apply to credit card invoices, charge account invoices, and other credit invoices of any kind.

Control of the Methods of Collection

Notice of lawsuit or collection letter?

Who has not received in the mail an apparent notice that a lawsuit has been filed against him to collect a debt? Close study would probably reveal that the notice was nothing more than a cleverly worded collection letter from a creditor or collection agency. Such billing and collection practices have become the targets of consumer protection laws such as the federal Fair Debt Collection Practices Act of 1977.

Fair Treatment Guaranteed. Enforced by the FTC, the Fair Debt Collection Practices Act is designed to ensure that people are treated fairly by debt collectors. The debts covered are personal, household, and family debts. These could be contracted in purchasing a car, using a charge account, obtaining medical care, and buying literally hundreds of items or services.

Under the Act, the consumer has the right to receive a written notice of the indebtedness within five days after a debt collector contacts him. The notice has to state the amount owed and the name of the creditor. The notice must also contain instructions on what the recipient can do if he or she believes that no debt exists.

Licensing of lenders

Many financial institutions that lend money to the public have to be licensed by the state. The licenses can be suspended or revoked for abuses of credit laws. This is, of course, an excellent way to control the loan business, if properly policed. If you have any information concerning abusive collection or billing activities, or deceptive practices engaged in by such companies, the state agency involved with the licensing of the institution should be notified.

Improper Billing and Collection. Like the collection letter that looks like a court summons, any deceptive method of debt collection is unlawful. To the extent that they are also unreasonable, those methods may involve the invasion of the *right of privacy* and result in legal action by the debtor. Notifying a debtor's employer of a debt or indicating that he is a "deadbeat," using the telephone to harass the debtor and his family, and hiring private investigators to follow, embarrass, and intimidate the debtor—all these are unlawful.

Many other methods of billing and collecting have been attempted. Today the consumer has the right to complain—and may have a right of action against the party employing such practices.

Control of Credit Reporting

Modern economies place great stress on a person's credit rating. The ability to get a job, to purchase what one wants or needs, and to live the good life may, consequently, depend on one's credit rating.

Is it wise to pay cash for everything purchased? The experts say No. More appropriately, young people, when starting out, are advised to borrow a minimum amount of money from a bank or other financial institution. They can pay the loan back as soon as possible. In the meantime they have a credit reference that they can use when applying for credit at a later date.

Until recently, a person applying for credit never knew that he might be investigated by a financial institution or a merchant. He would hear from his neighbors or his employer that someone was asking questions about him at home or at work. But he never knew what was said or what was finally reported to the company requesting the report.

Abuses by credit agencies

Many private agencies were engaged in securing credit information and supplying it, for a fee, to interested persons or companies. Naturally, abuses arose in the system. Primarily, the person who was being investigated did not know what was in his credit report. No one could know for certain whether he was ever denied a job, credit, or something else because of a bad credit rating—even though the credit report may have contained incorrect information.

In an attempt to correct the abuses, Congress enacted the Fair

Credit Reporting Act in 1970. The Act applies only to personal, family, and household credit, and not to business or commercial credit. Nevertheless, it gives the individual some protection with regard to his credit rating.

Right to Proper Information.   When an applicant for a job, insurance, or credit is refused because of a negative credit report, the law requires that he or she be advised of the name and address of the agency supplying the report. If no agency was involved, the person must be given a summary of the information received. The applicant then knows at least the name of the agency or the basis on which his application was refused.

Right of Privacy.   Under federal law, credit bureaus and investigative agencies cannot disclose information about a person's credit to persons who have no lawful use for it. The person being investigated must be advised of the fact that he is being investigated and of his right to know the results of the investigation. No longer can the report in such cases be kept secret from him. On request, a credit agency must also tell the consumer the names and addresses of the persons to whom it gave credit reports during a six-month period before the request. The agency must indicate to what employers such reports were given during a two-year period previous to the request.

Attack on Credit Report for Errors.   Specification of the right to correct errors in a credit report is perhaps the most important provision of the law dealing with fair credit reporting. The information contained in the credit report is ordinarily supplied by friends, neighbors, employers, and others who may or may not know what they are talking about. Thus these reports may be incorrect and even downright false. If not corrected, a bad report may follow an individual and cause him problems for years.

A limited right to require disclosure

At one time the consumer had no way to correct a report. Today he has a limited right to have an agency disclose to him, on request, the information in its files.

When a consumer claims that his report contains incorrect information, the agency must try to determine whether or not the claim is correct. If the claim is verified, the information in the agency's report must be amended. Corrections must be sent to all persons to whom the agency sent reports in the preceding six months and to employers who received reports during the preceding two years.

If the consumer and the agency cannot agree on the accuracy of an item in a report, the consumer has the right to submit a written statement of his position to the agency. The agency must send the statement with the report to anyone requesting information concerning the consumer. Again, the consumer's written statement must be sent to all to whom the agency had sent a report during the previous six months and to employers who received reports during the previous two years.

References to bankruptcy

Finally, the law provides for the elimination of old, stale items that are no longer applicable and which, if allowed to remain, could harm the consumer without justification. For example, a report containing information adverse or harmful to the individual's credit cannot be given out after three months from the date of the report unless it is determined that the report is still accurate. In addition, with certain exceptions dealing with loans, life insurance, and employment applications, any reference to lawsuits involving the consumer must be eliminated after seven years. Any reference to a bankruptcy must be eliminated after 14 years.

An agency must, in brief, maintain up-to-date records of court proceedings and inspect public records on a regular basis to ensure that the information it supplies is accurate.

What does this all mean? Simply this: the person denied a job, credit, or insurance should ask whether the denial was based, in any degree, on an adverse credit report. If it was, the consumer should immediately ask for the name and address of the credit agency supplying the information. The agency should be asked about the general nature of the information furnished—and correction of erroneous items and the elimination of stale items can be demanded. The consumer can then submit a written statement of 100 words or less if the agency will not correct the report as demanded; the agency must send that statement to all who received the report earlier, as outlined above.

The lesson: don't allow your credit rating to suffer because of inaccurate information.

Control of Issued Securities

Most of the consumer protection laws were enacted recently. Others were enacted some time ago. In the latter group are laws governing the issuance of corporate stock and other securities. Some of these merit attention here.

*Those "blue
sky laws"*

State Blue Sky Laws. To protect the public from the sale of worthless stocks or other securities, many states have adopted "blue sky laws." These outlaw fraudulent practices in the issue and sale of stock; require the licensing of brokers, dealers, and others dealing in securities; and mandate the approval of a state securities agency or commission before a stock can be sold to the public. Engaging in fraudulent activities involving corporate securities is a criminal offense under these laws.

Federal Regulation. In addition to the state laws, federal law recognized the need for regulation of the securities field as early as 1933. While the state laws deal only with transactions within a state, the Federal Securities Act of 1933 was adopted to control the interstate sale of, or dealing in, corporate stocks and bonds.

*To make an
intelligent
decision . . .*

The federal Act requires the filing and registering of a *prospectus,* a written statement about a stock to be issued, the company and its financial situation, and the company's officers and directors. Government regulations specify what information is to be included in the prospectus; serious penalties are imposed for violations of the requirements. A detailed review of these regulations is outside the scope of this book. But, essentially, they are intended to prevent anyone from selling or dealing in corporate securities, by use of the mails or otherwise, in interstate commerce without full disclosure of all information that an investor would need to make an intelligent decision to invest. This information is to be supplied in the prospectus.

There are some limitations on the applicability of the federal securities laws. These have to do with the number of shares to be issued, the number of persons who are offered the stock, and the total assets of the company involved. The limitations may eliminate a particular stock offering from the requirements of the federal laws. But in most large stock offerings federal registration is required.

Protection against the issuance of worthless securities was one thing; but it became evident that the public also needed protection against abuses by stock exchanges and certain stock brokers. In 1934 Congress passed the Federal Securities Exchange Act. Under that law, it became unlawful for any broker, dealer, or stock exchange to use the mails or any means of communication to effect any security transaction without proper registration of the particular stock exchange with the Securities and Exchange Commission.

The Act permits some exemptions, and certain activities are outlawed. The latter include fraudulent rumors to affect the price of a stock, continuous trading in a particular stock to create the impression of great activity and boost the stock's price, and similar practices. Restrictions on speculation in stock are also imposed. The Federal Reserve Board has the right to establish *margin requirements*—the extent to which money can be borrowed to finance stock transactions and the percentage that the total amount borrowed must bear to the total price. Control of the use of "inside information," which restricts insiders from making a profit on information that is not given to the public, is also mandated.

Full disclosure is not a guarantee of performance

These restrictions have been imposed on corporations, stock exchanges, and dealers. They also affect the consumer's rights. The consumer can obtain full disclosure of all information on a particular stock, bond, or other security so as to make an intelligent decision regarding investment. The law, of course, was not designed to guarantee the performance of any stock.

Control of Mutual Funds. The average investor is not in a position to investigate the past performances of corporations to determine whether to purchase their stocks. For that reason, mutual funds have stirred widespread interest among small investors. In recent years, the large institutional investors such as banks, trust companies, pension plans, and labor unions have also turned to mutual funds in increasing numbers.

The attraction of mutual funds lies in the fact that investment decisions are made for the investor by someone with more sophisticated knowledge of the stock market. Thus the risk of loss is spread over a broad range of investments. For example, the typical mutual fund portfolio includes stocks and bonds of utility companies, insurance companies, transportation companies, and manufacturing companies, among others. The investor purchases shares in the mutual fund itself. The fund then uses that money to purchase shares in the entire wide range of companies selected for investment.

Since mutual funds use investment counselors, it has sometimes appeared as if the fees charged by the counselors were excessive in comparison to the services rendered. The Investment Company Act Amendments of 1970 were designed to place restrictions on charges to investors for these services.

"Front loading" criticized

Another feature of mutual fund purchasing that aroused some criticism was the "front load." A consumer might agree to purchase mutual funds over a period of time, paying in annual or monthly installments. The funds with "front loads" would then take all commissions and other charges out of the front or early payments. If the investor cancelled out, or withdrew from the fund before completing his longterm purchase plan, he would have lost the entire amount paid as commissions or charges at the outset.

The 50 per cent limit

Under the present law, mutual funds cannot charge more than 50 per cent of the total charges and commissions against payments made by an investor in his first year in the fund. If the fund charges the maximum 50 per cent allowed by law in the first year, the investor has a graduated right of rescission. If he rescinds the contract within

45 days after notification of the charges, he can get back the value of his account and all amounts charged to its administration.

Regulation and control of the entire securities field will undoubtedly continue. The complex nature of the U.S. economy demands such controls. But investors and consumers should insist on full disclosure of the facts in all stock transactions. Anyone receiving false or misleading information should complain about it to the broker or company issuing the stock. If no action results, the securities agency or commission in the particular state will investigate the complaint. A lawyer can help if court action becomes necessary to recover a loss.

Stock markets involve risks. The risks make investing an exciting pastime. The laws seek only to eliminate fraud and misrepresentation.

Control of Insurance Companies. Insurance companies come under regulation in all 50 states. By statute, insurance company regulation is accomplished through control of their financing, the maintenance of reserves of money to meet policy owners' claims, control of companies incorporated in other states, and control of the performance of insurers within the state. Control and regulation are handled through state insurance departments.

Licensing of insurance brokers, agents

Statutes also provide for control over insurance agents and brokers in the advertising and soliciting of policies. Agents and brokers have to be licensed. Deceptive practices and other practices that may cause losses to the consumer, such as failure of a broker or agent to forward policy owners' premiums to the company, are prohibited. In some instances, these may be declared criminal activities.

Fraudulent insurance activity should be reported to state agencies. The many honest agents and brokers will not be affected, but will be able to maintain the professionalism of their field and organizations.

Control of Insurance Settlement and Claim Procedures. The test of a really good insurance company—whatever its field of specialization—is the method by which it handles claims and settlements. Advertising blurbs may have stated that the company pays all claims promptly and without a lot of red tape. In the event of a loss, the company's real character emerges.

Fortunately, the vast majority of insurance companies realize their responsibilities. They are reasonable and fair in their claims procedures. The number of fraudulent claims presented to insurance companies every year makes caution in the settlement of claims a must; but sometimes an overabundance of caution works to the disadvantage of the policy owner.

Liability may exceed policy coverage

In recent years the law has developed methods by which it forces companies to be fair. In effect, the law holds insurance companies liable to the policyholder for more than the coverage of the policy.

How is this done? Normally, the company's liability under any policy is strictly set at the limits specified in the policy. If an automobile policy has liability limits of $10,000 for each person injured, the company's liability to pay a claim against the policyholder for one person's injury cannot exceed $10,000. But suppose the injury is very serious. Suppose the company nevertheless refuses to settle a claim within the $10,000 limit despite the willingness of the injured person to settle.

In this case the policyholder may be sued and forced to go to trial. If a judgment is secured against him for more than the $10,000 coverage, he may be able to hold his insurance company liable for the entire amount of the judgment. But the defendant has to establish that the company's refusal to settle was unreasonable under the circumstances and opened the door to the greater judgment eventually awarded.

In another case a company, under a liability policy, refuses to defend a policyholder because the claim is not protected by the policy. The policyholder then has to hire a lawyer and defend himself. Whatever the result of the lawsuit, if it can be established that the company's refusal to defend was fraudulent or unreasonable, the policyholder can sue the company and recover the amount of any judgment plus any other loss suffered, including lawyer's fees. This is true even if the total amount exceeds the limits of coverage under the policy.

"Adjusting"
insurance claims

Claims under insurance policies are investigated by adjusters. These persons work directly for insurance companies or as independent claims adjusters retained on contract by the companies to handle certain types of cases. In rare cases an adjuster does such a poor job investigating a claim, or treats the person making the claim so shabbily, that the individual suffers frustration and even physical or emotional injury. In a 1970s court case, a widow sustained the loss of her home by fire. Because the company, through its adjuster, failed to investigate the loss properly, the company offered the widow only a fraction of the real value of the loss. The widow brought suit for the value of her home and for the physical and emotional injuries that she had suffered because of the company's unreasonable conduct. In a landmark decision, the court allowed a judgment in the total amount of the claim.

Consumers can and should continue to exert efforts to make the law work for them and to assert and win their claims. While faced with many fraudulent claims, insurance companies must accord to the valid claim the law's full right and protection.

The Poor as Consumers. Recent legislation enacted by Congress and some states, and backed by court decisions, has attempted to make certain that the law does not "favor the rich." Court decisions have sought to place the poor, insofar as their rights are concerned, in the same relative position as those better able to pay for legal advice.

Assistance to the poor has taken many forms. For example, the Supreme Court has decided that an attorney must be appointed for a poor or indigent defendant unable to pay for his own counsel. Even in less serious cases, including misdemeanors that may call for jail sentences, the court has to appoint an attorney for the poor defendant. This is a constitutional right.

The right to have
legal counsel

A 1963 Supreme Court case underscored the right of every defendant to have legal counsel. In *Gideon* v. *Wainwright,* the Supreme

Court reversed the decision of a Florida court because of the court's failure to provide counsel for a poor defendant. The decision holds the various states to the requirements set down in the Sixth Amendment regarding the right to defense counsel. The case became famous because the defendant, Clarence Gideon, wrote personally to the Supreme Court when the Florida court refused both to allow him to defend himself and to appoint counsel for him. On trial for burglary, Gideon was later acquitted.

Other types of protection for the poor involve the requirement of a public hearing before welfare payments can be discontinued, the requirement of counsel in divorce cases where the complaining spouse cannot afford a lawyer, and the elimination of the requirement of a jail sentence if the defendant cannot pay a fine. At one time the poor person faced with a "$60 or 60 days" judgment would have found himself in jail if he could not produce the $60. The person with funds would go free. Thus the constitutional rights of the poor were violated in such cases.

Other examples of how the law attempts to give equal protection to the poor might be cited. Public service corporations have been created to provide legal services for the poor. Neighborhood Legal Services agencies have been funded by federal and state grants for this purpose. Legal Aid Societies and Public Defender Associations have sought to provide adequate counsel for the poor, to educate the public in the need for such protection, and to seek continuing support from the government. Thus the fact that one person has less money than the next will not usually affect the right to protection. Local bar associations provide the names of lawyers and agencies that can help the needy.

Enforcement of the Rights of the Consumer

*The consumer
must cooperate*

Laws protecting the rights of the consumer have developed rapidly. But the expanded concepts of rights mean little if the consumer cannot or will not enforce those rights. A person who buys a small item costing little may hesitate to enter a complaint or bring suit because of the cost involved. To remedy this situation, the law has placed the responsibility for enforcement with various agencies and individuals.

The laws of the various states give the state attorneys general, or the administrators of the state consumer protection agencies, the power to bring actions against individuals or groups for fraudulent or deceptive practices in consumer transactions. Such an action may be brought on behalf of an individual or a group of consumers. The goal is usually to obtain cancellation of contracts and refunds of money lost because of the fraud or deception. In addition, the laws of many states permit suits for injunctions to provide legal prohibitions against the continued conduct of business by particular individuals or companies.

The consumer himself has the right to bring a lawsuit that may involve refunds and even penalties against an offending merchant. In some instances, the consumer can bring a class action suit—a lawsuit on behalf of himself and all members of the particular group of consumers who have suffered similar losses.

Local consumer protection agencies and state attorneys general can help in determining exactly what assistance may be expected in pressing a complaint.

"The squeaky wheel" principle

"The squeaky wheel gets the grease." That maxim applies in the field of consumer rights as in other fields. Reports of false advertising claims, mislabeling of products, and other deceptive practices should go to the FTC, which has both regional and field offices throughout the United States. The offices are listed under "Federal Trade Commission" in telephone directories. The FTC headquarters is located at 6th Street and Pennsylvania Avenue, N.W., Washington, D.C. 20580.

If you have been victimized by medical quacks, health claims, or mislabeled foods, drugs, or cosmetics, contact the Food and Drug Administration, listed in major telephone directories under "United States, Department of Health and Human Services." Or you can contact the FDA at its headquarters office at 5600 Fishers Lane, Rockville, Maryland 20852.

If meat and poultry products are involved in your complaint, contact the local office of the U.S. Department of Agriculture.

If the problem centers on the lack of proper sanitation of a restaurant or other business, contact your local health agency.

If you suspect that illegal sales or distribution of drugs or narcotics, such as stimulants, depressants or hallucinogens, are taking place, contact the local office of the United States Department of Justice, Drug Enforcement Section.

Help is usually available

To stop the receipt of unwanted mail, contact your local post office.

To report suspected violations of the Truth in Lending laws, contact the local Federal Reserve Board office. You will be directed to the proper agency to which you should complain.

The consumer has another remedy. He can contact a lawyer to find out what he, as an individual, can do to make the legal maxim, "caveat vendor"—"let the seller beware"—take on added meaning.

ENVIRONMENTAL PROTECTION: NO MAN IS AN ISLAND

As recently as the middle 1960s, it would have been unthinkable to claim that a large industrial plant should be told to bank its furnaces because it was poisoning the atmosphere, or because of the amount of smoke boiling from its smokestacks. The need for a free and prosperous industrial society was held to be paramount. Little real thought was given to the problems of the environment—or to the pollution caused by wastes, smoke, noise, and other pollutants.

WHERE TO GO FOR HELP
ON A CONSUMER PROBLEM[1]

Hundreds of agencies and organizations across the country provide help on consumer complaints and problems. Some are local, some statewide. Some, including those listed below with their areas of specialization, are nationwide.

Bureau of Consumer Protection, Federal Trade Commission, Washington, D.C. 20580. Deceptive advertising, illegal sales tactics, violations of the Truth in Lending law, and a host of other consumer frauds, deceptions, unfair sales, and trade practices.

Center for Science in the Public Interest, 1755 S Street N.W., Washington, D.C. 20009. Food and health safety, energy conservation, and good nutrition through publications and participation in government proceedings.

Center for the Study of Responsive Law, P.O. Box 19367, Washington, D.C. 20036. From mental health to aviation to coal mining.

Common Cause, 2030 M Street N.W., Washington, D.C. 20036. "Structure and process" issues to improve function and accountability of government. Also, in the early 1980s, tax reform, energy policy, consumer and environmental protection.

Congress Watch, 133 C Street S.E., Washington, D.C. 20003. Voting records, committee performance, and responsiveness by senators and representatives to their constituents and to the public generally.

Consumer Federation of America, Suite 406, 1012 14th Street N.W., Washington, D.C. 20005. Helps groups organize and act, testifies and lobbies on any proposed consumer legislation, and publicizes important issues.

Consumers Opposed to Inflation in the Necessities (COIN), Suite 413, 2000 P Street N.W., Washington, D.C. 20036. Fights inflation in food, energy, health, and housing.

Consumers Union, 256 Washington Street, Mount Vernon, New York, 10550. Publishes *Consumer Reports* magazine on products ranging from cars to contraceptives——for safety, convenience, effectiveness. Also participates in lawsuits on behalf of consumers.

Corporate Accountability Research Group, 1346 Connecticut Avenue N.W., Washington, D.C. 20036. Contests corporate power, violation of antitrust laws, seeks to make corporations accountable to shareowners and the public.

Council of Better Business Bureaus, 1150 17th Street N.W., Washington, D.C. 20036. Headquarters of the well-known Better Business Bureaus. Provides local BBB contacts.

Disability Rights Center, 1346 Connecticut Avenue N.W., Washington, D.C. 20036. Rights of the disabled through legal action and monitoring of federal actions.

Energy Action, 1523 L Street N.W., Washington, D.C. 20005. Watches federal energy legislation and publishes a newsletter.

Office of Consumer Affairs, 626 Reporters Building, Washington, D.C. 20201. Government agency concerned with all kinds of consumer problems, consumer education, and legislation.

Public Citizen Litigation Group, 7th Floor, 2000 P Street N.W., Washington, D.C. 20036. Lawsuits against corporations, government agencies on behalf of the public.

A book and a court case

That situation changed, to some extent at least, because of a book and a court case. The book was *Silent Spring* by Rachel Carson. Published in 1962, *Silent Spring* brought a powerful indictment against Americans' disregard of their country's ecology. The book found special fault with the wholesale use of pesticides, in particular DDT. The author painted a grim picture of an American earth denuded of much of its wildlife, of fields and streams poisoned by chemicals, of technology running destructively rampant.

In the court case, decided in 1965, a major utility was told to consider the environment when drawing up plans for a new plant. The Federal Power Commission had granted New York's Consolidated Edison Company a license to build the plant at Storm King Mountain. An appeals court ordered a reversal, noting that the company's plans had to "include as a basic concern the preservation of natural beauty and of national historic shrines."

It is recognized today that the impact of pollution on the environment directly affects each citizen at every moment of his life. If the air is polluted, if a next door neighbor's air conditioner keeps someone awake at night, if the property owner living on a higher street dumps water that erodes others' soil, everyone is eventually affected. Everyone has cause for real concern.

Young people first recognized the need for regulation and protection of the environment. They acknowledged first that the "quality of life" may be more important than the economics of a given situation. As the environment became a cause, small communities began to forbid the erection of large shopping centers within their boundaries. The shopping centers would have resulted in increased tax revenues, but they would also have had an adverse effect on the quality of life in the community. Changes in community planning, changes in zoning regulations, and many other changes indicated that the environment was receiving solid consideration. Principles were turned into law.

Environmentally, everyone is a "consumer"

Each individual is a "consumer" of his environment. Everyone uses it to bring quality into his life. As a consumer, each citizen has the right to an environment that is clean, enjoyable, and appropriate to the manner in which he lives. The resident of a congested city cannot, of course, expect that he could live in the same environment as someone living on a farm. Certain restrictions are imposed by society; but with those restrictions, consumers have a right to expect protection of their environments.

The federal Environmental Protection Agency (EPA) was formed in 1970 to give concrete form to many basic environmental concerns. The Agency has acted as a clearinghouse and headquarters for the national effort to ensure pure water and clean air. The Agency also works with state environmental commissions to enforce a long list of congressional mandates relating to ecology and the environment.

Control of Groundspace and Airspace

Unless given the right by the landowner, it is unlawful for someone to mine for coal or dig for oil under another's land. It is also unlawful for someone to build a house that projects over another's property line. A person owns to the center of the earth under his own property and up to the heavens—unless these rights have been conveyed away.

On airplanes
and hens

The right of flight over the land of another does exist. But the flight may not interfere with the proper use of the land or do damage to the structures on the land. This principle has led to many cases involving the condemnation or "taking" of property near airports, where the descent paths of landing planes bring planes so close to the ground that considerable noise pollution results. Farmers have complained that airplane noise may interfere with hens laying eggs, or cause injury to skittish livestock, or produce vibration damage in buildings. Noise may, in effect, destroy an owner's enjoyment of his property.

The courts have held airports and others liable in damages for such noise pollution and for "taking" the property from the owners in such cases.

Weather studies have brought other problems. Hurricane and tornado investigations, seeding clouds to produce rain, and other attempts at scientific control of the weather have been said to be altering normal weather patterns. The effects on the environment will undoubtedly be accompanied by problems of damage to the owners of land. In fact, many people believe that severe storms or drought may today rank as one result of tampering with the weather.

Control of Water Rights

American history suggests that the availability of clear, unpolluted water has immense environmental importance. The development of the West depended heavily on the availability of water. In consequence, laws were developed early to protect the sources and supply of water against waste pollution or appropriation by some persons to the exclusion of others.

The need for guaranteed supplies of water continues in many parts of the country. The continuing disputes over the Colorado River give evidence of deep concern.

*How water
practices and
regulations differ*

Water practices and regulations may differ depending on need. The person living on a lake or river usually has the right to use the water reasonably for his needs. But the person owning property

370 THE LEGAL GUIDE

above another on a river may interfere with the quality of the water or the quantity of flow, causing damage to the lower owner's property. In this case the lower owner may have the right to bring legal action for damages against the higher owner. Because of a lack of water, some states have permitted the use of water for irrigation or for watering cattle even though that use may affect others' enjoyment of the water supply.

The water pollution problem has been attacked by many state authorities. For example, dumping waste materials into waterways is restricted, as in voluntary spillage of oil from tankers off the seashore. Various federal statutes deal with this problem. The laws uniformly try to limit the negative effects of pollution on the water supply, on public and private beaches, on marine life, and on other areas of the environment.

Related problems involve the disposal of waste materials. Man today generates tremendous amounts of waste—throw-away containers, rubber and plastic materials, and other products. Laws have been passed to encourage recycling of such wastes and their reprocessing into other useful materials. Laws have restricted the use of nonreturnable containers. They have also encouraged and funded local and state pilot projects dealing with waste disposal, sanitary land fills, and treatment facilities under the guidance of the Department of Health and Human Services.

Pollution problems should normally be brought to the attention of local pollution control agencies.

Private Nuisance—The Neighbor's Air Conditioner

One person's free use of his land cannot, today, unreasonably interfere with another person's possession and enjoyment of his or her property. If it does interfere, a private nuisance may result.

Physical trespass
through
excavation

Note a typical example. If, while excavation is under way on adjoining property, an explosion occurs, throwing rocks and soil onto your land, a physical trespass may have occurred for which you can recover damages. Continuation of the activity would constitute a *pri-*

vate nuisance that you can stop by bringing suit for an injunction to prevent further blasting—and for any money damages you may have incurred.

The trespass does not have to be a physical one, however. A nuisance can take the form of any prejudicial use of property. Your neighbor's air conditioner that interferes with your sleep at night, or his high-fidelity record system which plays into the wee hours of the morning, are cases in point. A nuisance may also involve the more serious problem of smoke, smells, or fumes from industrial plants that interfere with your use and enjoyment of your property.

*Annoyance may
not constitute
damage*

The mere fact that you are annoyed by someone else's use of his property is not enough to create a personal, private nuisance. The law looks for damage to your property or your enjoyment of life, and balances that against the need to continue the problem activity for social or economic reasons. Thus, while you might be annoyed by smoke from the utility plant nearby, unless the amount of smoke is unreasonable, and the cost of abating the smoke is minimal, a balancing of interests may result in your inability to stop the smoke condition.

Since interest in environmental protection has increased tremendously in recent years, various governmental agencies have been given the authority to direct plant shut-downs because of extreme pollution of the atmosphere. Where private suits are brought against such companies, the courts may award damages while leaving the question of shut-down or continued operation to the local or other governmental agencies having specific authority. An appeal from a court decision is always possible, as is an appeal from an agency's ruling.

Often, an offending company can reduce the amount of interference or pollution without totally stopping operations. Where this is possible, a workable solution can usually be found. Where individuals have suffered physical damage to person or property, a lawyer should be consulted regarding the possibility of bringing suit.

Public Nuisance

A *public nuisance* involves harm done to the general public as opposed to an individual person. The general public in an entire area is affected; the usual remedy will be an injunction and an award of damages. A generally accepted condition for a public nuisance is that the public health, safety, or morals suffer damage. Sewage disposal areas that emit foul odors, disposal of industrial wastes in rivers, lakes, and streams, and similar activities have all been found to be public nuisances.

*To reduce
pollution by auto
and truck
engines . . .*

Recognizing the need for controls over public nuisances, Congress has enacted legislation such as the Clean Air Act and the National Motor Vehicles Emissions Standards Act. The aim has been to reduce pollution by auto and truck engines. In response, the automobile industry has moved toward production of an automobile engine that is substantially pollution-free. In addition, standards have been adopted with respect to various types of emissions, techniques, and devices to control emissions. The Environment Protection Agency is charged with general overall review and control of the program.

The EPA has not, for the most part, acted ruthlessly. For example, it has required auto manufacturers to install antipollution devices in cars. But it has delayed implementation of some standards to give the manufacturers more time for research and development.

State laws have also been enacted to control nuisances such as air pollution. Both state and local agencies are involved in air pollution control. A common indication of this concern is the inclusion of air quality reports in the weather forecasts distributed by the National Weather Service and by private forecasting services.

Control of the Right of Land Support

Because all land depends on adjoining land for support, the law requires that no excavation on neighboring land can cause a lot to subside or fall away from its natural position. The neighbor has to brace and support the excavation to prevent damage to the lot in its natural state. The neighbor will be liable for any damage, in most states, even though he has done everything possible to prevent subsidence or cave-ins.

A different rule may apply where a building stands on Lot A. This land is not regarded as being in its natural state. In order to hold a neighbor, owner of Lot B, liable if Lot A subsides, it must be established that the neighbor performed the excavation negligently.

Notice of excavation

Some states and local municipalities require that an adjoining landowner receive notice that an excavation will be begun on the property and that possible subsidence may result. This gives the property owner an opportunity to try to protect his property from damage. Where soil conditions are such that a landslide may carry away land, the excavator is required to take practical precautions. In urban areas, an excavator customarily conducts core boring tests, using soil experts, to determine whether a danger of subsidence exists before starting an excavation. Failure to do this can easily be found to be negligence, making the excavator liable for damage to the adjoining property.

Control of Natural Conditions on Land

Formerly, a landowner was not required to do anything with his land in terms of its effects on his neighbors so long as it remained in its natural state. For example, land on which a natural pond served as a breeding ground for mosquitos did not have to be filled in or drained.

Defenses against
weeds, bugs,
fire, infection

Under current law, many states and municipalities require that grass and weeds be cut, that wet areas where bugs, flies, and mosquitos can breed be filled in, and that the hazards of infection and fire be reduced. Not uncommonly, the owner of an unimproved lot will receive a notice from the local municipality directing that he cut the weeds, trim the trees, or fill in water holes. The reason may be that rodents or insects breed there, or that dandelion pollen is blowing onto the lawns of neighbors.

These new requirements have come about because of changes in public policies. The owner of property now has certain responsibilities to his neighbors even though his property is not improved, or built upon.

A property owner should make every attempt to "get along" with his neighbors. But he should insist on what is rightfully his.

Control of Noise

Noise as a pollutant? Yes! With the rise of commercial aviation, and the arrival of "jumbo jets" and supersonic transports, noise pollution has become a significant concern of federal and state policy makers. Noise is now considered a type of interference with the environment that requires controls.

The Federal Aviation Act attempts to control noise pollution by aircraft. Also, states have regulations on the noise from vehicles such as autos and motorcycles. Studies of the effects of noise on property values and the enjoyment of life are continuing under federal auspices. Undoubtedly, the entire issue of noise pollution will continue to influence the laws to be passed in the future.

The Right of the Consumer to Sue

Harm and the right to sue

Federal laws allow suits by private parties in federal courts to stop violations of federal legislation against air pollution. Suits are permitted even where the individual cannot show a particular harm to himself that differs from the harm done to any other member of the public.

In addition, various states have brought suits against other states, or citizens of other states, to end pollution in specific cases. The use of satellites to photograph pollution of waterways has proved effective in locating sources of pollution.

The citizen who wants to take an active role in the protection of his environment should attend meetings of the local zoning board. He can then be sure that the community in which he lives will develop as it should. Complaints can be directed to the state or federal environmental protection offices.

PROTECTION AGAINST PERSONAL INJURY
OR PROPERTY DAMAGE

The entire subject of consumer protection presumes that a fundamental right of the consumer is to be free from bodily injury or property damage resulting from defects in manufactured products. The rapidly expanding field of law known as "product liability" has to do with the liability of a manufacturer or dealer for injury or damage caused by defective products. The subject has been discussed in Chapter 7 from the point of view of insurance. It requires some additional analysis from the consumer-protection aspect.

Liability for
defective products

A manufacturer or seller can be held liable for a defective product in various ways.

Breach of Express and Implied Warranty

A person selling a product may give a form of guarantee that the goods will be of a certain kind, or operate in a certain way, or obtain certain results. He may advertise his goods in such a way as to lead the consumer to believe that the product will function as advertised. For example, where a merchant advertises a properly insulated electric motor, and the consumer receives electric shocks when using the motor, the merchant has breached his express warranty of proper insulation.

Responsibility for the quality of the product may be binding on the seller even though the implied warranty or guarantee came from the manufacturer. A parallel case would be the statements made on the label on a can of food.

Implied and express warranties: differences

An *implied warranty,* as opposed to an express warranty, is not made expressly. Rather, the law infers that it has been made by reason of the sale. The law reads the warranty into the sale. A merchant, in selling a product, implicitly warrants that it is fit for normal use and will pass freely in the marketplace. The merchant may regularly deal in soda pop. He warrants that the soda pop he sells is fit for normal use—consumption by the consumer. If a foreign body is found in the soda, or if the bottle explodes, causing injury to the consumer, a breach of the implied warranty of fitness for normal use can be presumed.

To avoid any question of liability for breach of an implied warranty, a merchant normally gives an *express warranty.* The warranty includes the stipulation that no implied warranties are made. However, unless the disclaimer of implied warranties is phrased precisely as required by state law, the disclaimer may not be valid and the consumer may retain his right to claim breach of implied warranty.

At one time, only the direct buyer could sue the direct seller for a breach of implied warranty. A husband who purchased an item that injured his wife would not be able to recover damages. Today, however, most states permit members of the buyer's family, his household, and certain other persons not directly involved in the sale to sue for breach of warranty, particularly where food, beverages, or drugs are concerned.

By statute in many states, the requirement of a direct sales relationship between seller and the person injured or damaged has been abolished—to the extent that a suit for breach of warranty can be brought by members of the buyer's family, his household, and guests.

A wife could recover for the defect in the product bought by her husband. So could other members of the family and guests on the premises, if they were injured. Recent trends in the law also indicate that the requirement of a direct sales relationship between the seller and the owner of damaged property is no longer necessary to make the seller liable for the property damage.

Limits on the right to sue for economic injury

Court cases appear to have placed definite limits on the consumer's rights to sue for damages—at least where economic injury is involved. In one 1977 case, *Illinois Brick Co.* v. *Illinois,* the Supreme Court held that a manufacturer could not be sued for price-fixing by anyone but the direct purchaser or purchasers. The consumer who bought a product from a middleman—a plumber, retailer, or other source—could not "go over the middleman's head" and sue the manufacturer directly.

By the early 1980s Congress had begun work on bills that would restore the consumer's right to sue manufacturers directly. The bills were viewed as aspects of the federal government's continuing antitrust activities. The consumer, it was reasoned, usually paid higher prices that covered artificially "fixed" product costs. The middleman then escaped unharmed. If the consumer could not sue, manufacturers might fix prices with impunity.

Strict Liability for Harm Caused by a Product

Manufacturer and dealer liable for defective products

In many states, the law permits a purchaser, consumer, bystander, or anyone else who is injured by a defective product to bring an action against the manufacturer or dealer of the product. In other words, once a defective or dangerous product causes harm, the manufacturer, wholesaler, or dealer has liability for any harm done. It does not matter that negligence may not be shown, or that a component part secured from another manufacturer was the defective part.

The liability rule is strictly enforced if the product was defective and caused injury.

An example will show how this strict liability concept works. If the blade on a rotary mower breaks off, flies across the yard, and strikes a neighbor or breaks his large picture window, he may have a good claim against the manufacturer and seller of the mower. He need not show that the manufacturer or seller was negligent in the making of the mower. Nor does it matter that he did not buy the mower.

This strict liability protection applies also to people who are injured by defective leased property. Recent court decisions hold that all forms of rental equipment, such as automobiles, trucks, power tools, and gardening equipment, are subject to the strict liability rules. Thus if a neighbor is helping you load a rental truck and is injured when the hydraulic tailgate malfunctions, he may have a right of action against the truck rental company and the manufacturer of the truck. He may not have to establish negligence or breach of warranty.

A disclaimer of warranty made by a manufacturer on specific goods has no effect on the right of the injured person to sue on the basis of strict liability. While the disclaimer may eliminate certain warranties from the sale, it has no effect in the strict liability case.

Liability for Negligence

The consumer may also sue the dealer or manufacturer for negligence—for failing to exercise due care in the preparation, manufacture, instructions, or other aspects of an item or product. Warnings have to be given regarding dangerous characteristics. Where the manufacturer should have understood that if he was negligent a person or class of persons would have been injured, then he may be held liable for negligence.

Safety regulations for consumers

Safety regulations have been drawn up for consumers in certain instances. Legislation involving safety features on automobiles—on seat belts, bumpers that absorb impact without damage, and so on—furnishes examples of safety regulations issued by governmental agencies that have the force of law. Violations of these safety regulations may be evidence of negligence. Without more proof, they may entitle the consumer or other person to recover for personal injury or property damage resulting from the safety violation.

Often a manufacturer will sell a product in a disassembled state and give instructions for its assembly and proper use. If the consumer puts the item together in accordance with the instructions and suffers an injury because of a malfunction, liability may be claimed for negligent instructions. If the consumer, using the product as directed, suffers injury or property damage, he may be able to recover for negligent instructions regarding use.

In summary, a consumer or other person injured by a defective product that was purchased from a manufacturer, wholesaler, or retailer may have a right to sue for property damage or personal injuries. Three theories underlie that right: the strict liability theory that is by far the easiest insofar as proof is concerned; the theory of breach of warranty, if the party injured falls within the appropriate group that, under local law, has the right to sue for breach of warranty; and the theory of negligence, if proof of negligence can be established.

Time limits may be imposed by local law on claims against manufacturers or dealers. These limits have to be met and satisfied. A lawyer can help a claimant determine the best procedures by which to enforce specific rights.

THE ULTIMATE PROTECTION: BANKRUPTCY AND ALTERNATIVES

The harried consumer has one other means of protecting himself. When his indebtedness gets out of control, he can declare bankruptcy. Alternatively, he can work out a personal repayment plan.

The uniform bankruptcy laws

Article 1 of the U.S. Constitution empowers Congress to enact uniform bankruptcy laws. In 1978, acting under that power, Congress passed the Bankruptcy Reform Act that became effective October 1, 1979. The bankruptcy laws are adjudicated by federal judges. Under the laws, debtors have a choice between two forms of voluntary bankruptcy: Chapter 7 and Chapter 13, both parts of the Bankruptcy Reform Act.

Chapter 7: "Straight Bankruptcy"

Under Chapter 7, a debtor declares what is called "straight bankruptcy," or liquidation. A portion of his assets is converted into cash that his creditors share. The debtor then receives a discharge that relieves him of further obligations.

The federal Bankruptcy Act allows the debtor to retain some of his assets. In fact, the Act for the first time lists the types of assets that would be exempt. They include:

—A $7,500 interest in a home and/or burial plot ($15,000 for a married couple). What if you don't own a home or burial plot? Federal law says you still can use the $7,500 exemption. In fact, you can add $400 to it and claim $7,900 worth of additional exemptions in any kind of property. Even if you do have a house and burial plot worth $7,500, you can claim $400 worth of extra exemptions in other property. You can use this exemption, too, to keep a refund on income taxes that you paid before the year you file bankruptcy.

—A $1,200 interest in *one* car or other motor vehicle.

—Any items worth up to $200 *each* in these categories: household goods and furnishings, clothing, appliances, books, animals, crops, or musical instruments.

—$500 in jewelry.

—$750 worth of books or tools that you need for your work.

—A life insurance policy.

—Health items, such as a hearing aid, that were prescribed for you.

—Social Security and veteran's benefits.

—Unemployment insurance proceeds.

—Pension and profit sharing plans.

Bankruptcy not
the total solution

Straight bankruptcy cannot, of course, solve all the problems facing an individual or family with an intolerable load of debt. But it can give you a new lease on life. The new lease will last only six years—no one can file again to have his debts discharged until six years have elapsed.

The federal bankruptcy laws provide that discharged debts must have been contracted in good faith. But it is often impossible to say which have been contracted in good faith and which in bad. It should also be noted that some states have in effect restricted the types and values of the assets that the debtor can exempt when declaring straight bankruptcy. In these states, the feeling is that the federal laws are too generous.

Chapter 13: Alternative Approaches

Chapter 13 of the Bankruptcy Reform Act offers alternatives that many persons view as superior to straight bankruptcy. Using Chapter 13, the debtor can rearrange his debt load so as to emerge with a more reasonable credit rating than he would have under straight bankruptcy.

Features of a
Chapter 13
repayment plan

Chapter 13 makes possible a budgetary plan. Called a "wage earner's plan," Chapter 13 actually applies to anyone whose principal source of income is derived from a salary, wages, or commissions. Filing under Chapter 13, the debtor is required to work out a repayment plan including the following features:

—A listing of all normal expenses each month.

—A compilation of total debts.

—Addition of 10 per cent to the debts to cover court costs.

—Dividing the total by 36 to ascertain what would be owing if the total were spread over 36 months.

—Adding in the monthly installments on all debts not covered in the second item above.

—Adding to the total debts normal monthly living expenses.

—Calling all creditors and telling them about the plan—and obtaining verbal agreements to the plan from most of the unsecured creditors or *one* secured creditor.

The debtor can then file. Before the Reform Act, a debtor had to obtain approval of a repayment plan from a majority of his creditors. Because most creditors, naturally, wanted 100 per cent repayment— or as close as possible to 100 per cent—Chapter 13 was seldom used before 1979. Today, any plan is acceptable if it meets two conditions: the creditors have to receive at least as much in payments as they would in a straight bankruptcy after exemptions, and the plan has to represent a good faith effort by a debtor.

What valuations are placed on a debtor's possessions? A "fair market value" standard applies. That means a Chapter 13 plan allows the debtor to pay off unsecured installment debts at low rates, without interest. Reduced payments may also be made on secured debts other than home mortgages.

15 THE GREAT AMERICAN NOVEL AND THE BETTER MOUSETRAP

The classic cartoon shows two gentlemen sitting outside a patent office. Each holds on his lap an identical strange-looking package. Each stares at the other with suspicion.

The cartoon symbolizes one aspect of American inventiveness and the problems involved in protecting that inventiveness against use by others. Writing the great American novel or building a better mousetrap takes much more than developing an idea and then transforming that idea into substance. Fortunately, the private enterprise system has created an atmosphere in which inventiveness has flourished. American-made products are copied, purchased, and utilized everywhere. The law has a definite place in the protection of the inventive

genius of authors, composers, critics, novelists, engineers, technicians, and others.

This chapter deals with the questions of copyright and patent protection that the law affords individuals and companies. It also deals briefly with trademarks. The protection extends to the creation of ideas, the utilization of ideas, and the production of an end product.

COPYRIGHTS

Under the Federal Copyright Act of 1976, an author or artist can obtain protection for his ideas and the exclusive right to control, publish, and sell his literary or artistic production. In addition to the copyright provided by federal law, copyright exists in the absence of statute. In this case any author, composer, or artist may retain the exclusive right to an idea or a composition until it is published. Once it is published, however, in the absence of a statutory copyright provided by Congress the exclusive right is lost forever. Publication involves the placing of the material before the general public for sale or for other use.

The copyright granted by statute to an artistic or literary creator protects him against appropriation of his ideas or work of art for his entire lifetime plus 50 years. All forms of literary or artistic expression, including records, musical compositions, plays, novels, sermons, pictures, and similar works, can enjoy copyright protection.

*How to obtain
a copyright*

To obtain a copyright, the creator of an artistic or intellectual work places a notice of copyright, his name, and the year of first copyright on the first and all other copies of the work. He can then publish the work and apply for a certificate of registration on forms provided by the Register of Copyrights, Library of Congress. As an alternative, he can apply for a certificate of registration on the unpublished work. A specific number of copies should accompany the application along with a small fee.

The "copyright seal" is a small letter "c" enclosed in a circle. Thus a typical copyright line would read:

© John J. Doe, 1980

Sound recordings are protected by placing a special notice on the label:

℗ Jones Recording Co., 1980

Using the © symbol in the copyright notice, the owner obtains simultaneous copyright protection in more than 60 countries that adhere to the Universal Copyright Convention.

While the work must be original with the author, it does not have to be absolutely new in the sense that it has never been thought of before. In order to be copyrighted, works must be the independent result of a mental or creative exercise.

If you have in your attic an old song that you wrote in your college days, it is possible that it might be saleable. To find out, write the song on paper, place a *copyright notice* on the bottom, publish the song, register for a copyright, and file the necessary documents with the Register of Copyrights in Washington. Following these steps should give you protection against anyone else who might copy the work.

When copyright protects

Remember the cartoon. Copyright does not give protection against someone else who may independently create a similar or identical product. If two works are identical, the person claiming originality in the later work has a difficult time proving originality.

Infringement of copyright occurs when a second work has copied, or plagiarized, from a previously copyrighted work. Since the copyright owner has the exclusive right to print, copy, adapt, and perform the composition, any action of anyone else in printing, copying, or publishing the work without proper permission constitutes infringement. The copyright owner then has the right to sue. To succeed in such an action, proof must be presented that the party sued had access to the copyrighted material and actually infringed it.

The Federal Copyright Act recognizes that most cases of infringement of copyright are innocent ones. Thus the Act provides for minimum damages in such cases. If the infringer is notified of the alleged infringement but does not discontinue the infringing activities, he will lose the benefit of the minimal damage provisions of the law. He may become subject to the full range of damages allowed.

In effect, when a claim of infringement is made, the party involved must decide whether to withdraw his material from publication or subject himself to possibly extensive damage claims.

The "fair use" rule

In order to promote the use of materials without undue restrictions, the law dealing with copyright has developed what is known as the "fair use" rule. Under the rule, the moderate use of copyrighted material by other than the author is permitted.

What constitutes "fair use" under the circumstances of any particular case has to be decided on the merits of each case. Generally, if the alleged infringer uses the previously copyrighted work in an attempt to substitute for it or take its place, and thus reduces the profits accruing to the copyright owner from the original work, there can be no valid claim to fair use. Beyond such a clear case, however, lies a vast area in which circumstances suggest what may be considered fair use.

A literary or artistic work can be promoted and exploited in many different ways. Newspapers, reprints, dramatic presentations, radio and television reproductions, musicals and other stage productions, recordings, hard- and soft-cover publications, reruns, and residual rights belong on the list. Thus the production and protection of artistic works involve much more than just their creation.

Lawyers, publishers, and other professionals can help ensure that an author or composer is properly protected, receives the royalties, and maintains ownership rights. Later adaptations of a work should not affect those rights.

That song up in the attic may find its way into a stage presentation, a musical comedy, a gold record, a folio of piano favorites, or, possibly, a movie.

PATENTS

The new or different mousetrap

A patent involves the protection of a physical expression of an idea or invention, usually for a period of 17 years. Unlike a copyright, a patent is not renewable without a special act of Congress. To be eligible for patent protection, the invention must consist of a new and useful article, a combination of materials, or a machine not previously known or used. The better mousetrap must, therefore, contain a combination of materials or design that makes it, in fact, a new or different mousetrap.

WHEN SENDING A PATENT APPLICATION . . .

A patent application must be filed with the United States Patent and Trademark Office. The patent application must include:

- an abstract, which is a form of summary of the entire disclosure;
- a detailed description that would allow one skilled in the art to practice the invention;

- the claims which describe the distinguishing aspects of the invention; and
- drawings, if possible, showing the preferred embodiment of practicing the invention.

U.S. patents are of three kinds. They include:

1. "Utility" patents, the ordinary electrical, mechanical, or chemical patents on processes, machines, manufactured articles, compositions of matter, or improvements on any of those kinds of items

2. "Design" patents covering the ornamental or artistic appearance of manufactured articles, machines, and so on

3. "Plant" patents covering an originally discovered, developed, and asexually reproduced new and distinct variety of plant

Utility, design, and plant patents

Utility and plant patents are granted for terms of 17 years. Design patents are granted for periods of three and a half, seven, or 14 years. The inventor can specify how long he wants the design patent to run.

If an idea has merit as an invention, the inventor should give it concrete form by designing it on paper. He should then describe the invention in words, including all its components and what it is designed to do. This description must go into minute detail; it will form the basis of the patent application. Nothing should be left out. The components and mechanics of the invention should be described from beginning to end.

After the preliminary work is completed, the sketches and written description of the invention should be placed in the hands of a *patent lawyer*. A family lawyer can usually recommend a patent specialist who will review both the sketches and the description and conduct a "patent search."

The patent search will determine whether any existing, previously issued patent involves the same (or similar) ideas, methods, or material compositions as the "new" invention. Costing, usually, $250 and up, the search will determine whether a new invention will infringe on any other valid patent already issued. The lawyer can also conduct searches to find out which patents have been issued to other inventors and who owns a particular patent at the time of the search.

A patent application should be filed within a year after the invention is described, used, or put up for sale by the inventor. The first inventor to file a patent application for the same or a similar invention will usually prevail where there is a contest. While it is sometimes difficult to establish the date of an invention, the inventor should maintain all his notes and records to show the progress of the invention, how it was conceived, and the method by which it was reduced to a practical, physical object.

Damages for patent infringement

In the event of patent infringement, damages are collectible for a period of six years preceding the suit. Triple damages may be awarded for intentional or willful infringement. Under some circumstances, an injunction may be issued against the infringer to prevent additional damage.

A physical device may not be patentable. But it may have a definite use for which the inventor may want protection. He may be able to license others to use the product, perhaps utilizing his own engineering talents or other know-how. Leasing or licensing should be provided for under strict agreements. Covenants would be included to indicate that the party using the object will not reveal or take it for his own use and will return it and all specifications and plans concerning it after the lease or license expires.

The subjects of copyright and patents, the protection of trade secrets, technological information, artistic and literary works, and similar matters are highly complex. They require the assistance of qualified professionals. The genius of American industry and the inventiveness of the American personality indicate that the need for this kind of protection will continue.

If you have written that song, if you have a short story that you have always wanted to publish, or if you have an idea for a better mousetrap, why not do something with it? Fortunes have been made on less.

Part V
SPECIAL PROBLEMS

The law as a general concept has been viewed as preserving society's fabric. But the law also enables people to adjust to new and different situations; it emerges in many cases as a tool that every citizen can use to cope with special problems.

As a coping mechanism, law does not lose its regulatory function. It has still to serve as that moderating influence that keeps the rights of one person inviolate while guaranteeing the rights of others to enjoy "life, liberty, and the pursuit of happiness"—within limits. In at least three different categories of situations, the law projects itself into many people's lives at one time or another:

- Defamation, which arises when one person attacks or limits the right of another to be free of unwarranted, untruthful assaults on his or her character
- Automobile accidents
- Involvement with the law because of a crime or misdemeanor

Auto accidents
and court time

Of these areas, the one involving auto accidents holds the lead insofar as numbers of cases are concerned. In fact, experts indicate that automobile accident cases take up a large proportion of all the court time in American courts at all levels. Auto accidents are traumatic in themselves. But they also lead under specific circumstances to civil or criminal actions, serious financial loss, and jail sentences.

What a person does and says immediately after an accident may determine entirely what happens to him later. It may even determine whether and how much he can recover for an injury or other loss. Thus Chapter 17 has special importance. But Chapter 16 should also be read with care if only because liability for libel or slander can be incurred unintentionally. The operations of the courts in criminal and other cases require some understanding, too, if the citizen is to remain up-to-date on some basic legal processes.

16 "IF YOU CAN'T SAY ANYTHING GOOD ABOUT A PERSON . . ."

In a crowded meat market, a woman customer says loudly that the market sells contaminated meat.

A man draws a recognizable picture of a neighbor, writes the name of a neighbor and the word "murderer" under it, and circulates it through the neighborhood.

A newspaper carries an item to the effect that a local department store is in financial straits.

The three hypothetical cases provide examples of libel and slander. Together, these two offenses constitute the offense of defamation of character. In most instances, defamation ranks as a civil offense,

or *tort*. The injured party can bring suit for damages. Less frequently, defamation may be a criminal offense, a misdemeanor, that is viewed by the law as a threat to the peace.

Before the invention of the printing press, the principal means of defaming a person was through the spoken word, or *slander*. With printed or written defamation, the legal concept of libel made its appearance. Today, *libel* is both a more serious and a more common offense than slander.

Libel and slander underscore some possible conflicts in the protections that the U.S. Constitution affords the American citizen. On the one hand, each person has the rights of freedom of speech and the press. On the other hand, those rights can interfere with another person's good reputation, privacy, or ability to earn a living. In trying to resolve this conflict, the laws of defamation are sometimes extremely complex.

This chapter will attempt to guide the reader through this complexity. The reader should remember that if he commits an act of defamation, he may be sued. At the same time a person who thinks he has been defamed should understand that he can bring legal action if he so chooses.

THE LAW OF DEFAMATION

When is a communication defamatory?

A communication is defamatory when it has the effect of, or tends to have the effect of:
harming the reputation of another;
lowering that person's esteem or standing in the community;
causing any persons to stop associating or dealing with him;
exposing a person to scorn, ridicule, or contempt; or
depriving a person of his job, or of his business if he is self-employed in a business, craft, or profession.

The content of a defamatory communication may take either of two forms. It may question a person's morality or integrity or it may brand the person with a loathsome disease that could cause people to avoid him. From another point of view, defamation may be either a statement of fact that charges a person with performance of a particular act or an expression of opinion about facts known or unknown, but which imply the commission of an act.

In general, before a suit can be brought because of a defamatory statement, all three of the following conditions must be met:

1. there must be publication, or communication, spoken or written, to a third party;
2. that communication must identify the particular individual either by name or in words that point to the person's identity; and
3. the communication must have a harmful effect that need not be tangible, as in provable financial loss, but may be merely an intangible affront to one's good name.

Two kinds of damages

A defamatory publication need not have malicious intent. But proof of such intent would strengthen a lawsuit. A defendant in a civil defamation suit cannot escape responsibility for his actions by claiming mental incompetence, as he could in a criminal case.

A defamed person usually tries to recover damages. In the normal case, he can then see himself as vindicated. Either of two kinds of damages may be awarded:

- General damages, where loss of reputation is presumed. In this situation, a case is called *actionable per se:* no special losses beyond a loss of reputation need to be shown. The loss of reputation is presumed to exist simply by virtue of the fact that the defamatory statement was published. General damages are typically token in nature, sometimes amounting to no more than six cents. The principle does matter.

- Special damages, where the person defamed can show he has suffered a particular loss, such as a loss of income or the prevention of a marriage. Special damages are awarded in addition to general damages. In order to receive special damages, however, a defamed person must show that special losses were incurred.

LYING DOWN ON THE JOB: A LIE?[1]

In the 1950s, his friends played a joke on John Cardiff of Brooklyn. The Brooklyn *Eagle* had published an announcement of John's death. He sued the paper on the basis that it not only falsely said he had died, but also said that he was lying "in state at 566-4th Avenue," which was his saloon. Still the court held that there was no libel. "At its worst, the publication might cause some amusement to the plaintiff's friends," the court said. "But it is difficult to see where his reputation would be impaired in the slightest degree and the law of defamation is concerned only with injuries thereto."

[1] From *Libel: Rights, Risks, Responsibilities* by Robert H. Phelps and E. Douglas Hamilton, revised edition. Copyright © 1966, 1978 by Robert H. Phelps and E. Douglas Hamilton. Reprinted with permission from Dover Publications, Inc.

He typically demands special damages in a specified amount at the time of filing suit. A jury may award special damages up to the amount specified by the plaintiff, but never more than that amount.

Differences Between Libel and Slander

*Libel more serious
than slander*

Libel is generally considered more serious than slander because the written or printed word has permanence while the spoken word does not. In addition, the commission of libel typically involves a more deliberate, studied attempt to defame. Slander is more subject to impulse. For these reasons, higher judgments for damages are awarded in cases of libel than in cases of slander.

Slander has, of course, been defined as spoken defamation. But with the advent of radio and television, the distinction between libel and slander has become somewhat hazy. The traditional definition of libel states that it involves publication of defamatory matter in the form of written or printed words, pictures, caricatures, statues, or other representations. These may appear in letters, circulars, petitions, newspapers, books, or other published works.

Spoken libel: a
new phenomenon

The electronic and other media have led to broader definitions of libel. Today, in fact, "libel" includes spoken libel. In one form of spoken libel, defamatory matter is broadcast or telecast—issued over radio or television. The speaker or actor must, however, read or follow a prepared script or written notes. In some cases ad libs can constitute spoken libel.

A second form of spoken libel involves an orally transmitted defamation to a reporter. Publication may take place in a press conference, an interview, or a telephone conversation. The speaker may be liable even where the printed account differs somewhat from the spoken communication—if the substance of the communication is essentially accurate. The speaker may be liable even if he did not ask the reporter to print his remarks.

The Right to Be Protected from Defamatory Statements

The right to protection against defamatory publications is rooted in the U.S. Constitution and in most state constitutions. Every individual is guaranteed freedom from unwarranted and untruthful attacks upon his character. An attack that is warranted or true may be another matter.

The law normally labels any allegedly defamatory story as libelous even if the plaintiff does not recover damages. Likewise, a libel can be true and still be defamatory. The law makes the same point in an-

398 THE LEGAL GUIDE

other way. At the beginning of a court case, the court assumes that the libel is false.

Defamatory Words

The words used in a defamatory publication establish the principal criterion for determining whether such publication is actionable. Various qualifications of this criterion should be noted:
the clear identification of the injured party
the kinds of acts attributed to that party
the social standing of the party
the occupation held by the party
the moral standards of the community at the time

General and special damages

Words That Are Defamatory Regardless of Actual Damage Done. A line may be drawn between general and special damages. A presumption that general damages are proper and deserved always exists in a defamation case. Proof of harm or loss must be shown before special damages will be awarded.

The distinction between libel and slander can be made more specific. In a case of libel, almost any publication is *actionable*—suit can be brought—for the recovery of general damages. In the case of slander, however, a publication is actionable without proof of damages under four specific circumstances:

When no proof of
damages is needed

- When a person falsely and unjustifiably suggests that another person is guilty of a crime that is chargeable by indictment and punishable by death or imprisonment
- When a person suggests that another person has a loathsome disease
- When a person accuses another of improper conduct of a business or profession
- When one imputes unchastity to a woman

Unless one of these conditions is present, a slandered person must prove injury or harm meriting special damages. For example, he must prove a specific loss in terms of income or opportunity.

Words That Impute the Commission of a Crime or Status of Immorality. Crime is the most common subject matter of defamation. It can result in the most comprehensive kind of damage to a person: to his personal reputation, his right to enjoy social contacts, and his ability to make a living.

The accusation or suggestion of a crime is clear-cut; it must refer to a criminal act that is subject to indictment and to imprisonment or the death penalty. Any act that does not meet that criterion is libelous. For example, if a man kills in self-defense, he has not committed murder. If someone accuses him of murder, the accuser can be sued for libel.

To say that a person has committed a crime is much more serious than to say that he has been accused or is suspected of a crime. A libelous reference can mention a crime by name, telling of pertinent facts, or it can simply describe a punishment. Thus, to say that a person is an ex-convict indicates that he was guilty of a crime.

Moral standards
change, vary

References to immoral acts may be still more ambiguous. Moral standards change from one year or decade to another. They also vary from one community to another, and from one group or social stratum in a community to another.

The phrase "the general public" admittedly expresses a fiction. However, it serves as a basis on which to decide what is libelous. In general, if a publication is intended to produce an unfavorable opinion in the minds of a large segment of a community's average, fair-minded people, that may constitute libel.

In 1900, describing a woman as a singer in a dance hall might have impugned her morality and would therefore have been libelous —if in fact she was not such a singer.

Words Tending to Injure a Person in a Profession or Business. Defamatory statements about persons in a profession or business may impute to them either criminal or immoral behavior. Such libels or slanders may injure not only individuals but partnerships and corporations as well. If a law office consisting of several partners is defamed, for example, the firm may sue. But individual partners may also bring suit. A defamation need not actually harm the reputation or business of a person; it may only tend, or be calculated, to do so.

Business or occupational defamations may take several forms:

• Charging a professional man with acts that are a breach of professional ethics

• Charging a person with general unfitness or with inefficiency in his occupation or business

• Charging a person or business with bankruptcy, insolvency, or other financial distress or embarrassment, whether past, present, or future

• Accusing a person or firm of fraud or dishonesty in one's line of work, in which case suspicion has the same effect as an outright charge of guilt

Three limiting situations

When can a person bring suit for this kind of defamation? Generally, the right to sue faces limitation in three kinds of situation:

- When the injured party has made, or is accused of making, a single mistake. "Anyone can make a mistake," and while it is held to be unfair to criticize a person for such an imperfection, it is also held that such a criticism does no real damage. However, an exception may be made to the general rule: the nature of the mistake may be such as to be open to criticism. If, for instance, a lawyer is accused of disclosing confidential information, an act that does not rank as a permissible mistake, that lawyer may sue for damages.

- When the act is illegal. If a person is accused of being an incompetent criminal, he may seek damages only for the imputed criminality, not for incompetence.

- When a person is not legally engaged in an occupation. A person not licensed as a physician cannot sue on the basis of a charge of incompetence.

In addition to individuals and corporations, nonprofit corporations and unincorporated groups can sue for defamation. Thus labor unions can sue; if they could not sue as organizations, each union member would have to sue separately.

Damages for financial losses

Business or occupational defamations are the hardest to defend against. Because of the financial losses that may be involved, a business or professional person can seek compensatory damages from the defendant.

Words Imputing Unfitness or Misconduct in a Public Office. Federal, state and local governments can legally be made the targets of defamatory statements. So can public officials in the act of carrying out government business. In their capacities as private citizens, however, public officials enjoy the same protections against defamation as do other citizens.

One exception to the latter protection may be noted: when some aspect of an official's personal or family life may have a serious bearing on his or her conduct in office. Thus the press did not libel Senator Eagleton of Missouri, a former vice-presidential candidate, when newspapers published reports that he had received psychiatric treatment for depression. The reports nonetheless cost Eagleton his candidacy.

Neither individuals nor the media stand under a legal restriction on criticisms of public officials or governments. Even if criticism consists entirely of lies, and the critic both knows he is lying and acts out of malice, he is still free to do so. Only one limitation exists: individual officials may not be named.

Third party involvement

Necessity of Certainty Regarding the Person Defamed.   A person cannot be sued for defamation unless he directs his damaging remarks toward particular individuals or groups. Aside from the person being defamed, only one other person needs to be involved—to identify the person being defamed. It is not even necessary that a so-called "average person" be exposed to the publication—only a specific person, or any person. Nor is it necessary that the audience—one person or many—personally know or be acquainted with the defamed person.

FAIR COMMENT AND CRITICISM: A NEWS AGENCY'S GUIDELINES[1]

The doctrine of *fair comment* has grown up in connection with slander and libel of public figures and elected and appointed officials. In essence, the rule holds that such persons have to expect more ——and harsher——criticism of their performance on the job than private citizens.

A newspaper may charge a city official with inefficient or incompetent handling of public funds. Because the official's performance is a matter of public interest and concern, the criticism would probably fall under the fair comment rule. But the comments must be truly stated, must be based in some kind of fact, and must be honest expressions of opinion.

So important is libel to newspapers, news agencies, and other information media that many of them instruct their employees in basic principles. Especially sensitive are those relating to fair comment.

The Associated Press, for example, warns its employees that ". . . whatever facts are stated, must be true" where comment and opinion are used with reference to matters of public interest or importance.

The AP also provides a summary of the fair comment rule:

Everyone has a right to comment on matters of public interest and concern, provided they do so fairly and with an honest purpose. Such comments or criticism are not libelous, however severe in their terms, unless they are written maliciously. Thus it has been held that books, prints, pictures and statuary publicly exhibited, and the architecture of public buildings, and actors and exhibitors are all the legitimate subjects of newspapers' criticism, and such criticism fairly and honestly made is not libelous, however strong the terms of censure may be. (*Hoeppner* v. *Dunkirk Printing* Co., 254 N.Y. 95)

---

1 From *The Associated Press Stylebook and Libel Manual* edited by Howard Angione. Copyright © 1977 by The Associated Press. Reprinted with permission from The Associated Press.

Establishing the Identity of the Person Defamed

You have gone hunting with old friend Jim. In the heat of pursuit you accuse Jim of murder. No third party hears the charge. You have not published slander.

The identity of a person can be established in a publication in a number of ways. These include, typically, a name, a nickname, a pen name, initials, or circumstances. Regarding the latter, pieces of information presented in a publication might enable a reader to arrive at the defamed person's identity with certainty. Identity is thus established circumstantially.

Direct and
circumstantial
identification

Similarity of names may mean similarity of identifications. For instance, if one chooses a fictitious name for the person being defamed, another person with that name could sue. If one accidentally used the wrong name, and another person happened to have that name, he could sue in every state but Illinois.

It may take more than one publication to connect a particular individual with a defamation. A newspaper one day may describe a police raid on a house of prostitution. The next day the same paper reports that a particular woman resides at that address. The woman may be able to sue on the ground that a reader can "put two and two together." This is an ambiguous area, however. Some courts will permit such a suit and others will not.

In defamation law, mention of a large group does not identify individuals. Under the law, defamatory talk is allowed where a professional, occupational, racial, religious, or ethnic group is concerned. One may refer to lawyers en masse in strongly negative terms, or use the traditional defamatory words for racial or ethnic groups.

A rule of thumb holds that when a group numbers fewer than 100, it is best not to refer to all members of the group even if no names are named. Qualifiers such as "some," or "many," or "most," or "certain" persons are preferable—and safer.

The Meanings of the Words Used. A publication may have more than one meaning. One meaning may be defamatory; another may not. As noted, standards vary with the times, the geographic area, and groups within a community. The first question is: What would the majority of average, reasonable citizens think of a particular publication?

If the words in a publication can have only one meaning—a defamatory one—the judge will usually be able to make the ruling on the case. If the judge decides that the meaning is not defamatory, then of course the trial ends.

The jury
may decide

Some judges let juries decide whether publications are defamatory. This may happen when the words are capable of having two or more meanings, a relatively rare occurrence.

Necessity for Intent and Malice.   In defamation, intent constitutes an essential element, and that intent must be malicious. Evidence of malice may be either expressed or implied. Where a person publishes a communication that appears defamatory on its face, malicious intent is presumed. A plaintiff does not have to prove the existence of other circumstances showing malice.

Defamation thus differs from other torts—minor offenses—in that intent and malice are presumed elements. However, the person who composes a defamation and the person who publishes it may be two different persons. The editor of a newspaper publishing a libel has the same liability as the reporter who wrote it. If he knew nothing of the publication, the newspaper owner is free of liability.

Another aspect of defamation law involves repetition of a defamation. The person who repeats or republishes a defamation has the same liability as the originator of the defamation. If a defamatory newspaper article is syndicated to various newspapers, each of these newspapers may be sued for libel. Each republication of a defamation constitutes a new offense even if the originator is named.

"Innocent
mistake" no
excuse

An innocent mistake on the part of a publisher, committed without malice, will not excuse him. But a defendant remains liable if he publishes a defamation without malice. In this case he may have any award of damages reduced if he can prove that he acted with proper motives and with a belief in the truth of what he published. The bad reputation of the plaintiff may also mitigate damages.

Necessity of Publication to Other People. Publication has some technical meanings. The sale of even one newspaper constitutes publication. Proof of distribution of that paper would be viewed as evidence of publication.

A sealed letter or other communication delivered to the plaintiff's spouse constitutes a publication.

In the case of letters, a libel becomes criminal rather than civil if it appears in a letter addressed to another. In criminal libel, a prosecutor rather than the injured party seeks damages. As in all crimes, the state has become, at law, the injured party.

Civil libel may be established if:

• the letter was forwarded to the plaintiff during his absence;
• the letter was intended for the eyes of the plaintiff's family and/or employees; or
• the letter was in fact read by them.

If it was not read by those persons, it cannot be considered a publication.

Defamation after death: criminal libel

When the person defamed is deceased, defamation may nonetheless take place on publication. This is a case of criminal libel, however, as the peace of the community is at stake. For example, if a president who died in office is called a traitor after his death, such a publication may incite riots. In general, criminal defamation is extremely rare.

DEFENSES IN DEFAMATION CASES

Certain defenses can be used to avoid liability for either civil or criminal defamation. One such defense, the statute of limitations, means that a plaintiff cannot bring suit after a specified period of time has elapsed. Among other defenses are:

- the defense of consent, where the defamed person actually consented to have the statement published;
- the defense of husband and wife, where spouses can publish defamations about one another (by common law, husband and wife are one person);
- the defense of privilege; and
- the defense of truth.

The last two appear most commonly in defamation cases. Privilege may be either absolute—without restriction—or qualified.

Absolute Privilege

*Two kinds of
absolute privilege*

Privilege as an absolute defense renders immaterial the motive of the publisher or the purpose of the publication. The two principal types of defenses arising out of absolute privilege are (1) statements made in court and (2) the official acts, reports, and records of public officials.

In the first instance, every participant in a court proceeding has the right to make, with impunity, any statement about a person regardless of intent or effect. Comments can touch on the judge, jurors, attorneys, prosecutor, witnesses, plaintiff, and defendant. The court setting provides complete freedom of speech.

In the second instance, a public official can make any statement about any person, regardless of intent or effect, while performing his official duties. If that condition is not fulfilled, the defense cannot be used. One official may be accused by another official of wrongful acts while both are taking part in legislative hearings. If the second official later makes the same statement off the floor, he may be compromising himself legally.

Qualified Privilege

Qualified privilege applies to persons not involved as described above. Qualified privilege cannot be used as a plea when malice is present. This kind of defense is typically employed by news media in two situations:

- Presenting authentic news reports of legislative, judicial, or legal proceedings of which there are official records
- Presenting fair comment or criticism of elected or appointed officials or of candidates for public office—as distinguished from reporting official activities

The so-called *"New York Times* rule" has a bearing on qualified privilege. It stipulates that publishing a defamatory statement about a public official justifies a lawsuit only when the writer knew it was false or wrote with reckless disregard of its truth or falsity. The news media also enjoy protection against suits by private parties where published statements involve issues of "public or general concern."

Truth as Justification

Truth constitutes the most complete, or perfect, defense in a suit. It is rooted in the right to free speech. But truth has not always been allowed as a defense. At one time, it could be used in civil cases more readily than in criminal cases. Today, truth may be raised as a defense in both civil and criminal defamation cases.

In most states truth ranks as a complete defense even where malice is involved. By the early 1980s, the following states held that malice could not be an issue in civil cases: Delaware, Florida, Illinois, Maine, Massachusetts, Nebraska, New Hampshire, Pennsylvania, Rhode Island, West Virginia, and Wyoming. But even in those states truth would probably serve as an adequate defense.

To be effective as a plea, truth must be proved in all its essential particulars. Half-truths will not exonerate a defendant. Accusing a man of perjury, for example, means not only that he testified falsely under oath, but that he did so willfully and knowingly. A publication containing errors may nonetheless be held to be truthful if it is true in its essentials. If a publication accurately reproduces a defamatory charge, the defense of truth will not apply even though the reproduction was accurate.

Evidence that
proves truth

Truth can be proved only through presentation of hard evidence such as documents or the statements of witnesses. Because most people and organizations—including newspapers—lack the powers of the

STATUTES OF LIMITATION FOR STARTING A CIVIL ACTION
AGAINST LIBEL OR SLANDER (IN YEARS)[1]

State	Libel	Slander	State	Libel	Slander
Alabama	1	1	Montana	2	2
Alaska	2	2	Nebraska	1	1
Arizona	1	1	Nevada	2	2
Arkansas	3	1	New Hampshire	2	2
California	1	1	New Jersey	1	1
Colorado	1	1	New Mexico	3	3
Connecticut	2	2	New York	1	1
Delaware	2	2	North Carolina	1	1
District of Columbia	1	1	North Dakota	2	2
Florida	4	4	Ohio	1	1
Georgia	1	1	Oklahoma	1	1
Hawaii	2	2	Oregon	1	1
Idaho	2	2	Pennsylvania	1	1
Illinois	1	1	Rhode Island	10	1
Indiana	2	2	South Carolina	2	2
Iowa	2	2	South Dakota	2	2
Kansas	1	1	Tennessee	1	½
Kentucky	1	1	Texas	1	1
Louisiana	1	1	Utah	1	1
Maine	2	2	Vermont	3	3
Maryland	1	1	Virginia	2	2
Massachusetts	3	3	Washington	2	2
Michigan	1	1	West Virginia	1	1
Minnesota	2	2	Wisconsin	2	2
Mississippi	1	1	Wyoming	1	1
Missouri	2	2			

police to ferret out such evidence, the defense of truth is seldom used.

To prevent legal problems, two questions should be asked before a possibly defamatory statement is published:

1. Is the matter actually defamatory? If not, there is no problem. If it is, a second question arises.
2. Have you a legal defense for publishing it? Only if you can answer affirmatively should you consider publication.

17 "DID YOU GET THE NUMBER OF THAT TRUCK?"

America has always been a nation on the move. The early movements westward, the drive for new horizons, and the ability of Americans to adjust to different climates and ways of life have been, perhaps, the most significant aspects of American traditions and history. Today, companies routinely move their executives or workers to new locations; the transferees have to make new plans, establish new roots, and find new homes. Millions of others move at whim, to find new jobs, or to relocate in retirement.

The automobile has played a distinct and dominant role in the development of the United States and its ways of life. The old "Model T" brought the automobile to the common man. That trend, continued, has probably had a greater influence on America's mobile society than any other factor.

America manufactures and uses more automobiles than any other nation of the world. Almost every American family has an automobile. More of the capital budgets of the various states go to road maintenance and construction than perhaps any other item on the budget. The possible exception may be welfare.

Inevitably, the passenger miles driven in any given year result in a high incidence of automobile accidents. Expectably, the automobile figures more than any other factor in accidental deaths and injuries. In consequence, trials of automobile accident cases have taken up a substantial portion of the time of American courts for many years. Various plans and programs have been designed to reduce the numbers of auto accidents tried in the courts. But today and for the foreseeable future the auto accident case will continue to be the most typical one appearing on the nation's court calendars.

What should a person do if he is involved in an auto accident? What should he do if he witnesses an accident? What protection can the individual purchase to protect himself in the event he is sued for an accident in which someone else is hurt or injured?

In the event of an
auto accident . . .

This chapter deals with the automobile accident, the procedures to follow in the event of an accident, and the types of protection which you can purchase to protect yourself against money claims.

AUTOMOBILE ACCIDENT PROCEDURES

Where an auto accident occurs, certain procedures are required by both common sense and the laws of most states. Regardless of who is at fault, both drivers in a two-car accident have to stop at the scene of the accident and supply names and addresses. They also give the names and addresses of the insurance agents and companies providing their liability insurance. Once this information has been exchanged, depending on the seriousness of the accident, the police may question the parties.

The Police Report

The police investigation at the scene of the accident is very important. The police report may be used in any lawsuit deriving from the accident. Thus the information supplied to the police officer has to be as accurate, clear, and complete as possible.

What the police report contains

The police report will normally include all pertinent details:
* The accident and its location
* A diagram of the scene and the locations of the vehicles immediately following the accident
* Any skid marks or debris that appear on the roadway
* The weather and road conditions
* The names and other information on all persons injured
* The approximate amount of any damage to the vehicles
* The various versions of the accident from the viewpoints of the drivers and passengers

A copy of the police report on a serious accident can and should be obtained from the local police, usually at minimum cost. The police version should be checked to make sure it is consistent with the facts. If it is not, a certified letter, return receipt requested, should be sent immediately to the police. The letter provides a correct statement of how the accident occurred as reported to the investigating officer.

The letter should contain a request that it be attached to the police report in the police files. If the police report is later used in court, the letter, written to correct an error in the report, can on request be used at the trial.

Many states require that an accident report be filed with the state public safety or motor vehicle department within a certain number of days following the accident. In these cases the accident will have involved personal injuries or property damage up to a stated amount. The report includes all the information set out in the police report along with information on the existence of liability insurance.

Most states provide that the information contained in these reports is confidential and cannot be used in any court trial that may arise out of the accident. Insurance information helps to fulfill the requirements of various state financial responsibility laws.

Reporting the Accident to the Insurance Company

*To be safe, call
your insurance
company or agent*

An accident should be reported immediately to an individual's insurance agent or company. This is particularly important where "the other person" may bring a claim for vehicle or personal injury. The accident should be reported even if no one appears to be hurt—or even if no one says he is injured. Waiting too long may mean that the insurance company will be unable to investigate properly. The company may even refuse to defend its client against the claim of a second party. Failure to report the accident promptly may actually violate a requirement of the policy.

A CHECKLIST OF THINGS TO DO IN CASE OF AN ACCIDENT[1]
MAKE SURE YOU PROTECT YOURSELF

What to do in case of an accident. How you act after an accident may strongly influence the settlement of the insurance claim, so it's important to observe certain procedures. Here are key things you should try to do, according to the Professional Insurance Agents of Iowa, an association of agents who sell property and other insurance.

—Seek medical attention for anyone who is injured.

—Don't discuss who is at fault. Admitting guilt might jeopardize your rights.

—Don't discuss the kind of insurance coverage you have.

—Obtain the following information: operator's license number; license plate number; year and make of car; name, address and telephone numbers of driver, passengers and witnesses, if any; car owner's name, address and telephone number if driver is not the owner; name, address and telephone number of the other driver's insurance agent and company. Give the same information about yourself to the other driver.

—If police come to the scene, get their names, badge numbers, and the office where the report will be filed.

—While the accident is still fresh in your mind, jot down details about road and weather conditions and other relevant circumstances.

—Notify your insurance agent and consult with him on how to proceed with your claim.

—Make copies of accident reports, if needed (see list below). Some states require the agent to sign the form. Make sure the form is sent to the proper agency within the prescribed period.

When you have to report an accident. In all states and the District of Columbia, any accident involving physical injury or death must be reported to the authorities. If there are no injuries, an accident report has to be filed when the estimated property damage exceeds the following amounts (in most states the minimum applies to the combined damage to all vehicles):

Ala.	$ 50	Ill.	$250	Mont.	$250	R.I.	$200
Alaska	500	Ind.	200	Neb.	250	S.C.	200
Ariz.	300	Iowa	250	Nev.	250	S.D.	250
Ark.	250	Kan.[2]	300	N.H.	300	Tenn.	200
Cal.	500	Ky.	200	N.J.	200	Texas	250
Colo.	250	La.	200	N.M.	100	Utah	400
Conn.	400	Me.	300	N.Y.	400	Vt.	200
Del.[2]	250	Md.	100	N.C.[2]	200	Va.	350
D.C.	100	Mass.	200	N.D.	400	Wash.	300
Fla.	100	Mich.[2]	200	Ohio	150	W.Va.	250
Ga.	250	Minn.	300	Okla.	100	Wis.	400
H.I.	300	Miss.	250	Ore.	200	Wyo.	250
Ida.[2]	250	Mo.	500	Pa.[3]	—		

[1] Reprinted with permission from the Professional Insurance Agents of Iowa.

[2] Accident report filed by police officer only.

[3] Damage limit has been replaced by the following requirements: "If an accident involves death, injury or any vehicle involved cannot be driven away under its own power without further damage or hazard to the vehicle or other vehicles on the roadway, the police must be notified. If police are unable to investigate accident, driver must report accident to the Bureau of Accident Analysis within 5 days."

Photographs and Injury Diary

Photographs and an injury diary may make it possible to reconstruct details later. If you are the party injured or damaged, and feel that you have a claim against the other driver, you should take photographs of both cars to establish their condition immediately following the collision. The photos would become important in a lawsuit to show the cars' physical condition and assist in arriving at a determination of how the accident happened.

The importance of photos

Photos should also be taken at the scene of the accident from various angles. The photos should show the directions in which the vehicles were traveling, the point of impact, the general neighborhood, the traffic controls in the area, including traffic lights and stop signs, and speed limit signs or other warning signs.

If you have suffered injury, you should maintain a diary. Entries should provide a record of all hospital stays by dates; every inpatient and outpatient visit; the names of all physicians, on staff or otherwise, who treated you; the dates and times of all visits to doctors' offices; the types of medicines prescribed; all your doctor bills, hospital bills, and drug and medication bills; the amounts of lost wages or earnings; the number of days you were laid up at home; the days you were totally or partially incapacitated and unable to perform your normal work; and the number of days or amount of time lost because of doctor visits or outpatient treatment at the hospital.

The diary can be very important. It obviously records facts. But it also serves to refresh memories of the accident and later events. Several years may elapse before a case comes up for trial. Remembering incidental things with the aid of a diary may make the difference between an adequate and a good recovery for injuries.

Medical and Hospital Benefits

Insurance under Blue Shield, Blue Cross, or some other private medical or hospital policy provided by an employer does not necessarily restrict claims for medical and hospital expenses. The injured party's insurance company may even have paid all basic claims. The laws of many states do not allow the party at fault to escape liability for these expenses by claiming that the injured party had provided himself with private insurance to pay his bills. The reason for this is that the person at fault ought not to be able to take advantage of the foresight of the injured person.

Including all bills

Personal accident records should therefore include every single bill even though all the bills were covered by insurance. These amounts should be included in the total amount of the claim.

Dealing with the Insurance Adjuster

The injured party should give written notice of a claim to the other party. Shortly afterward, if the party at fault has insurance, the adjuster for his insurance company will contact the injured party to make an adjustment or settlement of the claim as soon as possible for the lowest possible amount. This is his job; no one should be offended if the first offer in settlement is far below what is deserved or demanded. In this case negotiations should continue.

The adjuster needs a statement from the injured party as quickly as possible. But it is usually better not to give any statement to the adjuster before consulting with a lawyer.

Dangers in giving statements

Most people make the serious mistake of believing that they can "handle it themselves." They try to give statements that will not adversely affect their cases. They forget that taking a statement is an art, and that a trained adjuster can see things in a person's statement that the person himself would never see. In too many cases a statement comes back to haunt an accident victim at a trial. The statement may be written, put on tape, or given over the telephone. In each case the effect is the same.

If a statement must be given, it should be a written statement that can be checked thoroughly. All necessary corrections should be made before it is dated and signed. Taped statements, or those given over the phone, should be avoided because they cannot be corrected —or even replayed to ensure that they are accurate.

What, then, do you do when an adjuster calls you on the phone and asks if you mind if he records the conversation? You tell him, "Yes, I do indeed mind," and refuse to allow the conversation to be recorded. Any recording of the conversation after your refusal would be unlawful.

If the adjuster is advised that the injured party is represented by an attorney, he is required to deal with the lawyer through all phases of the claim. He cannot deal directly with the injured party without express instructions.

Cooperation with an Insurance Company

If contacted by the lawyer for the person injured, the party at fault should refer the lawyer to his insurance company. The party at fault should not deal directly with the other side. Nor should he give any statements to anyone representing the party injured. To do so could jeopardize his own protection under a liability policy.

A family lawyer might be brought into the case if the possible liability for the accident could exceed the limits of the policy. In such a case, the family lawyer will work with the insurance company lawyer. But the party at fault will have to pay for this lawyer's services.

When to Settle a Claim

Don't rush to
settle a claim

No one should rush to settle a claim. That rule of thumb has particular validity if an accident has resulted in personal injury. Unfortunately, many serious injuries do not become noticeable until many months after an accident has occurred.

Insurance adjusters are trained to secure settlements as quickly as is reasonably and fairly possible. In a clear case of liability, an adjuster may make an offer in the hope that the offer will be accepted, settling the case. The offer may be quite fair insofar as the condition of the injured person is known at that time. If final settlement is made, however, and if serious additional injury is discovered later, the injured person may have no right to recover anything further.

A formal, written "Release of All Claims" is normally required by the insurance company. The release is signed by the injured party and acknowledged before a notary public. It usually contains language that releases the party at fault and his insurance company from any further claims for any personal injury or property damage that may be discovered in the future.

Waiting has a purpose

It is important to realize that an adequate waiting period permits any additional medical problems to become evident. Normally, an injured person should wait until he or she is released from further medical treatment by the physician who has been treating the accident injuries. No claim should be settled without consultation with a lawyer first.

Statutes of Limitations

How can one decide when to sue or settle a claim? Most states have either a one-year or a two-year "statute of limitations" on personal injury cases. This means that a lawsuit to recover for injuries has to be started within one or two years from the date on which the accident occurred. Failure to bring suit within the time limit established in the particular state will normally terminate the right to sue. The period can, however, be extended if the party at fault waives the defense of the statute of limitations. Such a waiver is very difficult to establish.

In some states, suits based on certain types of claims must be filed within 100 days after the accident.

An injured party should have a pretty good idea before a year passes just how serious his condition is. He should know whether he can settle without a lawsuit. But his negotiations with the adjuster should not mislead him into believing that he does not have to file a suit in time to protect a claim.

A suit can be discontinued

Safety first: a suit can be discontinued once it is filed, but if not filed in time, the suit can never be filed.

Insurance policies typically require the insured to cooperate with the insurance company. If he is served with suit papers, the party at fault should immediately deliver them to the company so that it can prepare the necessary defense. The insured may also be required to sign various defense papers, to discuss the case with the attorneys for the insurance company, and to appear at pre-trial depositions. The latter are interviews, under oath, conducted by the attorney for the opposing party, with a court reporter present who transcribes all the questions and answers.

The insured may have to testify in court as part of his obligation to cooperate with the insurance company. Failure or refusal to cooperate may give the company a reason to deny any further coverage.

Elements of Damages

Four elements
of a claim

By 1980, 16 states had no-fault insurance laws of various kinds. In the other 34 states and the District of Columbia, the basic elements on which a claim should be based, or damages sought, include the following:
1. Out-of-pocket expenses, such as medical bills, the cost of drugs and medicines, nursing costs, and all other expenses.
2. Lost wages or lost profits and earnings (if self-employed).
3. An amount representing the pain, suffering, and inconvenience that were sustained.
4. An amount representing future disability and loss of earning power. If the injury results in a permanent disability, either full or partial, this amount represents the total loss of earnings anticipated over one's working life, measured by income at the time of the accident, work expectancy in years as determined by mortality or work expectancy tables, and, in certain cases, by experts concerning future earnings and increments in income that could normally be expected in the future.

While these are the basic factors in a claim, there are others. For example, pain and suffering may be expected to continue over one's entire life span. The laws of a given state may indicate that this should be taken into account.

Depending on state laws, it may be possible to demand a specific amount in a lawsuit—a sum representing all the elements noted above. Some states, however, do not permit demands in specific amounts. These states leave it to the jury to place a value on the claim as part of its verdict.

HOW TO PUT A VALUE ON YOUR CLAIM

Determination of what a claim is worth constitutes the most difficult aspect of any suit for personal injury damages. Establishing liability may, of course, be equally difficult. But how can a dollar value be placed on pain and suffering?

State laws affect
PI claims

What follows are some very general rules that apply to the basic personal injury claim. Each case, however, has its own peculiar facts that may change any basic formula. The laws of the several states will certainly affect these rules as they apply in any given case.

An example will serve to illustrate the basic rules. Suppose, as the result of an accident for which someone else is responsible, you accumulate $1,000 in total medical, hospital, and drug bills and $250 in lost wages. Your physician has discharged you from further treatment and has assured you that you should suffer no further discomfort or disability. In fact you feel fine. What is your claim worth?

You can rule out any claim for future disability or loss of earnings. Thus you can recover your out-of-pocket "special damages" of $1,000, as well as your lost wages of $250. For pain, suffering, and inconvenience, where there is no permanent pain, suffering, disability or loss of future earnings or earning power, and where the liability of the party at fault is clear, you can usually use the factor of two to four times the amount of the "special damages." That ratio is generally accepted by insurance adjusters as being reasonable.

The factor, it should be noted, can be different in different parts of the country. For example, the factor would be somewhat lower if the accident case is being tried in a rural area. It might be slightly higher in a large metropolitan area. The basic claim might thus be valued generally as follows:

Total medical expenses.....................	$1,000
Lost wages...............................	250
Pain, suffering and inconvenience:	
2 to 4 times $1,000	2,000 to 4,000
TOTAL	$3,250 to $5,250

If earning power
is reduced . . .

Changing the facts, and considering that the other party's liability is not clear, the settlement value for a plaintiff is reduced accordingly. If, however, permanent disability is involved, either complete or partial, reducing future earning power, the value of the claim would substantially increase. Loss of a limb or eyesight, disfigurement, or other serious, enduring problems would increase the value of the claim.

Assume that an accident victim suffered a 25 per cent disability that will be permanent. A physician will give testimony to that effect. The victim was earning $15,000 per year at the time of the accident; he could assume a working life expectancy of 20 years. The calculation of the claim could be made as follows:

Medical expenses	$1,000
Lost wages	250
Loss of future earnings, pain, suffering and	
inconvenience, 30 years x $15,000 =	
$450,000; 25% disability x $450,000 =	
$112,500, reduced to present worth	

Note that the total claim, because it reaches into the future, must be "reduced to present worth." This involves a calculation to determine what amount, if invested at the time of the trial or settlement at the then-legal rate of interest in the state, would yield the sum of $112,500 after 30 years. Some states require that this calculation be made by an actuary or other expert.

The above example does not take into account any permanent pain and suffering. Nor does it allow for normal increments in income over the 30 years of the victim's working life. But it illustrates the vast difference in the value of the claim where disability or permanent injury is involved.

Huge awards may
be deceptive

Newspaper accounts of huge sums awarded in personal injury cases can be deceptive. They can rarely be used as measures of the worth of other claims. Each case is different. One can only say, in general, that the more serious the injury, the higher the award.

THE TRIAL OF A PERSONAL INJURY LAWSUIT

Unlike radio and television programs that deal with courtroom trials, the trial of a lawsuit involving personal injuries is not, for the most part, dramatic or spectacular. Rather, the process unfolds as an orderly and, ideally, interesting presentation of facts and evidence. Rarely does a defendant break down on the stand and confess that he was not watching where he was going and that he caused the accident.

The trial of any lawsuit, like so many things in life, is not won or lost in the courtroom but in the painstaking preparation that must precede the trial. This includes complete investigation of the facts of the accident. It also includes interviews with witnesses and doctors, inspection of photographs and diagrams, expert witnesses, securing hospital records, and many similar tasks. The client can be of great help to the lawyer in his preparation of the case.

Before the Trial

Preparing to
go to trial

As the trial date approaches, the victim may become impatient with the manner in which cases are called. Since personal injury cases make up the great bulk of the trial calendars in many courts, the trial schedules may be congested. Often, cases do not move as rapidly as they should.

In order to bring cases to trial as quickly as possible, judges may insist—either by rule of court or in practice—that attorneys be ready to go to trial immediately when their cases are called. However, neither the judges nor the attorneys can be absolutely sure when a case will actually be called. Other cases may take longer to complete than expected, or may be settled "on the courthouse steps," thereby moving up a later case faster than expected. This means that the lawyers must have all the witnesses lined up to come to court on short notice —a great inconvenience to many participants, particularly the medical witnesses.

Each county may, of course, have a slightly different system. But the basic problems with trial schedules are the same. They require the sympathetic cooperation of the principals and witnesses in each case.

Assignment to a
courtroom
and judge

Once a case is ready for trial, it will be assigned to a particular courtroom and judge. Before the start of the case, assuming it is a jury case, the attorneys will take part in the selection of a jury. In most states, juries of 12 persons are chosen for all civil cases. In the federal courts, a jury of six is common.

THE TRIAL

With the jury selected, the trial begins. In the normal case the attorney for the plaintiff, the party bringing the action, introduces himself, the other attorney, and the judge to the jury, then delivers his opening statement. Here he outlines the case that he is about to present. After he has finished, the defense attorney may make his opening remarks. He may, however, wait until the plaintiff's case has been presented in full.

From "direct" to "re-cross-examination"

The plaintiff's attorney calls his witnesses in order. After the "direct examination" of his witness is completed, the defense attorney begins the "cross-examination." After the cross-examination is completed, the plaintiff's attorney may ask additional questions on "redirect examination." "Re-cross-examination" by the defense counsel may follow. The trial continues in this way until both attorneys and the judge—who also may put questions to the witnesses—have no further questions. The witness is then excused.

After the plaintiff's attorney has called all his witnesses and introduced into evidence all the exhibits, photos, and other documents, he *rests his case.* That means his part of the case, to that point, is concluded. The defense attorney then begins his case, makes his opening statement, and goes through the same procedures with his witnesses and exhibits. After he rests his part of the case, rebuttal witnesses may be called for the plaintiff, followed by any rebuttal witnesses for the defense.

After all witnesses and all exhibits have been heard or introduced into evidence, the closing arguments take place. These constitute a review of all the evidence and arguments in favor of the particular party. In some states, the defense attorney must give his closing argument first; other states require that the plaintiff's attorney speak first. After these arguments are concluded, the lawyers and the judge consult on the judge's instructions to the jury.

Since the jury decides on the facts that are in dispute, the judge must instruct the jury on the law to be applied to those facts. The attorneys may submit to the judge those instructions that they want to be included in the judge's instructions. At this time the judge rules on these requests and permits or denies some or all of the requested instructions.

The importance of instructions to the jury

Proper instructions to the jury are very important. If the judge makes a mistake and disallows a proper instruction, or gives an improper instruction, he may be establishing the basis for a reversal of the verdict and judgment on appeal to a higher court. The lawyers generally spend a great deal of time in preparing these instructions to the jury—and in trying to convince the judge that he should give the instructions they prepared.

Following his conference with the attorneys, the judge instructs the jury on the law. If the circumstances warrant, the judge reviews the evidence presented at the trial. The jury then goes to the jury room to consider its verdict in private. On reaching a verdict, the jury members return and state their verdict in open court in the presence of the judge, the attorneys, and, sometimes, the parties to the suit.

After the verdict, motions may be entered for a new trial, or for judgment in one principal's favor regardless of the jury's verdict. A judgment is then entered by the court in favor of the winning party. The motions are formal proceedings in which a party states his position that some error was committed in the trial of the case. The error presumably prejudiced him in the result reached by the jury. After the court makes a decision on these motions, the losing party has the right of appeal.

Where Death Occurs

Suits for "wrongful death"

Where personal injuries incurred in an accident have resulted in death, an action may be brought in most states for the "wrongful death" of the person killed. In this kind of lawsuit, beneficiaries such as a spouse, children, or the parents of the deceased, as identified under the laws of the state, sue to recover for the losses sustained through the death of the loved one.

Suits may also be brought on behalf of the estate of the deceased person to recover for losses that the deceased himself suffered and for losses to his estate resulting from the death. The laws of the various states differ as regards the amounts that can be recovered, and the beneficiaries who can recover, in wrongful death cases. Anyone faced with a situation involving the accidental death of a close relative should immediately consult a lawyer to ascertain what the laws say on these very important points.

INSURANCE AGAINST LIABILITY

The chapter on insurance dealt in general terms with liability insurance covering automobiles. This section will deal in more detail with the basic automobile liability policy and what it covers, whom it covers, and what protections are available under the policy.

First, in some of the states, and particularly since the passage of the "no-fault" insurance laws, it has become impossible to obtain a driver's license without evidence that the applicant has liability insurance coverage. In those states that do not have such requirements, financial responsibility laws on the books require the driver to provide proof that he is financially able to pay for any damages that he may cause in an accident. Sometimes some form of security, such as a bond, has to be posted. The bond would cover any judgment that might be rendered against the applicant.

A problem exists with both of these methods of establishing financial responsibility. Essentially, they do not protect the victim if the party at fault does not have the means to post bond or carry insurance. That party may lose his driving privileges, but that will be small consolation to the victim.

Limits of Liability

Protection against third-party claims

Automobile liability insurance protects the owner or driver against claims by third parties for property damage or personal injuries resulting from the use of the auto. The policy is stated in terms of limits of liability—for example, $10,000 for each person and $20,000 for each occurrence. That means that the coverage provided will not exceed $20,000 for all injuries resulting from one accident, regardless of the total number of persons injured. No more than $10,000 can be paid for each person injured.

Payment by the company is made directly to the injured party and is not paid to the insured. The company pays if the insured is liable. Under the typical policy, the insurance company is required to defend any claims brought against the insured. If the insured has insufficient coverage, however, the victim retains the right to sue for a judgment for the total amount of damage. If an injured party exhausts the total amount of insurance coverage carried by the party at fault, he can attempt to collect the balance directly from the insured.

Covered damages under auto liability policies extend to deaths and injuries as well as to physical damage to cars or other property. A policy may be described as 100/300/25. In the shorthand of the insurance industry, that means the insurance company will pay:

- up to $100,000 for injury to, or the death of, one person;
- up to $300,000 in the aggregate if more than one person is injured or killed in a single accident; and
- up to $25,000 for property damage.

Insurance experts believe that a good liability policy in the early 1980s should provide at least 100/300/25 coverage. Inflation could, of course, indicate a need for upward revision of those figures in coming years.

The auto liability policy protects the owner of the vehicle when he is operating it and anyone else operating it with the owner's permission. The policy may also protect the insured or his spouse, when either is driving someone else's vehicle, under "drive other car" coverage. Members of the household of the insured are normally covered by the policy. The courts liberally interpret the language of these policies to find that the individual involved was a resident or a member of the insured's household. Thus the policy would usually provide protection.

Exclusions from coverage

As with any other liability policy, there are exceptions or exclusions from coverage that generally appear in an auto policy. These include claims covered by the workers' compensation laws and claims involving areas in which certain commercial vehicles may be used.

The policy provision binding the insurance company to defend any claim made against the insured applies even though the company finds that the claim is false or fraudulent. If the company refuses to defend and the insured has to hire a lawyer, the company may have to pay both the amount of any judgment against the insured and the insured's costs and attorney's fees.

In addition to the liability insurance that is included in the standard auto policy, the insured can also elect to carry collision insurance. A form of property insurance, collision coverage pays for damage to the insured's own vehicle. "Collision" refers to the unintentional striking of another object, even if it is not another vehicle. Normally the collision coverage is purchased with a deductible feature: the first $100 or $250 of collision loss is paid by the insured and the insurance company picks up the balance.

Exclusions are usually written into the standard collision provisions. Among those are damages occurring when the vehicle is being operated in violation of the law, loss of personal property in the auto, and loss of use of the auto. As property insurance, collision coverage does not depend on fault on the part of the insured; the loss must merely be unintended.

The family and special package policies

The auto insurance policy may come in the form of a *family automobile policy* or a *special package automobile policy*. The first of these is the basic liability policy, which may contain various types of special coverage. Some of these are:

- *Medical payments.*   Since most people have separate medical and hospital insurance, additional coverage is generally unnecessary. But in no-fault states, every policy has provisions for medical payments.
- *Uninsured motorist coverage.*   The auto owner and his passengers are protected in the event of injuries incurred in an accident with a hit-and-run or an uninsured driver.
- *Comprehensive coverage.*   A policy with "comp" covers damage resulting from an event other than a collision. Examples are fire, vandalism, theft, and so on.
- *Wage loss and substitute service.*   In no-fault states insurers are required to include wage loss coverage for the loss of working time or services due to accident.
- *Safe-driving or merit-rating policies.*   Some companies provide for discounts on premiums for persons with clean driving records. But the system works in reverse too: persons with poor records find their premiums going up for the next three years.

No-Fault Insurance

A relatively recent development in the law dealing with personal injury liability caused by auto accidents is the "no-fault" insurance concept. No-fault began partly as an attempt to reduce the load of auto accident cases that are taking up so much of the nation's courtroom time. In 1970, Massachusetts became the first state to adopt no-fault insurance.

The "fault" system: more common

The more common system of determining liability is based on a finding of fault on the part of one of the parties to an accident. For example, it is necessary to show that one of the parties was negligent and that his negligence caused the accident. If he is not found to be negligent, then he is not responsible. His liability insurance company will not have to pay. It often takes a lawsuit to determine the question of fault; as a result, if the party at fault refuses to settle or admit his fault a trial becomes necessary.

No-fault insurance programs seek to eliminate fault from consideration in auto accident injury cases. The no-fault statutes require that every auto liability policy provide no-fault coverage. When an insured is injured while using the insured auto, the company providing the coverage will make payment directly to the insured without regard to whether or not he or the other driver was at fault.

The "threshold" in no-fault programs

No-fault insurance covers medical expenses and losses of wages suffered by an insured. But it does not provide for payment for pain and suffering, inconvenience, or disability or disfigurement except in certain cases. Most no-fault programs have built into them a "threshold," the amount of medical expenses that must be incurred before the insured can bring a lawsuit against the party at fault to recover damages for pain, suffering, disability, disfigurement, and other claims that can be brought under the present fault system of liability.

An example may be noted. A no-fault system in a given state contains a threshold of $2,000. This means that before the insured can sue the party at fault to recover for all his claims, the amount of his medical expenses incurred as the result of the accident must exceed $2,000. Some no-fault programs allow suit if serious permanent injury, disability, or disfigurement results regardless of the threshold.

Each no-fault system is different from all the others. Whatever the differences, each system has a threshold amount. Other factors of significance:

- All of them restrict the right to sue.
- All of them attempt to eliminate lawsuits for personal injuries stemming from auto accidents.
- Some of them require arbitration of disputes between the insured and the company concerning the no-fault coverage.
- Some of them direct that some reduction in auto insurance premiums be made by the companies, at least in the first year or two of the system.

It is difficult to generalize further about no-fault insurance. The system will probably, in time, find its way in some form into the laws of most states. No-fault may be enacted into law by Congress as well—as a means of pushing the states into adopting their own plans. But no-fault has been attacked because it "unconstitutionally" deprives individuals of their right to use the courts for redress of their grievances.

The Problem of the Uninsured Motorist

What happens if an insured owner and driver is struck by a vehicle driven by someone who does not carry liability insurance?

"Uninsured motorist" coverage

In order to protect the insured person, the statutes of many states provide for a particular type of insurance called "uninsured motorist" coverage. As noted, the policy containing this coverage provides that one's own insurance company will pay if the insured is injured by a motorist who does not have liability insurance. It must, however, be established that the uninsured motorist was at fault and would be held liable in a lawsuit. Uninsured motorist coverage differs, thus, from no-fault coverage and collision coverage because fault on the part of the uninsured motorist must be shown.

Some policies offer "underinsured motorist" coverage. It pays off if the other driver's insurance is too low to cover injury losses.

The driver who leaves the scene of an accident before he can be identified is also considered an uninsured motorist. The typical policy contains a provision that an injured party, if struck by a "hit-and-run" motorist, must report the accident to the police within 24 hours. A search for the driver must also be made. This requirement is intended to prevent the filing of fraudulent claims. The conditions must be fulfilled or the insured will not qualify for the coverage.

Only PI claims are covered

Generally, liability in uninsured motorist coverage is limited to a maximum of $10,000. Only personal injury claims are covered.

There must have been actual contact with the uninsured vehicle; the coverage does not apply if there was no such contact.

In the event of a dispute with the company regarding the claim or the amount to be paid, the policy normally provides for arbitration.

The victim of a hit-and-run accident, or the person struck by someone who does not carry insurance, should check his policy immediately. If he has uninsured motorist or "medical payments" coverage, he has some protection and can enter a claim if the other driver was at fault. If he does not have such coverage, he should probably get it right away.

LOSS OF DRIVING PRIVILEGES

Once considered a privilege, driving an automobile has become a virtual necessity. The salesman who delivers the milk every morning, the mail truck driver who brings the mail, the salesman who drives hundreds of miles a day all rely on their ability to drive to earn a living. For these and millions of others, suspension or revocation of driving privileges can qualify as a serious and very personal concern.

Suspension or revocation of driving privileges

The statutes that control motor vehicle usage in the various states provide for the suspension and revocation of driving privileges under specified circumstances. While these laws differ from state to state, such suspensions or revocations usually hinge on the violations of the laws dealing with vehicle operation—"moving violations" such as speeding, reckless driving, and driving too fast for conditions.

One little-understood aspect of this problem can lead to very serious consequences. To avoid going to court and losing time, people often voluntarily pay the fine when they receive a ticket for a serious moving violation. Rather than pay the fine, they should attend the hearing and contest the fine. They should do so especially if they believe they did not exceed the speed limit or otherwise violate any laws.

TEN RULES FOR SAFER DRIVING[1]

Speed. Observe posted limits but remember: most laws require lower speeds when maximum is dangerous.

Lanes. Keep right except when passing.

Right-of-Way. If no traffic signals, first vehicle entering intersection has it. In case of a tie, vehicle on your right has it. If no traffic signals, pedestrians have it at cross walks. Children conducted by school patrols have it. Emergency vehicles and funeral processions always have it.

Signals. Obey all traffic control signs; pedestrians and other drivers act on the assumption that you will.

Turning. Turn right only from the right lane, left from lane nearest center of road (except on one-way roadway). Always signal stops and turns.

Lights. Lower them when approaching another car. (It is courteous to lower them when following another car.)

Equipment. Keep lights, brakes, steering gear, tires, windshield wipers, mirror in good condition. Keep windshield, windows clear.

School buses. Stop when they load or unload.

Driver's license. Be ready to show it at all times.

Intersections. Always slow down and look to right and left regardless of signals.

[1] From *The Automobile Accident—What Should You Do?*, a pamphlet prepared and issued by Kansas Bar Association, 1334 Topeka Avenue, Topeka, Kansas.

Two separate proceedings

What is little understood is that a serious moving violation may involve two different proceedings. One is the criminal complaint for the violation, represented by the ticket. The other is a separate proceeding to suspend or revoke their driving privileges. Voluntarily paying the fine for the criminal moving violation may be treated as an admission of guilt in a later proceeding to suspend or revoke the driver's license.

Paying a moving violation fine is not necessarily the end of it. A notice may arrive later, asking the driver to appear before an examiner of the state motor vehicle department to determine whether cause exists for the suspension or revocation of his or her driver's license.

Paying a fine may also affect one's chances of collecting damages from the other driver later.

Fines and "point systems"

Many states have adopted "point systems." These assess points against an individual's driving record for violations. After amassing a certain number of points, the person may find that his driving privileges have been suspended or revoked. He may be required to attend safe driving classes as a condition of keeping the license or getting it back.

The intent of such laws is to control the reckless driver. But they affect deeply and directly those who depend on their ability to drive.

If you must drive to earn a living, before you pay a fine for a moving violation consult your lawyer to find out the effect of payment on any future proceeding that may affect your driving privileges. Despite the time and effort required, it may be better to attend a hearing on whether or not you did in fact violate the law.

To say that the automobile figures importantly in American life is to grossly understate the case. Production of the automobile creates and maintains jobs; its distribution and sales strengthen the economy; its repair and maintenance provide markets for many other products; the repair and maintenance of the highways it uses represent major parts of state budgets; and its ownership and use present problems to the motorist involving liability and livelihood. This discussion has been intended to pinpoint some of the problem areas.

This discussion was also intended to make it clear that there is, today, no such thing as a simple automobile accident. Claims and counterclaims can come out of the simplest "fender-bender."

18 "DAD, I'M CALLING FROM GRAND CROSSING POLICE STATION . . ."

Most parents have lived in dread of receiving a phone call like that mentioned in the title of this chapter. The newspapers, radio, and television are filled with stories of young people getting in trouble with the law, acquiring criminal records that could haunt them throughout their lives, and ruining their lives because of criminal activity.

What does a parent do when a child, relative, or close friend is accused of a crime? Where does he turn? What is involved in a criminal accusation and how is a child or adult released from custody? These questions are discussed in this chapter. Also included are basic rules that have to do with criminal procedures and practical pointers on how to handle the situation if it ever arises.

Supreme Court decisions have in recent years changed the entire complexion of criminal matters. The decisions touch on the need to

involve the police, on apprehension of a suspect, on advice to be given the person regarding his rights to remain silent and to have an attorney represent him. Legal representation may be called for in serious felony cases, and in less serious misdemeanor cases if they involve a possible jail term as a penalty.

The rules of several states and the federal courts require that the arrested person be taken before a committing magistrate without unreasonable delay after the arrest. Many other protections are available to the accused person.

It has been said that so much is done to protect the alleged criminal that the victim of the crime is ignored. Some maintain that something must be done to protect the victim. Some states have already taken steps in this direction by providing forms of compensation for the innocent person who has suffered serious personal injury or serious loss of property. Other states are considering similar legislation.

Under the American system of law a person is deemed innocent until proven guilty beyond a reasonable doubt. The laws, rules, and regulations devised over the years by legislatures and enforced by the courts have had as their primary objective observance of that fundamental rule.

Unreasonable detention is prohibited

In honoring the presumption of innocence, criminals may go free because of lack of evidence or because an accused did not have counsel. Evidence may be suppressed because of police failure to advise suspects properly of their rights. Other procedural factors may lead to an acquittal. The law does, in fact and in principle, deny to police the right to detain a suspect for an unreasonable length of time. Statements cannot be taken without advising the suspect of his rights. Both physical abuse and the subtle pressures of confinement without counsel degrade the presumption of innocence and create an atmosphere in which innocent persons may find themselves without protection.

It is, in sum, too facile to make generalizations that society protects criminals at the expense of innocent victims of crime. If that is your feeling, you might do two things. First, visit a jail or penitentiary in which people convicted of serious crimes are committed. You will most likely come out of that institution with a feeling of dread and a feeling of the hopelessness of the inmates there. Imagine, if you will, what it would be like for an innocent person to be committed to such an institution for any length of time.

Second, talk to the prison officials, prison chaplain, and others who are involved with the penal system. Many recommendations have been made regarding the rehabilitation of convicts, and some states have gone farther than others in this area. While prison officials will tell you that nearly every inmate claims to be innocent, the same officials will be the first ones to admit that the penal system is not perfect. Innocent people have been convicted of crime and have spent many years behind bars.

Conviction may be secondary to protection

Protection of the innocent must be paramount. Conviction of the criminal must, in the American system, remain secondary. By utilizing the protections provided for accused persons, and by recognizing the difficulties facing the police daily, we can minimize the chance of an unjust conviction of an innocent person. The procedures involved in arresting and convicting the guilty may at the same time be improved.

No system is perfect. Citizens have to live within the system as it develops and attempt to perfect it through experience and by continual study and investigation.

PRACTICAL INFORMATION TO REMEMBER

A phone call comes from your son. He says he is being held by the police for a crime. Your first concern must be to get him released from custody. Beside every person's home telephone, in plain view, should be the numbers of the fire and police departments, the family doctor, and the family lawyer. The lawyer can provide the telephone number of a bail bondsman who is both reputable and available on short notice.

Why is all this necessary? Pending the posting of the bond, and depending on the seriousness of the alleged crime, a suspect will nor-

mally be held. He should be released as soon as possible because it is a terrifying experience to spend even one night in a jail or prison. Many individuals who have spent only a single night in jail have been beaten and robbed, had their clothes stolen, and been sexually assaulted. Such experiences can stay with the victim for a long time.

That single phone call

The police will allow the detained person to make one phone call. The parent or other person receiving the call should immediately call his or her lawyer and then the bondsman. The attorney will talk to the police and will visit the suspect, advise him of his rights, and caution him to make no statement until the lawyer can find out what he is charged with, the circumstances of the arrest, and so on.

The lawyer's interview with the detainee will take place at the police station or lock-up where he is being detained. The lawyer will need the following information:

What the lawyer needs to know

- All the facts of the incident
- Whatever the suspect knows of the alleged crime

- The names and addresses of anyone who might be a witness
- The manner in which the arrest was made
- What was said to him by the police concerning his rights
- Whether the suspect gave any oral or written statement to the police at any time
- Details of any prior criminal record that the detainee might have
- Information regarding his job and where he works
- The identities of persons who might serve as alibi or character witnesses
- If no bondsman is available, the names of relatives or friends who could post bail
- Whether any personal business has to be attended to while the detainee is in jail or awaiting bond

What is Bail?

With bail, the authorities attempt to assure the presence or appearance of the accused person at a later date—in court, at a preliminary hearing, or at an arraignment—after his release from custody. Under the federal system, a person accused of a non-capital offense is entitled to bail. Eligibility for bail may, however, depend on the severity of the crime. In some states where the right to bail is governed by statute, the police official at the station where the accused is "booked" may release the accused on bail immediately.

*Where bail is
excessive and
arbitrary*

The amount of bail is based on similar considerations. The severity of the crime and the circumstances of the particular case have a bearing on the amount. If the amount of bail is excessive and arbitrary, the constitutional rights of the accused will have been violated and the bail may be released or reduced on application to the court.

Other considerations may be important. Those include:

- The circumstances under which the accused was arrested
- How severe a penalty might be imposed

- The general weight of the evidence against the accused
- The likelihood that the accused might attempt flight
- The probability of guilt
- The accused's ability to post bond (what is reasonable for the rich may be unreasonable for the poor)
- The physical condition of the accused and whether he would face serious health hazards if jailed
- The accused's prior record, if any, and his general character

ARREST AND THE BILL OF RIGHTS

In the United States people are governed by laws, not men. Three separate sections of the U.S. Constitution, the fifth, sixth, and eighth amendments of the Bill of Rights, protect the basic rights of the citizen under arrest.

Amendment V—No person shall be held to answer for a capital, or otherwise infamous crime, unless on a presentment or indictment of a Grand Jury, except in cases arising in the land or naval forces, or in the Militia, when in actual service in time of War or public danger; nor shall any person be subject for the same offence to be twice put in jeopardy of life or limb; nor shall be compelled in any criminal case to be a witness against himself, nor be deprived of life, liberty, or property, without due process of law; nor shall private property be taken for public use, without just compensation.

Amendment VI—In all criminal prosecutions, the accused shall enjoy the right to a speedy and public trial, by an impartial jury of the State and district wherein the crime shall have been committed, which district shall have been previously ascertained by law, and to be informed of the nature and cause of the accusation; to be confronted with the witnesses against him; to have compulsory process for obtaining witnesses in his favor, and to have the Assistance of Counsel for his defence . . .

Amendment VIII—Excessive bail shall not be required, nor excessive fines imposed, nor cruel and unusual punishments inflicted.

Cash deposit may be acceptable

Bail usually takes the form of a bail bond issued by an insurance company. Some of the states specify by statute the exact bond forms. In addition to requiring the payment of a premium for the bond, some bonding companies require other security to ensure the appearance of the accused at the later proceedings. A cash deposit or deposit of other property may be acceptable as a substitute for a bail bond depending on the nature of the crime involved. Where real estate is used as bail, a record to that effect is filed in the office of the county recorder of deeds.

The title of the real estate then shows that it is subject to a possible lien for the amount of bail specified. If the accused "jumps bail" and does not appear, the real estate remains subject to the lien.

The Preliminary Hearing

Both federal law and the laws of most states require that an accused be taken before a committing magistrate within a reasonable time after his arrest. This preliminary hearing gives the state or federal government an opportunity to establish that a crime has in fact been committed and that there exists reasonable and probable cause to believe that the accused committed it. The prosecutor in all criminal proceedings is the United States attorney or the state's or district attorney.

The state is not required, at the preliminary hearing, to establish that the accused committed the crime. There must only be sufficient basis for holding him.

The lawyer for the accused has the right to cross-examine the state's witnesses. But he need not call any witnesses to defend against the charges. Some states require that certain defenses that may be used at the trial of the accused, such as alibi or insanity, be raised at the preliminary hearing—or that notice be given to the prosecution that these defenses will be relied on later.

At the preliminary hearing the state may rely on a confession or admission of the accused. The defense that the confession or admission was secured by force or coercion, or resulted from delay in bringing the accused before a magistrate, should then be raised at once so that the same defense can be used at the trial. Some states require that these defenses go into the record as early as possible. The laws of other states may be more lenient.

The defense of illegal search and seizure

State laws differ, again, where an accused wishes to use the defense of illegal search and seizure by the police. The claim may be made that the accused's property or home was searched without a warrant in violation of his constitutional rights. The accused's person may have been searched illegally. Depending on the state, the evidence for such a claim may be suppressed. But state law may require that this defense be raised at the preliminary hearing or at the arraignment that follows.

Some legislation, such as the "no knock" laws, allows the police to enter premises and make a search without knocking if they believe a crime is being committed or is about to be committed. This right is not unqualified, however.

The validity of the arrest itself may also come into question at the preliminary hearing. The right of a citizen or police officer to make an arrest is usually spelled out in the state statutes; but the circumstances required for a lawful arrest may differ depending on the nature of the crime.

It is important that the accused be represented at the preliminary hearing by counsel. A lawyer will be provided for the accused if he cannot afford one. Both state and federal laws should be consulted for guidance on what defenses must be presented to avoid any problems at trial.

The Grand Jury and Its Functions

Handling minor crimes

Certain classifications of crimes are minor in nature. State laws normally allow these crimes to be handled at the magistrate, justice of the peace, or city court level. Minor crimes usually involve fines only and are usually misdemeanors. If, however, the crime is a serious one involving a possible imprisonment, or if the crime is a felony under the laws of the state, the case will generally be submitted to a grand jury for "indictment."

The indictment constitutes an accusation by a grand jury that the accused has committed the crime charged in the indictment. The grand jury is composed of citizens of the county or district where the accused is to be tried. Jury members listen to sworn testimony and review other evidence. They then determine whether or not the state, acting through the proper county official or the federal government, has made out an adequate case that a crime has been committed and that the accused person should stand trial. The crime needs to be established only in broad terms. The details of the crime are left for presentation at the trial.

In some instances the accused may want to appear before the grand jury in an effort to avoid the issuance of an indictment. This may be permitted where the accused has agreed to waive immunity from prosecution for his testimony. The accused has no absolute right to appear before the grand jury unless state law gives him that right.

Besides returning indictments against persons accused of crimes, the grand jury serves another important function. It may also be convened to investigate, on a broad scale, various types of criminal activity in the community. The jury then has the power to issue *subpoenas* to compel witnesses to attend and testify before it.

To avoid self-incrimination . . .

An accused has the constitutional right to avoid self-incrimination if he is subpoenaed to testify before a grand jury. Even in states where an accused must appear, he can refuse to answer incriminating questions unless he has been granted immunity from prosecution for the alleged crime. After the grand jury has considered the evidence, it will either return an indictment or refuse to do so.

If indicted, the accused becomes the defendant. He faces arraignment, the next step in the criminal procedure.

THE MIRANDA RULES:
ADVICE BEFORE INTERROGATION

In the 1966 case of *Miranda* v. *Arizona,* the U.S. Supreme Court reversed a state conviction because of the use at a trial of statements given to police during an interrogation. The high court specified that an accused had to be told before interrogation of four basic rights. The four:

- the right to remain silent

- the right to know that anything he might say could be used against him

- the right to have an attorney present during questioning

- the right, if he has no money, to be provided with a lawyer without charge

The so-called "Miranda warnings" came to be used nationwide after the 1966 decision. The effect has been that admissions or a confession made by a suspect during police interrogation are not admitted as evidence at a subsequent trial—unless the four warnings were given.

The Supreme Court has slowly moved away from strict adherence to the Miranda rules. Confessions secured without following the rules have, for example, been admitted in evidence on technical grounds. But police generally have instructions to give the warnings immediately after making an arrest for a crime.

The Arraignment

At the formal court proceeding called the arraignment, the indictment is presented and read to the defendant. The defendant has an opportunity to plead to the indictment.

The "not guilty" plea

Where any doubt exists in the mind of the court regarding the defendant's understanding of the charges against him, the court may only accept a plea of "not guilty." Where, however, the defendant is represented by counsel and understands the nature of the charges against him, the court will usually accept whatever plea he makes.

Before the arraignment, however, the attorney for the defendant usually talks to the state's attorney to find out how strong the state's case actually is and—sometimes—whether the state would accept a plea of guilty to a lesser crime. This practice, called "plea bargaining," has been attacked by some as a means of allowing a criminal to escape the law's full penalty by pleading guilty to a lesser crime. Both the defense and the prosecution find the practice acceptable in many cases. It is not illegal. Also, it allows for the completion of criminal proceedings without a full-scale trial, and enables the state to obtain a conviction when the evidence to convict a defendant of a more serious crime is weak.

Charges of plea bargaining are raised in many cases that receive wide public notoriety. But in fact the great majority of criminal cases are terminated in some manner before trial.

The defendant has, of course, the right to plead not guilty to any and all charges and to take his chances before the jury. In most cases a defendant who agrees to plead guilty to a lesser charge will want some idea of the sentence to be imposed by the court. Some judges refuse, however, to commit themselves in advance on a sentence; others may be willing to do so. Only with the assistance of an experienced criminal lawyer can the defendant estimate his chances to plea bargain and ascertain the probable sentence to be imposed.

Various considerations go into a decision on whether the state will accept a plea to a lesser crime than that charged in the indictment. The factors include the character of the defendant, the strength of the state's case, the defendant's prior criminal record, if any, the views and opinions of character witnesses, the reports of the behavior from parole officers, and the reports of other social welfare agencies. The latter may be used by the court to determine the questions of sentence and probation.

"Nolo contendere" in criminal and civil cases

A plea of *nolo contendere* indicates, in effect, "no contest." With such a plea the defendant states that he is not going to defend himself against the charge. It amounts to a plea of guilty in a criminal case. In a civil case, where a suit is brought for money damages suffered by others because of a criminal act, the defendant's liability may be reduced.

Proceedings Before Trial

A defendant who has pleaded not guilty to the charges in the indictment pending trial and who is out on bail, in most states, can make some requests. In preparing his case, for example, he may ask for the grand jury's minutes to see if any of his rights have been violated, can attempt to have the indictment set aside for some violation of the law, and may request a statement of the particulars of the crime charged. He may also demand that the court dismiss the charges as inadequate to sustain indictment.

Request for change of venue

A crime may have caused sufficient public outrage to raise the question whether the defendant could receive a fair trial in that area. The defendant may then move for a "change of venue"—meaning that he requests that the trial be held in another location away from the area where the crime was committed. He may also request a separate trial where he has been indicted for more than one crime, or where he has been indicted with another accused person if a joint trial of the defendants would work against him. He may also seek, during this period before trial, the reports of such experts as medical examiners. He may ask to be shown the physical evidence: the books, records, and photographs that the police have gathered.

Whether such requests will be granted depends on the laws of the state in which the case is pending. State laws differ markedly on what portions of the state's case a defendant may inspect.

DEFENSES AND PRE-TRIAL PROCEDURES

In most criminal cases, as noted, the defenses usually have to be indicated as promptly as possible. The preliminary hearing or immediately thereafter is not too soon. The first of these is the defense of *insanity*.

Four kinds
of defense

1. Insanity as a defense to a criminal charge constitutes a legal matter, not a psychological one. In other words the law defines "insanity" for its own purposes. A defendant must be found to have been within the legal definition of insanity at the time of the crime.

In a few words, insanity has been held to be a defect of reason resulting from a mental disease. That defect must prevent the accused from understanding the nature and quality of his act and the fact that it was wrong.

Most states follow that definition or some similar one. Other states hold simply that insanity means that the criminal act was the result of mental disease or mental defect.

The difference between the "right or wrong" test and the "mental disease or illness" test is highly important. Psychologists say that a defendant may be aware that what he is doing is wrong but nonetheless be unable, because of mental disease or defect, to resist performing the act.

Whatever the law of the state on this point, insanity must be raised as a defense early in the proceedings. Once it has been raised, the state has to attempt to establish the defendant's sanity. If an acquittal because of insanity results, the defendant may be committed to an institution rather than freed.

2. Like other defenses, an *alibi* must be raised as soon as possible. Some states require that this defense be specified by the defen-

dant at or before the preliminary hearing. In some cases it may be submitted in writing to the state's attorney. Once the defense is properly raised, the state must prove the alibi false.

3. *Illegally obtained evidence* constitutes a common defense in criminal cases. Evidence obtained as a result of an illegal search and seizure has to be excluded from a trial. The definition of illegally obtained evidence varies according to the laws of the particular state. But the Supreme Court of the United States has placed definite restrictions on illegally obtained evidence and the use of such evidence in court.

Wiretapping for evidence

Federal laws allow wiretaps where authorized by the Attorney General in writing. But the wiretap information, to be admissible as evidence, must have been secured in the precise way authorized by the statute. Some states have adopted procedures requiring a court order before telephones can be tapped to obtain evidence. With such an order or warrant wiretapping becomes legal. The information gathered can be used as evidence.

4. *Double jeopardy* can serve as a valid defense where the defendant alleges that he has already been tried for the same offense. The test is whether or not the prior trial of the defendant did in fact place him in jeopardy of conviction. If he was not, the defense fails. Where the prior proceedings had gone so far that testimony was heard after a jury was empanelled, that would constitute a previous "jeopardy" and serve as a defense to the later action.

The Writ of Habeas Corpus

Uses of habeas corpus

The great triumph of the English Common Law, from which American law is derived, is the *writ of habeas corpus*. Historically, this writ has been used to require the production of the person or "body" of the defendant. The writ was and is used:

• to prevent injustice;

- to prevent the continued imprisonment of persons who have not been charged formally with a crime;
- to test the validity of the criminal prosecution in all of its stages;
- to test the arrest warrant; and
- to test the right of the police or state's attorney to refuse to allow the defendant's attorney to interview his client.

The writ is generally issued when the defendant's attorney makes application to a judge in a court of record in the district where the defendant is being held. A "court of record" is a court that has a clerk to keep a record of all its proceedings. The judge signs and issues the writ. A hearing is held on the facts stated in the writ regarding the allegedly illegal or improper acts of the authorities.

The writ of habeas corpus is entitled to top priority to bring the defendant before the court on the basis of some illegal detention. Under the federal system, federal judges may issue writs where a defendant alleges that his federal constitutional rights have been violated by his detention by state authorities. But usually the federal court will require that all of the defendant's remedies in the state courts be exhausted first, including his application to a state judge for a writ.

Extradition

In a typical case a person charged with a crime in one state flees that state and is later found in another state. The federal Constitution requires that the accused be extradited at the request of the executive authority of the accusing state. In this process the accused is moved to the state having jurisdiction of the crime.

Formalities for extradition

Certain formalities have to be observed in extradition. These include certification of the indictment or charge and signature by the governor or chief judicial officer of the state demanding the return of the fugitive.

Extradition of accused felons is provided for by treaty among the nations of the world. The nation to which the felon has escaped is required to surrender him to the nation demanding his return for trial. Not all countries have extradition treaties with the United States, however. Thus fugitives, including political dissidents, may escape to those countries so that they cannot be forced to return against their will.

TRIAL, SENTENCING, AND AFTER

Assume that a defendant has been convicted of a crime in a proper trial. He may then enter a motion for a new trial for one or all of the following reasons, as they apply to his case:

*Reasons for
moving for a
new trial*

- The jury received improper evidence in or out of court.
- The jury itself did not act properly, as where a juror argued with counsel during the trial.
- The court did not properly instruct the jury on the law governing the case and on the effect of the law on the evidence after the defendant's attorney took the necessary exceptions to the court's instructions to the jury.
- The jury verdict is clearly against the evidence and the law.
- The defendant can show by affidavit that he has found new evidence that would have produced a different verdict—if the evidence was not available at the trial and was discovered after the trial ended.

These motions for a new trial are argued by the lawyers before the court. They may result in an appeal by the defendant if he is refused a new trial. In many cases the lawyer for the accused has to take exceptions—or raise objections—during the trial to procedural or other matters. Without the objections, a later appeal may be impossible.

While new trial motions or an appeal is pending, the court may withhold sentencing the defendant until the motion or appeal is decided. In such a case the defendant will remain free on bond. However, sentence may be imposed, depending on the seriousness of the crime, while the motion or appeal is pending.

The Sentencing Process

A major problem area in criminal law focuses on sentencing. The judges who pass sentences are human beings. Since they have different temperaments, personalities, and views of the seriousness of various crimes, no uniformity exists among them as regards sentencing.

*Judge has latitude
in sentencing*

This situation has led to much criticism. To their credit, criminal court judges have formed professional associations and have attended seminars and educational programs on the subject of proper sentencing. The problem continues to exist because the laws of the states are not the same. The laws usually give the judge wide latitude in imposing sentences consistent with specific crimes and the records of defendants. If the law, for example, sets the penalty for second degree murder at five to 20 years in prison, the judge is free to impose any term within that framework.

Some states require that judges sentence only to the maximum period of the penalty. The state correctional department can then determine the actual length of the sentence, up to the maximum imposed, depending on the record and behavior of the defendant.

*The pre-sentence
report*

Whatever the procedure, the judge has help, in most states, in the difficult job of sentencing. State probation departments and behavior clinics will make pre-sentence investigations of the defendant, look into his or her background, find out whatever it can about the defendant, and file a report with the court. This report often becomes the basis of the sentence that is imposed on the defendant. If the report is favorable, the defendant can usually expect to receive a minimum sentence.

In this area the defendant's attorney can also be of significant help. So can the defendant's family, even after conviction. The family lawyer and the family should work closely with the probation office or behavior clinic to make available all needed information on the defendant. The pre-sentence report will then be entirely fair to the defendant.

In some states the attorney for the defendant is permitted to see the pre-sentence report before it is given to the judge. In other states the attorney cannot read the report. At the sentence hearing, the judge will have the report before him. Usually he will allow counsel and the defendant himself to make any statement they may wish to make that might affect the sentence. A statement may touch on the defendant's character, his family's need for support, his lack of a prior criminal record, and any other facts that might favorably affect the sentence.

SEVEN MAIN STEPS IN A CRIMINAL JURY TRIAL[1]

Criminal trials held before juries generally follow a well-established pattern. They begin with selection of the jury and proceed through six other steps—to sentencing if the verdict is guilty. The seven steps or stages:

SELECTION OF JURY
- a. Challenges
    1. Cause
    2. Peremptory
- b. Completion of jury
- c. Oath

THE TRIAL
- a. Opening statements by counsel (not evidence)
- b. Evidence
    1. Testimony of witnesses
    2. Exhibits
    3. Depositions
- c. Closing arguments by counsel (not evidence)

JUDGE'S ADMONITIONS TO THE JURORS DURING TRIAL
- a. Admonitions to jurors not to discuss the case among themselves or with anyone else, until the case is finally submitted to the jury for verdict

JUDGE'S INSTRUCTIONS ON THE LAW
- a. Instructions to jurors on the law after completion of testimony and arguments

DELIBERATIONS BY JURY
- a. Selects foreman
- b. Weighs evidence
- c. "Beyond reasonable doubt" must characterize guilty finding

THE VERDICT
- a. Criminal case—unanimous

SENTENCING
- a. Judge pronounces sentence

[1] Adapted from *Juror's Manual*, State Bar of Michigan, 306 Townsend St., Lansing, MI 48933.

Probation lasts a specified period

If all these factors bear strongly in the defendant's favor, and if his prior record allows it, the judge may suspend the sentence. The defendant is then placed on probation for a specified period during which he will be required to report to the probation office and stay out of trouble.

The Parole Process

Once a defendant has been convicted and imprisoned, he may become eligible for parole, or conditional release from prison, after serving a minimum sentence. Most states have parole boards that pass on the eligibility of convicted persons for parole. In many cases, the application for parole is made by the convict. But it may also be made by the attorney, prison social worker, or others.

The parole board will consider such things as the convict's behavior in prison, whether or not he has a job waiting for him, and whether he has shown that he can rehabilitate himself in civilian life.

The parole board hearing may consider medical, psychological, and other evidence. It may consider evidence offered by the state in opposition to the parole request. If the convict is then paroled, his activities will be restricted. He will be required to remain in the area and he will be required to report periodically to the parole officer assigned to his case. He cannot associate with known criminals or carry any weapons. A violation of any of these restrictions may result in the termination of parole and the parolee's return to prison to serve the balance of his sentence.

THE YOUTHFUL OFFENDER AND THE JUVENILE DELINQUENT

Delinquency age established by state

Special consideration has been given in criminal law to the youthful offender and the *juvenile delinquent*. Traditionally, the law has presumed that a person below a certain age—14, 16, or some other age established by state law—was not capable of committing a crime. Thus when a juvenile is apprehended for a crime, he is not charged with a particular crime. Rather he is charged with being a juvenile delinquent.

The juvenile delinquency laws help to prevent the minor from acquiring a criminal record. A hearing is usually held before a juvenile court judge. In former years, this hearing was not considered a criminal trial, and the juvenile was not given all the constitutional protections accorded an adult defendant. However, the Supreme Court has decided that a juvenile delinquent has the same constitutional rights as an adult accused. Among these rights is the right to counsel at the hearing to determine whether he is in fact a delinquent.

The juvenile delinquency procedure does not emphasize punishment. Rather, it seeks to help the delinquent child to adjust. Thus the juvenile court judge has considerable discretion in sentencing the juvenile. He may be placed in the custody of parents, sent to a reform school or similar institution, or sent to a foster home or a school operated by or for the state or county. Such an arrangement is intended to encourage rehabilitation. In imposing sentence, the judge will consider the offense involved, the juvenile's background, home life, past trouble with the law, and the institutions to which the juvenile can be sent.

A "youthful offender," by contrast, is a person who, in the eyes of the law, is old enough to be capable of committing a crime but whose age indicates that he should not be treated as an adult criminal. This treatment depends on the age of the accused, the nature of the crime, his background, and, often, the results of physical and mental examinations.

The preliminary hearing

The laws of most states provide for a preliminary hearing to decide whether an accused person should be treated as a youthful offender. The accused may be required to make formal application to the court for such treatment. But the court may, on its own, treat the person as a youthful offender.

To ensure privacy, the trial of a youthful offender is usually held in the judge's chambers rather than in open court. The offender must previously have waived the right to a jury trial and agreed to such a procedure. If the court finds that the accused person is a youthful offender, sentence may include sending the youth to an institution or home or placing him or her on probation. If the case involves a first offense, the youthful offender procedure can help provide the youth and his family with an opportunity to start again.

Basic criminal procedures have been detailed here for one reason: to show that the law is intended to give everyone protection in the event of a criminal charge.

If your son calls you from Grand Crossing police station, don't panic! Call your family lawyer.

INDEX

architect, services of, 74-76
arraignment, 445-446
arrest, rights under, 440-442, 444
assumed names, for business, 310
automatic premium loan clause,
166-167
automobile, insurance for: *see*
insurance, liability

bail, 439-441
"bait and switch" advertising,
338-339
bankruptcy
straight, 380-383
"wage earner's plan," 382-
383
Bankruptcy Reform Act, 380, 381,
382
bar associations, 20, 21
lawyer directories, 21, 32
Tel-Law, 36
bar examinations, 20
Bill of Rights, U.S., 7, 16, 440
Blackstone, Sir William, 7
"blue sky laws," 356
bonds
bail, 441
corporate, 318
fidelity, 180
"fiduciary," 262
personal, for mortgage, 84
for redevelopment, 125
surety
bid, 181-182
construction, 80, 81
contract, 181
labor and material pay-
ment, 80
maintenance, 182
performance, 80, 182
broker, real estate, 95, 96, 99,
100, 101
building contract, 77, 78-80

completion date clause, 79
termination for cause, 80
building permit, 116-118
burglary and theft, insurance for,
180
burial, of body, 281
burial grounds, 282-283
business organizations
corporation, 313, 316-321,
324-329
joint venture, 323-324
partnership, 311-315, 322-
323, 330
sole proprietorship, 309, 311
voting rights in, 326

Camara v. *Municipal Court*, 41
canon law, 6
Canons of Professional Ethics, 20
Carson, Rachel, 366
case law, definition of, 8
cash value, of life insurance, 156,
161-162
certificate of limited partnership,
323
certificate of occupancy, 119
change of venue, 446-447
Chartered Life Underwriter
(CLU), 331
*Chartered Property and Casualty
Underwriter* (CPCU), 331
children
in divorce, 200-201, 208-210,
211
guardian for minor, 243
rights for, 290
Circuit Courts of Appeal, 12, 13
civil law, 11-12, 13-14
Civil Rights Act of 1964, 289
Clean Air Act, 372
"closed shop," 292, 295
closing, final, 59, 67-68, 96
closing sheet, 67